Rethinking the Psychoanalysis of Masculinity

Drawing on a broad range of psychoanalytic, cultural and social influences, the author examines the concept of toxic masculinity for how it brings into focus a widespread anxiety about toxicity throughout daily life: In nature, society and personal relationships.

Aggressive, misogynistic masculinity has become a major topic in recent years, spreading throughout popular culture, the media and research. Often called 'phallic,' it simmers in everyday life and hits the headlines for turning florid and violent in maintaining its dominance, especially towards women. But at the extreme, phallic masculinity has recently crystallized in a very different form, as *toxic* masculinity, and 'toxic' has become the near-universal epithet for all forms of extreme destructiveness in a 'toxic culture.' It has brought into focus, and named as masculine, an anxiety over toxicity in every corner of everyday life. Exploring toxic masculinity in depth brings out a misogynistic current that pervades individual and social realms, but also throws a sharp light on normal masculinity. By elaborating on the roots of this toxicity, Figlio is able to draw out a different, more positive alternative for masculinity, with particular reference to the underlying fears around fertility and the seminal.

With a strong research and clinical base, this book is essential reading for all psychoanalysts and psychoanalytic psychotherapists and cultural and social theorists interested in exploring concepts of masculinity.

Karl Figlio taught history of science and medicine at Cambridge and was the founding director of the Centre for Psychoanalytic Studies, University of Essex. He is a clinical associate, British Psychoanalytical Society; a Senior Member, Psychoanalytic Psychotherapy Association, British Psychotherapy Foundation; a Professor Emeritus, Department of Psychosocial and Psychoanalytic Studies, University of Essex; and in private practice.

'The psychoanalytic understanding of male sexuality has tended towards overemphasising the penis, and scotomotising the testicles. The dominance of this discourse has served to maximise exploration of the phallic and minimise interest in the generative aspects (the seminal), both clinically and socially. Karl Figlio, a highly respected psychoanalytic clinician, has spent his professional life exploring the boundaries between psychoanalysis and culture. This book is exemplary in this respect showing the interpenetration of the individual and the social. It makes a profound contribution to our understanding of male sexuality and is particularly timely, as toxic male sexuality is an increasingly dominant feature of our world.'

David Bell *is a psychoanalyst and former president of the British Psychoanalytic Society and currently chair of its applied section. He retired in 2021 after 25 years as a consultant at the Tavistock and Portman NHS Foundation Trust*

'Toxic masculinity is a concept now reached for as if it were a given, not a matter for enquiry. This scholarly and original book offers a fresh look at the roots of masculine identity, linking the other fashionable theme of masculine fragility to the defence provided by the phallic omnipotence at the heart of what we mean by toxic. Figlio argues with vigour and eloquence for a more complex understanding of male anxieties, emphasising the procreative power of the male and the inevitable dread of failure to create. This builds a bridge to shared thinking about what we humans most desire and fear the loss of, men and women.'

Margaret Rustin *is a child, adolescent and adult psychotherapist, Tavistock and Portman NHS Foundation Trust and British Psychoanalytic Society*

'Professor Karl Figlio has broadened my professional and personal horizons with this highly original book. By introducing *seminal masculinity*, he is venturing beyond the traditional limitations of thinking about men in reductionist, phallic terms. With its important theoretical elucidations enriched by carefully selected clinical material and links to timely social issues, this groundbreaking work contributes greatly to deepening our thinking about masculinities.'

Sebastian Thrul, *senior psychiatrist and head of the clinic for Gender Issues at Psychiatrie Baselland, Switzerland, and host of the podcast* New Books in Psychoanalysis

'Karl Figlio brings a fresh perspective to the debates on masculinity. He argues that "toxic masculinity" represents a triumph of the negative aspect of a more complex and inherently ambivalent masculine configuration which he terms "seminal masculinity". While seminal masculinity embodies a life-giving and reparative capacity, toxic masculinity aims omnipotently to dominate, control and anhilate the feminine. Toxic masclinity cannot make use of feminine sexuality and receptivity, so identity is also impoverished, while often "hiding in plain sight" in the familiar stereotype of phallic masculinity. Its misogyny is also a primitive form of replacement ideology.'

Sharon Numa *is a fellow of the British Psychoanalytical Society*

Rethinking the Psychoanalysis of Masculinity

From Toxic to Seminal

Karl Figlio

Routledge
Taylor & Francis Group

LONDON AND NEW YORK

Designed cover image: La Cassette Bleue © Getty Images

First published 2024
by Routledge
4 Park Square, Milton Park, Abingdon, Oxon OX14 4RN

and by Routledge
605 Third Avenue, New York, NY 10158

Routledge is an imprint of the Taylor & Francis Group, an informa business

British Library Cataloguing-in-Publication Data
A catalogue record for this book is available from the British Library

Library of Congress Cataloguing-in-Publication Data
Names: Figlio, Karl, author.
Title: Rethinking the psychoanalysis of masculinity : from toxic to seminal / Karl Figlio.
Identifiers: LCCN 2023029377 (print) | LCCN 2023029378 (ebook) | ISBN 9781032596839 (hardback) | ISBN 9781032594651 (paperback) | ISBN 9781003455790 (ebook)
Subjects: LCSH: Masculinity--Psychological aspects. | Psychoanalysis.
Classification: LCC BF175.5.M37 F543 2024 (print) | LCC BF175.5.M37 (ebook) | DDC 155.3/32--dc23/eng/20230928

ISBN: 978-1-032-59683-9 (hbk)
ISBN: 978-1-032-59465-1 (pbk)
ISBN: 978-1-003-45579-0 (ebk)

DOI: 10.4324/9781003455790

Typeset in Times New Roman
by MPS Limited, Dehradun

Dedicated to my Parents

Rose and Dominic Figlio

Contents

Acknowledgements

Chapters 2, 4 and 7, revised and extended, are drawn from: Figlio, K. (2010) Phallic and Seminal Masculinity: A Theoretical and Clinical Confusion. *International Journal of Psychoanalysis* 91(1): 119–139.

Chapter 11 is a revised version of: Figlio, K. (2010) The Financial Crisis: A Psychoanalytic View of Illusion, Greed and Reparation in Masculine Phantasy. *New Formations* 72: 33–46; also in Bennet, D. (ed.) *Loaded Subjects: Psychoanalysis, Money and the Global Financial Crisis*. London: Lawrence and Wishart, 2012, 34–51. https://journals.lwbooks.co.uk/newformations/

My thanks to the publishers for permission to make extensive use of these sources.

I am grateful to my wife, Eva Stina Lyon, for her support, advice and incisive commentary throughout this project, and to Sebastian Thrul and Sharon Numa for their encouragement, helpful comments and permission to quote from personal correspondence and conversations.

I am indebted to my patients, particularly to 'Miss Collins' and 'Mr Harris,' who have kindly allowed me to make extensive use of our work. I am also grateful to 'Max' and his mother, who have allowed me to reproduce their discussions of the imminent arrival of his baby sister (all pseudonyms). In writing a psychoanalytic book, one also becomes – once again – very aware of, and grateful to, the network of analysts, supervisors and colleagues, whose contributions are deeply embedded in one's thinking.

Preface

This is a psychoanalytic book, rooted in clinical and theoretical psychoanalysis. But it aims for a dialogue with other fields around topics through which they converge. Masculinity and the masculine in relationships are among those areas of convergence. I began to explore the neglect in psychoanalysis of the unique male, seminal function, and of the psychological correlates of this function some time ago. It began with a book publised in 2000, *Psychoanalysis, Science and Masculinity*, and more focally in a paper, Phallic and Seminal Masculinity (2010). My aim was to establish an observational field in which the experience of masculinity could more clearly be seen clinically and discussed theoretically.

Tracing the history of this neglect has been an important part of the project. Freud's (1923) interpolation of a phallic stage in the psychosexual development of male and female led to a phallic monism, in which the female was said to think herself a genitally deficient male. Repudiation followed on the heels of Freud's theory, and controversy stormed around it. Despite the early interventions by women psychoanalysts, such as Karen Horney, Helene Deutsch and Melanie Klein, however, the decisive turning point was more apparent as a 'maternal turn,' attributed to them by Janet Sayers in her 1991 book, *Mothering Psychoanalysis*. Other psychoanalytic writers, both men and women, have continued their work of directing attention away from phallic aspects of genitality, into the deep interior of female sexual anatomy, physiology and psychology. Phallic monism sits uneasily in psychoanalysis these days; even today, there remains a puzzlement that it has not been, in Rosemary Balsam's language, consigned to the 'ash pit of history.'

Curiously, however, this monism overshadowed *both* male and female sexual characteristics, and the maternal turn left men to one side with their non-descript phallic sexuality. In the wake of the maternal turn, however, psychoanalytic thinking did begin to attend to the male, but in a particular way. If female sexuality was better defined by a psychology centred on her interior, then so, too, for the male: His psychology was also a psychology of an internal genital space. Now, 'internal' rather than 'external' (phallic) sexuality seemed important in men as well as women. In popular culture, men were urged to become 'new men,' through an awareness of their feminine side.

But what is this feminine side? What do we mean by 'internal'? And anyway, men have continued to dominate public life with their traditional, competitive – phallic – masculinity. The masculine stereotype has peaked with the label 'toxic masculinity,' which names the extreme of this stereotype, a misogyny, often to the point of violence against women. The #MeToo movement forced into public awareness the extent of this, especially sexual, violence. Moreover, 'toxic,' with its 'masculinity' often unspoken but just under the surface, has come to name every form of egregious behaviour as well as the pollution and degradation of our natural and social worlds.

The rapid and seemingly universal spread of *toxic* masculinity (at least in Western, English-speaking culture), combined with the equally universal repugnance named by 'toxic' in countless spheres of life, leads back to a basic feature of masculinity. Masculinity is at a fundamental level inherently ambivalent: Fertile, life enhancing but also destructive. I argue that this ambivalence inheres in semen: The substance and its symbolic elaboration. Moreover, it is deeply internal, carried by projective identification, a phantasy of relocating in a repository parts of the self that have become intolerable to it: Inside a union; inside the feminine; inside the female. It can destabilize as it fertilizes. It can undermine– poison – the fertility of the union of individuals, our relationship to nature and relaionships between social groups.

This book explores seminal masculinity as a source of faith in the contiuance of life, plagued by instability, but also the pollution of nature and an extreme and apparently unlikely social case study. When the banking crisis of 2008 threatened to collapse economies across the world, an unstable, even destructive masculinity of trading financial products leaped into public awareness and spawned research as well as popular commentary. I published a paper on it in 2012: 'The Financial Crisis: A Psychoanalytic View of Illusion, Greed and Reparation in Masculine Phantasy.'

The strange thing about the toxic masculinity of traders of financial products was that it actually fit the stereotype of *phallic* masculinity: Self-made, flamboyant, distinctly not feminine, risk-taking men. The persistent, entrenched misdescription of toxic masculinity in blatantly phallic terms, however, does make sense psychoanalytically. It is a defence – but a defence against what? What could be more unwelcome to consciousness than phallic masculinity? In my view, it deflects awareness from its deeper, more ominous – seminal – root. The label 'toxic' itself adds to this defence, because it lies in plain sight, an obvious part of the stereotype of the misogynist, typically phallic, male.

But what inheres in seminal masculinity, so deeply concealed beneath this defensive overlay? I argue that it is desolation. The fertility of seminal masculinity is stalked by an ominous dread of the collapse or the destruction of life by the negative, toxic power of this same vitalizing capacity. Together they embody a seminal ambivalence. Phallic masculinity, by contrast, rests on the omnipotent phallus. It can recover and its magic spreads everywhere. The assured conviction of authoritarian, populist politics, climate-change denial, environmental poisoning, racism and economic chancing can seem to overcome pessimism. Movements with this character also tend to be misogynistic in that they are typically populated by men – who also dominate women.

I take up this alignment among movements and direct my analysis to their character as reactive men's groups. I hypothesize that they share a primal, unconscious nucleus of reactivity to a sense of having an identity stolen, which can be revised into a conscious 'replacement ideology.' It is not just reactive, however: Seminal ambivalence creates an ominous, retaliatory, feminine object. The (depressive) desolation of undermined fertility carries with it a (paranoid-schizoid) persecutory current (in Melanie Klein's theory), which only more deeply embeds the risk of retaliation and a reactive posture. The feminine object must then be repeatedly attacked to keep it under control. My argument suggests that misogyny might provide a template for this reactivity, rooted in the complexities of Klein's 'femininity phase': An entanglement with the maternal, which the boy struggles to resolve and which, as she says, can lead to a particular, demeaning aggressiveness towards women.

We need historians and social scientists to nail the case down in its nuances and different situations. Some work has been done and the contours are becoming clear. In a recent book, *The Traces of History*, the historian, Patrick Wolfe, shows that historical situations structure specific forms of colonization of peoples, but there remains a mode of suppression that cannot be encompassed by these strictures. The often-violent erasure of peoples is not just a residue so far unexplained: It is at the core. It aims to conquer not just another people's land or resources, but their identity. It bespeaks an inner desolation, also recast by projective identification, to be conquered as an external object. I compare it to Freud's *Civilization and its Discontents* (*Das Unbehagen in der Kutur*, which would more accurately be translated as *The Unease in Culture*): An undefinable, perhaps ominous, uncanny sense of inner disconsolance.

This inner mechanism is at play, I argue, in toxic masculinity with its phallic cover. The dramatic confrontational aggression of phallic masculinity promises victory. That includes victory over its own destructiveness, a frame of mind that reinforces the optimistic belief that technology will undo the damage caused by technology. The recasting of toxic masculinity as phallic while retaining the label 'toxic' allows a manic triumphalism to cover the desolation of seminal ambivalence. As with any effective defence, the phallic overlay ensures that 'toxic' registers as actually toxic only in The Unconscious. With prescience and a novelist's imagination, P. D. James has portrayed such a collapse in *The Children of Men*. Semen had simply given out. No children had been born in years, and society was falling into boredom, even sexual boredom; into hopelessness; into shallow evasions of the truth; and into violence. Life – at least human life – was simply winding down.

I follow Freud in believing that we must work with a well-defined conceptual framework. It must also be dispensable as we look more widely and deeper, and learn more, but we need it as a torch in the dark. I see phallic masculinity as a paranoid-schizoid defence in Melanie Klein's theory and seminal masculinity as depressive and therefore reparative, bringing life and concern for its objects, but also the dread that destructiveness or reparative inadequacy could damage or destroy life. Toxic masculinity is misogynist because it poisons the interior or the feminine and the feminine as the female. Because everyone begins inside a mother, misogyny might be seen as the template of hate-based prejudices.

But with Freud, I also take the 'pathological' to be an extreme of the 'normal.' It shines a sharp beam on the normal, sometimes so sharp that it needs to be turned down to allow the dark to come to light. Although my way into current views of masculinity, in its misogyny and destructiveness, has been through its toxicity, I come back, in the conclusion, to 'ordinary' masculinity. We will see the struggles of a boy just under four years old to accommodate the 'surprise' of a little sister and his wish to be an 'ordinary boy' with no plight with which he was expected to acquiesce. So, although there is a misogynist streak in masculinity, there is also a loving streak. I conclude that both are carried, concretely and symbolically, in its seminality.

Again with Freud, I take the ego to be a bodily-ego and the body to be a projective surface of the psyche; that is, it displays itself and deploys itself, spatially, through the body: 'Space may be the projection of the extension of the psychical apparatus' (Freud 1938). I also take the view of the philosopher, Richard Wollheim, that, under duress, the psyche breaks up from an unreflective, experiential unity to become more spatial, as it sees (feels) itself to be in pieces. We see in clinical psychoanalysis that high anxiety can be dispersed into parts of the body. It is as if the mind had broken up into internal objects, embedded and localized in the body, as a regression to the bodily structures that were, in early development, the precursors of internal objects. They are then ready for expulsion into repositories.

From this angle, whether in the pathological extreme or in the normal, differences between male and female become significant, as each can serve as a projective repository for the other. Following J. O. Wisdom, I think that, in the extreme, the repository facilitates the repudiation of a portion of the self; in the 'normal,' it acts as a complement, allowing male and female to enhance each other. In this book, I am mainly concerned with the use made of the feminine by the masculine, including the forceful pressing of the feminine into the female.

The body is not, however, a neutral, passive repository of ego projections, just as, in early development, it is no accident that we make early relationships with external objects through the mouth and oral apparatus and later relationships through the genitals and genital apparatus. Seminal, including toxic, masculinity makes sense in this body-ego setting. Semen is a vitalizing fluid. Sometimes it lacks this capacity. Sometimes it pollutes. It also carries a symbolic load. Popular culture and clinical accounts reveal this duality and the anxiety that it brings with it. The duality of seminality and its phallic overlay is striking once one looks for it clinically and in many social and cultural situations.

I define masculinity as seminal projective identification. Unlike the phallic stereotype of masculinity, grounded in penetration by the penis, masculinity in this definition is by seminal incursion, not by penetration. It is by merging with the interior of its repository, whether to fructify, to control, to house the 'bad self' or to pollute. This focus also captures the masculine yearning for the feminine that is the target of misogyny. It brings out the quality of *having* and *being* the repository, while resisting the loss of self into the repository.

Yet, for all that this book is rooted in the concept of a bodily-ego and in there being a feature of masculinity that is intrinsic to the biological male, it is not a thesis about gender identity. The relationship between mind and body is complex, specifically in the forms of identification of mind with body, and the harmonies and dissonances of those identifications. The narrowness of my conceptual model aims for clarity within its objectives and scope, not for comprehensiveness. A well-defined model will necessarily be partial and could be scrapped, but for now, it allows research to proceed.

Part I raises a question: What do we mean by masculinity? It introduces the idea of seminal masculinity and the toxic masculinity that has become the nearly universal epithet for egregious misogyny and a crystallization of toxicity in countless areas of nature and society. Part II takes up a reaction in psychoanalytic thinking to the internal world of the female. It reviews evidence for a male internal genital space, equivalent to a female internal genital space. It raises the question: What do we mean by 'internal,' as the elusive object of insatiable curiosity and mastery? Part III re-examines the phallic dimension of masculinity and of phallic monism – the theory that there is one phallus as the harbour of one libido and that its primary location is the penis. Phallic monism has been repudiated, but an outgrowth of it – parthenogenic phantasy – remains significant as a collaborative defence against the incestuous dimension of the Oedipus complex.

Part IV shifts the focus squarely to seminality in its positive and, in the idea of seminal ambivalence, in its negative – toxic – aspects. Part V extends the exploration of seminal ambivalence and toxic masculinity to misogyny and to misogynist currents in society, such as reactive men's and anti-environmentalist movements. It also includes, as an extensive case study, the 2008 financial crisis.

In the Conclusion, we pick up points for further elaboration and shift our focus from pathology to the normal. In line with Freud's view, we will see the extreme of the pathological as sharpening the image of the normal and ordinary, opening them to clearer analysis. Our view of Freud also becomes more ordinary as he becomes a man who struggled with the feminine.

Finally, a note about evidence and the focus and structure of the book. Its roots are clinical observation and psychoanalytic theory. At the same time, some social situations provide natural experiments in which the seminal level seems demonstrable. The 2008 financial crisis was one of those instances. Certain features of environmental scepticism provide another. I address both clinical and social instances and draw out their misogynist character as a common theme. The thesis develops over the course of the book, and only in the conclusion does it focus specifically on being 'ordinary.' In that sense, it builds and, I hope, gets more persuasive as it goes along. At the same time, each chapter aims to provide enough background and direction to be self-standing and could be read on its own.

Part I

Becoming Masculine

Chapter 1

The Uniquely Masculine

The Duality of Masculinity

It has become difficult to say what we mean by masculinity. At one extreme is the brazen stereotype of 'phallic masculinity,' which has become a major topic in recent years, in popular culture, the media and research. It simmers in everyday life and hits the headlines for turning florid and violent in maintaining its priority, especially towards women. At the extreme, phallic masculinity has crystallized as *toxic* masculinity: The near-universal epithet for a phallic maleness, idealized in a particular male stereotype, sustained by a demeaning, often violent, misogyny.

But among the many versions of masculinity, there is also a masculinity that complements femininity. It is concerned for the object of its love: 'depressive' in Kleinian terms, hopeful in its fertility and devastated by the dread of infertility. It is a 'seminal masculinity,' mostly displaced by the more familiar 'phallic masculinity,' which sits on top of it, defending against it. The public image of maleness is phallic, but the root of masculinity is seminal.

The idea of *toxic* masculinity brings to the surface, without drawing attention to it, a deep, unconscious association between seminal masculinity and contamination, revealing an ambivalence in seminal function. It is fertile, life enhancing and reparative, but it is also poisonous and undermines life. On the positive side of ambivalence, the idealized – phallic – penis can penetrate and arouse, but beneath the phallic level, it is semen that enlivens. On the negative side, the phallic penis invades and demeans, parading as the object of envy, but semen pollutes. Phallic masculinity, for all its self-aggrandizement and misogyny, is more tolerable than the mixture of fragile hope and utter desolation of seminal masculinity. Indeed, toxic masculinity has brought to a focus an anxiety over a toxicity in every corner of everyday life, poisoning nature and society, as well as personal relationships.

When we speak in general of masculinity, we are almost certainly speaking of phallic masculinity and reactions to it. The phallic defence is reinforced by a culture of phallic masculinity that holds it in place. There are other cultures and countercultures of masculinity, which surface from time to time; the 'new

DOI: 10.4324/9781003455790-2

man' of the 1980s might be seen as a counterculture to phallic masculinity. Tom Castella asked, 'Whatever happened to the term New Man,' on the occasion of a conference at the London South Bank Centre in 2014 (https:// www.bbc.com/news/magazine-25943326; accessed 30 March 2022). He refers to other evocations of being a man as well: New lad, metrosexual, *übersexual*. But they all neglect the obvious, fundamental, procreative dimension of being a man, and the equally obvious, genital equipment of a man: The inseminating penis; the testicles; the prostate gland and associated structures.

When 'seminal' does occur, it is in the abstract. There is a collective unseeing – perhaps a scotomization – in the over-use of the word 'seminal' in every sense but its actual meaning. With 'seminal,' we praise the creative, influential, original, productive, inspiring, fruitful contributions of women and of men, while we simultaneously ignore the seminal contribution to procreation and the psychic reality of masculinity that goes with it. There are seminal contributions, seminal ideas and seminal moments, but not a seminal contribution to procreation and no mention of the structures and functions that subserve it.

Even a paper on 'primary femininity' by a female analyst speaks of the 'seminal contributions' of Karen Horney (Mayer 1995, 19). In a similar vein, the philosopher of psychoanalysis, J. O. Wisdom (1992), says in his book on Freud and women in society, that *scientific hypotheses* are *born*, and that 'We mainly hear about the great scientific hypotheses that have succeeded,' he says. 'We hardly ever hear about the seminal *ideas* that gave them birth' (13; my emphasis). He does not, however, discuss seminal function as the essence of masculinity or receptiveness to semen as the essence of femininity.

Michael Diamond (2013, 16), a major contributor to the psychoanalysis of masculinity, says:

> The phallic ego ideal is thus based on the boy's unconscious denial of differentiation in the service of his grandiose wish for maintaining the unlimited possibility inherent in the omnipotent, idealized union with his maternal object. The *seminal issue* for most men is how this *early preoedipal phallic narcissism and phallic omnipotence becomes integrated into an ongoing and evolving sense of masculinity* (my emphasis; indeed, it *is* a seminal issue – specifically – as masculinity matures into a procreative capacity).

The displacements from seminal masculinity to phallic masculinity, and from the obliteration – the castration of procreative function – to cutting off the penis, eclipse an awareness of procreative structures and functions, along with the nature of the (castration) threat to them and the phantasies that they all engender. The male seems simply to lack an internal procreative space with structures and processes uniquely male and equal in importance to those in the female; and the anxieties associated with them remain marginalized, misrepresented or unrecognized in clinical work. Recent recognition of an internal male genital refers more to a receptive femininity in the male than a uniquely male attribute.

The Masculine Dilemma: Masculine Femininity

Along with the currents of masculine misogyny, epitomized by toxic masculinity, the realization has hit home, that becoming a man, especially a man who recoils from hating women and who can enjoy fathering, is a process fraught with impediments. John Munder Ross, a psychoanalyst who has devoted decades to understanding what he calls *The Male Paradox* (1992), characterizes being a man in a negative way. He sees it as a struggle against forces that pull against maturity. '[A] man defines himself in opposition to three polarities: child, woman and beast' (15). We might say that a man struggles against the regressive attraction to a childhood with mother and against an attraction to being a woman himself.

A boy often lacks, whether physically or emotionally, the support of a father with whom he could identify: A secure internal father would support him in these three oppositions. The symptoms of paternal absence are clear on the surface. For example, boys show its impact in poor performance at school, in inhibiting feelings and a reluctance to seek help with illness (for a review of research on fathering, see Flouri 2005). Beneath the symptoms, becoming a man involves moving from an infantile relationship with mother to a relationship with women, regardless of sexual orientation. It ideally retains a caring and generosity that reciprocates the caring and generosity of the mother, without being ensconced inside her. It builds on mitigating the envy, jealousy, demandingness and uninhibited aggression of childhood.

Such a complex process raises an important question: Does the father, who could exemplify adult masculinity, leave, by his absence, a residue of a defiant, infantile attitude towards 'mother' – mother found in all women. In the adult man, such a posture is dangerous. An adult male caught up in an infantile struggle with femininity, which can be felt but not articulated, can turn to action with his powerful body. Whether as a flaw inherent in masculinity, or an aspect of the social relations in which boys become men, there might be a deeply engrained, seemingly structural abuse of the feminine of girls and women.

But the emphasis on fathering is lopsided. From a Kleinian angle – the theoretical and clinical basis of my book – an absent father does not fully account for the distorted masculinity behind misogyny. Melanie Klein (1928, 191; my emphasis) drew attention many years ago to the 'excessive aggression' in male attitudes towards females, lodged in a psychic stage more primitive than that between oedipal males. In Klein's view, the difficulty, especially for the boy, of early feminine identification and ambivalence towards it – the femininity phase – led to an especially aggressive attitude towards women, in comparison to that towards other men.[1]

A tendency in boys to express *excessive aggression*... has its source in the femininity complex. It goes with an attitude of contempt and "knowing better", and is highly asocial and sadistic; it is partly determined by an attempt to mask the anxiety and ignorance which lie behind it. In part it coincides with the boy's protest (originating in his fear of castration) against the feminine role, but it is rooted also in his dread of his mother, *whom he intended to rob of the father's penis, her children and her female sexual organs.* This excessive aggression unites with the pleasure in attack which proceeds from the direct, genital Oedipus complex, but it represents that part of the situation which is by far the more asocial factor in character-formation.

The working-through of this early ambivalence towards the mother is the source of the male's later capacity for generosity in his genital relationship with a woman. Thus, although Klein says that aggression towards the female, based on the anxieties of the femininity phase, is extreme, she also suggests that their mitigation provides the foundation for mature love. A man's sexual relationship with a woman capable of reassuring him of the reparative power of his penis seems to be more important than his identification with his father, in bringing him into adulthood (Klein 1937, 313–316). She also refers in various places to the reparative power of semen.

But Klein's concept of the femininity phase also needs to be supplemented by understanding why a male cannot be satisfied with being a male. Whatever progress the boy makes in growing beyond the sadism of this phase owes to his engagement with his mother and the mother in his female partners. Identification with the father, and the development of his super-ego, do not seem to be adequate in this maturation. We are left with an insecurity of masculine identity, which seems to be an intrinsic instability, rather than a consequence of an absent father.

Perhaps it is concordant with an insecurity of masculine identity that the psychoanalytic enquiry into being a man has followed an interest in the nature of woman. There is a substantial literature on theories of femininity, and, until recently, a lot of the attention given to masculinity has been tied to the revision of theories of female sexuality and gender identity. The attention to female sexuality has reversed the masculine dominance of phallic monism in psychoanalysis: The theory that there is only one gender in a phallic world – that the female is a deficient male. The non-phallic dimension of masculine sexuality runs alongside this recasting of female sexuality, as if an adaptation to it. Recent psychoanalytic writings on masculinity have seemed dedicated to having its share of this non-phallic, feminine dimension, no longer to be marginalized as the phallic narcissism and omnipotence of the masculine character. As the psychology of the female fought free of a phallic base into a uniquely female base rooted in uniquely female anatomy and physiology, the psychology of the male tended to import this newly asserted femininity into the character of the non-phallic male.

Britton (2001, 57) notes that

[t]he "father complex" reached its zenith ... about the same time as the "female castration complex" was promulgated ... Then the pendulum swung and some analytic theorizing made mother all-important, [which] led to the undervaluation of those aspects of psychic function associated with an internal father, such as objectivity.

Previously (Figlio 2010a), I examined the consequences for psychoanalytic theories of masculinity of the development of psychoanalytic theories of female sexuality since Freud's late papers on the topic. Freud built on a phallic monism, in which femininity was borrowed from a masculinity based on the penis. By contrast, later literature on female sexuality established a primary femininity, against which phallic monism was a defence. The literature on a primary female sexuality is rooted in the material and psychic reality of female internal space. The 'female internal genital' refers, not only to the vagina and womb, but also to the nervous innervation of the clitoris, which brings the deep structure of the vagina into relationship with the phallic clitoris. The diminutive female penis of phallic monist thinking is, in fact, an integral part of female internal anatomy, physiology and psychic reality (see Zachary 2018) for a detailed scrutiny of the literature on female sexuality, including its anatomical base). Following this literature, so, too, did the male acquire an internal genital space, located in the scrotum, testes, prostate and connecting structures (reviewed in chapter 2).

Although this literature has tended to repudiate a dyadic, oppositional view of gender, in which female means deficient, castrated male, it has nonetheless included along the way an oppositional, dyadic stance, in which the boy, through identifying with the father, dis-identifies from the mother: Father separates the boy from immersion in the mother. It has moved on to replace these ideas with a 'post-modern' notion of gender and sexuality as fluid and more a performance of selfhood than a heritage or encumbrance, whether biological or psychological (see vol. 54 of the *Journal of the American Psychoanalytic Association*, which includes a special issue on masculinity; see also Diamond 2006, 2015, 2021; Dimen and Goldner 2006; Marí and Thomson-Salo 2013; Johns 2002 speaks of disidentification, but not of an oppositional view).

Diamond (2021) provides an up-to-date, comprehensive overview of developments in the theory of masculinity. He divides them into three waves, through which the psychoanalytic theory of masculinity has been released from phallic monism and has integrated the 'other' into the masculine psyche, 'both in terms of the concrete, flesh-and-blood other and the culturally based, symbolic other' – the first other, being the mother (12).

- first wave: 'beyond the male protest and psychic bisexuality';
- second wave: 'disidentification and repudiating of the feminine';
- third wave: 'receptivity [and] the male's essential lack, yearning and dependency.'

For Diamond, mature masculinity is based on an integration in the healthy male of phallic functioning and feminine receptivity. Such an integration depends on the boy's identification *with* his mother and *by* his mother (78; Laplanche 2007); that is, on his mother's unconscious attitude towards her son's masculinity. It also depends on his identification *with* and *by* his father (51), as well as on his father's protectiveness towards his maleness and on the parents' unconscious attitudes towards each other's gender. Altogether, it involves a set of unconscious triangular identifications among the two parents and the child rather than on a dyadic differentiation of male from female.

Diamond further postulates that the boy's difference from his mother renders him for ever insecure, in a primordial vulnerability from his earliest unrepresentable and unsymbolizable experience of his mother. The phallic stance of the male, which for Freud was the normal primal state, becomes, for Diamond, an ever-insecure attempt to overcome his primordial vulnerability. Diamond rejects the disidentification theory, according to which the boy, in becoming male as not-female, is still embedded in a dyadic concept of becoming male. As the boy turns away from mother, he takes her femininity with him into his masculinity in gendered ego ideals, maternal as well as paternal. The mature male cannot escape into maleness, but must live with his primordial insecurity, repeatedly securing his masculinity, affirmed in it by the set of triangular identifications. I would add that the relationships among the figures surrounding the boy are also – perhaps primarily – internal, as successful single parenting shows. Mother, for example, carries an internal father/partner who, in favourable circumstances, supports her generosity to her son.

I agree with Diamond's analysis, but my thesis is anchored in a different tradition. In the Kleinian tradition of my work, Donald Meltzer (1988, 63) says it is 'only very late in development that the aesthetic of the father and his genital appears as a force in development, through the emergence of introjective identification with the internal mother's view of him.' So far, Meltzer is consistent with Diamond. But he continues: With the 'next baby' conflict, the father's genital becomes a 'tool-of-procreation,' which establishes the role of the father with a 'genuine glory comparable to that of the mother.' The son's mature masculinity is modelled on the internal relationship between what Meltzer calls the 'testicular father' and the mother who accepts his testicular offering. The feminine receptivity, to which Diamond refers, is, for me, the receptivity to the masculine seminal substance and function, material and symbolic.

Similarly, I agree that the repudiation of Freud's theory of phallic monism (1923; 1925a; 1931) has been decisive and that the literature on masculinity shares this repudiation (or indifference) with that on femininity (Balsam 2018; Breen 1993, 32). But I claim that phallic monism remains robust as a *defence* and that it retains its strength because of what it defends against. I aim to show that it defends against the depressive anxiety of seminal function, its psychic reality and its roots in *male* 'internal' space. Releasing the female from phallic monism also frees us to explore its source in masculinity itself, and to see the dilemma of masculine identity as accepting not only his feminine receptivity, but also his seminal anxiety.

The Masculine and Phallic Monism

Phallic monism is narcissistic and *gender-indifferent*; it is an omnipotent phantasy, as is the 'organ' – the phallus, not the penis – in which it is 'located.' 'Castration anxiety' applies to the phallus, not to the penis. Seminal function, by contrast, is uniquely masculine and divides the sexes and genders. Its near absence from the psychoanalytic literature suggests a tacit agreement to disregard masculinity, despite the attention that recently has been given to it. Attributing phallic narcissism to the penis has provoked the feminist reaction to it – quite rightly – but should not side-track us from recognizing phallic monism as an omnipotent phantasy – in my view, as a defence against the depressive anxiety of fertility and its failure.

But what makes phallicism so powerful a defence, and is it restricted to the male? I argue in chapter 5 that it is a collaborative defence, sustained by male and female together. It is lodged, however, primarily in the penis because the penis so aptly expresses narcissism. The penis (and the clitoris) inflates by engorgement as an expression of excitement; it is visible; it is itself, yet part of the whole body; its inflated state seems, of itself and by itself, to produce the emission, which in a non-phallic world, is associated with fertility. It is, altogether, an alter-ego-double, which can be imbued with omnipotence and magic.

The 'mistake' in psychoanalytic thinking of calling castration the cutting off the penis is so obvious, so well-known, that it demands an explanation. Lying on the surface of such an account is Freud's clear association of the phallic stage with the assertion of maleness. The visible penis with its erectile capacity, compared with the barely visible clitoris, stamps maleness on all sexuality, but mainly *it stamps gender identity with narcissism*. In phallic monism, cutting off the penis annihilates the foundation of gender identity of the male (secondarily of the female). Cutting off the penis, as the locus of phallic power, obliterates phallic power, narcissism and omnipotence. But why call it castration, when castration refers to cutting off the testicles, in popular as well as technical thinking? Calling it castration embeds the confusion of phallic with penis, and therefore with male as phallic and with female as deficient male.[2]

For Horney (1926), a phallic stage in the female aptly expressed the male's terror of feminization, a terror that Freud (1933) took to be the ultimate limitation to psychoanalysis, the bedrock that it could not break down. One could say that the female phallic stage was a girl's image reflected in a mirror held up to her by masculine phallic narcissism. *His* narcissism finds a way to impose itself on *her*. A good deal of his masculinity is sustained through this imposition. He presses his renounced femininity – the shadow of his masculinity – into her by an attributive projective identification (Britton 1994), depleting her of her own femininity and impressing her with an idealization of the phallus. But simultaneously, his phallic narcissism repudiates his own, actual, non-phallic – seminal – masculinity: The psychic concomitants of the production of semen by the male internal genital.

Masculinity (as well as femininity) loses its essential qualities into a phallic monism. The seminal dimension of masculinity, so intrinsically and exclusively male, is curiously absent from discussions about men, whether loving or misogynist. It is also absent from the psychoanalytic literature, where phallic and anti-phallic ideas abound, and where castration refers to cutting off the penis rather than the true meaning of cutting off the testicles. In my view, this displacement can be ascribed to the dread of the existential significance of semen, as a source of life and, in its ambivalence, also an agent of death. It is absorbed into a phallic defence, the omnipotence of which rescues masculinity from despair. This phallic defence shifts the dread of extinction into a threat of a penis castration, which the next erection can undo with sublime grandiosity. Phallic masculinity is, in this sense, squarely in the paranoid-schizoid position, described by Klein (1946).

It follows that this 'mistake' is not at all a mistake, but an unconsciously intentional displacement from seminal function to phallic narcissism. The more debate centres on phallic monism and female castration, and the more it is disputed for its monism and its masculine bias, the less is this seminal function in evidence. Displacement from seminal masculinity to phallic masculinity, and from actual castration to cutting off the penis, eclipse an awareness of procreative structures and functions, and the phantasies that they engender. The male seems simply to lack an internal procreative space with structures and processes uniquely male and equal in importance to those in the female; and the anxieties associated with them remain marginalized, misrepresented, or unrecognized in clinical work. It keeps us thinking about phallic monism when we need to understand masculinity.

The assimilation and mitigation of phallic narcissism into mature masculinity is a *seminal* issue, not just metaphorically: Semen is the vehicle of that assimilation – the material and symbolic location of genital phantasies. But also, evolving masculinity involves more than integrating phallic narcissism. It includes the depressive concern for the object and the reparative healing of ambivalence, which is also expressed as a seminal anxiety.

So, there are two non-phallic dimensions of masculine sexuality: A male internal genital space, equivalent to the female internal genital space, and the specifically masculine material and psychic reality of semen and insemination.

There is some literature on the former (which I will review in Chapter 2) but the latter is nearly absent from the psychoanalytic and popular literature.[3] Parallel with this gap, there is virtually no literature on the psychological dimension of male infertility (Keylor and Apfel 2010). Here, in my view, is the rock bottom male vulnerability against which phallic monism defends. I am not downplaying the male vulnerability to his feminine, receptive, caring dimension. What I am stressing is the uniquely male attribute of seminality. A deficiency in seminality is a deficiency in his identity as male. To the extent that his masculinity is bonded to such an attribute, so too is his anxious sense of complete collapse. For that reason, seminality is linked to hope and to desolation. It is squarely in the territory of Klein's depressive position, as is the phallic defence against it squarely in the territory of the paranoid-schizoid position.

An Observational Field for the Masculine: Observing Seminality

Seminality has to be observed with the mind's eye, in an interior space for which dimensional thinking is inadequate. We commonly speak of the internal world, of the baby and father's penis inside the mother, of the wish to return to (inside) the womb, of projecting into the object. But perhaps the common-sense use of inside misleads us into using visual images for a more primal urge recover a lost state, of which we have only an intimation. 'Inside' is, in my view, a comforting version of an ominous wish to acquire a state of 'before': Before object relations, before awareness: An uncanny, indescribable non-state, which I put with Kant's thing-in-itself and Bion's 'O.' I have elsewhere called this idea 'getting to the beginning of the beginning' (Figlio 2003).

A particular, primal, process of enlivening and repairing takes place 'there,' attracting the unending wish to be there, at the origin of oneself. Misogyny is also rooted there, when the impossibility of being there is intolerable and when the mystery of procreation is replaced by the phantasy of procreation by masculine activity in the womb as a workshop.

We have lacked an observational field, within which observations of the seminal dimension is possible. Let us consider the idea of an observational field: A setting and an attitude – an apparatus – in which we might 'see' this otherwise absent seminal masculinity. Fogel (2006, 1139) draws attention to this kind of problem. Aiming to expand the rigid concept of masculine and feminine into polarities of bisexuality, he makes the point that '[p]ersistent gender stereotypes and unnecessarily limiting theoretical formulations … may mask subtle countertransference and theoretical blind spots … .' But he does not include seminal function among the many characteristics of the masculine pole.

Distortion of the observational field for seminal masculinity was first mooted in path-breaking work by Anita Bell in the 1960s. She noted that

[up] to the present time, we have interpreted castration anxiety in relation to the phallus. In so doing we have unwittingly maintained a taboo about the testicle and scrotal sac. Until the taboo is lifted and the role of the testicle and scrotal sac fully explored, we must assume that the analysis of the male castration complex and male homosexuality has been incomplete. (1961, 283) ... We seem to have been overly zealous in offering phallic interpretations, thereby reinforcing the very defences we want to analyze – repression, denial and displacement to the phallus (Bell 1965, 189).

The recent tendency to repudiate phallic monism has aimed to diffuse concepts of gender identity but has not unearthed the deeper stratum of seminal masculinity. It is, therefore, important to back up and bear in mind that both occur in clinical material. We need to be ready to see phallic monism, in order to recognize its transitional and defensive functions.

Two vignettes from the analyses of boys poignantly show the insertion of a phallic defence into their seminal enquiry.

At about 2 ¼ years, having earlier accepted parents' explanations of bodily differences; and during toilet training, having been able to assuage emerging fears of losing his penis, as he lost faeces; 'the increasing importance of his penis [in the phallic-narcissistic phase] made it necessary for him to resort to defensive denial of his mother's lack of a penis. At this time [about 3 years old], *he asked increasingly sophisticated questions about conception, pregnancy, and birth. He was given simple answers, but was now unable to accept his parents' explanations as readily as he had done previously. Instead, he maintained in conversation with his mother: "When I was born I came out of your penis"'* (Edgcumbe and Burgner 1975, 173; my emphasis).

Another boy, just under five years "[h]aving worked towards a theory of conception, in which a man put his penis and seed into the woman, whose womb was horrific and red, and in which the man's penis would be broken off,... concluded that he had spare penises" (Hampstead Index).[4]

Of course, the pleasures of masturbation and the threat to the penis might be more immediate than the role of semen for the child, but the sensory-based vulnerability of the testicles is also immediate, and the phantasy of the mother's reproductive capacity might reasonably be matched by the phantasy of the father as a unique being like himself.

'Seeing' the internal male genital is, therefore, central to my argument. There is evidence of this equivalent male internal anatomy and psychic reality. For example, the inguinal canal is homologous with the vagina, and there are reports of masturbatory stimulation of the inguinal canal by retracting the testicles by the spermatic cord that passes through it. I have also highlighted the uniquely masculine dimension of masculine sexuality, which was not an internal genital space, but the production and implantation of semen; and by implantation, I mean to emphasise not just the discharge of semen but the psychic reality of implanting it – and the male himself, physically and psychically – in the female (see chapter 2 and Figlio 2010a for documentation). It is on this basis that Ferenczi (1924) spoke of a form of self-castration in sexual intercourse. The male, he argued, identified not just with his penis, which could be lost inside the female, but with his semen, which was lost in the female. Ejaculation was self-castration (29).

Ferenczi's account of identification with semen might seem improbable, but once in mind, it opens a new terrain of observation. We can now 'see' that, with genital generosity, semen is given to, not lost in, the female; that without generosity, semen is extracted from, overcome by, the female internal genital. We can also trace the ambivalence of the male towards the female, back through psychoanalytic theories of masculinity, ultimately to semen: What is given generously to fill the internal space of the female, repairing and impregnating her, can also be injected to poison her. This aggression is not phallic – it is not conveyed by physical attack by the penis: It is internal, an infection. Penetration as healthy phallic narcissism is shadowed by penetration as violation; seminal generosity is shadowed by seminal corrosion.

There is a profound, specifically seminal, ambivalence of good and bad semen. It is not the psychically sophisticated ambivalence of love and hate, but a primal ambivalence, in which the capacity to procreate and restore life can also destroy it at its moment of origination, a source of a deep-seated dread that the very springs of life could be undermined, leaving desolation behind. The primal ambivalence in semen, through which the male identifies with the female, suggests the need of an observational field in which we see 'inside' differently. Inside the female is not topographical, as with the penis inside the female, but an invisible interior merging or diffusion, in which destructive phantasies take the form of pollution, contamination and poisoning (see chapter 3).

Klein refers to the boy's fear of injury to his 'inside,' as well as to his penis, arising from a phantasy of retaliation by his mother and the internalized father's penis (1945). In this formulation, mother contains creative internal organs that arouse his envy. The boy, too, has an 'inside' that, he wishes, could be like hers. He fears for his 'inside,' attacked in retaliation for his attack on her 'inside.' But in Klein's formulation, while mother retaliates from her *inside*, he injures with his – external – *penis* as a ballistic weapon and as a vehicle for oral and excretory attack. Although Klein does refer in passing to 'urine and semen being destructive' (1961, 357), for her, the male mainly attacks with a phallic and excretory organ, not with the semen that comes from his internal, complex genital (also Ferenczi 1924, 37, 64).[5]

I draw attention to this seminal dimension of ambivalence, which Klein clearly has in mind, because she also speaks of seminal reparation. The semen that destroys is the impetus for reparation. Altogether, then, seminality embraces the uniquely male functions of generativity, destruction and reparation, located 'in' the complex male genital. Seminal ambivalence is primal ambivalence. It is foundational, a psychic element or unit. What creates also destroys. Being an ego, an agent, is ambivalent. As a core duality, seminality is an instrument of life and death drives. In the overall picture of non-phallic masculinity, seminality and its organs must be seen in their own right, next to the feminine receptivity of the male, which has been the main focus in reformulating masculinity from phallic to non-phallic.

Toxic Masculinity

The label, 'toxic masculinity,' has been applied to an egregious misogyny, and it gives us a clue about its roots.[6] Harrington (2021) reviews various cultural settings in which this label expressed dissatisfaction with stereotypes of the hard, unemotional man: A diffuse ascription gathered and sharpened into 'toxic.' It has come to stand for every sort of male abusiveness, as a character trait of masculinity. Harrington points out that it is often undefined and that, in its lack of specificity, it can stand for an equally unspecified, pejorative side of masculinity: Toxic masculinity as the dark side of a mythic essential manhood.

The magnetic power of toxic masculinity to draw every kind of male denigration of femininity under one label suggests an attribution – whether justified or not – of a fundamental character to masculinity. That warrants a searching investigation. Why *toxic* masculinity? Shepherd Bliss, the apparent inventor of the term in the 1980s, had in mind a medical idea of the polarity – toxic/healthy – which would suggest the possibility of recovery from the sickness of a toxic state (Harrington, 347). The medical idea of recovering from sickness, suggested by Bliss, would more readily evoke the idea of an infection, treated with antibiotics: A contagious disease, not a toxic state.

Although toxic masculinity was invented in the 1980s, it took off only in 2011 (see Google ngram viewer). The upsurge occurred not long after 'toxic assets,' which began its ascent in 2003, just ahead of the banking crisis of 2008. The banking crisis was provoked mainly by these toxic assets. There was particular concern for so-called 'collateralised debt obligations' (CDOs) and financial 'derivatives,' which were forms of selling packages of debt on to other banks or insuring them. As the packaging of debt moved further away from the original institution and client, it became more difficult to assess the assets from which the debt could be repaid. An inherent instability in the financial system was known about for some time and dismissed. When it came, it was a major event. Good assets were found to be worse than worthless: They were poisonous – 'toxic' – 'assets.' The banking crisis spawned research into the masculine culture in banking, along with coverage in the popular press (Figlio 2010b). Then came the eruption of toxic masculinity.

But 'toxic' and 'toxicity' had been embedded in culture long before toxic masculinity. They began their ascent into English in the already in the 1870s, presumably with a rising sensitivity to pollution, then took of sharply in the 1960s. Rachel Carson's *Silent Spring* has captured this sense of injuring nature since it was published in 1962. 'Toxic waste' began its accelerating rise shortly after, in 1965. These days, many things that go wrong are called toxic: Toxic waste, toxic culture, toxic influence, toxic language, toxic debate, toxic impact, toxic information, toxic atmosphere, toxic beauty culture, toxic funding cuts, toxic debt – not just toxic masculinity (the list is endless; even a casual survey of newspaper reports will quickly confirm the dissemination of toxic everything into everyday language; also see Google ngram viewer).

Sally Weintrobe (2021, 261–262) points to a toxic aggression directed at nature, which bespeaks a paranoid-schizoid anxiety, and which hints at an underlying depressive anxiety.

> After just eighteen months in power, Trump's new administration had repealed seventy-six environmental protections (forty-six successfully, the rest facing legal challenge [several of which could be seen literally as toxic, affecting water, air and soil] ... Might survival anxiety also lie beneath this triumph and be driving these savage sadistic attacks.

We have begun either to fear that nature can no longer survive this destructiveness, or to deny it. I think the idea of a phallic attack incudes a defence against an unconscious phantasy that we use nature as a pre-mother, overwhelmed by the insidious, internal contamination by human aggression. It has created an uncanny 'Ominous in Nature' (Figlio 1996), as a subliminal awareness of a depressive desolation.

Toxic masculinity crystallized these currents of feeling and an unconscious association with masculinity. It subsumed other toxicities, giving them a masculine tone. A culture of a hard masculinity has also been found in fundamentalist movements, which burgeoned in the English language from 1974. Smith (2019) has documented the connection between the violence of terrorism and a history of male violence towards women. The masculine culture of the Taliban, of Iranian fundamentalism and of the terrorist cults affiliated to Al Qaeda have no soft edges; they are hard and relentless. We could add Christian and Jewish fundamentalism – fundamentalism in general – as cultures of masculinity because the leaders are exclusively male and because the terrorist sects are exclusively male. Stein (2002, 413) argues that terrorists, typically male, regress to a homo-erotic relationship with a tyrannical father, submitting to him in an act of love and merger, which is also sustained through misogyny. More generally, links appear in the popular press and elsewhere between contemporary populism, white supremacism and the incel movement, with a misogynist leaning.

But still, why *toxic* masculinity? Toxic means poisonous, contaminating, polluting. What is toxic is insidious: Not an assault from the outside, not an impact on, but an erosion from the inside. Toxic undermines life. It makes sense only with respect to the well-being of life. Toxic often suggests an effluent of waste that must be separated from the processes of the healthy organism, of which it was once part. There are also toxic effects of products marketed for beneficial purposes, such as weed-killers, sometimes foisted by deceit on unsuspecting customers. Toxic reminds us that the bad is mixed into the good. I think it suggests an amalgamation of human feelings attitudes and behaviour, just as it alerts us to the poison that medicines become if we overdose. In psychoanalysis, that amalgam of good and bad is called ambivalence. Male fertility and the organs, processes, and substances of male fertility – penis, testicles, spermatic structures, prostate gland – produce semen, which is the seat of a primal ambivalence.

Toxic Masculinity and Primal Ambivalence

This primal ambivalence contaminates the good object, as understood in psychoanalysis; that is, the infant's phantasy of a primal – maternal – goodness on which its life depends. The anxiety of contaminating the good object is an anxiety that goodness cannot be separated from badness and cannot be protected. It is a source of guilt and the motive of the reparative phantasy that the good object can be improved: Not restored – that would be magical – but made better, brought into ordinary good-enough reality.

Primal ambivalence might be overlain by phallic anxiety and its magical properties, but it remains a sink of dread. The closest psychoanalytic representation I have found is a comment by Bion, that 'good smells are felt to be turned into bad by the destructiveness with which they are savoured' (1992, 48). The immediate sensation of savouring, apart from the ancillary muscularity of biting or chewing, can infiltrate the goodness of an aroma and sour it. Similarly, semen, in the moment of engendering or repairing life, like a moment of savouring, can infiltrate the goodness of an insemination and contaminate it.

Phallic masculinity defends against this deeper bedrock of depressive anxiety. It is characterized by paranoid-schizoid mentation: The ego is threatened by persecution and defends itself by attack on an object that then becomes retaliatory. This sort of anxiety is often confused with guilt, but they are not the same. The ego feels belaboured in both, but harassment by persecutory objects invites defensive aggression – destroy the object – while harassment by guilt proper is a desolation at the collapse of life and the originating urge for reparation. Phallic masculinity is a masculinity of performance and prowess; seminal masculinity is one of fertility and lineage, hope and dread. The dread of seminal failure, unlike phallic failure, is a dread of the loss of hope that the ego can generate and sustain life.

The catastrophe of ambivalence, which can generate life and destroy it, is squarely in the depressive position, described by Melanie Klein (1935).

Without it, there is no life; with it, comes concern for the object as the target of hate as well as love, or retreat into phallic triumphalism. It is, however, a primal ambivalence, before love and hate have any meaning. It is lodged at the core of the ego, in an ambivalence in the origination of object relations. It reaches an albeit denied recognition through the label, toxic masculinity. The insecurity of male identity, the loss of faith in the capacity to sustain life, the shame of infertility – these debilities that shadow adult masculinity – are also thresholds for the boy as he matures into adulthood.

Masculinity oscillates between persecutory and depressive – phallic and seminal – poles, with an anxiety appropriate to each. The former is triumphal; the latter is depressive in the Kleinian sense. The former combats destructiveness with its own weapons; the latter aches with the realization of human destructiveness. The former embodies hope through destroying destructiveness; the latter carries a seed of regeneration, nurtured by the hope for a conception. The former is omnipotent; the latter reality-orientated and object-related, in its waiting for love to renew human life: Male insecurity plays on the vulnerability of the testicular father against which the phallic father presses forward in a defensive posture. In this situation, seminality is eclipsed and garnered by phallicism. What I call toxic masculinity is the intrusion of phallic masculinity, with its heroic posturing, into the masculinity of fertility, with its hope for life in the face of desolation.

The Pathological Highlights the Normal: A Methodological Note on Misogyny and Gender

I follow Freud's dictum, that the pathological – the extreme, if we want to avoid the idea of pathology – sharpens the view of the normal – or ordinary – by the exaggeration of its features. Toxic masculinity is such an extreme, in which toleration of the fecundity of the mother and the mystery of union and conception is lost. The imperative to be 'inside' the space of this intimacy, countered by the dread of dissolution into it, combine to establish masculine identity through misogyny: By demeaning, ultimately extinguishing, the feminine. This dreadful ambivalence is so fundamental, that, in my view, misogyny is the template for other hatred-driven masculine prejudices. It takes us back to Klein's femininity phase as the process through which a loving, embracing relationship if the masculine with the feminine is facilitated or impeded.

I will not enter into the current controversies over gender and sexuality. The relationship between them is as old as the philosophical mind-body problem. The sense of identity, concordance, dissonance or disconnection between gender and anatomy is complex. Wisdom (1983, 1992) suggests that psychoanalysis might have taken – still might take – a different course, had it begun with divergence of gender from an androgynous core, rather than from bisexuality and phallic monism. [7]

Wisdom also, however, points to a basic anatomical and physiological feature, which is also fundamentally relational. The penis inserts and ejaculates semen. In that sense, it is active in a way neither the breast nor the clitoris is active. The vagina and the mouth may actively suck, and both penis and breast can be sucked, but the penis and ejaculation are uniquely male.

I will define masculine and feminine on this basis. The male, in his masculinity, is characterized by the anatomy and the physiology to generate semen and to put it into the female, who has the anatomy and physiology, not only to receive it, but to assimilate and unite with it, and to nurture the union into a child. But, along with Freud, I am concerned with the psychoanalytic psychology. I see masculine as active, in the sense of giving semen and penetrating, not with the penis, but with projective identification, and feminine as receptive. Receptivity can be active, as in embracing and incorporating. But the feminine is receptive, not just in receiving, but in conceiving.[8] I will avoid 'male' and 'female,' 'man' and 'woman' as much as possible, unless it strains common-sense to avoid them. I will speak of 'masculine' and 'feminine,' to single out this particular meaning of active as seminal and receptive as conceptive.

Referring to the extreme to highlight the ordinary, I describe and analyze a specifically masculine unstable identity through a hostile, demeaning attitude towards women. It is the masculine tendency, typically more pronounced in men. It is the masculine that is misogynistic and the feminine that is the target of misogyny. By the misogyny of the masculine, I refer to the tendency towards a phallic defence and its implementation through projective identification. By vulnerability of the feminine, I refer to her receptivity to projective identification, in particular, to attributive projective identification. The phallic defence includes a conscious narrative and, as such, conceals the seminal-conceptive level as a depressive level, haunted by dread and desolation.[9]

Notes

1   There is a particular perversity in misogyny when it is found in the betrayal of the protectiveness that we also associate with masculinity. When, for example, police attack women, the tolerated and barely hidden abuse known in the low conviction rate for rape, erupts into public awareness. That misuse of legitimate and expected protectiveness is, for example, an egregious betrayal of trust in the father.

2   The misnomer in 'castration' is a form of defence. The displacement from testicles and fertility to penis and phallic omnipotence carries the testicles and fertility with it but remaining unconscious. It functions similarly to negation (*Verneinung*: To say 'no'; Freud 1925b), in that it allows the Unconscious into consciousness without recognizing it. Freud says of negation, that it allows the intellectual content into consciousness, stripped of affect, so it has (no) meaning (the content seems meaningless).

3   The parental couple may have a sexual and procreative relationship, but the seminal uniqueness of the father – half of what makes them different from each other and a couple – is missing. Moreover, as Green has pointed out (Green 1995,

877), the Kleinian concentration on the breast equates the penis with the breast, and therefore with nourishment more than with procreation. Green is partly right: Klein does refer to the procreative and reparative penis and semen, but somewhat in passing (e.g., 1950, 45). Britton (1989, 85, 99) also mentions procreativity, and the difficulty in recognizing the 'parents' sexual relationship, their different anatomy, and the child's own nature' (86). Meltzer (1973, 67–73) speaks of the 'testicular father.'

4   A precise citation is not possible. The Hampstead Index project is described in detail and utilized for research by Dreher (2000). The author is grateful to Professor Peter Fonagy for permission to quote from it.

5   There are fourteen references to poison in *The New Dictionary of Kleinian Thought*, but none refers to semen (Bott Spillius et al. 2011).

6   'Toxic masculinity' is a curious misuse of 'toxicity.' Toxicity is a property of a substance: Poisonous, polluting, contaminating. Yet it has become the ubiquitous label for masculine misogyny as a phallic atrocity against the female. In my view, this misuse is not accidental: It serves the unconscious aim of avoiding the very thing that it names: Toxicity, the pollution of life into desolation. To attack the origin of life in the female, in order to extinguish or corrupt it, is the fundamental misogyny. This misuse of a concept is the same as using castration to designate cutting off the penis – the home of the phallus – rather than the testicles, which are the home of male fertility. It seems also to be a variant of Freud's 'negation.' Also, Freud (1895, 169) drew attention to a 'boundary idea,' which represents repressed thoughts, 'because, on the one hand, it belongs to the ego and, on the other hand, it forms an undistorted portion of the traumatic memory.' I think 'toxic masculinity' has spread so widely *because* it gives voice to an unconscious idea, on the condition that it remains unrecognized.

7   Wisdom argues that psychoanalysis has been handicapped by lodging our thinking about sexual and gender difference in terms of bisexuality, with its presupposition of male and female. He suggests it might have been better had Freud begun with androgyny as an undifferentiated core, rather than an androcentric and bisexual core. Androgyny implies unity of gender at the beginning. From androgyny, sexual difference and a variety of genders would differentiate and 'personality exchange' would distribute gender qualities back and forth by projective and introjective identification. Equality is never breached, as opposed to the active/passive gender attribution built into bisexuality. Freud (1910, 94) referred to myth, in which gods were androgynous, and to hermaphrodism (1930, 105 n. 3) as a possible original sexual state. Androgyny refers to an ambiguous gender, while hermaphrodism refers to bearing both male and female genitals. Freud seems not to have distinguished them clearly, which leaves bisexuality similarly unclear.

8   Having drawn attention to the active nipple, I would add that the breast can also function as an organ of projective identification. But semen remains quite different from milk. Both get 'inside,' but semen, unlike milk, gets inside the very origination of life and of its failure or destruction.

9   Wisdom (1983) also points out that men are more sensitive to any attribution of femininity to them, than women are to an attribution of masculinity to them. Interestingly, in a general PEPWEB search, under 'what are you looking for?', there are 1457 hits for 'boys fantasy of female genital' and only two hits for 'girls fantasy of male genital.' The fascination – and the anxiety? – is very much the opposite of what one might expect from the theory of phallic monism, based on penis envy, and in line with Wisdom's singling out the greater sensitivity to gender attribution in males than in females, and specifically to an anatomical reference for gender identification.

References

Balsam, R. (2018) 'Castration Anxiety' Revisited: Especially 'Female Castration Anxiety'. *Psychoanalytic Inquiry* 38(1): 11–22.

Bell, A. (1965) The Significance of the Scrotal Sac and Testicles for the Prepuberty Male. *Psychoanalytic. Quarterly* 34: 182–206.

Bion, W. R. (1992) *Cogitations*. London: Karnac.

Bott Spillius, E., et al. (2011) *The New Dictionary of Kleinian Thought*. London/New York: Routledge.

Breen, D. (ed.) (1993) *The Gender Conundrum: Contemporary Perspectives on Femininity and Masculinity*. London/New York: Routledge.

Britton, R. (1989) The Missing Link: Parental Sexuality in the Oedipus Complex. In Steiner, J. (ed.) *The Oedipus Complex Today Clinical Implications*. London: Karnac, 83–101.

Britton, R. (1994) Publication Anxiety: Conflict between Communication and Affiliation. *International Journal of Psychoanalysis* 75: 1213–1224.

Britton, R. (2001) Forever Father's Daughter: The Athene-Antigone Complex. In Trowell, J. and Etchegoyen, A. (eds) *The Importance of Fathers*. London/New York: Routledge; revised, as Phallic Idealisation in Women. *In Sex, Death and the Superego: Updating Psychoanalytic Experience and Developments in Neuroscience*, 2nd edn. London/New York: Routledge, 2021, 50–61.

Carson, R. (1962) *Silent Spring*. Boston: Houghton Mifflin.

Diamond, M. (2006) Masculinity Unravelled: The Roots of Male Gender Identity and Shifting of Male Ego Ideals throughout Life. *Journal of the American. Psychoanalytic. Association* 54: 1099–1130.

Diamond, M. J. (2013). Evolving Perspectives on Masculinity and Its Discontents: Reworking the Internal Phallic and Genital Positions. In Mari, E. P. and Thomson-Salo, F. (eds) *Masculine and Feminine Today*. London: Karnac, 1–24.

Diamond, M. J. (2015) The Elusiveness of Masculinity: Primordial Vulnerability, Lack, and the Challenges of Male Development, *Psychoanalytic Quarterly* 84: 47–102.

Diamond, M. (2021) *Masculinity and Its Discontents: The Male Psyche and the Inherent Tensions of Maturing Manhood*. London/New York: Routledge.

Dimen, M. and Goldner, V. (2006) Gender and Sexuality. In Person, E., Cooper, A. and Gabbard, G. (eds) *The American Psychiatric Publishing Textbook of Psychoanalysis*. Washington/London: American Psychiatric Publishing, 93–114.

Edgcumbe, R. and Burgner, B. (1975) The Phallic Phase – A Differentiation between Preoedipal and Oedipal Aspects of Phallic Development. *Psychoanalytic Studies of the Child* 30: 161–180.

Ferenczi, S. (1924) *Thallassa: A Theory of Genitality*. NY, New York: Psychoanal. Q., 1938; repr. London: Karnac, 1989.

Figlio, K. (1996) The Ominous in Nature. *Free Associations* 6(2): 276–296.

Figlio, K. (2003) Getting to the Beginning: Historical Memory and Concrete Thinking. In Radstone, S. and Hodgkin, K. (eds) *Regimes of Memory (Routledge Studies in Memory and Narrative, vol. 12)*. London: Routledge, 2003, 152–166; pb *Memory Cultures: Memory, Subjectivity and Recognition*. New Brunswick/London: Transaction, 2006.

Figlio, K. (2010a) Phallic and Seminal Masculinity: A Theoretical and Clinical Confusion. *International Journal of Psychoanalysis* 91(1): 119–139.

Figlio, K. (2010b) The Financial Crisis: A Psychoanalytic View of Illusion, Greed and Reparation in Masculine Phantasy. *New Formations* 72: 33–46; also in Bennet, D. (ed.) *Loaded Subjects: Psychoanalysis, Money and the Global Financial Crisis.* London: Lawrence and Wishart, 2012, 34-51.

Flouri, E. (2005) *Fathering & Child Outcomes.* Chichester: John Wiley & Sons.

Fogel, G. (2006) Riddles of Masculinity: Gender, Bisexuality, and Thirdness. *Journal of the American Psychoanalytic Association* 54: 1139–1163.

Freud, S. (1895) Draft K. The Neuroses of Defense (A Christmas Fairy Tale), January 1, 1896: [enclosed with letter]. *The Complete Letters of Sigmund Freud to Wilelm Fliess, 1887–1904*, edited and translated by Masson, J. M.: Cambridge: Belknap Press, 1986, 162–169.

Freud, S. (1910) Leonardo Da Vinci and a Memory of His Childhood. *The Standard Edition of the Complete Psychological Works of Sigmund Freud* 11: 57–138.

Freud, S. (1923) The Infantile Genital Organization: An Interpolation into the Theory of Sexuality. *The Standard Edition of the Complete Psychological Works of Sigmund Freud* 19: 139–145.

Freud, S. (1925a). Some Psychical Consequences of the Anatomical Distinction between the Sexes. *The Standard Edition of the Complete Psychological Works of Sigmund Freud* 19: 241–258.

Freud, S. (1925b) Negation. *The Standard Edition of the Complete Psychological Works of Sigmund Freud* 19: 233–240.

Freud, S. (1930) Civilization and Its Discontents. *The Standard Edition of the Complete Psychological Works of Sigmund Freud* 21: 57–146.

Freud, S. (1931) Female Sexuality. *The Standard Edition of the Complete Psychological Works of Sigmund Freud* 21: 221–243.

Freud, S. (1933) New Introductory Lectures on Psycho-Analysis. *The Standard Edition of the Complete Psychological Works of Sigmund Freud* 22: 1–182.

Green, A. (1995). Has Sexuality Anything to Do with Psychoanalysis? *International Journal of Psychoanalysis* 76: 871–883.

Harrington, C. (2021) What Is "Toxic Masculinity" and Why Does It Matter? *Men and Masculinities* 24(2): 345–352.

Horney, K. (1926) The Flight from Womanhood: The Masculinity-Complex in Women, as Viewed by Men and by Women. *International Journal of Psychoanalysis* 7:324–339; reprinted in *Feminine Psychology*. NY: Norton, 1967, 54–70.

Johns, M. (2002) Identification and Dis-identification in the Development of Sexual Identity. In Trowel, J. and Etchegoyen, A. (eds) (2003) *The Importance of Fathers: A Psychoanalytic Re-evaluation.* Hove/New York: Brunner-Routledge/Taylor and Francis.

Keylor, R. and Apfel, R. (2010) Male Infertility: Integrating an Old Psychoanalytic Story with the Research Literature. *Studies in Gender and Sexuality* 11(2): 60–77.

Klein, M. (1928) Early Stages of the Oedipus Conflict. In *The Writings of Melanie Klein*, vol. 1. London: The Hogarth Press and the Institute of Psycho-Analysis, 1975, 186–198.

Klein, M. (1935) A Contribution to the Psychogenesis of Manic-Depressive States. In *The Writings of Melanie Klein*, vol. 1. London: The Hogarth Press and the Institute of Psycho-Analysis, 1975, 262–289.

Klein, M. (1937) Love, Guilt and Reparation. In *The Writings of Melanie Klein*, vol. 1. London: The Hogarth Press and the Institute of Psycho-Analysis, 1975, 306–343.

Klein, M. (1946) Notes on Some Schizoid Mechanisms. In *The Writings of Melanie Klein*, vol. 3. London: The Hogarth Press and the Institute of Psycho-Analysis, 1975, 1–24.

Klein, M. (1950). On the Criteria for the Termination of a Psycho-Analysis. In *The Writings of Melanie Klein*, vol. 3. London: The Hogarth Press and the Institute of Psycho-Analysis, 1975, 43–47.

Klein, M. (1961). Narrative of a Child Analysis: The Conduct of the Psycho-Analysis of Children as Seen in the Treatment of a Ten Year Old Boy. In *The Writings of Melanie Klein*, vol. 4. London: The Hogarth Press and the Institute of Psycho-Analysis, 1975.

Laplanche, J. (2007) Gender, Sex, and the Sexual. *Studies in Gender and Sexuality* 8: 209–219.

Marí, E. P. and Thomson-Salo, F. (eds) (2013) *Masculinity and Femininity Today*. London: Karnac.

Mayer, E. (1995) The Phallic Castration Complex and Primary Femininity: Paired Developmental Lines towards Female Gender Identity. *Journal of the American Psychoanalytic Association* 43: 17–38.

Meltzer, D. (1988) *The Apprehension of Beauty: The Role of Aesthetic Conflict in Development and Violence*. Strath Tay: The Clunie Press.

Ross, J. M. (1992) *The Male Paradox*. New York: Simon & Schuster.

Smith, J. (2019) *Home Grown: How Domestic Violence Turns Men into Terrorists*. London: Riverrun.

Stein, R. (2002). Evil as Love and as Liberation. *Psychoanalytic Dialogues* 12: 393–420.

Weintrobe, S. (2021) *Psychological Roots of the Climate Crisis: Neo-Liberal Exceptionalism and the Culture of Uncare*. London/New York: Bloomsbury.

Wisdom, J. O. (1983) Male and Female. *International Journal of Psychoanalysis* 64: 159–168.

Wisdom, J. O. (1992) *Feud, Women, and Society*. New Brunswick/London: Transaction Publishers.

Zachary, A. (2018) *The Anatomy of the Clitoris: Reflections on the Theory of Female Sexuality*. London: Routledge.

Part II

The Interior World

Chapter 2

Male Internal Genital Space

Freud's theory of a phallic stage became controversial on two grounds. First, it was a phallic monism; that is, it applied to both males and females: For males, centred on the penis; for females, centred on the absence of a penis and the envy of the male for his penis. Secondly, he thought it was a developmental stage, part of normal psychosexual development. Today, psychoanalysts think of it as a defence, not a developmental stage, common in males, rare in females. Not surprisingly, in the case of females, psychoanalysis has concentrated on an internal genital space, only recently attending to an internal genital space of the male.

It goes unrecognized that Freud earlier thought that phallic genitality was the external manifestation of complex, internal genital structures and function. His self-analysis ended with a dream of dissecting his own pelvis. Apart from the phallic intrusion of the dissection, a key part of the dream involved a log cabin with two children lying next to two men on benches, which he approached in a weakened state, his legs giving way, suggesting phallic castration. He associated the cabin with the adult figures to an Etruscan tomb he visited, but he laid stress on the children, who would replace two planks that would allow him to cross a crevasse. They were the future: Two children in the womb, next to two adults in the tomb (Bonomi 1998, 45; Freud 1900, 413, 452–455, 477–478).

Freud did not interpret, for us at least, these procreative aspects. Nonetheless, he said

> The quality of fears, fantasies, and misconceptions about the male inside genital structures has led me to believe that even in early childhood sensations of an uncanny nature may arise not only from the testicles but also from accessory genital pelvic organs (489).

This strand of Freud's thinking has a distinctly modern ring to it, though even today, with the phallic stage far less prominent than it was for him, the idea of an internal male genital is not common and castration still refers to cutting off the penis, not the testicles (Figlio 2010). Freud (1937) is partly

DOI: 10.4324/9781003455790-4

responsible, because he marginalized his own recognition of an internal male genital next to his phallic monism, and he saw a core resistance to the feminine as an unavoidable obstacle to psychoanalysis, without connecting this resistance to the male's own – feminine, we might say – vulnerable interior. In the bright light of day, the phallic penis casts a shadow on the internal genital of both male and female, the 'uncanny nature' of which becomes a menace in the interior depths of the body.

It seems Freud touched a nerve in his retreat into phallic monism, turning a blind eye, in a scotomization that serves as a defensive stance against this shadowy internal world of the male. Kestenberg (1977, 404) drew attention to this diversion, led by Freud, and saw in it the male anxieties that drove a flight from an unstable internal genital.

> Most analysts followed in Freud's footsteps and consistently refrained from the analysis of inner genitals in men. They shifted their attention from the inner-genital, reproductive organs to the sphere of faeces inside and from the pre-oedipal to the negative oedipal phase in which the boy's anal-passive wishes are revived. They shifted their attention from the inner-genital reproductive organs of the woman to her wish for an external attribute—a penis—and from her pre-oedipal to the negative oedipal phase in which she wishes to impregnate her mother. In my view, *the wish for a baby is derived from all pregenital phases*; it culminates and is organized in the inner-genital phase and is revived—as a substitute for the phallus—in the phallic-oedipal phase ... It is remarkable that not a single analyst has concerned himself with [the inner genital space of the male, such as the] role of the prostate and seminal vesicles in the psychology of men. It is equally remarkable that men, whose fathers complain about the symptoms of prostatic hypertrophy in advancing age, ignore their own apprehension about suffering the same fate as they grow older. Is there a universal fear of exploring man's essential inner reproductive organs? Is man's fear of getting too close to his inner genitalia related to his inclination for distance empathy? Is that also the reason why we have so little information about the role of the pre-oedipal father in the lives of infants ... Are men afraid to encroach upon this domain of women, not only because of the threat of castration, but also because women guard their intimate relationship with their infants and refuse to share it with men?... (Kestenberg's emphasis).

Kestenberg suggests that males distance themselves from females, and denigrate them, not because females lack a penis, but because an internal dimension – including their own – arouses anxiety.[1] It is a dimension they cannot bring into perception. In 'Analysis Terminable and Interminable,' Freud (1937) spoke of a 'bedrock' in analysis – an elemental level, based on castration anxiety, that cannot be further analyzed. For the male, that is a repudiation of femininity, so solid that it must have biological roots.

Suggesting that the male does not want to be a female to another male, he adds that 'What [men[reject is not passivity in general, but passivity towards a male' (252, n.1). Steiner (2020) reflects on Freud's pessimistic conclusion that analysis comes up against a bedrock resistance, in a combination of the death drive and the repudiation of femininity. The absent penis and the thinly veiled receptive orifice of the female render her a suitable repository for the male's projection into her of his unseen internal space. I would add that his unseen, and unseeable, internal space is also inconceivable, literally beyond comprehension and of an 'uncanny nature' (Freud).

The projection of the obscure, dark world of the interior in the female makes her into a fascinating terrain for exploration as well as a frightening foreign land. I speak, rather, of the feminine, because 'she' is not any actual female, but an abstract attribution. He can be the inveterate explorer, as long as he retains his phallic dominance. Having projected his dark interior into femininity, his 'fantasies about a penis inside a woman, frightening as they are, are reassuring by their implication that his own hidden structures are phallic, linked to the outside, and controllable from the outside ... In exploring women men try to find out what their own inside is like [from the distance established by projection' (Kestenberg 1968, 488, 489). She becomes a terrain to be mapped.

Despite the readiness of psychoanalysts to follow Freud in marginalizing the recognition of the internal male genital space, a body of observations has established a credible base for continuing research. Studies on male internal genital space usually refer to the path-breaking work of Anita Bell (1961, 1965). She argued that boys were aware of their internal genital, which was the site of confused, but nonetheless perceptible, sensations. Because of the anatomical proximity of anus, testicles and penis, defaecation aroused anxiety at also losing the testicles, and the anxiety was displaced onto the penis, whose existence could be confirmed and whose manipulation and enlargement were pleasurable and reassuring. Phallic anxiety comes later and acts as a defence against internal anxiety (1961, 185, 266; also, Edgcumbe and Burgner 1975, 173; Tyson 1986, 6; Bell's theory should be read next to Ferenczi's (1924) on the libidinal links to urethral and bowel functions).

> We must not forget that the pregenital anxiety felt by the little boy about loss of feces and testes is the forerunner of the later occurring phallic castration anxiety. The boy is likely to think that if the testicle can disappear, the phallus may do so too. With the development of phallic primacy, the older fears of loss of feces and testes tend to influence phallic castration fears in an unconscious way. Since with few exceptions the boy can see his phallus change but not disappear, it is quite possible that the mechanism of displacement—from testes to phallus—has its beginning here ... Boys regard a trauma or blow to the developing testes as extremely

dangerous. "You can die from that", we are told; or it is said that after a blow the testes will swell and burst, causing death. I have several times come upon the fantasy that if a boy cohabits with a girl his testicles will die, or fill up and burst and then he will die. One ten-year-old thought that a man can make only two children because after it gives out its seed each testicle shrivels and dies. Here we have fears of castration in which boys refer to the testicles rather than to the phallus … It is more than likely that the deeper roots of the male's castration anxiety lie in his fears about the loss of his testes… We seem to have been overly zealous in offering phallic interpretations, thereby re-enforcing the very defenses we want to analyze—repression, denial, and displacement to the phallus … and completely neglected the rest of the male genital, which constitutes two-thirds of the whole (Bell 1965, 185, 186, 188, 205).

Moreover, Bell and others observed that the boy compared his testicles with mother's breasts and fertility (189, 191; Stärcke 1921, 186; Yazmajian 1966a, 308–309; 1967, 87; Putnam reported a scrotal phantasy as a feminine symbol, in Jones 1912, 53 n.6).

This line of thinking has been developed most thoroughly by Kestenberg (1968), who postulates an 'inner genital phase' as well as 'inner genital structures' in boys and girls. Both boys and girls relieve the inchoate, confused sensations, excitement and imaginations of something going on inside, identified with mother, by externalization. But the boy, with his visible as well as focally sensitive penis, more readily and completely externalizes inner feelings and anxieties onto the penis, including castration anxiety, and disposes of the awareness and the anxieties surrounding his inner genital by projection (Kestenberg speaks of the penis 'as conveyor and transformer of diffuse visceral sensations' (492).

Discovering the differences between the sexes furthers an association of femininity with 'bloody holes' and masculinity 'with intactness' (505). 'The internal route from the testicles to the penis is equated with the female birth canal and with the tube that connects the bladder to the outside' and the boy 'imagines that the baby is delivered on the side of the body through the inguinal ring which he equates with the birth canal' (508). These associations bring out an anxiety, kept under control by phallic reassurance. 'Men are reluctant to talk about their testicles, but even more reluctant to acknowledge the role of the prostate, seminal vesicles or spermatic cords. Fears and fantasies connected with anal penetration tend to be expressed in terms of feminine identification and castration fear' (488).

The male's concern for the inside of his body and his wish to control his genitals leads to his 'interpreting his inside as a secure framework for the penis' (503), which is reminiscent of Hans' troubled assertion that his penis was 'fixed in' (see chapter 4). A penis could be 'torn out at the roots,' as several of Kestenberg's patients feared (495), displacing anxiety outwards, in the penis, but also revealing its roots inside the body, which secured a phantasy of regeneration of the internal genital.

Following Bell's and Kestenberg's work, several other analysts developed the idea of a male inner space as the seat of procreative capacities of similar status to those of the female; of anxieties at loss or damage, equivalent to castration anxiety; and of diffuse, inchoate sensations. Fogel (1998, 662) says that 'castration anxiety arises when any crucial part of mature psychic life is threatened.' The phallus defends against the vulnerability of an inner 'generative space,' which is a primary, 'cloacal' fantasy, in which a plethora of feelings and fantasies to do with creativity occur (675–688). Cloacal fantasies are common to male and female: For the male, a body-based location of his feminine parts (695; cf. Freud 1905, 196).

For Fogel, the alternative to phallic masculinity seems to be a capacity similar to femininity (see also Diamond 2006), whereas, for Kestenberg and others, the alternative is an inner masculinity, akin to what I am calling 'seminal' masculinity. Friedman (1996, 202), for example, notes that 'in psychoanalytic theory the testicles have no separate libidinal cathexis and castration fears are considered solely from a phallic reference point.' Against this accepted view, he presents a substantial body of clinical evidence, showing the development of symptoms around anxieties centred on loss of the testicles, including the consequences of cryptorchidism. One conclusion he draws is that the male body image, which has been taken to be unproblematic – based on the penis – is not so secure. With Bell and Kestenberg, he argues that it is undermined by testicular anxieties. Phallic masculinity is a defence against them, a defence that leaves these inner anxieties unrecognized, and, without an adequate integration of the phallic and testicular dimensions of castration anxiety, only insecurely mitigated.

Unlike the penis, the testicles could be lost for ever, disappearing into an inner space that is both beyond monitoring and is female. Stereotypes of masculinity reinforce this phallic defence, in which the male penetrates. It is a desire further reinforced by fears of being penetrated, which, for Elise (2001) and others, gives a phallic shape to anxieties concerning internal space.

Boys and men are aware of movement of the testes in the scrotal sac and inguinal canal. Bell (1961), Friedman (1996) and Yazmajian (1967; 1983) report on the anxiety that the testicles could retract, lodge in the inguinal canal and even enter the abdomen or, in phantasy, disappear. Boys phantasize that the testicles can wander around the body (a male equivalent of the archaic belief that the womb wandered). Friedman reported the case of a four-year-old boy, who was aware of testicular retraction, and developed a model in which they moved into the stomach via the inguinal canal, where babies were made by mixing them with food and faeces, then moved into the intestines, to be born anally (1996, 246). Yazmajian (1966a; 1967) provided clinical evidence of testicular retraction in dream material, and of exacerbation of testicular anxieties by cryptorchidism (for extensive clinical material on testicles, concentrating on family constellation and on testicular move-ment, see Myers 1976).

These authors also report on testicular masturbation by pressing the tes-ticles into the inguinal canal, which can be interpreted as an attempt both to mitigate testicular castration anxiety and to identify with the female. They report the common association of testicles with breasts and, in the case of the four-year-old boy, an imitation of the mother through a complex theory of making and giving birth to babies. Glenn (1969) shows the extent to which boys do have pleasurable feelings in, and associations to, their testicles, even if more diffuse than in the penis. He explores situations in which testicular castration fears, perhaps because of injury or over-stimulation in childhood, become more significant than phallic castration fears. There is evidence, therefore, of a sensory basis for seminal castration anxiety, just as there is for phallic castration anxiety (Bell 1965; Friedman 1996, 242–246; Kestenberg 1968, 489; Yazmajian 1966a; 1983).

These studies bring out aspects of masculinity based on a more diffuse idea of the male genital. It is more complex than the penis alone, and it supports a function quite different from penetration. Yet, as Steiner (2020) points out, there remains a desire to possess a penis as the desire for the easy route of phallic omnipotence, in the face of the reality of dependence and need – certainly the need of the envied mother. And, he argues, men denigrate femininity because they idealize it, then envy it.

> Freud's view of a "struggle against a passive or feminine attitude" is in fact a struggle against the adoption of a receptive position, which although feminine in its imagery, is equally important for both men and women to accept[,] not only in relation to the breast in infancy, but also in order to be receptive to the thoughts and feelings of others through a capacity to receive and contain projections … The resistance to progress delineated by Freud can thus be thought to arise from the predilection to phallic omnipotence on the one hand and from the reluctance to adopt a receptive position on the other (91).

For Steiner, feminine is not passive but receptive, and masculine is not active, but tending to the phallic. In its phallicism, males, in their masculinity, abhor feminine receptivity and denigrate the femininity of women as a way of refusing to accept femininity in themselves. In my view, the abhorrence of receptivity that Steiner sees in phallic masculinity also reflects a dread of an internal male genital space, and his recasting female passivity as female receptivity gives us a clue to an additional feature of this dread of his own interiority. Receptivity suggests, not just vulnerability, but openness to, even desirous of, receiving. The idea of an internal male genital, projected into the female, suggests the same wish to take in, to do what is attributed to the female. In that sense, an internal male genital space invites being filled, and it drives a male wish, countered by dread, to dissolve into the female. Ferenczi (1924) identified this wish in the male's identification with his penis, but more so in his identification with his semen. The penis can be retrieved and recharged with libido lost to the female, semen cannot: It dissolves into her, along with masculine identity.

Moreover, the particular dissolving into the female is also conceptive: Something happens, in which the 'masculine' male loses himself into something new, the child – in phantasy – over whom he has no claim and in whom, though he might see resemblances, he does not exist. I follow Meltzer, in distinguishing between the phallic father and the testicular father: The father who penetrates to get inside to replace mother's creativity and the father who nourishes mother's creativity. Meltzer also distinguishes between the quantitative father and the creative father. The quantitative father operates in a paranoid-schizoid mode in asserting his superiority over mother; the creative father bears her creativity and contributes to it.

> It is only very late in development that the aesthetic of the father and his genital appears as a force in development, through the emergence of introjective identification with the internal mother's view of him. This limited apprehension of its aesthetic quality greatly facilitates the conception of the import of the male genital as a weapon rather than a tool. Only with acceptance of the "next baby" conflict does this weapon concept yield place to the tool-of-procreation and establish the role of father in any degree of genuine glory comparable to that of the mother. Usually this is a very late acquisition indeed. Consequently ideas of male superiority can be firmly placed as paranoid schizoid phenomena, based as they are on quantitative (size + power) rather than qualitative (goodness, creativity, utility, courage, etc.) criteria (Meltzer 1988, 63).

Masculine 'inside' is testicular. It is modelled on the relationship between the testicular father and the accepting mother. It is not a paranoid relationship, but deferential to the creativity of the internal parents. It is not submissive, but a non-defensive acceptance of being known (by the internal parents) without yet knowing them. In Kleinian language, it is an introjective identification with the parental couple, which we can also call the internal parental couple. Having that couple inside as an introjective identification is the same as being inside the internal parental couple because it is an identification based on union.

I suggest we speak of the tolerance – or the dread – of masculine seminality and its creative union with conceptive femininity. The internal organs of seminal masculinity – the organs of the male internal genital space – do not 'fix in' the penis but produce semen and participate in procreation. Unlike phallic masculinity, which can always be assuaged, seminal masculinity could be lost into a mysterious internal space. Unlike the boy's penis, which differs only in size from father's, semen is absent. The shape and appearance of the pre-pubertal testes and scrotum also differ from those of the adult (Yazmajian 1966b).

Moses Laufer (1976) argues that, for the adolescent, the mature male genital refers to the capacity to impregnate a woman, and that the wishes and prohibitions connected with this seminal function bring internal incest conflicts to a head. Semen appears suddenly, like a male equivalent to menstruation, in a *first* experience: The experience of ejaculation. Something absolutely new breaks into consciousness, and it can be traumatic: An absolute breach of the continuity of experience; an eruption of overwhelming internal forces, boding good or ill (Kestenberg 1968, 463, 492); sometimes inducing a psychotic episode (Anna Freud Centre 1981, 81; Ladame 1995, 1148). Bird (1957, 258, 265) reported the case of a young man whose first serious relationship with a woman stirred up intense feeling and also a sense of unreality, which were traced to castration anxiety (that he would ejaculate blood) and which rendered previous, seemingly untroubled oedipal observations and feelings (about his mother) suddenly and frighteningly unreal. They were traced to memories and phantasies about his first ejaculation. He had been masturbating, when

suddenly he lost control and felt himself wet ... Before [this relationship with a woman], although admitting he had been upset by his first ejaculation, he had always insisted he knew nothing terrible had happened—he knew the wetness was not blood or urine. Now it was different. Now he remembered with great feeling what it had been like: he had been sure that it was blood and that he had seriously injured his penis ... Immediately upon his first ejaculation a great many things changed. Fantasies of all kinds which he had had for years, without much conflict, suddenly became very disturbing. For example, he had had, without shame or fear, fantasies of intercourse with his mother and of impregnating her; then, after the onset of ejaculation, these fantasies brought him real fear that something of that sort might actually take place.

Ejaculation had made his sexual strivings and ensuing oedipal conflicts real to him, seemingly marginalized until his post-pubertal relationship brought them back. His anxiety had initially arisen from the internal male genital, focused on semen-as-blood. Only later, in a sexual relationship, did it collect onto the terror of a castrated, bloodied penis. One might say that he seemed, retrospectively, as in Freud's deferred action (*nachträglichkeit*), to have imbued his first ejaculation, which was unintelligible and traumatic, with an emotionally immediate and overwhelming oedipal significance. He could, of course, also see that his penis remained unbloodied and intact, but the underlying, seminal anxiety, pressed through.

The inside of union, which insemination enacts, gives a particular urgency in being inside. It leads to the question, 'What do we mean by "internal" or "inside," and the wish to be, and the dread of being, inside?' In everyday perception, inside is geometrical, a Euclidean space marked out by three dimensions: Length, breadth, depth. That is how we see the world and our bodies in this world. But clearly, the male has no internal space, in this sense, to match that of the womb and vagina of the female; no place in which another being can reside. Phallic masculinity aims, by projective identification, to control an alien feminine being who embodies a mysterious place beyond dimension. The ego, always searching for perceptual reality, strives to transform ultimate reality into a dimensional internal space – to transform the feminine into a container of an inside a physical space, a terrain, captured by the explorer that conquers by occupying. It is characterized by size and power, enacted by the phallic penis. It contrasts with the testicular space, which an animate relationship of introjective identification with the parental couple, enacted in a seminal coupling.

In chapter 3, we will take up the idea of 'inside' in greater detail. I argue that 'inside' as a three-dimensional space within a container, continued and modified over time, is a transformation of a realm beyond representation into a thinkable, visualizable form. The very necessity of this transformation requires what I call a 'reduction of dimensionality.' Such a reduction, essential as it is to thinking, leaves a residue beyond representation. The mysterious union of the parental couple, with its fertility, lies in this 'beyond,' as does primary narcissism and what Bion (1992, 372–373) calls the irrepresentable 'and.' This overflow is the object of yearning, and it can never be satisfied, because it remains beyond representation. There are two main approaches to it: To tolerate it, and not to expect it in a relationship; or to find it intolerable and seek to dominate it. I associate the former with seminal masculinity and the latter with phallic masculinity. We will take up seminal masculinity in chapters 7 and 8, and phallic masculinity in chapters 4, 8, 9, 10 and 11, where we will see it as the basis of misogyny and toxic masculinity.

Note

1 Freud has been accused of misogyny, which we will take up in chapter 12. The focus of this book is on misogyny in toxic masculinity, but I have tried to show that it is an extreme of a characteristically masculine struggle with the feminine. It need not become denigrating or violent but is, for mother, father and son, a turbulent process. That was Freud's struggle, but it is a masculine struggle. Sebastian Thrul (2023) has carried forward the strand of thinking to which Kestenberg refers, from the angle of paternal, pre-oedipal involvement, which is avoided by concentrating on the oedipal/post-oedipal boy.

References

Anna Freud Centre (1981) Scientific Forum on the Superego: Its Early Roots and the Road from Outer to Inner Conflict as Seen in Psychoanalysis. *Bulletin of the Anna Freud Centre* 4: 77–117.

Bell, A. (1961) Some Observations on the Role of the Scrotal Sac and Testicles. *Journal of the American Psychoanalytic Association* 9: 261–286.

Bell, A. (1965) The Significance of the Scrotal Sac and Testicles for the Prepuberty Male. *Psychoanalytic Quarterly* 34: 182–206.

Bion, W. R. (1992) *Cogitations*. London: Karnac.

Bird, B. (1957) Feelings of Unreality. *International Journal of Psychoanalysis* 38: 256–265.

Bonomi, C. (1998) Freud and Castration: A New Look into the Origins of Psychoanalysis. *Journal of the American Academy of Psychoanalysis* 26: 29–49.

Diamond, M. J. (2006). Masculinity Unraveled: The Roots of Male Gender Identity and the Shifting of Male Ego Ideals Throughout Life. *Journal of the American Psychoanalytic Association*, 54: 1099–1130.

Edgcumbe, R. and Burgner, B. (1975) The Phallic Phase – A Differentiation between Preoedipal and Oedipal Aspects of Phallic Development. *Psychoanalytic Studies of the Child* 30: 161–180.

Elise, D. (2001) Unlawful Entry: Male Fears of Psychic Penetration. *Psychoanalytic Dialogues* 11: 499–531.

Ferenczi, S. (1924) *Thallassa: A Theory of Genitality*. NY, New York: *Psychoanal. Q.*, 1938; repr. London: Karnac, 1989.

Figlio, K. (2010) Phallic and Seminal Masculinity: A Theoretical and Clinical Confusion. *International Journal of Psychoanalysis* 91(1): 119–139.

Fogel, G. (1998) Interiority and Inner Genital Space in Men: What Else Can Be Lost in Castration. *Psychoanalytic Quarterly* 67: 662–697.

Freud, S. (1900) The Interpretation of Dreams. *The Standard Edition of the Complete Psychological Works of Sigmund Freud* 4 & 5.

Freud, S. (1905) Three Essays on the Theory of Sexuality. *The Standard Edition of the Complete Psychological Works of Sigmund Freud* 7: 123–245.

Freud, S. (1937) Analysis Terminable and Interminable. *The Standard Edition of the Complete Psychological Works of Sigmund Freud* 23: 209–254.

Friedman, R. (1996) The Role of the Testicles in Male Psychological Development. *Journal of the American Psychoanalytical Association* 44: 201–253.

Glenn, J. (1969) Testicular and Scrotal Masturbation. *International Journal of Psychoanalysis* 50: 353–362.

Jones, E. (1912) The Symbolic Significance of Salt in Folklore and Superstition. *Imago* 1: 361–454; repr. in *Psycho-Myth, Psycho-History*, vol. 2. NY: Stonehill, 1974, 22–109.

Kestenberg, J. S. (1968) Outside and Inside: Male and Female. *Journal of the American Psychoanalytic Association* 16: 457–520.

Kestenberg, J. S. (1977) Psychoanalytic Observation of Children. *International Review of Psychoanalysis* 4: 393–407.

Ladame, F. (1995). The Importance of Dreams and Action in the Adolescent Process. *International Journal of Psychoanalysis*, 76: 1143–1153.

Laufer, M. (1976) The Central Masturbation Fantasy, the Final Sexual Organization and Adolescence. *Psychoanalytic Studies of the Child* 31: 297–316.

Meltzer, D. (1988) *The Apprehension of Beauty: The Role of Aesthetic Conflict in Development and Violence*. Strath Tay: The Clunie Press.

Myers, W. (1976) The Psychological Significance of Testicular Problems. *Journal of the American Psychoanalytic Association* 24: 609–629.

Stärcke, A. (1921) The Castration Complex. *International Journal of Psychoanalysis* 2: 179–201.

Steiner, J. (2020) *Illusion, Delusion, and Irony in Psychoanalysis*. Abington, Oxon/New York: Routledge.

Thrul, S. (2023) The Young Man and the Sea: Reflections on Male Infantile Development, Fatherhood and Psychoanalytic Training. *British Journal of Psychotherapy* 39(2): 380–392.

Tyson, P. (1986) Male Gender Identity: Early Developmental Roots. *Psychanalytic Review* 73(4): 1–21.

Yazmajian, R. (1966a) The Testes and Body-Image Formation in Transvestitism. *International Journal of Psychoanalysis* 14: 304–312.

Yazmajian, R. (1966b) Reactions to Differences between Prepubertal and Adult Testes and Scrotums. *Psychoanalytic Quarterly* 35: 368–376.

Yazmajian, R. (1967) The Influence of Testicular Sensory Stimuli on the Dream. *International Journal of Psychoanalysis* 15: 83–98.

Yazmajian, R. V. (1983). On a Retractile Testis and an Infantile Umbilicus Phobia. *Psychoanalytic Quarterly*, 52: 584–589.

Chapter 3

Being Inside
The Topography of the Interior

What Does Inside (the Mother) Mean?

In this chapter, we will explore the idea of 'internal' or 'inside.' It is important because we speak of internal objects, of the internal world, of the inside of the mother's body, of conception by entering the woman's body, of the yearning to return to the inside of the mother, of returning to the womb. Freud – and psychoanalysis more generally – ground curiosity in the wish to explore this inside, seeking to find where babies come from and what father puts into mother, or the 'primal scene' of parental intercourse. We look inside the way we might search in a room for a lost object or secret happening.

'Inside' is intrinsic to our notion of life: Living things have an inside, in the form of what the 19th-century physiologist, Claude Bernard, called the *milieu interior*. The internal environment is a self-stabilizing, homoeostatic, system in living organisms, increasingly withdrawn from the external world as they ascend in evolutionary development (Jonas 1966). Inanimate objects usually do not have an interior, and when they do have an inside, it is not a homoeostatic system, maintained apart from the outside or surface by an internal, self-regulating system: It is just a location away from the surface.

The idea of a living inside puts our thinking onto another track. We are looking for something deeper than inside as a place. The spatial framing of where an object might be or where something might take place transforms a more primal mystery of origin into an imaginable – specifically visualizable – form. It transforms an inconceivable primal state into a conceivable location within dimensions. Space as a place in which objects are arrayed, and time as the duration of an experience, sustain an emotional and epistemological distance between us as observing subjects and the objects we observe, including ourselves. Vision, in particular, establishes distance between subject and object and between objects (Jonas 1966). This conceivable, dimensional, transformation approaches, but does not comprehend this deeper reality, which is beyond dimensions.

Among the objects we might observe are males and females. As we saw in chapter 2, psychoanalysts have typically drawn a difference between male and

DOI: 10.4324/9781003455790-5

female on the basis that the female has an internal, reproductive space, while the male does not, and each has a psychology consistent with its space. The female reproductive organs are internal; the baby originates and develops in her internal space, and we can 'see' it happening – now, literally. Female psychology is inward-directed, for example, in a sense of vulnerability to penetration, as if she needs to protect what is inside her or prevent something bad getting inside her. The male, in this three-dimensional world, does not have an inside. He has a tool for getting inside. The penis is emblematic of an object in external space and male psychology is outward-directed, for example, in seeking to penetrate.

This simplistic difference has been challenged, mainly with respect to female psychology, but not with respect to the meaning of 'internal.' The critique often aims to repudiate Freud's characterization of sex and gender difference as male/masculine/active (penetrating) vs female/feminine/passive (penetrated). It aims either to detach a psychology of gender from an anatomy of sex or to show that the female 'external' organ – the clitoris of phallic monism – is deeply embedded in her 'internal' space (for recent overviews, see Balsam 2018; Zachary 2018). In a similar critique, we have come to speak of a male internal genital space and corresponding psychology, analogous to the female internal genital space. We focused on this male internal genital space in chapter 2. In this chapter, we will develop a different, more fundamental idea of 'internal,' which refers – ultimately – to a domain *beyond* and *before* an internal, dimensional space: A pre-objectal space, at the origin of life and of the ego: A realm of the enigma of 'natality' (Arendt 1958).

Of course, we cannot experience this realm prior to the ego, in the empirical sense of a world of objects in space, one in which the ego senses objects and can sense itself as an object. Rather, such a realm is a ground against which the ego sets itself apart. The ground itself lies outside empirical reality, and we have to use a different language to speak of it. Maybe we could say we have an intimation or an intuition of it, or that we have a sense, though not an empirical sense, of approaching it or becoming it, getting to know it.

The idea of an empirical reality known only within a frame, only having meaning against a ground, brought into relief as if moulded in this ground, like a cameo, is a Kantian idea. Kant (1781/1787, B310)[1] spoke of the 'noumenal' world of the 'thing-in-itself,' as opposed to the 'phenomenal' world of empirical reality. For Freud, the ego emerges from such a realm beyond empirical reality, which he called primary narcissism. The ego does not pre-exist: It comes into being and maintains itself in being. We are driven to think what that could mean: What realm exists for the ego without the ego yet being present to it, an ego aware of this realm and of itself as an imminence (intuition for Kant), also sensing itself as an object in the three-dimensional world in empirical reality.

Two ideas set out by Freud (1938) among a list of thoughts for further consideration are relevant to the idea that the dimensional realm in which we live intimates more than it can represent, and in this intrinsic inadequacy, it incites a perpetual yearning for (whatever) it (could be).

> August 3rd: The ultimate ground of all intellectual inhibitions and all inhibitions of work seems to be the inhibition of masturbation in childhood. But perhaps it goes deeper; perhaps it is not its inhibition by external influences but its unsatisfying nature in itself. There is always something lacking for complete discharge and satisfaction ... and this missing part, the reaction of orgasm, manifests itself in equivalents in other spheres, in absences, outbreaks of laughing, weeping, and perhaps other ways.—Once again infantile sexuality has fixed a model in this.

> August 22nd: Space may be the projection of the extension of the psychical apparatus. No other derivation is probable. Instead of Kant's a priori determinants of our psychical apparatus. Psyche is extended; knows nothing about it.

I take there to be a connection between these two successive, and apparently unrelated ideas. The sexual theory needs revision, to include an internal sense of unfulfillment as an inherent insufficiency that, to the ego, knowing only its agency – its capacity to act in a perceptual, spatial world – might appear as a restriction. That insight could be expanded to spatiality. Without spatiality, there could be no psyche, and since spatiality, paradoxically, is also the ground of its very existence, psyche cannot know nothing of it. And yet, the ego is unsatisfied, feels restricted – that there is a beyond, the nature of which it tries to comprehend while aware of its being nonsensical even to imagine it.

The idea of an ego that emerges brings with it, in the dimension of time, the idea of a beginning. It is fruitless – Kant and Freud would think it a non-question – to ask what lay just before the beginning, just as it is fruitless to ask what lay just before the Big Bang, or whether we could know of our own coming into existence, or of the founding of spatiality by the ego that inhabits it. We either tolerate the enigma or are driven to question it anyway. In this case, we are locked within empirical reality, and believe we can get to the beginning of ourselves – all the way back, to the 'beginning of the beginning' (Figlio 2003), not only to imagine ourselves there, as in one formulation of the Oedipus complex (Freud 1910, 173), but, so to speak, to fabricate ourselves. Such a state becomes a quest for certainty. Often, we reach for it by religion or myth. With the idea of a Big Ego Bang, we can say that, godlike, we created ourselves out of a chaos in which we had sunk, or might sink. Such a position of wresting the ego from chaos, in my view, lies behind misogyny, in which the masculine ego wrests itself from the chaos of the feminine by producing itself (explored in chapter 9).

Behind and before Dimensionality

The copula, 'and,' points to such an unrepresentable idea. Conception is an 'and,' a union that defies representation by words, enticingly suggestive, such as 'intercourse' or the word 'conception' itself. These words appeal to visualization. They point to an empirical reality, to an imaginable scene, as if one were an observer. They also hint beyond themselves to an intimation of such a world beyond representation, an overflow, suggesting the idea of a unique beginning, but one that we could get to, glimpse and know (Figlio 2000, 1).

On this basis, let us revise the concepts of masculine and feminine. With Chasseguet-Smirgel (1986), I think the pair represents difference and its union as an essential feature of reality. How 'the pair' grounds the idea of being, whether concretely as in a child, or abstractly, as in the 'nature' of ... , remains the enigma of 'and.' At the intersection between an inconceivable ground of reality, and a conceivable, empirical reality, 'feminine' seems to represent the inconceivable ground behind and before an object-related – 'masculine' – yearning for a primal state as a yearning to be 'in' there. The inconceivable state is signified by Bion's 'O' or by primary narcissism.

Conceiving thereby becomes both the beginning of pregnancy and the possibility of thinking, of formulating an idea, of representing reality in language. They go together. Hannah Arendt uses 'natality' to speak of the absolute novelty of birth, but also of the absolute novelty of the moment of speaking. It is a coming into being in and to ourselves. We experience our being in such a moment, flowing from nothing into something, which we can fix in our minds on a birth. Conception/conceiving is a moment of novelty, in the moment of 'and.' Calling the biological moment, 'impregnation,' or the ideational moment, 'linking' of thoughts, transforms it from the novelty of 'and' into the conceptual world of represented reality in language.

To be 'in' a three-dimensional space, like a box, recasts in conceivable terms, as in geometrical co-ordinates, the pre-dimensional, pre-objectal, primal union of 'and.' It transforms a primal state of union, not just of masculine and feminine, but of zygote with placenta (Hustvedt 2019, 237–238), into an object inside a containing structure. Ferenczi (Anon. 1933, 378) was thinking in this area with his formulation of the masculine return to the feminine. As with Freud, the penis entered the vagina, but Ferenczi it carried further, into a merging. Semen, he said, entered the womb, along with the male, identified with his semen. In the blending of semen with the womb, the masculine return to the primal state is fulfilled. In the conceivable language of dimension, however, the feminine remains a place, the womb a structure that houses the conception in which the foetus emerges inside her.

The wish to explore 'inside' aims to retrieve, upgraded into an idea – *nachträglich* – the dawning of awareness as the nascent ego forms by separating itself from a nascent object. In the background is Kant's 'thing-in-itself.' For Kant, the thing-in-itself was not an object beyond what could be known, but the precondition, in reason, for experience. The framing of experience within dimensions could only be thought as a contraction of a formless field into a shape defined by co-ordinates. As a precondition for experience and therefore for the empirical world in the only way we can know it, it is also the precondition for objects, in the only way we can know them. Bion took up this idea as 'O,' which could not be known empirically, but could be intimated in the movement of becoming 'O.' It is a primal form of Freud's (1919) 'uncanny,' as a haunting by a sense of strange familiarity with primitive thinking that, in consciousness, we believe we have surmounted. For Freud, objects come into being for the ego, as the ego comes into being for itself, as subject next to object.

We grasp perceptual reality in representations, and only incompletely. Representations bring reality into boundaries within which one can speak of it, render it coherent as conscious experience, establish fixed ideas of objects and of persisting relationships among them. But representations always leave something out, always diminish what they represent. In doing so, however, they also point beyond themselves, fixing in our minds an intimation of a reality that overflows our representations. Kant categorized these two moments of reality into appearance (phenomena) and the thing-in-itself (noumena). Phenomena appear to us within a three-dimensional frame: That is the way we grasp them, that is how we occupy the world. Noumena are intuitions, not facts of nature as a reality apart from us. This reality is the world of the thing-in-itself. We can name its otherness to us but not lay claim to it as an existence in itself.

Freud's (1900, 111n.1) dream navel seems very close to this idea. Every dream, he said, arose from some node that could not be represented, but which drove the representations of the dream. Bion (1965) called noumena, 'O,' and distinguished between 'knowing in K' and 'knowing in O': The former grasped at knowing, comprehending it; the latter was more of a residing with an immediacy of a non-sensual sort. He implied, as did Kant, that we do not grasp it as an object world but retain a stance of humble belief without comprehension, but by intuition. We cannot come to knowledge of the noumenal world through empirical knowledge, because it is not an objectal world, but we register an intimation of this ultimate domain and get to know in a continuing becoming. Mawson (2019) developed this theme as a clinical methodology, in which the analyst, and the analytical moment, remained in a state of becoming.

There is a paradox in this distinction between the phenomenal and the noumenal, or between knowing about and 'knowing in O.' We are still driven to believe we do comprehend this world of ultimate reality. Such a position of certainty is an arrogance (Bion 1967). The Oedipus myth, in his reckoning, was not primarily about incest, but about the arrogance of claiming certainty and of pursuing such a certain truth no matter what the consequences. In my language, we have a dim awareness of it in an anti-noumenal 'feeling of certainty' (Figlio 2017). The more certain one's *apparent* comprehension, the more we grasp irritably for the noumenal, the more it is undermined and replaced by the assertion of certainty. By contrast, the more uncertain and humble we are, the greater an intimation of the noumenal, the more wonderment revitalizes endless curiosity. In a popular misconception, science is often seen as grasping at certainty, a stance that provokes a repudiation, typically from fundamentalist or populist groups that are certain of their own views.

Previously (2000), I coined 'the reduction of dimensionality,' to express the paradox of bringing knowledge into the dimensions of the phenomenal yet intimating the noumenal. It can seem like a seduction into believing completely in the ring-fenced – disenchanted – world of perceptual, empirical reality. Reducing infinity to three dimensions is paradoxical. The far side of three dimensions extends beyond imagination; four dimensions stand at the edge of imagination, with the fourth dimension of time still within the conceivable frame of space-time. Beyond four dimensions, imagination fails: We can only construct a frame of five or more dimensions by mathematical formulae, as they extend to infinity.

Reducing three dimensions to two dimensions stays within the conceivable and is easy to imagine: Just think of looking at one surface of the object, then at another surface, until, having looked at every surface, one builds up a mental picture of the three-dimensional object. The act of imagination reconstructs what was lost from the reduction of dimensionality. Reducing two dimensions to one dimension is harder, in that we must do more mental work than looking at the surfaces of an object, one by one. Now we must create a surface from a line. To begin with, the line is a point extended in one dimension. Then we stretch it sideways. We can do it mathematically, but we gain some common-sense belief in it by looking at a pencil line on paper, where we extend a point that seems to have width, no matter how minimal.

For Bion (1965), geometry hovers on the boundary between, on the one hand, a 'beyond,' in space, and 'before' or 'after,' in time, the existence of which we cannot demonstrate, and, on the other hand, empirical reality. We can grasp the 'facts' of the empirical world with our senses, while an ultimate reality, a ground of their existence we can only – and must – postulate. The width of a drawn line can support an imagination of a flat surface, in the limit reduced to one dimension, because imagination is, at base, visual and therefore in space. Similarly, we can imagine a relationship between a line and a point. Seen end-on, a line seems to recede into infinity, or the gap between two lines becomes infinitely small – a dot, which, on paper, occupies a two-dimensional space while simultaneously representing the infinitely small, down to non-existence.[2]

Visualizing nature is an important stage in the development of science – in particular, the form of visualization that I connect with a reduction of dimensionality. In the portrayal of nature, the reduction of dimensionality can be traced historically to the use of perspective to represent a three-dimensional world on a two-dimensional surface, and also to the general reductive movement of scientific naturalism, in which complex phenomena are represented by matter in motion alone, or by models with a limited and manageable array of parameters.

But reducing the dimensionality of external reality also empties the object in the process of objectifying it, exchanging an unforeseeable, more comprehensive, future knowledge for what can be manipulated now. In the extreme, it becomes what I have called 'The Idea of the Inanimate' (Figlio 2000, 102–114), in which the subject loses any sense of an interior as a self-replicating, self-regulating core of a living object. It is then no longer a subject, and even no longer animate (Jonas 1966 offers a model for trying to capture in language the intrinsic interiority of living organisms).

The Topography of Object Relations

Every mapping into geometrical space – every act of picturing – leaves a gap between what was present in an intimated reality, as in Bion's 'O' or infinity and what appears in the mapped space: The finitude of geometrical space. I take Bion to include emotion in that infinity, which is why knowledge, K, is one of the emotional links, with love (L) and hate (H) and why he assigns a + or − to each of them. He seems to push us into representing a multi-dimensional world of emotion, in which emotion is an intention towards an object, not the object itself, and in which we preserve discriminations of intention; for example, -L is not the same as H and anti-knowledge, -K, is not the same as hating knowledge. But the contraction of reality into dimensional space cannot represent the infinitude of emotion. It requires emotional work to tolerate the painfulness of this gap and to rehabilitate the displaced emotional space that has been mapped.

For example, photographs – the ultimate picturing of nature – often create a nostalgic mood that is absent in paintings, because this emotional work is not apparent in the picture as a physical object. The viewer, along with the photographer, dissolves into the picture, leaving a sense of loss in the viewer, who has no photographer-subject with whose emotional work he or she can identify. A good photograph gives the viewer a glimpse into a scene, a feeling of being there, at a unique, private moment, unnoticed by the participants. By contrast, the surface of a painting shows the work of the painter and provides a focus for identification with a subject who has laboured over emotional expression (on the importance of the painted surface, see Wollheim 1987). Bearing the reduction in dimensionality and repairing lost meaning makes an open, generous relationship to nature possible; not bearing it enhances the frustration of exclusion from the mystery of the painting and the temptation to triumph over it, sometimes by destroying or denigrating it. The same applies to or understanding of nature and of the primal scene.

Let us return to geometry as a prime example of a reduction of dimensionality. Geometrical space is both visualizable and abstract. With Bion (1970, 10), let us ask what is mapped onto a dimensional space, and whether it is possible to restore a meaning lost in the mapping.

> I shall now use the geometrical concepts of lines, points, and space (as derived originally not from a realization of three-dimensional space but from the realizations of the emotional mental life) as returnable to the realm from which they appear to me to spring. That is, if the geometer's concept of space derives from an experience of "the place where something was" it is to be returned to illuminate the domain where it is in my experience meaningful to say that "a feeling of depression" is "the place where a breast or other lost object was" and that "space" is "where depression, or some other emotion, used to be."[3]

But the reduction of dimensionality into a frame bounded by co-ordinates cannot transform the emotion of absence without loss, and one cannot recover the emotion transformed into geometrical co-ordinates. Bion implies that geometry is more than a tracker and memory aid: He speaks of transformation, and we are invited to think of what is retained and recoverable in transformations. In my view, not only is there a gap between the transformed object and the original, leaving an unrepresented residue: The reduction of dimensionality, in establishing a domain of empirical reality, also posits a missing dimension that cannot be encompassed within the co-ordinates. The gap between Bion's 'knowing in K,' as knowing phenomena, and 'knowing in "O"' as intuiting noumena, renews the belief in an ultimate reality.

More generally, we might say that any attempt to possess the object – to encompass it by force, so to speak – opens a gap between what can and what cannot be represented within the reduced dimensions; and 'by force' includes projective identification. I would go further to say that the reduction of dimensionality is inherent in empirical reality and that the unknowable noumenal overflow is not just a residue that cannot be encompassed by empirical reality: It is enhanced – spurred on – by the reduction of dimensionality, as the source, object and drive of curiosity. But the gap provokes two different reactions. In the first, the deficiency of representation is tolerated along with a yearning, linked to wonderment, to know the object, so to speak from the inside. In the second, the deficiency provokes hatred of the object and the attempt to master it by projective identification: To claim the object and to degrade it as a hated part of oneself. Here lie the seeds of misogyny (taken up in chapters 9–11).[4]

The science of human anatomy systematically reduces the dimensionality of the animate and psychic domains to structure and the inanimate. Consider, for example, the double reduction of empathy, first to the activation of mirror neurones (physiology), then to the structure and innervation of mirror neurones (anatomy). In doing so, it implicitly calls attention to what it occludes. Empathy remains a mystery to the anatomy and physiology of mirror neurones. We find a psyche-based, psychoanalytic methodology for studying empathy in countertransference.

In a psychoanalytic frame, knowing an other-as-subject evolves from identifications, not from geometrical location.[5] For Freud, identification began with incorporation – literally, eating the object – and psychically elaborated, as introjective identification, along with psychosexual development. Eating is just the entry point, the visualizable experience of ingestion. But the enigma then begins: What happens to the food? It is not surprising that among the phantasies of the creation of babies is their origination in a transformation of food (more in chapter 6).

Klein distinguished another form of identification – projective identification – based on a phantasy of inserting ego-alienated aspects of the self into the mother as the primal object, to eliminate them, to protect them and to communicate through them (elaborated by Bion 1967). Britton (1994) differentiated projective identification into 'acquisitive projective identification,' by which parts of the object are acquired by the subject, and 'attributive projective identification,' by which the object is commandeered to house rejected parts of the ego (akin to Klein's original definition).

Introjective identification, by contrast, does more than acquire parts of the object: It enhances the ego by assimilating the object, whereas projective identification restricts the ego as it restricts the subject by using it as an object. It aims to make the subject more an object and more under the control of the ego. Introjective identification is insecure, uncertain, dependent on the reliability of its other-as-subject-world. Projective identification is secure in its stance of certainty and arrogant in its objectification of the subject-as-other. It presumes to take what it wants and eliminate what it does not want.

Introjective identification is akin to intuition, bringing it close to knowing in 'O.' It is a form of loving, in which attributes of the object enrich the ego without possessing it or claiming to know it as it knows itself. Projective identification enters the object, 'knows' it by a phantasy of depleting it of its contents. In a reduction of dimensionality, it instigates an arrogance of certainty, a knowing attitude that pretends to leap beyond getting to know a reality, into believing in having comprehended it. Instead of knowing as phenomenal knowing – knowing about – it claims to know in 'O,' to penetrate to the core of reality. Knowing is always phenomenal, but knowing in 'O' recognizes the enigma that is beyond knowing and this humility revises knowing about from an arrogant comprehension into an ever-awed, unending but not relentless, exploration of the world. 'O' sits on the other side of a boundary that cannot be bridged, no matter how pellucid our empathic glimpse of it might be. Knowing in 'O' is a constant becoming (Mawson 2019). It is not certain but humble.

To go back to the sexual dimension of the Oedipus story, incest is an action steeped in the belief that it can replace parental intercourse. It is a mistake. It does not achieve the union that it purports to imitate, whether in phantasy or in behaviour. To enact the phantasy of the primal scene is arrogant in the omnipotent phantasy of imitating and thereby replacing the parental couple and it is profoundly deficient. The more relentlessly it is pursued, the more deficient it is experienced and the more compulsively it is pursued.

But there is an additional mistake: To believe that parental intercourse *is* the mystery, the scene that we all crave to witness, and in which we can participate by imitation. It is to mistake the activity that can be seen in space and time for the mystery of union, as if the primal scene revealed to our senses that union – the 'and,' which strives for representation.

Phallic Monism and the Topography of the Interior

Freud formulated a version of what I have called a reduction of dimensionality, in the theory that came to be called 'phallic monism'; that is, that the young girl is not aware of her vagina – of her inside – but only of her clitoris, which she glimpses on a boy. There is, in effect, only one genital – the male genital – and female sexuality, grounded in this visible male anatomy, is driven by penis envy. She resolves the contradiction between desiring a penis and having a baby in the phantasy of making a baby from father's penis.

Critics of phallic monism have argued that a 'primary femininity' based on a distinctive anatomy of the female genital refutes Freud's phallic monism. It grounds a distinctively female sexuality in an internal genital, which includes the innervation of the clitoris in surrounding deep structures and the vagina as an internal space surrounded by sensitive structures (Zachary 2018). Their reference to deep innervation also suggests a space beyond dimension. Critics also include psychoanalysts (whose work we reviewed in chapter 2), who think of phallic momism as an unwarranted circumscribing of the male genital by excluding a male internal genital space.

We will take up phallic monism, in its relevance to both male and female, in Part III. In this section, I want to connect it to the question at hand: What do we mean by 'inside'? In the confusion of phallus with penis, it enacts the reduction of 'inside' to the spatial metaphor that we have examined, in which an object is enclosed within a structure in a three-dimensional frame. That is how we see the world and our bodies in this world. It is difficult to think of inside in any other way, and several psychoanalytic concepts are prone to inclusion within it. Think of 'container/contained/containment,' 'holding,' keeping someone 'in mind,' 'internal world,' 'internal object,' 'projecting into,' 'acting out/acting in' or the internal space of the vagina. They all appeal to our immediate comprehension of 'inside' in visual, spatial terms.

The idea of a male internal genital presses us to recognize that spatialization misrepresents its referent. By including male seminal structures and function and their part in fertilization, it edges towards representing conception as a realization of the unrepresentable 'and.' Spatialization, by contrast, confers an illusion of mastery of what lies 'inside.' As a three-dimensional frame, it inadequately encompasses the 'and' of conception and thereby also enhances the enigma by what it cannot master. In the creation of a domain of mastery by setting out a boundary, spatialization also sets our gaze on the unmasterable beyond the boundary, as in Freud's beyond (*Jenseits*) the pleasure principle. By saying that we cannot speak of what lies beyond spatialization, we hypostasize it, mystify it, banish it and defend against it, all at once.

In subtly subsuming meaning within a spatial frame, we also introduce the idea of measure, of quantitative difference instead of qualitative difference. Container/contained/containment, for example, refers to a capacity – alpha-functioning – not to a structure that confines an object by a surrounding it, or holding it, as a mother's arms around her infant. Now within a spatial frame, we are led to push the essence of these concepts beyond our measurements, in the very attempt to master their obscurity or to defend against the implication of keeping them in mind.

Phallic monism achieves just such a reduction of dimensionality, which defends against what it also posits. What is this shunned – and highlighted – referent? Jones (1927) thinks it is incest: Male and female joined in intercourse evokes an incest phantasy. Because phallic monism allows only one genital, there is no masculine in intercourse with feminine, therefore, no evocation of incest. I would put the emphasis differently. I would say that phallic monism eases the distance between intercourse and incest, making it a matter of degree: A quantitative distance rather than a qualitative difference that signifies male and female. Distance rather than difference can seem to elide the root of incest as a psychological fact, pushing behind intercourse. But intercourse can evoke an incest phantasy while denying it. It can slip into incest and back. That is what defences do.

Defences are built on omnipotence. As a form of omnipotence, defence – phallic defence in this case – is a form of narcissism. One feature of narcissism is that it is unstable and erodes itself, and in eroding itself, it relies on intensifying the very defence that undermines it, becoming a negative spiral. Take as a vivid example, Oscar Wilde's *Picture of Dorian Grey*. Dorian Grey appears to remain unageing while his picture, hidden away, ages in a grotesque way. His narcissistic self-idolization can continue only as long as the reality (of ageing) can be projected. The sequestering of his two states, in which one is as ugly as the other is beautiful, is unstable. The more it goes on, the worse it gets, until the two aspects of himself come together only in a catastrophe. He destroys himself in the moment he destroys his grotesque aspect, in his portrait.

The narcissistic self cannot live with itself because to be a self is to be in reality, and being in reality erodes the self-complete perfection of narcissism, just as Dorian Grey – in reality – ages. Narcissistic perfection builds on there being a repudiated other to serve as a repository into which depleting aspects of itself can be ejected. The other must both be there and not be there, hidden as was Dorian Grey's portrait, yet present to continue as a repository: Needed to be present and not present at the same time. In Britton's (2021) formulation, there is a 'narcissistic problem of sharing space' – more a dilemma, I would say, in that needing and eliminating the other is a contradiction, which cannot be resolved within narcissism.[6]

The idea of space captures the dilemma. The narcissist experiences the other as an intruder into his uniquely personal and universal space. As long as the intrusion remains within the reduced dimensionality of space, it remains a kind of claustrophobia: A sense of concrete invasion, which provokes a wish to put a distance between the self and the other, even to the point of attacking the other. As long as it is a matter of distance, the danger of incursion *into* the ego cannot be escaped. A common plea is to 'get away to be on my own' but the certainty of getting away by moving away is an omnipotent phantasy, fed by an unacknowledged recognition that it is just an assertion, unconsciously claiming an omnipotent defeat of the intruder. Such triumph in the defeat of reality underwrites the claim while risking itself in the face of reality.

This insecure world of quantity calls for the father in the mind of the mother, who can, as an object of identification, stand for a stable reality based on objectification: On recognizing a world of objects, including the ego as an object to itself through the superego. This father restricts the mother's claim to her child as a part of herself and mitigates her power as an internal object in the child's mind. In a world of quantity, this objectification is reduced to a measure: Of dimension in an abstract, geometric sense; of being bigger and staying bigger, or being smaller. In the illusion of substance as bigger and smaller, the bigger – the male – is ceaselessly in danger of being swallowed by the smaller – whether the female or another male – as the smaller strives to exist by enlargement. It is an inherently unstable world of quantity rather than quality.

Beneath the phallic world lies the narcissistic collapse into world with no dimensions; above it lies a world of qualitative differences between objects, where substance, quality, objects, not dimension, matters. Men/fathers are different from women /mothers, whether or not they are bigger than women. And children emerge from their mothers, not as extensions of their mothers, or parthenogenically, as body parts, but as natality on conception, *de novo*: As an emergence from neither, but from an 'and.'

Meltzer (1973, 67–73) distinguished between the father of bigger and smaller – the 'quantitative father' – and the father of an object(ive) world – the 'testicular father' – who was neither bigger nor smaller than mother but was complementary in a world of creativity and repair rather than triumph and domination.[7] The quantitative father may be bigger than mother, and any individual, quantitative man might be bigger than another quantitative man, but he remains insecure, because there are no boundaries between bigger and smaller. Bigger can only re-assert itself against usurpation by a smaller who grows bigger. He is identified with his penis: He can swell up but then lapse into detumescence, again and again.

The quantitative father exists in a domain of reduced dimensionality. He is a geometrical man, in that his size could be plotted with co-ordinates in an attempt to capture his essence. But this very reduction of dimensionality also constructs a phenomenal world that evokes a sense of a realm beyond it, from which, for Bion, it has been extracted: A world known by K, which intimates knowing in 'O.' Meltzer (1988, 63) speaks of an aesthetic quality, which I take to be an attempt to represent in language a world of the father that overflows ordinary experience.

> It is only very late in development that the aesthetic of the father and his genital appears as a force in development, through the emergence of introjective identification with the mother's view of him. This limited apprehension of its aesthetic quality greatly facilitates the conception of the import of the male genital as a weapon rather than a tool ... Consequently [until this late acquisition] ideas of male superiority can be firmly placed as paranoid-schizoid phenomena, based as they are on quantitative (size + power) rather than qualitative (goodness, creativity, utility, courage, etc.) criteria.

Note that Meltzer ties the genital father to an introjection of the mother's view of him. The boy who can imagine a genital father, and hence his own genitality, as opposed to their shared phallic masculinity, has assimilated lovingly his parent's love of each other, in a genital union. This is Meltzer's aesthetic world, rather than a narcissistic world, and it is nurtured by the girl's capacity, now as a mother, to transcend her reduction of dimensionality to a quantitative, narcissistic, base.[8]

The masculine 'inside' is testicular, allowing a creative union with the receptive – conceptive – feminine. It is not a paranoid relationship but one developed from a deferential relationship with the creativity of internal parents. In Kleinian language, it is an introjective identification in a couple, based on their creative parental couples, that facilitates a lineage of introjective identification between masculine and feminine. The testicular father with mother is a qualitative, non-geometric, animate relationship of introjective identification, enacted in a seminal coupling. It is different from an inside by projective identification, which is a form of control from inside a geometric space, in which the feminine encompasses the masculine but is controlled by the masculine, from the inside. It is quantitative, in the sense of size and power, enacted by the penis, possessed by the male and envied by the female.

Dahl (1996), for example, concludes in her study of penis envy, that 'recognition of anatomical difference in the light of the oedipal narrative ushers in a new dilemma stimulated by the question of what meaning, if any, to assign to bodily, especially genital, differences. [Having a penis could achieve a] state in which all wishes are realizable and no superego retaliation occurs' (321). 'Penis envy should be understood ... not as the bedrock of what it is to be feminine, but rather as a compromise formation involving both drive and defence created by the dilemma of the inherent immutability and limitations of the body' (323). Recognition of difference and limitation can constitute a narcissistic threat, in which the fact of the body is a limitation that can be experienced narcissistically, in which 'more' or 'less' matters. The boy might be 'fancier' in his possession of a penis, but in a narcissistic world, quantitative – more or less – world, rather than a qualitative world, no-one is secure (320).

Chasseguet-Smirgel takes on both phallic and non-phallic aspects of inside. She addresses the phantasy of the mother's womb as both a world with objects inside – a quantitative, dimensional world – and a pre-object world of yearning, which overflows the constricted, dimensional world in its urge to get back inside. In this sense, she is elaborating Freud's thinking, in which the ego is historical – that it comes into being in the coming into being of its objects – and supplementing Klein's thinking, in which the ego is object-relating from the outset (where 'outset' is left ambiguous). She (1986, 77) hypothesizes that

> there exists a primary desire to discover a universe without obstacles, without roughness or differences, entirely smooth, identified with a mother's belly stripped of its contents, an interior to which one has free access. Behind the fantasy of destroying or appropriating the father's penis, the children and the feces inside the mother's body, a fantasy brought out by Melanie Klein, and, according to her, specific to the early stages of the Oedipus conflict, can be detected a more basic and more archaic wish, of which the return to the smooth maternal belly is the representative. It is a question of rediscovering, on the level of thought, a mental functioning without hindrance, with psychic energy flowing freely. The father, his penis, the children represent reality. They have to be destroyed so that the mode of mental functioning proper to the pleasure principle may be recovered. The fantasy of destroying reality confers on the fantasy of emptying the mother's belly its primordial role. It is the contents of the belly which are equivalent to reality, not the container itself. The empty container represents the unfettered pleasure.

I think the unfettered pleasure of freely flowing psychic energy is also a non-dimensional idea. It is this state, unknowable and unimaginable, that is the very basis of thinking in terms of objects – albeit, necessarily within dimensions. In her analysis, this state – the state of reality – is an obstacle to the fantasy of getting to the pre-object state. But this fantasy is also a perversion, a delusion in which the inconceivable is not only conceivable but attainable by clearing away the obstacles. She allows the possibility that there might be a normal version, as a ground to the reality of the object, but what she can demonstrate – and she offers several clinical examples – is the perverse fantasy of rolling back the imposition of reality on such a primordial state.

Misogyny: The Master of Conception

In this chapter, I have built on the idea that 'inside,' as we commonly understand it, is a space within a container. In Kant's formulation, we only know empirical, phenomenal, reality – the reality of objects – within a three-dimensional frame (plus time). Dimensionality constitutes empirical reality, grounded *a priori* in the transcendental idea of space as a logically necessary precondition of knowing it. This reality of a thing-in-itself, noumenal reality, is logically necessary to the very concept of, the conceivability of, empirical reality. It is not an empirical reality, but an intuition, from which we can abstract empirical reality as a limitation into the boundaries of three dimensions. Bion embraced this Kantian frame with his idea of 'O' or of infinity, from which empirical reality was abstracted as a limitation.

I have suggested that we also think of 'O' as referring to an overflow beyond empirical reality and that our intimation of it is a yearning that has no object. It cannot be satisfied, only attenuated, by experience. The reality of which we can think or imagine, which we believe to be the object that will satisfy our yearning, appears before us as an illusion of potential satisfaction. It is not an object at all, but 'O.'

There are two psychoanalytic concepts that, in my view, aim to circumscribe 'O' while it remains an enigma. One is primary narcissism, the other is the parental couple. Primary narcissism refers to a realm that, as critics point out, is impossible: A pre-objectal state of pure subjectivity. The parental couple is the fertile couple, the conceiving couple, 'in' which the enigma of origination – natality – occurs. Both concepts point to a ground unlimited by any parameter of empirical reality, an *a priori* necessity for the idea of a being who is now here, but who was not here, and from which empirical reality emerges as a coming into being. We can't think the 'being' of our empirical reality without the natality of which we are a realization. Without it, we would not be ourselves, but an extension of another being.

What does this framework have to do with misogyny, an ugly threat to females in the real world? We will take up this theme squarely in chapters 9 and 10. For the purposes of the current chapter, I will simply suggest that misogyny reduces 'O' to the female/mother; further, to the place in which being emerges and is sustained. As a place, she is the disappointing object that pretends to offer admission to the realm of an absolute, pre-objectal intimacy, 'in' which his unique, irreplaceable being would be realized – but from which he is excluded. The Oedipal myth casts this disappointment into a story in which the son imagines he is present at his own conception, indeed, he is part of the mysterious union that conceived him, but from which he is excluded by father.

The Oedipal myth brings out the son's demand that he not only be the unique being inside mother but that he also be the agent of his own creation. Natality becomes masculine activity inside the space of the mother. With the female reduced to the place in which he created himself, where he was nurtured, from which he was delivered and into which he seeks to return, he is unique. Yet he is replaceable, against which he can struggle. His imagined agency in producing and sustaining himself in the presence of the feminine remains inadequate next to his yearning to merge into – to be – the absolute, pre-objectal, complete realm of 'O' as his unique heritage. The resulting ego instability opens him to the dread of dissolving into her and into his extinction. The masculine ego then aims to recoup its agency by asserting itself against the feminine nest that it also craves. It takes the form of action: Action against the feminine, action in demeaning the feminine, action to extinguish the feminine. In the limit, it becomes, in the Unconscious, the equation masculine = – feminine. Action also becomes production. As we will see in chapters 5 and 6, it feeds a collaborative phantasy of parthenogenic creation.

This account aims to represent the unconscious dynamics of misogyny. In my view, it is the template of misogyny. Scaled up into a masculine social movement, misogyny is organized under the banner of 'replacement ideology,' the socially sustained belief that masculinity is under threat of extinction, replaced by femininity as a feminist conspiracy. Historical circumstances provide the specific settings and the perceived threats to masculine identity. Toxic masculinity is, for example, often associated with a reaction to waves of feminism, in which masculine identity had previously seemed secure, but was then disrupted and undermined.

Notes

1   'B' refers to the second edition, 1787, and 310 refers to the page number in that edition. It is pp. 318–319 in this unified edition. The noumenal world of the thing-in-itself was, for Kant, a logical idea, necessary *a priori*, a transcendental, as opposed to transcendent, idea. Space, for example, is a necessary idea: What is left once all sensible qualities have been removed. In that sense, it cannot be known by any association with sensible qualities. As I am using it, in line with what I take to be Bion's usage, there is a confusion between this logical necessity and sensible cognition. Strictly speaking, our knowing is restricted to the sensible realm, no matter how abstract, but I am assuming that the *a priori* grounding of the idea of necessity leaves us with an unquenchable sense of deficit and an urgency to transcend the limitation of the sensible realm. In that sense, even logic, as in mathematics or knowing of any sort, is driven by emotion. Perhaps I misuse Kant's concept of intuition, in allowing an intuition of the existence of such a

realm that remains outside knowledge, in essence, not just in being unattainable. The *Critique of Pure Reason*, however, is a monumental exercise in showing us what we, as human beings, not God, cannot know. It would be omnipotent to know, yet anyway we try, and, arrogantly, claim to know, as an omnipotent, narcissistic defence against our limitation. I argue throughout the book, that this defence underlies misogyny.

2   Bion also spoke of a reduction of infinity into a narrative structure of thinking. Myths, such as the Oedipus myth, for example, were structures of thinking that encompassed – albeit inadequately – grounding existential realities.

3   Vermote (2019, 126) puts Bion's use of geometry nicely.

> To Bion geometry, for instance, did not originate because geometrical forms reflect reality; it originated to provide a means of getting hold or creating a space so that infinity becomes bearable.

4   Richard Wollheim (1969) argues that the more the mind develops, the less spatial it becomes; that it is only in a regressed state that we have a conception of the mind, and in having a conception of it, we tone it with spatiality: The mind has an image of itself and becomes a scene of action. The more we think, the less spatiality we demand in making things conceivable. That is true of the world as understood by physics, which has moved well beyond the visualizable, and of the mind as understood by psychoanalysis, where we observe the mind under stress fragment and disperse into parts of the body. The more intolerant of thinking, the more the world and the mind break into schismatic sectors, topographically located.

5   This statement is incomplete. An objectifying pole of knowing is positional, with objects localized in dimensional space. It is in a dialectical relationship with the residue of the unrepresentable: Together forming the paradox of the 'inside' of the other, which induces an insatiable urge to return. One could speak of continuously changing 'subjective objects.' As we will see, I ground misogyny and its consequences in an intolerance of this paradox. In chapter 12, we will see little Max struggle – normally and successfully – with it.

6   There is a distinction to be made between a destructive narcissism, as I am using it here, and 'normal,' 'healthy' or 'libidinal' narcissism. Healthy narcissism is an ego feeling of affirmation, esteem, and satisfaction with one's personality, which is carried forward from the earliest experience as a reservoir of libido (Federn 1929; Grunberger 1979). More recently, in the Kleinian school, Rosenfeld (1971) and Britton (2008; 2021, 112–115; 118–120) have held to the existence of both libidinal and destructive narcissism. They all share, however, a recognition of a normal ego and an ego that cannot tolerate dependence, and overrides it in an illusion of autonomy as superiority. Surmounting dependence on an object by narcissism can be more or less triumphal, denigrating and annihilating to the object, and more or less drawn into a perverse relationship with exciting internal objects that substitute excitement for the experience of degrading dependence.

7   In modern Western culture, the idea that children emerge from conception rather than parthenogenesis might seem too obvious to warrant further thought. Pregnancy means there is a father; genetics puts it beyond doubt: A male and a female complement each other, induce the formation of the foetus and supply the material of its genetic core. But in the unconscious, conception is shadowed by the parthenogenesis as an omnipotent phantasy implicit in narcissism. Myth as well as clinical evidence makes the point vividly. I have explored these themes in Figlio (2000).

8 Meltzer also speaks of an 'aesthetic conflict,' which is an ominous, primal ambivalence in the infant's perception of its beautiful mother. Such an intrinsic, primitive conflict seems akin to the primal, existential ambivalence that I describe in chapters 1 and 8.

References

Anon. (Ferenczi) (1933) Ontogenesis. *Psychanalytic Quarterly* 2: 365–403.

Arendt, H. (1958) *The Human Condition*. Chicago: University of Chicago Press.

Balsam, R. (2018) 'Castration Anxiety' Revisited: Especially 'Female Castration Anxiety'. *Psychoanalytic Inquiry* 38(1): 11–22.

Bion, W. R. (1965) *Transformations*. London: Heinemann; Karnac 1984.

Bion, W. R. (1967) On Arrogance. In *Second Thoughts: Selected Papers on Psycho-Analysis*. London: Heinemann, pp. 86–92.

Bion, W. R. (1970) *Attention and Interpretation*. London: Tavistock; Karnac, 1984.

Britton, R. (1994) Publication Anxiety: Conflict between Communication and Affiliation. *International Journal of Psychoanalysis* 75: 1213–1224.

Britton, R. (2008) He Thinks Himself Impaired: The Pathologically Envious Personality. In Roth, P. and Lemma, A. (eds) *Envy and Gratitude Revisited*. London: Karnac, 124–136.

Britton, R. (2021) Narcissistic Problems of Sharing Space. In *Sex, Death and the Superego: Updating Psychoanalytic Experience and Developments in Neuroscience*, Second Edition. London and New York: Routledge, 121–133.

Chasseguet-Smirgel, J. (1986) The Archaic Matrix of the Oedipus Complex. In *Sexuality and Mind: The Role of the Father and Mother in the Psyche*. New York/London: New York University Press, pp. 74–91.

Dahl, E. (1996) The Concept of Penis Envy Revisited: A Child Analyst Listens to an Adult, *Psychoanalytic Study of the Child* 51: 303–325.

Federn, P. (1929) On the Distinction between Healthy and Pathological Narcissism. In Weiss, E. (eds) *Ego Psychology and the Psychoses*. London: Imago, 1953; Karnac, 1977, 323–364.

Figlio, K. (2000) *Psychoanalysis, Science and Masculinity*. London: Whurr; Philadelphia: Brunner Routledge, 2001.

Figlio, K. (2003) Getting to the Beginning: Historical Memory and Concrete Thinking. In Radstone, S. and Hodgkin, K. (eds) *Regimes of Memory (Routledge Studies in Memory and Narrative, vol. 12)*. London: Routledge, 2003, 152–66; pb *Memory Cultures: Memory, Subjectivity and Recognition*. New Brunswick/London: Transaction, 2006.

Figlio, K. (2017) The Mentality of Conviction: Feeling Certain and the Search for Truth. In Mintchev, N. and Hinshelwood, R. (eds) *The Feeling of Certainty: Psychosocial Perspectives on Identity and Difference*. Cham: Palgrave Macmillan, 11–30.

Freud, S. (1900) The Interpretation of Dreams. *The Standard Edition of the Complete Psychological Works of Sigmund Freud* 4 & 5.

Freud, S. (1910) A Special Type of Choice of Object Made by Men (Contributions to the Psychology of Love I). *The Standard Edition of the Complete Psychological Works of Sigmund Freud* 11: 161–175.

Freud, S. (1919) The 'Uncanny'. *The Standard Edition of the Complete Psychological Works of Sigmund Freud* 17: 217–256.

Freud, S. (1938) Findings, Ideas, Problems. *The Standard Edition of the Complete Psychological Works of Sigmund Freud* 23: 299–300.

Grunberger, B. (1979) *Narcissism: Psychoanalytic Essays*. Madison: International Universities Press.

Hustvedt, S. (2019) What Does a Man Want. In *Mothers, Fathers, and Others*. London: Sceptre, 2021, 225–253.

Jonas, H. (1966) *The Phenomenon of Life: Toward a Philosophical Biology*. New York: Harper & Row.

Jones, E. (1927) The Early Development of Female Sexuality. *International Journal of Psychoanalysis* 8: 459–472. In *Papers on Psychoanalysis*, 5th edn. London: Baillière, Tindall and Cox, 1948; London: Karnac, 1977, 438–51.

Kant, I. (1781/1787) *Critique of Pure Reason: Unified Edition*, translated by Pluhar, W. Indianapolis/Cambridge: Hackett.

Mawson, C. (2019) *Psychoanalysis and Anxiety: From Knowing to Being*. London/New York: Routledge.

Meltzer, D. (1973) *Sexual States of Mind*. Strath Tay: Clunie Press.

Meltzer, D. (1988) *The Apprehension of Beauty: The Role of Aesthetic Conflict in Development and Violence*. Strath Tay: The Clunie Press.

Rosenfeld, H. (1971) A Clinical Approach to the Psychoanalytic Theory of the Life and Death Instincts: An Investigation into the Aggressive Aspects of Narcissism. *International Journal of Psychoanalysis* 52: 169–178.

Vermote, R. (2019) *Reading Bion*. Abingdon, Oxon/New York: Routledge.

Wollheim, R. (1987) *Painting as an Art*. London: Thames & Hudson.

Zachary, A. (2018) *The Anatomy of the Clitoris: Reflections on the Theory of Female Sexuality*. London: Routledge.

Part III

The Phallic World

Chapter 4

Phallic Defence in the Boy

The Repudiation of Seminality[1]

The Magnetism of the Phallic Defence

My objective in this chapter is to dig beneath the outward, phallic display of masculinity as the secure anchor of the male psyche and its dominance in society as a lineage of masculinity. I aim to show that there is a core instability that pushes the bravado of its phallic presentation in front of it. We will build on the theme of previous chapters, on the masculine internal, seminal world and the idea of 'inside,' laying stress on the phallic defence as a cover over a depressive collapse of hope in the capacity to engender, sustain and repair life itself.

Ever since Freud interpolated a phallic stage between pre-genitality and genitality, it has been a source of controversy that has confined psycho-analytic attention, whether in support or in repudiation. A female phallic stage has been roundly rejected, while a male phallic stage remains more credible. We begin by following Karen Horney's lead on how male and female phallic defences are related. Horney (1926) rejected Freud's theory of a phallic stage in the female. She pointed out that a phallic stage in the female aptly expressed the male terror of feminization, a terror that Freud (1933) took to be the ultimate limitation to psychoanalysis, the bedrock that it could not break down. A female phallic stage was a male invention, the girl's image reflected in a mirror held up to her by masculine phallic narcissism. *His* narcissism finds a way to impose itself on – in – *her*, to sustain *his* masculinity. In more recent theory, he presses his renounced femininity – the shadow of his masculinity – into her by projective identification, depleting her of her own femininity and impressing her with an idealization of the phallus.

There is an unexpected feature of phallic omnipotence, which adds to its stability as a defence: It is inherently unstable, and because it is unstable, it is repeated. So, strange as it may seem, the persistence of the phallic defence follows from its evanescence. An erection of the penis represents a narcissistic expansion; the detumescence of the penis represents its collapse, only to be restored with the next erection, and again.

DOI: 10.4324/9781003455790-7

But what does a phallic defence defend against? Klein (1932, 251) makes it clear that male castration anxieties are rooted in his interior.

> Fear of castration... becomes, in the male individual, a dominating theme that overshadows all his other fears to a greater or less extent. But this is precisely because one of the deepest sources to which disturbances in his sexual potency go back is his anxiety about the interior of his body. The house or town which the boy is so keen to build up again in his play signifies not only his mother's renewed and intact body but his own.

Edgcumbe and Burgner (1975, 173) show, in a child analysis, the transformation of an internal genital anxiety into a phallic anxiety. At about 2 ¼ years, a little boy (whom we met in chapter 2), had earlier accepted his parents' explanations of bodily differences. During toilet training, he was able to assuage emerging fears of losing his penis as he lost faeces. But

> the increasing importance of his penis [in the phallic-narcissistic phase] made it necessary for him to resort to defensive denial of his mother's lack of a penis. At this time (about 3 years old), he asked increasingly sophisticated questions about conception, pregnancy, and birth. He was given simple answers, but was now unable to accept his parents' explanations as readily as he had done previously. Instead, he maintained in conversation with his mother: "When I was born I came out of your penis."

Bell (1965) acknowledges boys' anxieties connected with the internal genital, including the dire belief that 'if a boy cohabits with a girl his testicles will die, or fill up and burst and then he will die ... ' (186) but noted that we 'have tended to overplay the role of the phallus ... and *completely neglected the rest of the male genital*, which constitutes two thirds of the whole' (205; my emphasis).

We have, therefore, solid evidence of male anxieties at the vulnerability of their internal bodily world, and of its displacement onto the penis and its transformation into a phallic narcissistic defence. I build on this tradition. I argue that phallic narcissism repudiates the male's own, non-phallic – seminal – masculinity: The psychic concomitants of the production of semen by the male internal genital. Masculinity loses its essential qualities in phallic monism. As we will see in chapter 5, male and female phallic defences collaborate to avoid the psychic catastrophe of the failure of fertility and of the 'and' that it embodies. Together, they replace desolation, at the loss of the capacity for reparation and the regeneration and sustenance of life, with a manic transcendence. I am primarily concerned with the male, which leads me to distinguish between the phallicism of the penis and the seminality of the male 'internal genital.' It is the thesis of this book, that the destructive extreme of phallic narcissism is a defence against ambivalence in seminality, the destructive pole of which is the 'toxic masculinity' that contaminates the interior of the female and, through it, life itself. Phallicism, with its omnipotent regenerative power, avoids seminality, in both its positive and negative poles.

The classic case of a phallic defence in a boy is Freud's (1909) Little Hans. Let us look again at this boy's castration anxiety. We will see, not only a phallic defence, but his fascinating – seminal – phantasies of procreation, his rich imagination and curiosity, and his need – at times sceptical – of his father to work out what masculine and feminine might mean.

Phallic Castration Anxiety in the Boy: Looking Again at Little Hans

In this famous case of Little Hans, Freud pursued the analysis in terms of castration anxiety. It is worth a re-examination for two reasons: First, Freud pursued not just Hans' phallic, castration anxiety, but also his phantasies of procreation; secondly, Freud does not refer to begetting.[2] Hans' procreative phantasies, in Freud's analysis, were primarily maternal, not paternal. Freud does note Hans's preoccupation with having babies and his puzzlement over the role of fathers in having babies: 'Hans knew in his unconscious where the baby came from and where it had been before' (129). But the riddle of where babies came from was bound up in a phantasy of violence involving father, which surfaced, not only in his fear of horses (father) biting him and falling down (dying), but also in a conscious fantasy that brought a resolution of his phobia. In this fantasy, a plumber 'took a big borer and stuck it into [his] stomach' (65, 128), and later 'took away [his] behind with a pair of pincers, and then gave [him] another, and then did the same with [his] widdler' (98). Freud interpreted his phatansy as father boring into him with his big penis and putting Hans into his mother's womb (128) and, as the plumber/father, giving him a bigger penis. Internalizing his father's penis enhanced his masculinity (100).

Hans brought it all together in a symptomatic act with a doll, in which he *'had pushed a small penknife in through the opening to which the little tin squeaker had originally been attached, and had then torn the doll's legs apart so as to let the knife drop out. He had said to the nurse-maid, pointing between the doll's legs: "Look, there's its widdler!"'*(84, Freud's emphasis; also see 130). Freud attended only to father's asking whether Hans thought that babies were inside mother and were pushed out. The episode seemed also to have alluded to an identification of the baby with a penis pushed into the mother, as in the case of the borer, to which Hans juxtaposed another hypothesis, that babies might grow from eggs, and a question: What constituted his relationship to his father (84–87).

Hans puzzled over the role of fathers in the origination of babies, but Freud and Hans' father stuck to his wish to replace father in mother's affection and father's retaliation. They held fast to the threat to Hans' pleasure in being with mother and using his penis as babies put inside her, which had begun with his mother's castration threat at his pleasure in touching his penis, followed by his fear of being bitten by a horse. They attended to his wanting to achieve the 'revival of pleasures he had enjoyed when he was looked after as an infant ... called up by all that he saw his mother doing for [his baby sister],' and ignored his wanting to have children of his own and to know how they came about (57, 132).

Hans pondered over what father did to produce babies, other than to bore into mother, and, therefore, what else might have secured his belonging to his father, or what structures and functions might have underlain paternal capacities, but these serious questions remained undeveloped. His father 'not only prevented his being in bed with his mother, but also kept from him the knowledge he was thirsting for' (134).[3]

Freud speculated that Hans might have worked out what fathers did in having babies, had he listened to [his own] 'premonitory sensations' of excitement in his penis when he thought of it (134). But such excitement leads mainly to a phallic definition of masculine function and to oedipal castration anxiety. And here Freud made a strong theoretical claim: The threat of extinction had to be based in sensation. The penis was the gathering point of narcissistic cathexes: Of pleasure in oneself and the (castration) anxiety of losing that pleasure – pleasures and threats occasioned by touching – and transcended by accommodating to external reality through not touching and through desexualized pleasures.

But phallic sensations and castration anxiety left two issues out of consideration: The contribution of the father to having babies and the sensations and phantasies arising from the internal genital space of the male. Freud said of the former, that, along with the 'female orifice,' it 'remain[s] undiscovered by the sexual researches of children' (1905, 197); he rarely referred to semen or to begetting, and semen didn't figure in the analysis of Little Hans. Of an internal genital space in the male and its sensory base, he said nothing.

Instead, his theory of castration anxiety refers to the phallic stage, before testicular function, but at a time when sensations in the penis established it as an erotized organ, which could be lost and could serve as a fixation point in regression. And if it corresponded – now, as then – to a cultural stereotype of masculinity, as well as to a fixation point, then alternative representations would not be apparent, because neither analyst nor patient had the language for pursuing an investigation outside these bounds. The male would seem simply to lack an internal procreative space and processes uniquely complementary to those in the female and, therefore, also to lack internal objects of either envy or admiration. By default, analyst and patient would represent internal resources with female imagery and would represent invasion, occupation, usurpation and intrusion with male imagery. The uniquely male contribution to procreation, equivalent in value to the female's, and even awaited by the female, would go unnoticed.

We can see how, in Hans' case, a theory of phallic masculinity obscures seminal masculinity with its self-aggrandizement. It is a form of narcissism, and its castration is a narcissistic loss. Narcissism lends itself to quantitative thinking – more or less – rather than to the qualitative thinking of properties. As a world of 'more or less,' narcissistic thinking dissolves qualitative difference into gradations, ultimately into the continuity of infinite gradations. Narcissism gathers auto-erotisms into the first sense of being and, as a narcissistic being (Freud 1914), it is immediately lost into the mirroring but competing narcissism of its objects. The penis as phallus stands at the fulcrum between self-recognition through an alter-self-father (the self becoming bigger) and castration by the penis-father; and between fragmentation by loss into the object-world and restoration by it (Freud 1911, 61; Green 1990, 59, 60; Laplanche 1980, 61–65).

So, for example, Hans said, 'And everyone has a widdler. And my widdler will get bigger as I get bigger; it's fixed in' (Freud 1909, 34, 131–132). Hans and his father had been discussing Hans' fear of a horse's big widdler, which he transferred from his fear of father and his (presumed) big widdler. It is reasonable to interpret his comment as a reassurance that he could see that he had a penis and would retain it as he grew up to be like father (see also Bell 1961, 266). His fear of a big widdler was the core of his phallic anxiety, but it also opened a path into adulthood through the visual reassurance of continuity and becoming bigger. Freud noted that Hans' phantasy, in which the plumber father (who previously had bored into him) gave him a new and bigger widdler, signalled his overcoming his castration anxiety and made a major contribution to his recovery (131). A widdler was (a measure of) life itself, not a male property: 'When she [even his sister] grows up [her penis will] get bigger alright'(11).

The Penis at the Threshold between Primary Narcissism and Object-Relating

The penis is often confused with the narcissism of the phallus: The former, an organ; the latter, a terminology for an inexpressible notion of being (Birksted-Breen 1996; Laplanche and Pontalis 1980, 312–314). The penis can serve as the phallus because it is vulnerable to castration, but also offers consolation against castration. As the locus of intense sensory awareness – visual, tactile, kinaesthetic, internal – it gathers together the pleasure of sensation and the anxiety at its threatened loss; and it offers repeated assurance that the threat of its loss can be transformed again into the pleasure of its presence (especially in erection, Lax 1997, 132).

Freud did recognize a pre-genital source of castration anxiety, in the loss of faeces as the first detachable part of the body, which is later referred to the penis when observation of the girl suggests that it, too, is detachable (Freud 1917). But he re-asserted the phallic concept of castration anxiety against the idea that the fear of losing the penis genitally represented an earlier anxiety of loss. 'I have nevertheless put forward the view that the term "castration complex" ought to be confined to those excitations and consequences which are bound up with the loss of the *penis*' (Freud 1909, 8 n.2; Freud's emphasis; also see 1923b, 144 n.2; 1926, 129–130). Neither the trauma of birth, nor of weaning, nor of separation of faeces could menace the self as a subject, already aware of itself in relation to a threatening object. He argued that the penis was the location of the most intense narcissism, as if it were both an extension of the ego and a primordial object. It was, so to speak, a little self that could represent for the self, of which it was an extension, the experience of menace (castration), by being detached and attacked or depleted of its narcissism, and of menacing (castrating) by identification with another penis that will deplete it. Displaced onto a wholly external object (a horse-father, for Hans, who menaced him by having both a bigger penis,[4] which could drain his penis, and teeth, which could bite it off), the castration threat could be avoided, on the model of a phobia.

In his later reformulation of the concept of anxiety, Freud (1926) saw the root of castration anxiety as 'signal anxiety,' through which the ego organized a defence against the inchoate, indeterminate primary source of anxiety as a pre-psychological trauma. Following Ferenczi, he said that, in copulation, the ego returned through the penis to its primal state inside mother's protection. Castration anxiety, as signal anxiety, captured all the earlier forms of separation. The 'blissful experience' of mother referred to her protection against the traumatic, economic (instinctual) dislocation of birth, which was repeated and retrospectively managed as weaning, defecation and, ultimately, as phallic castration anxiety.

In this line of thinking, the oedipal threat to the penis transforms a primitive disruption of narcissism into a conflict between, say, father and son. Father's threat at this primitive level is not to cut off the son's penis, but to extract his son's narcissism, as it gathers into the penis, by mirroring it with his own. For Green (1990, 56–65) and Laplanche (1980, 61–65), the castration complex is inherent in the very nature of narcissism. The narcissistic gathering of autoerotic cathexes into a unity initiates the emergence of consciousness, and with it, a sense of estrangement, an immanent rift in the 'psychic surface' (Green) or 'narcissistic envelope' (Laplanche), the force of which will be projected into 'father' and will be experienced as a separation from an object. Similarly, Figlio (2000, 78, 127, 133) refers to the boy's penis as an irregularity in the 'narcissistic surface' which puts narcissism at risk and simultaneously salvages it. The penis as a reservoir of this narcissism does not disappear (Bell 1961, 266).

The phallus puts pre-genital anxieties into a new register. On the border of the narcissistic envelope, the penis, as the organ of the phallus, reaches inside narcissism and captures the inarticulable quality of anxiety, anchoring it in the penis as an object, also external to the narcissistic envelope. It can garner a new stock of its narcissism by depleting other objects, as in the 'one penis phenomenon,' and even treating castration as an illusion (Laplanche 1980, 61–65, 133–134, based on Rank 1924, 20–22). Indeed, Laplanche (1980, 117) queries whether there can be a castration anxiety, or whether such a concept aims to reconstruct anxiety itself, which is objectless and outside experience, as a coherent history (see chapter 3 on a primal, non-objectal, non-dimensional ground state).

As a narcissistic emblem, the phallus has no material reality: It is not an object and has no dimensions. We can use words for it, such as 'expansion,' 'elation,' 'fullness,' but not objectal words. The penis stands in for the phallus as a visible representative of narcissistic expansion, deflation and, again, expansion; and it is a source of masculine pride, but it is not itself a narcissistic emblem: Not the phallus of the phallic stage. The phallus, as a narcissistic emblem, underwrites a sense of being, but not a specificity of being – not being a man as opposed to being a woman or having any substantive, male endowment: That is object-related. The phallus and its anatomical representative are, therefore, also sources of masculine insecurity in the moment of offering security.

When we substitute structures and functions for phallic expansion and contraction, we aim to transform an inconceivable experience of 'being,' as elation, into the world of dimension and perception. In so doing, we create a phallic illusion of recapturing a primal, dimensionless state. That is because erectile organs are sites of transformation. They serve as seats of narcissism, mimicking a dimensionless sense of expansion and fullness. This fundamental, erotic exhilaration creates an illusion of a self-generated withdrawal from external reality, seeming to annul the constraining external reality of an object-related experience.

The boy's penis is the prime site for such a transformation. It is an anatomical and functional structure, geographically separate from the surrounding bodily topography, charged with narcissism. Indeed, its anatomy and physiology outfit it for this role. It literally fills with narcissism. When stimulated and erotically charged, it engorges and replicates primitive feelings of pleasurable fullness, which we might think of as an extension of oral satisfaction. And it fills as the result of sphincter activity, which suggests an analogy with the orifices at the interface between inside and outside.

Eugenio Gaddini (1972, 45) describes the extension of orality as follows.

After the oral zones, the erogenous zones capable of building up a psychical organization under their primacy are, on careful consideration, not only zones in which the inside of the body communicates with the outside, but also seats of coordinated neuromuscular organization, made up of striated muscles, whose functioning is from birth biologically pre-ordained. The sphincters and the male and female erectile sexual organs can, in this sense, be considered, in the early phases of life, as a part of the pre-ordained biological organization for the external discharge of aggressive energy. On the economic level, they therefore contribute to the oral homeostatic function.

This merging of passive, narcissistic completion and active, muscular object-relating is similar to what happens in feeding at the breast. The passive filling of the mouth and belly follows upon the active closing of the lips, like a sphincter, around the nipple and milk in the mouth. The mouth actively introjects the breast as an object but does so in the service of restoring the narcissistic fullness of the belly and the mouthspace that surrounds the continuity of baby and breast within a narcissistic envelope. The lips treat the breast as an object and the breast treats the lips as an object, while narcissism merges them into a unity. The object-relatedness of a muscular act blends with the narcissism of fullness. So too, the sphincter of the penis fills the penis with pleasurable narcissism. It restores the body's narcissism through adding the pleasure of the full penis to it.

At the same time, the full penis, with its muscularity, becomes an object to the ego, disrupting the narcissistic expansion of self-feeling that its fullness provides (on narcissistic expansion, see Grunberger 1979, 6, 43, 123). It is, so to speak, a segment of a narcissistic surface but also an object that can be detached and catastrophically lost – castrated – and therefore in an intermediate position between narcissism and object-relating. It is a topographical site on the body that represents both. It becomes, therefore, a prime site of the conflict between them: Being at one with itself, in the pre-objectal realm, and in the object-related world, probably equivalent to Grunberger's (1989) concept of the 'monad': An extension of foetal narcissism in the external world.

Although the penis is the largest erectile organ, it is not the only erectile organ. Not only is the clitoris erectile, but so are the nipples. In the theory of phallic monism, the clitoris disappoints the girl because it is smaller than the penis; it is this visual comparison, in which everything is reduced to dimension, that turns her to the wish to have a penis. But the illusion of capturing the penis, fed by the visual comparison of size, captures the essence of narcissism. It is unstable. There is no difference in substance, no qualitative difference: Just more or less, just superiority or deficit.

In comparing the clitoris with the penis, the girl might feel deficient; but the boy would feel deficient in comparing the penis with the nipples, were it not for its greater size. In this case, the visual comparison of size once again captures the essence of narcissism; once again, it snares the self in a narcissistic dimension. It reveals that, in being bigger, the penis, is not qualitatively, substantively superior: It only represents an unstable narcissistic self. In that fragile situation, with its illusory core hidden by visual comparison, the penis could suddenly be unmasked: Revealed to be as inferior to the nipples, as it claims to be superior to the clitoris. Even the visual comparison would lead to the same revelation. As the girl's nipples and breasts develop, their growth presages capacities that the boy clearly lacked, while the boy remains unclear what his penis might be for, apart from his pleasure.

We can draw together these two psychoanalytic observations – the penis-clitoris and the penis-nipple – into one psychological disposition. As sites of narcissistic expansion, all erectile organs have a common phallic property. In an oral phantasy, in which penis and the nipple are equivalent, there is no specifically masculine function and therefore nothing specifically masculine about the penis. Although it has become a psychoanalytic commonplace to compare the penis with the nipple and to note that the penis derives its significance from the nipple, the comparison has not been based on their being erectile. It has, therefore, not made clear the instability of phallic monism as a foundation for masculine identity, precisely because it is narcissistic and does not specify anything uniquely male. Only when it offers semen does the penis separate itself from the nipple, which offers milk. Without these two, different secretions, they both would offer only an extension of narcissism to their recipients.

Let us work backwards, conceptually and developmentally, to try to capture – or at least intimate – the matrix from which a sense of self emerges. Selfhood is subjective and objective at the same time. It combines 'being' as the ground of aliveness, and object-relatedness, including taking the ego as an object. [5] We might then, with Gaddini (1974; 1976) speak of 'father' as an emerging object of identification inside the 'being' of mother. Father is an unsettling disturbance, an irregularity or blemish inside a mother who was previously perfect, fused with the as yet unformed perfect self of the child. Gaddini calls her an 'extraneous mother.' For the girl, this father remains an object, outside her primary identification and identity; but for the boy, this father is essential to his primary identification and identity. His self-consciousness, his sense of a masculine self, in his identification with father, is unsettled in its core, because the nucleus of father-object is an extraneous mother, an irruption in mother, not a wholly separate locus of identity.

Being and Doing (Imitating and Incorporating) at the Birth of Object Relations

We have been treating narcissism, not just as a primal state, not (yet) disturbed, not (yet) in a field of objects, but as pre-objectal 'being.' Probably, we should not (yet) speak of an experience of being, because experience presupposes an ego that has it. We are, instead, seeking an intimation of being that is not so much before, as beneath the ego, as a ground. Originating object relations would, in this understanding, form around an identification that comprised two poles: A non-objectal pole, coalesced with primary narcissism; and an objectal pole, in which non-ego and the ego itself are recognized as objects. The sense of self comprises these two poles: 'being' and object-relating.

Since object-relating is active, we can, with Winnicott, speak of 'being' (non-objectal pole) and 'doing' (objectal pole). Taking up, first, the non-objectal pole: Winnicott (1963, 180) distinguished a primal selfexperience, which he called the experience of omnipotence, from defensive omnipotence, which he called simply omnipotence. He thereby shifted the emphasis from omnipotence as a repudiation of the other, to omnipotence as a fleeting primal experience of self – never a state, for that would quickly require the repudiation of external reality to sustain it, but a fleeting experience; one might better say, a ground of experience.

I think an *experience* of omnipotence might be misleading for specifying a prior, primal situation. To 'have' an experience, an ego must pre-exist, and an ego can impose a defence. A *prior* situation refers to 'before' in time and also to a logical as well as substantive precondition for an ego. Perhaps it is akin to Bion's '0' or Kant's 'thing-in-itself,' a ground against which we can think and speak of perceptual, dimensional, experience – the idea we considered in chapter 3. I will call such a required precondition, 'omnipotence,' and distinguish it from defensive (experience of) omnipotence. Winnicott (1971, 99) seemed to have such a primal state in mind, with his distinction between 'being' and 'doing.' 'After being – doing and being done to. But first, being.' He said of these two polar positions:

a   the baby *is* the breast (or object, or mother, etc.); the breast is the baby ...;
b   the baby is confronted by an object (breast, etc.) ... [O]ne can see that baby ≡ breast is a matter of being, not of doing, while in terms of confrontation baby and breast meeting involves doing (1966, 191–192; Winnicott's emphasis).

Omnipotence, as opposed to defensive omnipotence, is a dimensionless condition, because it does not imply an object or an action towards it. Only in engaging with or relating to an object does the notion of dimension comes into play. There is, therefore, no bigger or smaller, no comparison; and no feelings that go with comparison, agency and control, such as triumph or denigration. Grunberger (1979, 6, 43, 123) calls it 'narcissistic expansion,' to suggest a dimensionless feeling of pure eros. In this respect, it is interesting to note the prevalence of words such as 'boundless' to describe attitudes, such as generosity, which do not attempt to control the object; and to note also that they equally describe primary narcissism, as opposed to defensive, secondary narcissism.

Let us now turn to the objectal pole and the nascent ego, with its emerging/ created object, and apply it to understanding father as the primal object. For

Eugenio Gaddini (1974; 1976) father is an irruption into mother. He suggests that, at the most primitive level, the primal father as an emerging object is a disturbance – a disturbance in primary narcissism[6] (for Winnicott, being is associated with a female element, doing with a male element). Primary narcissism implies omnipotence: Nothing exists outside its realm, and, when an object appears, so does the need completely to master it. The nascent ego will response to this objectal disturbance, either to accept it or to re-create it as an aspect of itself; that is, to restore primary narcissism.[7]

These fleeting primal moments, in which narcissism and object-relating co-exist, are prior to the laying down of identifications that, as Freud (1923a) described, build up the ego with its object-world. Eugenio Gaddini combines psychoanalytic and early infant-observational methods, to argue that the concept of identification is used too broadly. It does not discriminate between two processes: Introjection, which implies a process modelled on oral incorporation, in which the ego contains objects in an internal space; and imitation, a primitive repudiation of objects as reality other to the ego, which attempts omnipotently to recapture the illusion of the boundless self of primary narcissism.

For Gaddini (1969), there are two forms of perception, related to these two processes: The more primitive, for which the skin surface and the musculature are used as organs of perception through imitation, which aims to resettle the body from a disturbance without recognizing the external, objectal source of the disturbance; the other, based on incorporation, for which any perceptual organ and any orifice might substitute for the mouth, and all perception is a form of oral incorporation.

At first the infant perceives by modifying his own body in relation to the stimulus. In this way, the infant does not perceive the real stimulus, but the modification of his own body... The primitive imitative perception seems to lead to the hallucinatory image, to the fantasies of fusion through modification of one's own body, and to imitations, in the direction of the wish *to be* the object. Oral incorporation seems to lead to fantasies of fusion through incorporation and to introjections, in the direction of *having*, of *possessing*, the object (20, 22; Gaddini's emphasis).

Gaddini distinguishes 'two areas of mental experience,' corresponding to these two attitudes towards the object, and defines them as the 'psycho-sensory ... and the psycho-oral areas respectively' (1974, 63). The former resettles the body-ego into primary narcissism; the latter holds objects as other to, and inside, the ego. I associate the imitative, narcissistic relaxation with Winnicott's 'being,' and the active encompassing of the object through perception with 'doing.'

The importance of imitation in comparison with early identifications was brought home to me by an observation of a baby of less than two weeks. His mother sat him on her lap facing away from her. I could see his face clearly, but they could not see each other's faces. He held his left thumb effortlessly in his mouth and gummed it vigorously but not greedily. His fingers were extended towards his right eye. His mother, saying he mustn't get his fingers in his eyes, brushed gently over his forehead. It wasn't clear whether she actually pushed his hand away and his thumb out of his mouth, but that was the effect. His left hand now moved to the same place on his face, as if repeating, with his hand, the movement she had just made. She wiped his lips with a cloth. His left hand went to the right side of his face, fingers extended and palm outwards, as if warding off a blow. He settled and yawned. She yawned and said he was making her sleepy.

Both forms of perception are in play here: An imitative (psychosensory) reconstitution of external reality within the baby's omnipotence, in which both mother and baby settled into a blissful state, unconcerned with external, perceptual reality, and a (psycho-oral) introjection of the thumb as an external object. Even the psycho-oral experience was largely removed from external reality, however, so one would not call his thumb-sucking an identification with mother (he was not facing her). But he was on the way towards identification. The psycho-sensory root will remain at the core of the self, but ultimately, identification by the maturing male psyche will require an object with a masculine identity. It will allow the male to relate to a woman, not in a phantasy of boundless mother-infant euphoria and not in a smashing of the Oedipus complex, but in a genital identification with father (Chasseguet-Smirgel 1986, 70–71; Freud 1923a, 32; 1924, 177).

Insecurity in the Birth of Male Identity

Following this line of thinking, we can see that becoming a self rests on combining two poles of (at first potential) experience: 1) 'being,' as a (psycho-sensory) intimation of omnipotence, in a narcissistic resettlement of the body through a perception by imitation; and 2) 'doing,' as a (psycho-oral) objectification by introjecting an object. For the girl, the psycho-oral foundation of identity in her identification with mother endures, in harmony with her psycho-sensory grounding of selfhood. For the boy, his psycho-oral identification is at odds with his psycho-sensory grounding of identity and its evolution, as he identifies with the father as an object that disturbs his psycho-sensory intimacy with mother. His evolving identity is further unsettled because his capacity to resolve his 'femininity phase' is more influential than his incorporation of, and genital identification with, father Klein (1928, 191–192).

The view I have developed seems at odds with the usual idea that the father and the paternal super-ego provide the solid foundation for the boy's ego and the realization of his ideal, and that the girl is in a less secure situation, deprived of the same capacity to realize her ideals. Klein, for example, said that the reality associated with the boy's identification with father promoted a creativity that was not common in women, for whom the (paternal) ego ideal was not achievable in external reality. Yet beneath this conventional surface, I think one can discern a more radical view, consistent with my argument that narcissism – phallic narcissism, ultimately – robs men of a deep sense of security in relation to their (paternal) ego-ideals and their relationships with other men.

The boy lacks a secure base derived from his mother, both because of the hardship of the femininity phase and because the penis as phallus, at the border of his narcissistic envelope, represents what he can lose of his (psycho-sensory) 'being' as well as losing a treasured object. The internal father as the extraneous mother is a disturbance in narcissism and thus a source of anxiety, marking an ambiguous moment of self-creation and self-loss. Father, as an extraneous mother may also not offer a secure object of (psycho-oral) identification, and in addition, can become a double that depletes him (the one penis phenomenon). Later, this phallic dilemma is lodged more squarely in his penis, threatened by castration anxiety. The boy's penis at this moment represents the ambiguity of his identity, as an irregularity on the narcissistic surface of the body-ego, intensifying the psycho-sensory experience of the omnipotent self, putting it at risk (castration anxiety) and reaching towards the object-world. The penis as the locus of phallic defence does not represent for him an enduring ideal, but teeters on the edge of revealing the phallic defence as an illusion.

I have argued that the sameness and difference of boy and father are concentrated in the penis because it is the organ that expresses both boundless narcissistic oneness and object mastery. As a narcissistic emblem, it is non-objectal. In the one penis phenomenon, there can only be one, in the sense that recognizing another penis would deplete the subject's penis of its narcissistic base. This narcissistic castration anxiety is supplemented by a castration threat to the penis as an object. The penis is the site at which father and son are at once aspects of each other and distinct from each other: The moment of an omnipotent attempt to re-experience narcissistic completeness, challenged by the instability inherent in narcissism, and the moment of the birth of self into external reality.

Such a dilemma is clear in the following daydream reported by a man.

> He said he had an idea for a film. A man was walking absent-mindedly in a park, when he came across a fenced-in playground. A child was playing inside and, as the man watched the play in a reverie, he began to recognize the boy as himself when he was a boy. But his pleasant, nostalgic daydreaming was disturbed by the anxious thought that, if the boy were he, when he was young, then there would be only one penis between them.

In this fantasy, there is a basic polarity. At one pole, there is the narcissism, in which the penis as narcissistic emblem reconstitutes egoexpansion.

The man and the boy together are like the touching of mother and child in an expansion of the narcissistic surface – two droplets of water that coalesce. At the other pole, the recognition of the penis as an object predominates, in the form of the suspicion that the boy and the man each has his own penis. At this pole, the penis as object challenges the delusion of the penis as a narcissistic emblem. Just before, there was only the child, unselfconsciously playing in a maternal envelope. The anxious moment of awareness creates the child as an object of the father's watching as simultaneously it creates the father inside the child's awareness of himself and of his (maternal) environment. The just-lost narcissism comes into representation through the father who will complete himself with the penis of the son. This is the early form of castration anxiety.

Since the core of the father is the extraneous mother and identification comprises a narcissistic identity moment and an object-related moment, the alignment with father leaves the nascent self in a precarious state. In his narcissistic moment, his 'being' with mother, he is assimilated to a disturbed, extraneous mother. In his object-related moment, he identifies with a father with a similar disturbance. Father is, therefore, likely to appear in his unconscious as his double and to add to a sense of estrangement.

Father, in his difference from mother, is a nascent object, appearing as a disturbance to the narcissistic moment of identification for both boy and girl. But while the narcissistic identity pole of identification can remain with the mother for the girl, secured by father in his difference from her narcissistic identity pole, the boy is drawn away from mother and his narcissistic identity pole, towards his father-object. His alignment, as with the girl's, is with father as extraneous mother, but he is more disturbed by it, because the ground of his identifications has been away from the narcissistic identity pole of the mother towards an unstable father-object. He cannot fall back on his narcissistic identity pole because his identification is shifted towards the father, whose lineage is similarly insecure. He is, therefore, left in disturbance in both his narcissistic (psycho-sensory) and his incorporative (psycho-oral) poles.

The absent father, as a psychological reality, not necessarily a physical reality, fits this model. In any event, the internal father does not match the public image of paternal authority. Strong evidence of this mismatch shows up in misogyny and its ramifications into resentment- and hate-driven prejudice. At the core of misogyny, I argue, is the repudiation of unique masculinity: What I call seminal masculinity.

The Phallic Repudiation of Seminality

My objective in this chapter has been to dig beneath the outward presentation of masculinity as the secure anchor of the male psyche and its dominance in society as a lineage of masculinity. I have aimed to show that there is a core instability and that this core instability promotes the bravado of its outward presentation. Phallic masculinity attacks femininity, but that attack, in all its violence, aims to keep phallic narcissism in play, in its power to subdue. We are bound to ask, subdue what? The uncontrollable in the female? It is true that Male supremacist movements of various stripes – members of the 'manosphere' – blame feminism for provoking them into reacting to restore their lost authority (Johanssen 2022). But the need to quell an opposition is a delusional creation, which throws into sharp relief its basis in narcissistic aggrandizement. Misogyny shares the delusional creation of an enemy with racism, antisemitism, fundamentalism (Figlio 2018). I will argue in chapters 9 and 10, that misogyny crystallizes a core identity around hatred. Beneath it, for all humanity, is the anguish of the erosion of fertility as a depressive quality, in Klein's concept of the depressive position.

Depressive, genital masculinity involves the ego in concern for the object, concern for the mother and her fertility. It involves his generosity, assimilated from his relationship with his generous mother and generous father. It brings with it the awesome dread of an incapacity to sustain her fertility: To engender, sustain and re-invigorate life with his sexuality – with his seminal masculinity. His insecure masculine identity, an insecurity in the lineage of genital, seminal masculinity, undermines his faith in his seminal capacity and invites a phallic transcendence, girded by phallic potency and superiority over femininity and seminality.

To establish a male lineage, the son must identify with father. If the lineage is to produce and reinforce genital masculinity, and not pregenital pseudo-masculinity, then the relationship between father and son must be properly an identification and not an imitation. Imitation is narcissistic and repudiates reality; identification recognizes reality. In the oedipal context, imitation repudiates father's existence and binds the son to his mother in a phantasy of fusion; identification with father frees him to relate generously and lovingly to women. But Gaddini's model, in which father emerges as a disturbance in mother, suggests that father as the anchor point to reality is unstable at the core. His capacity to secure the ego's hold on reality must come later, as an achievement of genitality; or, in the language of this book, of seminality (to be explored in chapter 7). Phallic masculinity is inversely related to this genital achievement.

The penis as an instrument can offer pleasure and in its phallic allure can offer a share in narcissistic aggrandizement. Both can fail but can be re-kindled. The seminal dimension is different. It enlivens, reassures or destroys on the inside, in all the meanings of inside that we have explored in chapter 3. In its failure and in its destructiveness, it is the masculine embodiment of depressive desolation. Semen is the substrate and the symbolic bedrock of the male's contribution to sustaining life and, in the ambivalence of seminality (to be explored in chapters 8 to 10), it carries toxic masculinity.[8]

Next to these seminal attributes, phallic narcissism and phallic castration anxiety, for all their thrall and menace, seem shallow. They also offer the comfort of simplicity: 'the idea that the constitution of the feminine sex was due to a castration, which would explain all the insufficiencies felt by her or all the inferiorities attributed to her, in the face of the male, who would not miss an occasion to oppress her in order to defend against his own, masculine castration anxiety' (Green 1990, 110–111; my translation). Such a phallic monism offers an apparently simple, masculine account of psychology and culture: A theory, according to which the girl used to have a penis (Abraham 1920, 339–340; Horney 1926). It is a theory that garners critical energy to itself, whether held or reviled, of female and male alike, of the culture at large and of psychoanalysis. It must function as a powerful defence, which gains strength as an unconscious collaboration of masculine and feminine.

Notes

1 This chapter is based on Figlio (2000), chapters 7 and 8, and Figlio (2010)
2 As I pointed out in chapter 1, every sort of inspiration is 'seminal,' in psycho-analysis as well as popular culture, but male procreative capacity is disregarded by both. Again, the unconscious can speak loudly because it is unrecognized.
3 Etchegoyen (1988) argued that Hans colluded with parental pressure to support phallic monism; Hinshelwood (1989) studied the transference in Hans' 'sessions' and argued that the absence of transference awareness channelled the analysis in this direction; Midgley (2006) has analyzed various re-readings of *Little Hans*).
4 In the one penis phenomenon, which I have observed clinically, father and son share a single penis, and compete over who owns it.
5 It is interesting to note that sense organs, including the nose, eyes and ears, which seem passively to register a sensation and therefore could not discriminate between an internal and an external sensation, are also fitted with muscles, which makes it an active encompassing of an object. Their muscularity reinforces the functional analogy drawn by Gaddini between perception and introjection, as in the ana-tomical analogy between an organ of perception and the active mouth, which grasps the nipple as it also fills with milk (narcissism). Even the iris of the eye actively opens to the sight of emotionally engaging images, just as the mouth does (Hess, 1975).
6 This construal is built into the etymology of an 'object.' In its earliest meaning, it referred to an accusation, an obstruction, something thrown in front of the mind; later something exciting emotion, towards which effort is directed, a subject of cognition, external to the mind.
7 For Freud (1900, 567 and n. 1; 1913, 75–99; 1920), the pleasure principle drove the nascent ego to relieve the burden of excitation. The restoration of primary nar-cissism resettles the disturbed ego in the moment of its emergence. In Beyond the Pleasure Principle, Freud (1920) took up the drive for mastery as a reaction to helplessness, including the swamping of the ego in trauma, as in his analysis of the compulsion to repeat and the 'Fort'/'Da' game. The overwhelmed ego struggled to bring excitation within a manageable range, in the realm of the pleasure principle.
8 In Figlio (2000), I argued that even nature becomes a target of phallic attack, the ultimate attack on mother (nature), mitigated by the belief that 'she' will rebound with every new illusion of our capacity to carry on, unaffected, as if not noticing the damage was another triumph over weaker, feminine, others. The phallic dimension of man's relationship with nature, as well as with femininity, conceals a

depressive anxiety that the capacity of 'mother nature' to survive and regenerate can be eroded by a slow, internal toxicity, which is the negative side of seminal masculinity.

References

Abraham, K. (1920) Manifestations of the Female Oedipus Complex. In *Selected Papers on Psycho-Analysis*. London: Hogarth Press, 1927, 338–369.
Bell, A. (1961). Some Observations on the Role of the Scrotal Sac and Testicles. *Journal of the American Psychoanalytic Association* 9: 261–286.
Bell, A. (1965) The Significance of the Scrotal Sac and Testicles for the Prepuberty Male. *Psychoanalytic Quarterly* 34: 182–206.
Birksted-Breen, D. (1996) Phallus, Penis and Mental Space. *International Journal of Psychoanalysis* 77: 649–657.
Chasseguet-Smirgel, J. (1986) The Archaic Matrix of the Oedipus Complex. In *Sexuality and Mind: The Role of the Father and Mother in the Psyche*. New York/ London: New York University Press, pp. 74–91.
Edgcumbe, R. and Burgner, B. (1975) The Phallic Phase–A Differentiation between Preoedipal and Oedipal Aspects of Phallic Development. *Psychoanalytic Studies of the Child* 30: 161–180.
Etchegoyen, R. (1988) The Analysis of Little Hans and the Theory of Sexuality. *International Review of Psycho-Analysis* 15: 37–43.
Figlio, K. (2000) *Psychoanalysis, Science and Masculinity*. London: Whurr; Philadelphia: Brunner Routledge, 2001.
Figlio, K. (2010) Phallic and Seminal Masculinity: A Theoretical and Clinical Confusion. *International Journal of Psychoanalysis* 91(1): 119–139.
Figlio, K. (2018) Fundamentalism and the Delusional Creation of an Enemy. In Krüger, S., Figlio, K. and Richards, B. (eds) *Fomenting Political Violence: Fantasy, Language, Media, Action*. London: Palgrave, 2018, 149–166.
Freud, S. (1900) The Interpretation of Dreams. *The Standard Edition of the Complete Psychological Works of Sigmund Freud* 4 & 5.
Freud, S. (1905) Three Essays on the Theory of Sexuality. *The Standard Edition of the Complete Psychological Works of Sigmund Freud* 7: 123–245.
Freud, S. (1909) Analysis of a Phobia in a Five-Year-Old Boy. *The Standard Edition of the Complete Psychological Works of Sigmund Freud* 10: 1–149.
Freud, S. (1911). Psycho-Analytic Notes on an Autobiographical Account of a Case of Paranoia (Dementia Paranoides). *The Standard Edition of the Complete Psychological Works of Sigmund Freud* 12: 1–82.
Freud, S. (1913) The Theme of the Three Caskets. *The Standard Edition of the Complete Psychological Works of Sigmund Freud* 12: 289–302.
Freud, S. (1914) On Narcissism: An Introduction. *The Standard Edition of the Complete Psychological Works of Sigmund Freud* 14: 73–105.
Freud, S. (1917) On Transformations of Instinct as Exemplified in Anal Erotism. *The Standard Edition of the Complete Psychological Works of Sigmund Freud* 17: 125–133.
Freud, S. (1920) Beyond the Pleasure Principle. *The Standard Edition of the Complete Psychological Works of Sigmund Freud* 18: 1–64.

Freud, S. (1923a) The Ego and the Id. *The Standard Edition of the Complete Psychological Works of Sigmund Freud* 19: 1–66.

Freud, S. (1923b) The Infantile Genital Organization: An Interpolation into the Theory of Sexuality. *The Standard Edition of the Complete Psychological Works of Sigmund Freud* 19: 139–145.

Freud, S. (1924) The Dissolution of the Oedipus Complex. *The Standard Edition of the Complete Psychological Works of Sigmund Freud* 19: 171–180.

Freud, S. (1926) Inhibition, Symptoms and Anxiety. *The Standard Edition of the Complete Psychological Works of Sigmund Freud* 20: 77–175.

Freud, S. (1933) New Introductory Lectures on Psycho-Analysis. *The Standard Edition of the Complete Psychological Works of Sigmund Freud* 22: 1–182

Gaddini, E. (1969) On Imitation. In *A Psychoanalytic Theory of Infantile Experience: Conceptual and Clinical Reflections*. London: Tavistock/Routledge, 1992, 18–34.

Gaddini, E. (1972) Aggression and the Pleasure Principle: Towards a Psychoanalytic Theory of Aggression. In *A Psychoanalytic Theory of Infantile Experience: Conceptual and Clinical Reflections*. London: Tavistock/Routledge, 1992, 35–45.

Gaddini, E. (1974) Formation of the Father and the Primal Scene. In *A Psychoanalytic Theory of Infantile Experience: Conceptual and Clinical Reflections*. London: Tavistock/Routledge, 1992, 61–82.

Gaddini, E. (1976) On Father Formation in Early Child Development. In *A Psychoanalytic Theory of Infantile Experience: Conceptual and Clinical Reflections*. London: Tavistock/Routledge, 1992, 83–89.

Green, A. (1990) *Le complexe de castration* [The Castration Complex]. Paris: PUF.

Grunberger, B. (1979) *Narcissism: Psychoanalytic Essays*. Madison: International Universities Press.

Hess, E. (1975) *The Tell-Tale Eye: How Your Eyes Reveal Hidden Thoughts and Emotion*. New York: Van Nostrand Reinhold.

Hinshelwood, R. D. (1989) Little Hans's Transference. *Journal of Child Psychotherapy* 15: 63–78.

Horney, K. (1926) The Flight from Womanhood: The Masculinity-Complex in Women, as Viewed by Men and by Women. *International Journal of Psychoanalysis* 7: 324–339; reprinted in *Feminine Psychology*. NY: Norton, 1967, 54–70.

Johanssen, J. (2022) *Fantasy, Online Misogyny and the Manosphere: Male Bodies of Dis/Inhibition*. London/New York: Routledge.

Klein, M. (1928) Early Stages of the Oedipus Conflict. In *The Writings of Melanie Klein*, vol. 1. London: The Hogarth Press and the Institute of Psycho-Analysis, 1975, 186–198.

Klein, M. (1932) *The Psychoanalysis of Children*. In *The Writings of Melanie Klein*, vol. 2. London: The Hogarth Press and the Institute of Psycho-Analysis, 1975.

Laplanche, J. (1980) *Problématiques II: Castration–Symbolisations* [Problematics II: Castration–Symbolizations]. Paris: PUF.

Laplanche, J. and Pontalis, J.-B. (1980) *The Language of Psycho-Analysis*. London: Hogarth and the Institute of Psycho-Analysis.

Lax, R. (1997) Boys' Envy of Mother and the Consequences of This Narcissistic Mortification. *The Psychoanalytic Study of the Child* 52: 118–139.

Midgley, N. (2006) Re-Reading 'Little Hans': Freud's Case Study and the Problem of Competing Paradigms in Psychoanalysis. *Journal of the American Psychoanalytic Association* 54(2): 537–559.

Rank, O. (1924) *The Trauma of Birth.* New York: Harper & Row, 1929.

Winnicott, D. W. (1963) Communicating and Not Communicating Leading to a Study of Certain Opposites, reprinted in *The Maturational Process and the Facilitating Environment.* London: Hogarth/Institute of Psycho-Analysis, 1965, 179–192.

Winnicott, D. W. (1971) *Playing and Reality.* Harmondsworth: Penguin.

Chapter 5

Phallic Monism
A Defensive Collaboration

Phallic Stage as a Monism

Freud's concept of a phallic stage postulates a common developmental pathway for girls and boys, which precedes genital maturity: In that sense, it is a phallic *monism*. He rarely used the phrase, phallic monism, but did set out clearly the idea of there being only one gender until full genital sexuality was established. Before then, in the interpolated phallic stage, male and female shared a conviction that the penis was the organ of libido.

In phallic theory, however, an attraction to the penis should be seen as a quest to embody libido. Freud was clear on this point. Phallic referred to libido and there was only one libido, not a male and a female libido. Perhaps this monism of libido could be recast in terms of Freud's (1920) dichotomy between Eros and Thanatos. There is only one life force. Eros brings life by increasing unifications; Thanatos depletes life.

Moreover, in defining 'masculine' as active and 'feminine' as passive, Freud (1915) was speaking the language of the drives, not of attitude or behaviour. Passive did not mean submissive, but the drive turned back on its source.[1] But a confusion does begin with the idea that the penis is the primary organ of phallicism. It is, after all, active in pressing eros – excitement and also semen – into the female. To equate Eros with the penis is an arrogation, an omnipotent bid, but the equation does carry a certain truth: The penis presses forward the drive of Eros; the vagina seeks to be filled with Eros. In that sense, phallic monism tends to be thought of as a monism of the penis.

The problem lies in the assumption that the girl, in this theory, envies the organ that, in comparison with her diminutive clitoris, she lacks. In her phallic monism, the girl phantasies that she possesses father's penis and can fashion a 'penis baby' from it. Unsurprisingly, monism of the penis has attracted intense criticism, often based on the case for primary, feminine psychosexual characteristics, such as awareness of the vagina and the intricate innervation of the clitoris into the deep structure of the female genital (see Zachary 2018 for an extensive review).

DOI: 10.4324/9781003455790-8

But suppose we drop penis envy. Then phallus refers to a phantasy of omnipotence, a monism in being held jointly by male and female. Castration names phallic loss. Castration anxiety is phallic anxiety: An anxiety specified within psychoanalysis, not within biology, where it refers to ablating the testicles. In psychoanalysis, with the phallus embodied in the penis, the boy's castration anxiety refers to cutting off the penis and the girl's to disappointment at her absent or diminutive penis, but only because, in this confusion of phallus with penis, phallus becomes the sole property of the male, and the female is co-opted into it. There are two sexes but only one phallus. It seems more naturally to belong to the male, because of the apparent embodiment of the phallus in his visible penis. Phallic monism therefore consolidates the identity of the male, while it sets the female at odds with herself.

If we stick with the omnipotent phallus, we can think of a collaborative defence. The idea of possession and dispossession of an omnipotent phallus defends against the actual collaboration of masculine and feminine in a fertile union. Their collaborative phallic defence creates the idea of a parthenogenic baby – the penis baby – in place of the baby of fertile union, for both male and female. 'Active' vs 'passive' as attitudes or positions leads us away from this point, into a controversy that recycles inside itself.

Freud (1925, pp. 257–258) did give occasion for confusion. He did imply a stereotypical feminine of submission to the masculine, for example, in saying that the female was less morally developed than the male, less a leader in civilized society. And he did locate the phallus in the penis, by referring to castration as cutting off the penis. If the testicles were included, they were, for Freud, secondary. But he also stated the imperative to keep psychoanalytic methods and findings separate from those of biology. Phallic monism is a psychoanalytic finding – a finding of its methodology, quite apart from the anatomy and physiology of reproduction. Findings could always be refined or overturned, but they must be findings of a clearly defined – psychoanalytic – method.

In a letter to Carl Müller-Braunschweig, a member of the Berlin Psychoanalytic Society, in 1935, Freud made the following point, in response to the critical reaction to the theory of phallic monism (see Burnham 1971, 329).

I object to all of you [e.g., Horney, Jones] to the extent that you do not distinguish more clearly and cleanly between what is psychic and what is biological, that you try to establish a neat parallelism between the two and that you, motivated by such an attempt, unthinkingly construe psychic facts which are unprovable and that you, in the process of so doing, must declare as reactive or regressive much that without doubt is primary. Of course, these reproaches must remain obscure. In addition, I would only like to emphasize that we must keep psychoanalysis separate from biology just as we have kept it separate from anatomy and physiology; at the present, sexual biology seems to lead us to two substances which attract each other.

Freud's determination to maintain an independent, psychoanalytic base for knowledge of the psyche, throws into relief the complexity of relating mind to body, gender to sex, libido to gender and sex. He pointed out (1905, 219 n. 1, added in 1915) that it is

essential to understand clearly that the concepts of "masculine" and "feminine", whose meaning seems so unambiguous to ordinary people, are among the most confused that occur in science. It is possible to distinguish at least three uses. "Masculine" and "feminine" are used sometimes in the sense of activity and passivity, sometimes in a biological, and sometimes, again, in a sociological sense. The first of these three meanings is the essential one and the most serviceable in psycho-analysis. When, for instance, libido was described in the text above as being "masculine", the word was being used in this sense, for an instinct is always active even when it has a passive aim in view. The second, or biological, meaning of "masculine" and "feminine" is the one whose applicability can be determined most easily. Here "masculine" and "feminine" are characterized by the presence of spermatozoa or ova respectively and by the functions proceeding from them. Activity and its concomitant phenomena (more powerful muscular development, aggressiveness, greater intensity of libido) are as a rule linked with biological masculinity; but they are not necessarily so, for there are animal species in which these qualities are on the contrary assigned to the female. The third, or sociological, meaning receives its connotation from the observation of actually existing masculine and feminine individuals. Such observation shows that in human beings pure masculinity or femininity is not to be found either in a psychological or a biological sense. Every individual on the contrary displays a mixture of the character-traits belonging to his own and to the opposite sex; and he shows a combination of activity and passivity whether or not these last character-traits tally with his biological ones.

Let us note two points in Freud's characterization of masculine and feminine. First, as we noted, he argues for one libido, active in his drive-based theory: Libido is active in that it cathects the object (*besezten* is the German: To occupy, as in a telephone connection). Freud makes it clear that psychoanalytic knowledge is based on psychoanalytic findings. The history of these *Besezntungen* is the history of the transferences that make up the ego, and they are the object of psychoanalytic enquiry. To be the object of a drive is passive in the phenomenological sense, but no less active in psychoanalytic theory since a drive can be turned around (Freud 1915). Freud's formulation became the basis of object relations, in which this interchangeability between subject and object has been developed.

Secondly, it follows from psychoanalytic psychology that the masculinity of the active and the femininity of the passive have nothing to do with the sociological attribution of passiveness to the female. But it is also true that Freud does stray across these neat categories, and one instance concerns me here. He acknowledges the biological meaning of masculine as characterized by spermatozoa and feminine by ova. But he subtly slips from these attributions, so deeply and unambiguously embedded in male and female, to attributing activity to the 'more powerful muscular development, aggressiveness, greater intensity of libido [, which] are as a rule [but not necessarily] linked with biological masculinity'. He does not carry forward the unique characters of masculine and feminine. More generally, partly down to Freud's slippages among the three categories, and his interpolating a phallic stage (1923), the theory of phallic monism, and the controversy it has incited, have preoccupied the psychoanalytic world and its critics.

I want to add a comment on the biological meaning of masculine and feminine, from which Freud backs away with the caveat that there are animal species in which the muscular, aggressive partner is the female. If we think of the breast as similar to the male genital, in that the nipple is akin to the penis, and the breast-organ is akin to the testicles, then the nipple and the muscular capacity to eject milk is akin to the penis with its muscular capacity to ejaculate semen. But with genitality comes their profound and specific difference: Milk is nourishing but does not participate in natality: That is lodged in the ova and sperm, which Freud points out, but displaces with his caveat about sexual aggressiveness across species.

Fertility, which is the focus of this book, is specific, in two ways. First, when it is lost, life is lost, bereft of the magical restoration of the phallic world. Secondly, the male loses it in a uniquely male way, in the incapacity of semen. Unlike the narcissism of the phallus, which is quantitative – a universe of more or less – fertility is qualitative – a universe of substance and difference.[2] (Phallic) castration anxiety is a form of denial of castration, and in that respect, it is magical. It imports the dread of the loss of life into awareness under cover, barely outside awareness; seen everywhere, but disguised, throughout society, even, as we will see in chapters 9–12, in the dread of environmental, cultural or economic deterioration.

Phallic Monism as a Defence Against the Depressive Collapse

Freud did not resolve the disparity between the phallicism of psychoanalytic findings and the seminal findings of biology. The bedrock, unique quality of genitality, for the male, lay in his biology, in his capacity to generate semen and to inseminate the uniquely female capacity to generate and harbour an ovum. Of course, Freud knew what castration meant, and perhaps he also accepted that the bedrock, male castration anxiety was the loss of fertility. Yet, referring to gender identity, he concluded (1933, 113) that science had nothing to offer the understanding of masculine and feminine, and he made clear that castration anxiety in psychoanalysis was a feature of the phallic stage (1923, 144). At the same time, he pointed out that it was 'remarkable what a small degree of attention the other part of the male genitals, the little sac with its contents, attracts in children. From all one hears in analyses, one would not guess that the male genitals consisted of anything more than the penis' (142 n. 1).

We had examples, in Chapter 4, of child analysands narrowing their internally rooted anxieties to the penis. There was also some concern, however, that analysts filtered out any other source of anxiety. In my view, this restricted focus, with its neglect of castration proper, has deeper roots: That the narrow, phallic focus reflects a defence, lodged in the culture, against a depressive, seminal anxiety of desolation. What I call seminality is not just a physiological function, embedded in male anatomy, but a psychic capacity, in which he is not an agent, but the bearer of a material and symbolic union with his sexual partner (Meltzer 1973, pp. 64–73). Moreover, I argue that insemination embodies a more primitive urge than returning to the womb: It embodies an intimation of a return to an inconceivable place beyond the womb, to a place where life begins and where it might also fail to survive or be destroyed by a primal ambivalence.

Phallic monism provides a psychic retreat (Steiner 1993), a haven from the utter desolation of the unremitting anxiety of failing to sustain life. The male believes his phallic supremacy is located in his penis, with its visible, demonstrable capacity to recover. The female, to the extent that she suffers the same anxieties, shares the same phallic defence. In the phallic universe, life is created magically by and from the phallus, seemingly visible in the penis and created from the penis. Putting penis envy aside, it is a phantasy of parthenogenesis in place of sexual union, which marginalizes the psychic forces of ambivalence and reparation. For the male, who is the topic of this book, ambivalence is at the source of conception, in his semen. Depressive anxiety, in the male, is seminal anxiety.

We can trace this relationship between phallic and seminal anxiety in the oedipal constellation, in which the father restrains the boy's incestuous wishes with the threat of phallic castration. Castration anxiety is, in Klein's (1946) language, paranoid-schizoid. The ego and its objects are split in phantasy into good and bad, and the bad can be projected and faced in the external world. Protecting the good penis can be reinforced, as Little Hans did, in loving and desiring his loving father, while simultaneously hating and fearing the death-dealing father. The triumphal inflation of the good penis(self) is sustained by the projection of the split-off, bad penis(self) of the castrating father, and in the omnipotence of defence, the castrated ego can be recouped by attacking and stealing from the castrating object. The oedipal boy preserves his penis by competing with the father's bad penis and from mother's claim to it, each stealing from the other.

But Klein (1932, 251) moves to a deeper, depressive, anxiety. The boy identifies with his mother's damaged and restored body. The threat to his penis extends into his own damaged and restored interior. That identification with the damaged and restored maternal body moves his paranoid-schizoid anxiety in the direction of depressive anxiety.

> Fear of castration … becomes, in the male individual, a dominating theme that overshadows all his other fears to greater or less extent. But this is precisely because one of the deepest sources to which disturbances in his sexual potency go back is his anxiety about the interior of his body. The house or town which the boy is so keen to build up again in his play signifies not only his mother's renewed and intact body, but his own.

We could add, the interior of all bodies, including nature (to be explored in chapters 10–12).

Klein (1948, 30) also brings out the non-phallic, depressive dimension clearly in distinguishing a specific anxiety owing to a threat to reproduction. But although she refers to depressive anxiety, with respect to reproductive function, she does not distinguish seminal function from the power of the phallus. Instead, she refers ambiguously to 'the genital', which is similar to the common reference to the penis or phallus.

> Turning to another essential danger-situation which Freud mentioned in his paper on Masochism, *i.e.* the fear of castration, I would suggest that the fear of death enters into and reinforces castration fear and is not "analogous" to it.

> Since the genital is not only the source of the most intense libidinal gratification, but also the representative of Eros, and since reproduction is the essential way of counteracting death, the loss of the genital would mean the end of the creative power which preserves and continues life.

Depressive anxiety refers to a more integrated ego and an object damaged in phantasy by destructive attacks. It is a guilt-ridden concern for the object, toned with desolation, signifying threat to the object and spurring reparative urges towards it. Klein clearly distinguishes this depressive concern for the damaged object (mother's insides, including father's penis) from the paranoid-schizoid anxiety that mother and father will attack and steal his penis in retaliation for the child's attacks on their penis.

Egle Laufer (1986, 71) refers to penis envy in the female, but attributes it and the female castration complex, not to a desire to possess the penis, but to a sense of a deficiency between pre-oedipal omnipotent phantasy and adult female sexuality. In this state, she views herself as 'not having a body that enables her to become a man', who can satisfy mother. Her analysis recognizes a sense of deficiency, a form of phallic monism, but it opens up a qualitative dimension, in which specifically female reproductive capacity is the core of female identity. Similarly, Birksted-Breen (1996) distinguishes between the phallus, which is magical, and possessed in phantasy by either male or female, from the penis-as-a-link, which refers to the reproductive capacity of the couple, not of an individual – therefore to the distinctive oedipal positions. Winnicott (1935, 136) saw a manic defence in a depressive woman's wish to be a man as an erection. Erection on its own is a phallic defence.

Quoting Freud, who said that the 'positive striving to possess a male genital' arises from penis envy in the female and the struggle against passive femininity in the male, John Steiner (2020, 91) argues that 'it is more appropriately thought of as a wish to possess omnipotent phallic superiority and is a desire prevalent in both men and women as a defence against dependency and need'. For Steiner, 'there is nothing passive or inferior about femininity'. The struggle is against receptivity associated with femininity. But it is 'a capacity that leads to some of the most important and valued qualities that we associate with femininity in both men and women. They include creativity and the capacity to engage with an internal world associated with images of pregnancy and care for others.'

> When the female genital becomes the focus of envious anal and urethral attacks it leaves behind a kind of battle scene of mutilated and defiled body parts, so that being feminine and receptive became associated with feelings of vulnerability to phallic attacks combined with repellent images of mutilation and contamination with faeces and urine … [T]hese images associated with sadistic attacks directed at receptive femininity give rise to the preference for the excitements of phallic triumph as well as to feelings of revulsion towards feminine receptivity. (p. 95)

I will put Steiner's account of phallic defensiveness next to Diamond's. Diamond, like Steiner, thinks that the integration of the denigrated and projected feminine receptivity is essential to the maturation of masculinity. They both stress the temptation of omnipotence to overcome the vulnerability of being masculine in the limited sense of needing the feminine, if masculine is to mean creative, caring, mortal, dependent: To live in the actual world of human beings.

There is, however, a difference between them. For Diamond (2021, 89), phallic masculinity denigrates the receptive feminine in its defence against the terror of 'the boy's abrupt sense of defectiveness during his oedipal experience of separation, entailing feelings of helplessness, weakness and vulnerability [and] of being engulfed by the archaic feminine [which cannot be represented and expressed]'. For Steiner, envy of the mother's receptive, creative, reproductive capacity violates the receptive feminine, including the female genital, and provokes paranoid-schizoid, retaliatory anxiety. The excitement of phallic narcissism defends against this anxiety. Diamond's model is based on privation. The boy lacks the receptive feminine and his phallic defence aims to deny it. The Kleinian model is conflictual, ambivalent, and the masculine phallic defence aims to transcend it by a phantasy of omnipotence and excitement.

I accept Steiner's and Diamond's views of the denigration of femininity in its receptivity and the importance of integrating it into the psyche of male and female. For both authors, the male lacks a crucial, feminine, receptive, dimension in his psyche. His unbalanced state makes matters worse, because he attacks the feminine that he misses. I lay stress on the depressive anxiety that lurks in the background for male and female alike. Paranoid-schizoid defence against depressive anxiety by a phallic monism is a shared defence against the vulnerability to depressive collapse – of fertility and life – that stalks the union of masculine and feminine. I see phallic monism as a psychic retreat (Steiner 1993), a defence shared by males and females, which offers a haven from the anxiety of the depressive anxiety of the Oedipus complex.

Ernest Jones adumbrated such a retreat already in 1927. For Jones, as for Freud, 'the psychoanalytical concept of castration, as distinguished from the corresponding biological one, refers definitely to the penis alone – the testicles at most being included in addition' (461). Jones accepts the phallic theory, in which boys and girls alike

> tend to view sexuality in terms of the penis alone ... [Analysts should be] sceptical in this direction. The concept of "castration" should be reserved, as Freud pointed out, for the penis alone and should not be confused with that of the "extinction of sexuality", for which the term "aphanisis" is proposed. (470–471)

Note that Jones distinguishes a fundamental collapse – aphanisis – from the covering anxiety of (phallic) castration. He speaks of a fallacy in equating the importance of the penis in male sexuality with the essence of sexuality, as well as in attributing this male preoccupation with that of the female.

> [T]he prominence of castration fears among men tends sometimes to make us forget that in both sexes castration is only a *partial* threat, however an important one, against sexual capacity and enjoyment as a whole. For the main blow of total extinction we might do well to use a separate term, such as the Greek word "aphanisis". (461)

Both male and female dread the same thing. The threat of aphanisis is the threat of oedipal retaliation for incestuous wishes. To put it bluntly, one can forgo either oedipal object or sexual capacity. The male can retain his sexual capacity by giving up mother as his sexual object; the girl faces the same alternative, with respect to father. The anxiety may reside in sexual organs, but it is sexual capacity, including its sublimations, that are risked. Both sexes fear privation, the

> deliberate deprivation on the part of the human environment [which] alone may be an adequate cause for the genesis of guilt ... and with it the superego is as it were artificially built up for the purpose of protecting the child from the stress of privation, i.e., of ungratified libido, and so warding off the dread of aphanisis that aways goes with this ... by damping down the wishes that are not destined to be gratified ... [N]on-gratification primarily means danger ... (463)

For Jones, aphanisis is the bedrock oedipal anxiety: The *total collapse* of sexual desire in both sexes, including the sublimations or displacements of sexual desire (as in the case of a patient who feared the loss of aesthetic enjoyment which he had substituted for sexual gratification, 461). It is the loss of libido, which is the loss of the life force. But incest is not just a trans-gressive desire: It is the omnipotent phantasy of replacing father or mother in the parental couple, including the mysterious creativity of parental union. The collapse in aphanisis, is a threat, a retaliation by the internal parental couple on sexual creativity, not just desire, which haunts all couples as an oedipal anxiety. Such a total collapse of sexual creativity is a collapse of the capacity to engender, sustain and repair life – for the male, a seminal collapse.

In separating aphanisis from castration anxiety, Jones clearly delineates the depressive dimension of the Oedipus complex. While castration anxiety expresses the paranoid-schizoid threat to the boy's penis in his aim to replace the father, this threat is illusory: The penis demonstrates it recuperative capacity and, in its narcissism, the capacity to steal itself back from the father. Aphanisis, by contrast, is the depressive threat of total collapse, which falls on the arrogant phantasy of creating oneself. Both Freud and Jones point to this aspect of the Oedipus complex. 'Incest' signifies a usur-pation that straddles both domains: Violating the paternal prohibition and arrogating the creativity of union. Each form of incest brings its retaliation: Phallic castration and depressive collapse.

Penis Pride, Penis Envy and Phallic Monism

Not surprisingly, phallic monism met criticism as soon as the ink dried on the paper. Horney (1926) said that it expressed the male's terror of feminization, not the nature of femininity. Freud based the case for phallic monism, in part, on the belief that girls only became aware of the vagina as a result of oedipal resolution. They were, at first, only aware of the clitoris, as a site of excitation and of inferiority to the penis. Horney (1933) countered, that the girl feared internal damage more than did the boy; she had no equivalent to the penis, the visibility of which secured the boy's confidence in remaining undamaged.

There was no escaping the biological difference between male and female in the profile of anxiety of each. Although the girl suffered forms of anxiety analogous to that of the boy, 'they take on a specific character from that proneness to anxiety which is part of the biological makeup of girls ... [A]ny fantasy of gratifying the tension produced by vaginal sensations (i.e., the craving to take into oneself, to receive) gives rise to anxiety on the part of the ego ... [B]ehind the "failure to discover the vagina" [Freud] is a denial of its existence' (158, 160). Freud was wrong to think that the girl at first knew only of her clitoris. Instead, she repressed an awareness of the vagina, because of the anxiety attached to the vulnerability of her internal world[3], which she replaced with anxiety attached to the external, observable clitoris.

Phallic monism, the female castration complex and penis envy have been marginalized by sustained criticism ever since. As Rosemary Balsam (2018, 41) put it, 'Why are these terms not simply in the ash pit of history by now?' (in addition to Balsam, see, for example, Chodorow 1994; Figlio 2010; Sayers 1991; Wieland 2000; Zepf and Steel 2016). Phallic monism, however, remains a clinical finding, but not a developmental stage, not to be confused with penis pride and not born of penis envy. As we will see later, girls sustain the boy's penis-pride as well as submit to it. Phallic monism is different from penis pride. It is an omnipotent defence, employed by male and female alike, against seminal anxiety. Let us get a better idea of it by looking at it squarely from the angle of the female.

Freud (1933) points to a difficulty for the female in psychosexual development: Unlike the boy, who retains his object choice as he moves from mother to a woman, the girl typically changes her object choice from mother to a man. But this turning is not just from preference: It is also driven by an enduring ambivalence towards the mother. As a result, many women remain 'tenderly dependent on a paternal object ... with an intense attachment of long duration' until late in life (119). It includes the wish to 'get mother with child and the corresponding wish to bear her a child [but also] the fear of being murdered or poisoned' (120). Turning from mother to father was not a simple change of object but was 'accompanied by hostility; the attachment to mother ends in hate' (121).

There was, for Freud, no shortage of grievances against mother: Too little milk; too limited a period of sucking; losing the breast; milk turned to poison; jealousy of a new rival; maternal frustration of genital pleasure. But disappointment – inevitable regardless of maternal devotion – would be experienced by boys as well as girls, so what disappointment would belabour the girl in particular? 'I believe we have found this specific factor ... After all, the anatomical distinction ... must express itself in psychical consequences [but] it was a surprise to learn from analyses that girls hold their mothers responsible for their lack of a penis and do not forgive her ... ' (124).

So although castration anxiety of the female, in Freud's formulation, follows from penis envy, it does not originate solely in penis envy, and psychoanalysis has since put it aside. The grievance at deprivation – that mother withholds something valuable from the daughter for herself – originates in ambivalence towards the mother. It is symmetrical with the castration anxiety of the boy, whose ambivalence in relation to the father threatens him with castration anxiety. Unlike the boy, the girl cannot reassure herself by looking at the penis: See it swell, recede, and swell again; fondle it for pleasure and associate that pleasure with seeing it; gain reassurance of its continued existence, amplified by exhibiting it for mother's admiration.

But the boy's reassurance can fall to castration anxiety just as the girl can believe she is witnessing castration in herself. Phallic monism as a defence is a magical retreat into a haven secured against reality and its disappointments for the male as well as the female. She would not be suffering penis envy but representing the belief in a magical transcendence of the limitations of reality by a *penis in itself as a representation in perceptual reality of the phallus*. The male as *possessor of the penis would be secondary*. Indeed, she might proclaim that the male only has the organ, which *he* so esteems, by *her* tolerance; or because she has given it to him; or that the organ is just the visible trace of the magical phallus that offers a narcissistic defence. I will give examples of each of these versions of the significance of the penis.

Freud does not state this view of provisioning the male with a penis, but he opens such a possibility in the case of women who transfer their ambivalence towards their mothers to their fathers and then to their husbands. Upon the birth of a child, they might identify, as mothers, with their mothers, and force their husbands to be the male child that embodies their penis. Freud emphasizes the female wish to have a penis from the male. But we will reformulate it as Britton's 'Athene complex', paired with his 'Antigone complex', in which female power can replace penis envy with her capacity to endow the male with what *he* takes to be pre-eminent.

We see an early experimentation with the penis among girls in child analysis and observation. Kirsten Dahl (1996, 309) remarks that 'child analysts may disagree about the role envious fantasies about the penis play in the construction of gender and the Oedipus complex, but there is little disagreement that such fantasies, wishes, and fears are part of the mental life of young girls.' Girls do not interpret genital difference as a defect, but their communications 'seem to reflect intense intrapsychic conflict [and she has] been struck by the clarity with which material concerning reactions to the genital difference between the sexes is presented in the analyses of young girls in contrast to the lack of clarity, even obscurity, of such clinical material in the analyses of adult women' (308). She compares four- to six-year-olds with adult women. What stands out vividly is not the sense of genital defect in the girls, but their astonishment and imitation of the bravado of boys. I present two extracts.

[In a nursery school playground,] a group of boys was playing a loud, exciting socio-dramatic game while riding around on trikes. Several girls were at the water table. Suddenly, one of the girls picked up a squeeze bottle and laughingly called to the other girls, "Look, we can make water too!" The other girls also grabbed squeeze bottles and immediately began to parade around holding the bottles between their legs and excitedly squirting water into the air. With much giggling, they shouted, "We're making peepee. We can do it too! Look at us!" ... Finally one girl rushed at the boys, squirted them and shouted, "You *can't* do it! We *can* do it!"[Later], fearing an outbreak of hostilities between the boys and girls, the teacher intervened. (306; Dahl's emphasis)

In another case, Clarissa had a doll, named 'First Class', who, like herself, was angered by some boy dolls.

Clarissa said angrily about one of the boy dolls, 'He's a show off, "peepee" boy, and First Class doesn't like that. He makes her mad.' Later in this session Clarissa made the boy doll dance about, gaily calling attention to himself. Then she announced that First Class felt very jealous of "the peepee boy". I wondered whether First Class was mad because she wanted to be able to show off as the boy did. Clarissa responded gravely, "Yes, she does – she wishes she could be fancy on the outside like a boy and she's not and she gets so *mad* about that!" ... The mother depicted in these fantasies curtailed the little girl's activity and exhibitionism. [L]ater ... material emerged to suggest that she now viewed mother as envious and potentially damaging to her daughter's feminine desires to be beautiful, to be loved by a man, and to have children. (307; Dahl's emphasis).

Dahl (321) concludes that 'recognition of anatomical difference in the light of the oedipal narrative ushers in a new dilemma stimulated by the question of what meaning, if any, to assign to bodily, especially genital, differences.' Having what the boy has can be equated with realizing all wishes without superego retaliation ... Penis envy should be understood ... not as the bedrock of what it is to be feminine, but rather as a compromise formation involving both drive and defence created by the dilemma of the inherent immutability and limitations of the body' (323). Recognition of difference and limitation is a narcissistic threat (320). The fact of the body is a limitation that can be experienced narcissistically and in narcissism, 'more' or 'less' matters. The boy might be 'fancier' in his possession of a penis (320), but in a narcissistic, quantitative – more or less – world, rather than a qualitative world, no one is secure.

Squitieri (1999) calls attention to a defensive enrolment of the male body (not necessarily the penis) in women with a fragile sense of self. For them, the body may not only be a mysterious, receptive cavity, but an unreliable organism, an unreliable anatomy (646). She has found, clinically, that such a fragility can lead to the protective idea of being 'a man somewhere' (646), though knowing that not to be the case.

[W]hen the discovery of anatomical difference follows a traumatic separation process, the female child tries to link the previous sense of the unreliability of her self to the perception of her pierced body. This equivalence lays the foundation for the building up of a defence that might circumscribe anxiety and provide a recognisable container. (648)

She presents the analyses of four women, covering a spectrum from neurotic to psychotic. The neurotic woman was professionally successful, but felt unable to hold her body together: That it would flow away through menstruation. Her father died when she was four and was not available for positive identification. Her dream material vividly portrayed male protectors (650).

Normally, the discovery of anatomical difference spurs curiosity. Squitieri gives a lovely example of the conversation between a 2½-year-old girl and her mother, other relatives and friends, as she pursues without anxiety her interest in her genital. But, Squitieri explains, if earlier experience of separation from mother had been unbearable, then difference might be equated with a mutilated self in a mutilated body (657; in Kleinian terms, we might emphasize the conflict of the femininity phase). 'Female anxiety about being deprived of phantasies with important self-protecting functions seems to be the female equivalent of male castration anxiety' (658). Women might seek to secure a psychic fragility in the solidity of the body, but when that solidity dissolves, or seems undermined, they call upon phantasies of male protectors. Miss Collins, whom I present in Chapter 6, suffered a fear of pregnancy – her internal contents? – leaking away; in her view, not only did I – father? – offer no protection: I exacerbated it.

These authors draw attention to the undermining of a secure feminine identity by a conflictual relationship between mother and daughter, whether in external or in internal reality. The flight to the male body, which might be a flight to the penis, is a flight from an internal fragility into a promise of protection by an other who is different, visibly so. Of course, the father-male-object to whom the girl flees is also a phantasy, no matter how lodged in the external reality of an available father it might be. In that sense, it is a flight to an idealized father with whom she is at one. But, as Freud (1933, 120–125) described, she might be fleeing to father from an ambivalent relationship with mother, 'resolved' by a prolonged, tender relationship with him. She might also identify with her mother, thereby making her own husband (now a version of her mother's son) into her child, now her phallic possession. Then the male and his penis can become the idealized possession of the daughter, perhaps dependent on her for his/its sustenance.

These two positions have been described by Britton (2001) as the Athene-Antigone Complex. He speaks of a

psychological deviation or overvaluation [sometimes] found in the analysis ... of women ... I think of it as a phallic idealisation in women; in men it has a counterpart in … "phallic narcissism" … Phallic idealisation is the location of inflated self-regard in phallic narcissism in men with a preoccupation with the phallus as an exhibiting rather than reproductive organ … In women the investment of desirable superiority in masculinity and its manifest localisation is in the penis. (50)

These women, he argues, idealize their fathers as relief from difficulties in the mother-infant relationship. Embedded in this idealization, such a woman might not define herself as wife, mother or sister. Instead, she

derives her significance by being the re-incarnation of [father's] power like Athene [born fully armoured from the head of Zeus], or the guarantor of his posterity like Antigone [daughter-servant to Oedipus] (51) … In the former there is a triumphant denial, by phallic identification, of being an ordinary woman, and in the latter, a more subtle female denigration of womanhood via masochistic, self-disparagement. With their phallic idea-lisation and their devaluation of femininity, they exemplify the 'female castration' or "masculinity" complex (52).

In the Athene complex, the woman shares a magical instrument – the phallus – with the father or analyst, as in Birksted-Breen's (1996) formula-tion. By 'attributive projective identification' (Britton 1994), she maintains an illusion of father's omnipotence, which she shares, thereby avoiding a cata-strophic encounter with reality. But then, the collapse of the illusion is not just a loss: It is 'the phantasy of having been literally or symbolically "cas-trated"' (Britton, 54) … In some women this state of psychic castration fol-lowing disillusion is rapidly projected into the father. He is then seen as infirm, impotent and in need of his daughter's ministrations (55). And Antigone is born.

Mother is left out of the Athene-Antigone complex. She is not, however sought, nor is the father. What is sought, by male and female, is the 'rela-tionship of the primal scene couple' (Britton, 56). For the male, heroizing intellect or power or daydreams of sexual adventure might aim to make up for the sense of inferiority in not taking part in the primal scene. For the female, romantic fiction might predominate, but also the idealization of the father and the penis with the denigration of mother's breasts and womb.

In the Athene complex, the woman idealizes and identifies with the omnipotent paternal penis; in the Antigone complex, she ministers to the father from whom she has taken the penis. The oedipal dimension – 'the relationship that can never be had' (2002, 56) – is replaced by the narcissism of the phallus, which, in phantasy, can be had. And it can be shared by father and daughter outside the primal scene, outside incest phantasy – removed from the threat of aphanisis. That narcissistic transformation renders the girl vulnerable to the catastrophic disillusionment that she experiences concretely as castration, but it also renders father vulnerable to her disillusionment in losing the phallus and falling into enfeeblement. Together they can live with a shared phallus.

A Collaborative Defence

In the phallic world, the parental relationship, as Britton says, is replaced by the omnipotent penis, and is, therefore, annulled. Oedipal exclusion, as it is typically conceived, becomes exclusion from possession of the idealized, omnipotent penis. Such a state of exclusion can be called penis envy or envy of mother's breasts and womb, but both lose their qualitative distinctiveness to narcissism; narcissism is the world of more or less: Of quantity not quality. Narcissism is gender-indifferent: Penis = self = a quantitative inflation or diminution by extracting more or less from the other. And as a shared phallus, the phallic couple exclude reality, which would be a catastrophe rather than a mourned loss. An excluded 'third', such as a sibling, can sustain the omnipotent phantasy. What goes missing in this conjoint phallic defence is the parental union of complementary functions.[4]

Jones suggested something similar in proposing that the incest of intruding into the primal scene would lead to a total collapse of desire, in aphanisis. For Jones (1927), the phallic stage was a defence shared by boy and girl, which appeared to be a normal developmental stage because it satisfied the defence against oedipal desire for both. For both, the more the penis is a phallic object on its own, rather than part of a genital, the more it becomes an omnipotent phantasy. In phallic – narcissistic – terms, male and female differ, not on what is specific to each, but on the quantity of what is common to both. But if common to both, then each can extract it from the other. In that sense, a woman is a deficient male or *vice versa*, a conflict well captured in Britton's (2021) concept of 'Narcissistic Problems of Sharing Space'. Difference itself – the difference between male and female – evokes in both the wish to be the other and a powerful repudiation of the difference, intensified by denying the wish (Boehm 1930, 457, 466, 469). For the male, the female's Athene-Antigone complex serves his phallic narcissism, whether by Athene's amplifying their shared phallus or by Antigone's continuous reparative regeneration of his phallic narcissism. For the female, the male's phallic narcissism offers her Athene-Antigone a haven in an idealized world of the phallus.

Phallic castration anxiety stands in front of oedipal castration anxiety, defending against the primal scene phantasies that evoke the incest prohibition. In phallic monism, boy and girl share a phallic defence: They unconsciously collaborate, each reinforcing the other's phallic defence. In this joint project, they share a paranoid-schizoid world of existential anxiety, projection of the source of threat and fear of retaliation for aggression; for example, the girl's projection of mother-daughter ambivalence into the (father) male; the boy's projection of internal insecurity into the (mother) female.

The paranoid-schizoid world of the phallic defence should be distinguished from the depressive world that underlies the incest prohibition. The oedipal world of the incest prohibition is the world, not of parental intercourse, but of fertility, procreation and the creativity of union; also, a world of concern for the object – the baby, as itself the embodiment of a creation. The oedipal catastrophe of violating the primal scene and retaliation covers over the depressive anxiety of the extinction of life.

Castration anxiety, therefore, includes two forms: Phallic (paranoid-schizoid) castration anxiety and fertility (depressive) castration anxiety. Phallic monism as a collaborative defence avoids the defining and mating of masculine and feminine. For male and female, man and woman, procreative partners, the mating of masculine and feminine is depressive. That is what is avoided by omnipotent, paranoid-schizoid phallic defence. Phallic defence is monistic – there is only one phallus – not because only males have the envied penis, but because the phallus is a magical, omnipotent instrument, albeit easily represented by the visible penis, with its capacity to mimic the phallus and represent it in the world of time and space.

Notes

1   Horney (1932, 142 and n. 13), an opponent of phallic monism and of attributing passivity to women, is clear that the girl's 'desire to receive … is not to be equated with passivity'. Receptivity is active in acquiring what it passively receives, and it does not just receive. As uniquely masculine as seminality is, so uniquely feminine is receptivity in the capacity to conceive.
2   Of course, sperm can be more or less motile, and sperm counts can be higher or lower, but the baseline fact of insemination as a unique, male function remains.
3   Abraham (1922) reported a woman's dream, in which her father created her vagina by pushing a pole into her.
4   But, as Freud said, defensive phantasies can also be transitional, in that object love originates in the overflow of narcissism, in which the first object is a version of 'me' (1914; or as someone with similar genitals, 1911, 61). For the girl, the appropriation of father's penis is therefore also a compromise that 'makes the transition from narcissistic self-love [penis baby] to object-love [actual baby] possible' (1917, 129).

References

Abraham, K. (1922) An Infantile Theory of the Origin of the Female Sex. In *Selected Papers on Psycho-Analysis*. London: Hogarth Press, 1927, 333.

Balsam, R. (2018) 'Castration Anxiety' Revisited: Especially 'Female Castration Anxiety'. *Psychoanalytic Inquiry* 38(1): 11–22.

Birksted-Breen, D. (1996) Phallus, Penis and Mental Space. *International Journal of Psychoanalysis* 77: 649–657.

Boehm, F. (1930) The Femininity-Complex in Men. *International Journal of Psychoanalysis* 11: 444–469.

Britton, R. (1994) Publication Anxiety: Conflict Between Communication and Affiliation. *International Journal of Psychoanalysis* 75: 1213–1224.

Britton, R. (2001) Forever Father's Daughter: The Athene-Antigone Complex. In Trowell, J. and Etchegoyen, A. (eds) *The Importance of Fathers*. London/NY: Routledge; revised, as Phallic Idealisation in Women. *In Sex, Death and the Superego: Updating Psychoanalytic Experience and Developments in Neuroscience*, 2nd edn. London/NY: Routledge, 2021, 50–61.

Britton, R. (2021) Narcissistic Problems of Sharing Space. In *Sex, Death and the Superego: Updating Psychoanalytic Experience and Developments in Neuroscience*, Second Edition. London/NY: Routledge, 121–133 (originally published in 1990, not in English, in the *Brazilian Psychoanalytic Journal*).

Burnham, L. (1971) Freud and Female Sexuality: A Previously Unpublished Letter. *Psychiatry* 34: 328–329.

Chodorow, N. (1994) *Femininities, Masculinities, Sexualities: Freud and Beyond (Blazer Lectures)*. Lexington, Ky: University Press of Kentucky.

Dahl, E. K. (1996) The Concept of Penis Envy Revisited: A Child Analyst Listens to Adult Women. *Psychoanal Study Child* 51: 303–325.

Diamond, M. (2021) *Masculinity and its Discontents: The Male Psyche and the Inherent Tensions of Maturing Manhood*. London/NY: Routledge.

Figlio, K. (2010) Phallic and Seminal Masculinity: a Theoretical and Clinical Confusion. *International Journal of Psychoanalysis* 91(1): 119–139.

Freud, S. (1905) Three Essays on the Theory of Sexuality. *The Standard Edition of the Complete Psychological Works of Sigmund Freud* 7: 123–245.

Freud, S. (1911). Psycho-Analytic Notes on an Autobiographical Account of a Case of Paranoia (Dementia Paranoides). *The Standard Edition of the Complete Psychological Works of Sigmund Freud* 12: 1–82.

Freud, S. (1914) On Narcissism: an Introduction. *The Standard Edition of the Complete Psychological Works of Sigmund Freud* 14: 73–105.

Freud, S. (1915) Instincts and their Vicissitudes. *The Standard Edition of the Complete Psychological Works of Sigmund Freud* 14: 109–140.

Freud, S. (1917) On Transformations of Instinct as Exemplified in Anal Erotism. *The Standard Edition of the Complete Psychological Works of Sigmund Freud* 17: 125–133.

Freud, S. (1920) Beyond the Pleasure Principle. *The Standard Edition of the Complete Psychological Works of Sigmund Freud* 18: 1–64.

Freud, S. (1923) The infantile genital organization: an interpolation into the theory of sexuality. *The Standard Edition of the Complete Psychological Works of Sigmund Freud* 19: 139–145.

Freud, S. (1925). Some Psychical Consequences of the Anatomical Distinction between the Sexes. *The Standard Edition of the Complete Psychological Works of Sigmund Freud* 19: 241–258

Freud, S. (1933) New Introductory Lectures on Psycho-Analysis. *The Standard Edition of the Complete Psychological Works of Sigmund Freud* 22: 1–182

Horney, K. (1926) The Flight from Womanhood: The Masculinity-Complex in Women, as Viewed by Men and by Women. *International Journal of Psychoanalysis* 7:324–339; reprinted in *Feminine Psychology*. NY: Norton, 1967, 54–70.

Horney, K. (1932) The Dread of Women: Observations on a Specific Difference in the Dread Felt by Men and Women Respectively for the Opposite Sex. *International Journal of Psychoanalysis* 13: 348–360; reprinted in *Feminine Psychology*. NY: Norton, 1967, 133–146.

Horney, K. (1933) The Denial of the Vagina: A Contribution to the Problem of the Genital Anxieties Specific to Women. *International Journal of Psychoanalysis* 14: 57–70; reprinted in *Feminine Psychology*. NY: Norton, 1967, 147–161.

Jones, E. (1927) The Early Development of Female Sexuality. *International Journal of Psychoanalysis* 8: 459–472. In *Papers on Psychoanalysis*, 5th edn. London: Baillière, Tindall and Cox, 1948; London: Karnac, 1977, 438–51.

Klein, M. (1932) The Psychoanalysis of Children. In *The Writings of Melanie Klein*, vol. 2. London: The Hogarth Press and the Institute of Psycho-Analysis, 1975.

Klein, M. (1946) Notes on Some Schizoid Mechanisms. In *The Writings of Melanie Klein*, vol. 3. London: The Hogarth Press and the Institute of Psycho-Analysis, 1975, 1–24.

Klein, M. (1948) On the Theory of Anxiety and Guilt. In *The Writings of Melanie Klein*, vol. 3. London: The Hogarth Press and the Institute of Psycho-Analysis, 1975, 25–42.

Laufer, E. (1986) The Female Oedipus Complex and the Relationship to the Body. *Psychoanalytic Studies of the Child* 41: 259–276; In Birksted Breen, D. (ed.) *The Gender Conundrum: Contemporary Psychoanalytic Perspectives on Femininity and Masculinity (New Library of Psychoanalysis)*. London: Routledge, 1993, 67–81.

Meltzer, D. (1973) *Sexual States of Mind*. Strath Tay: Clunie Press.

Sayers, J. (1991) *Mothering Psychoanalysis: Helene Deutsch, Karen Horney, Anna Freud And Melanie Klein*. London: Hamish Hamilton.

Squitieri, L. M. (1999) Problems of Female Sexuality: The Defensive Function of Certain Phantasies About the Body. *International Journal of Psychoanalysis* 80: 645–660.

Steiner, J. (1993) *Psychic Retreats: Pathological Organisations in Psychotic, Neurotic and Borderline Patients*. London: Routledge.

Steiner, J. (2020) *Illusion, Delusion, and Irony in Psychoanalysis*. Abington, Oxon/NY: Routledge.

Wieland, C. (2000) *The Undead Mother: Psychoanalytic Explorations of Masculinity, Femininity and Matricide*. London: Rebus; Routledge, 2002.

Winnicott, D. W. (1935) The Manic Defence. In *Through Paediatrics to Psycho-Analysis*. London: Hogarth and the Institute of Psycho-Analysis, 1975, 129–144.

Zachary, A. (2018) *The Anatomy of the Clitoris: Reflections on the Theory of Female Sexuality*. London: Routledge.

Zepf, S. and Steel, D. (2016) Penis Envy and the Female Oedipus Complex: A Plea to Reawaken an Ineffectual Debate. *Psychoanalytic Review* 103: 397–420.

Chapter 6

Parthenogenic Procreation

A Concrete Model of Procreation

Parthenogenic procreation is an oxymoron, in that parthenogenesis is not procreative and procreation is not parthenogenic. In putting them together, I mean to bring into sharp the point of difference that defines the theme of this chapter. Theories of the origination of children abound, in mixtures of myth, naturalism and science. Although they typically involve sexual intercourse, the intercourse does not always signify procreative sexual union, even within a wholly naturalistic account. The meeting of ovum and sperm and sexual union are the same, biologically, but not psychologically. Concrete theories, in which children are made from body parts or excreta remain beneath adult sexual knowledge. They are forms of parthenogenesis (literally, virgin origin, or more generally, without sexual intercourse). There can be biological pro-creation with psychological parthenogenesis, and the parthenogenesis can be transitional, on the way to procreation.

There is substantial clinical evidence that parthenogenic theories abound in modern Western culture, as unconscious phantasy. One phantasy has been called the 'penis-baby', which has been derived from female penis envy and castration anxiety and has shared the fate of phallic monism: It has been, in Balsam's (2018, 14) words, consigned to the 'ash pit of history'. But in my view, that is also to throw the baby out with the bath water. This historical alignment does not eliminate it as a clinical finding, the validity of which is clearer, if seen, on its own, as an unconscious parthenogenic creation model of baby-making. The parthenogenic baby is phallic in being magical, but not necessarily based on the penis. It can be a monism, that is, a gender-indifferent phantasy held as a collaborative defence by male and female alike. Whatever its organ or other material base, it need not derive from penis envy or castration anxiety, and as a phallic defence, it also plays a transitional role in the development of genitality. Klein (1945, 418), for example, saw the penis-baby as a feminine wish, pre-sumably, therefore, not as pseudo-masculine.

The penis-baby is a phallic idealization that complements phallic narcis-sism in the male. It is jointly held, by male and female, and, as we saw in

DOI: 10.4324/9781003455790-9

Chapter 5, it is embedded in the culture as a collaborative defence. Little Hans offered a vivid account of the birth of a baby from the penis, though not of its theft. Boehm (1930, 455–456) speaks of a *male* penis-baby phantasy, lodged in a *male* anxiety – *his* castration complex, although believed by females as well.

> Boys (like girls) imagine that in the act of procreation the man (or boy) loses his penis, has to let it be incorporated into the woman, who hides it away and turns it into a child. But the boy either does not suspect or will not admit the fact that she has no penis; he believes that she receives the child in addition to her own penis. He thinks she swallows up the penis (possibly the testicles too; these then form the breasts or the penis of the child). Or else the mother receives the father's penis through a hollow penis of her own and gives birth to the child through a kind of special tube. The thought of the act of procreation increases the boy's castration anxiety, for he imagines that it involves the loss of his penis.

What we see in parthenogenesis at the core of the penis-baby is a limitation in symbolization of origination: Of natality, of the emergence of new life, of ensoulment. We can see it, however, as a way of getting to grips with the inconceivable idea of a beginning, of origination, and of the union that initiates the origination. As I argued in Chapter 3, natality is inconceivable, so we fall back on processes we can imagine or even carry out, such as fashioning an object into a new shape (in Chapter 9, we will look at what Bion 1992, 372–373 called 'the crisis of "And and You"'). When does new life appear and by what manner of activity? And when does living matter become sentient?

There has been a history of thinking that sexual intercourse produces a baby by a kind of craftsmanship, or that intercourse simply implants a tiny, preformed human, carried in the sperm. We can imagine such processes, which happen by an action, in a frame of time and space. In so-called pre-formation, for example, which had some currency in the West in the 17th century, intercourse only opened the womb to placing the child inside it. There are also traditions in which it is believed that intercourse facilitates or is the setting for the fulfilment of agents outside the couple, perhaps ancestors (I explore various formulations in Figlio 2000, 164–185). These theories of childbearing excluded the beginning of life in the union of the parental couple. A sense of mystery surrounds that moment, which remains beyond and before comprehension, which we into we enter by an omnipotent phantasy of being present at our origination. In an oedipal formulation, the boy wishes to be at his origin by becoming his own father and giving himself as a gift to his mother (Freud 1910, 173) at the 'beginning of the beginning' (Figlio 2003).

We see the complexity and obscurity of the problem at the heart of Judeo-Christian religion. The King James Bible says, 'In the beginning God created the heaven and earth.' He did not have to *do* anything; He 'let' it happen, but the idea of a maker is embedded in the text. In a modern re-examination of the text, Everett Fox (1983) diminishes the comparison between God's creating and human fabrication: 'At the beginning of God's creating of the heavens and the earth.' In his commentary, he says, '**creating:** Indicative of God's power and not used in reference to humans, although later in the chapter such words as "make", and "form", do appear' (11 and n. 1; author's emphasis).

For Hannah Arendt (1958, 176, 177, 178):

> In man, otherness, which he shares with everything that is, and distinct-ness, which he shares with everything alive, becomes uniqueness ... Speech and action reveal this unique distinctness [which] rests on initiative ... With the creation of man, the principle of beginning came into the world itself ... It is in the nature of beginning that something new is started which cannot be expected from whatever may have happened before. This character of startling unexpectedness is inherent in all beginnings and in all origins ... With respect to this somebody who is unique it can truly be said that nobody was there before.

Speech draws humans into society, in which action has a 'revelatory character', without which it would 'lose its subject, as it were; not acting men but performing robots would achieve what, humanly speaking, would remain incomprehensible ... In acting and speaking [together], men show who they are, [a] disclosure [that] can almost never be achieved as a wilful purpose ... (178, 179)'.

In the common moment of speech and action, a unique subject is revealed, who initiates, rather than just produces, as a robot could do. And the appearance of this subject is an instance of origination. But the ability to conceive of such a unique moment of origination, to grasp a 'beginning' of life, especially individual, sentient life, fails. Where can we search for models of origination? We retain, repressed, concrete theories of the origination of children, covered by our advanced knowledge of conception, pregnancy, foetal development and childbirth, but never comprehended by it. Perhaps we hold on to a belief in our comprehension of the idea origination – make it conceivable – by various mental tricks. Words like 'union', 'marriage', 'intercourse', 'emergent', 'nascent', 'love', 'genitality', suggest that we are in on an origination, subjectively, that they are within our experience, but do not actually give us access to it.

Freud (1908, 222) speaks of the child's awareness of his/her parents in a state of being married. But the child advances his understanding of the origination of babies in the married state with theories from his own experience, such as urinating into each other. Perhaps Grown-ups feel savvy with their advanced knowledge yet remain as bemused as children about the origination of children: Not about the sexual act, with which they are familiar and link definitively with pregnancy, but about the emergence of a new life in a new body. Freud reminds us of a reluctance to give up primitive sexual theories, and they tended to be concrete, a-symbolic, visualizable, such as the belief that sex is urination and babies are like feces, expelled from the bottom.

I suggest that one example of savvy-posturing is sexual swearing. It flagrantly sprays concrete references to sexual, or near to sexual, parts, such as arsehole, cunt, prick; sometimes joining disparate functions, such as fannyarse or dickhead. It parades immature sexual knowledge arrogantly, as if it were superior to mature reality-based knowledge. It ridicules maturity, by combining body parts that are not joined anatomically or psychically in reality-orientated thinking. It hides the insecurity of not knowing what an adult 'should' know by arrogantly debasing it. A patient recalled a teenage form of ridicule that circulated in his school, called 'slipping'. The abuser would publicly and mockingly call a classmate by the first name of his mother, in the presence of girls and boys alike. The patient was puzzled by it but shared the buzz, no doubt because it implied a sexual intimacy with the victim's mother. It claimed adult sexual knowledge and parental privilege by exposing the victim's oedipal desire and mocking his exclusion, crushing a child's sexual knowledge and desire.

Such a debunking can also have more innocent roots. In analytic sessions, I have come to think that sexual words interlaced in a narrative can simply imitate bits of adult speech. They do not aim to debase, nor do they intend sexual content. Instead, they express an embarrassed failure adequately to grasp what they are trying to say, just as a child might overhear parents speaking of what the child only inadequately comprehends. The gap points to a mystery, animated because it is a mystery, in an illusion of an understanding attributed to adults, even in the mind of an adult.

So, too, with concrete theories of procreation. They reduce the mystery of parental intercourse and the origin of babies to a model that the child can comprehend and in which, in phantasy, he/she can participate. The penis baby is a parthenogenic model, a conceivable account of procreation as a production of new life. It is not surprising that it remains a clinical phenomenon that stands on its own, apart from penis envy and female castration complex. It is consolidated in the girl's mind as a phallic defence, organized as a detour around oedipal resolution, especially when the girl's phantasy of having baby puts her into conflict with mother as a procreator or the owner of the penis. It can also represent a transitional phase in the particular situation, in which a woman seeks mitigation of ambivalence in the mother-daughter relationship through an extended, idealized father-daughter relationship. She will not be free of conflict: With mother, over the penis that is mother's right; or with father, if he is weakened by the loss of part of himself in the narcissistic world of more or less. But she can, in this detour, have a baby.

The Parthenogenic Baby

For Freud (1908), the fundamental facts of human sexuality did not inform early genitality for either sex. Just as the girl, in his analysis, had not yet discovered her vagina, so too, the boy had not yet discovered semen.[1] Neither girl nor boy knew of the fertilization of the ovum by sperm. The male as well as the female begin with the parthenogenic phantasy that an omnipotent phallus makes the baby, to the recognition of the limited, complementary, fertilizing contribution of each sex to a mysterious conception.

I have argued that the phallic defence is an unconscious collaboration, jointly sustained by male and female, to repress the dread of the collapse of fertility: A collapse of life itself. I now add that it includes the penis baby as such a collaborative phantasy.[2] It can represent a transitional phase in the particular situation in which a woman seeks mitigation of an ambivalent mother-daughter relationship through an extended, idealized father-daughter relationship. It offers an alternative route, neither a developmental stage nor based on penis envy.

For Klein as well (1932, 227), there is a transitional quality. She says that the more the daughter's psychosexual structure leans towards the anal-sadistic phase, the more she believes she has fashioned a baby from her own feces, which are a product of her omnipotence and narcissism. But the more she tends towards a genital structure, the more she believes that babies are the joint issue of intercourse. The penis baby has a reparative component, but its concreteness channels reparative urges into repatriation of a stolen object; that is, it supports a retreat from depressive to paranoid-schizoid anxiety (Klein 1952, 78).

The more genital, the more reparative is the intercourse. In her (1945, 418) formulation, the penis baby is not a product of penis envy – a derivative of her wish for a penis – but a claim to father's penis from the inside of mother, as a feminine wish.

> Though the little girl at one stage assumes that her mother possesses a penis as a male attribute, this concept does not play nearly as important a part in her development as Freud suggests. The unconscious theory that her mother contains the admired and desired penis of the father underlies, in my experience, many of the phenomena which Freud described as the relation of the girl to the phallic mother.

> The girl's oral desires for her father's penis mingle with her first genital desires to receive that penis. These genital desires imply the wish to receive children from her father, which is also borne out by the equation "penis = child". The feminine desire to internalize the penis and to receive a child from her father invariably precedes the wish to possess a penis of her own.

We could reformulate Klein's position and say that the more conflicted the girl's relationship with her mother, the more her genital desire for the penis will tend to the phallic idealization, to theft of the phallus and to paranoid fear of maternal retaliation (Chasseguet-Smirgel 1986). So too, then, the more she would seek father's protection (Dahl 1996; Squitieri 1999) and also need to bolster his phallic idealization as she also uses it as a shield. At the same time, it offers a route into genitality, especially as a reaction to ambivalence in pregenital development. These two positions converge, in that ambivalence threatens the internal world – its fertility and reparative capacity – in both male and female.

Clinical Cases of the Parthenogenic Baby

Otto Fenichel (1936, 5) reported a case, which I think, is an example of Britton's Antigone. This case gains in evidential value as independent validation because it was reported well ahead of Britton's formulation and because Britton does not refer to it. Fenichel's patient identified with a friend of hers to such an extent that, at a time when he was impotent, she

> had the feeling: without me he can't do it at all. Her expressions of affection always resulted in her snuggling up to the man's body like a small part of the latter. When her friend left her she experienced a "sore feeling" in her back, as though her back had grown onto him and had now been torn loose. When, finally, she produced dreams of men who instead of a penis had a small child pendant from the abdomen, there was no longer any doubt as to her identification with a penis. In the fantasy of hanging like a penis from the man's abdomen, we had a kind of father's body fantasy ...

Before presenting the next clinical case, I want to gather the elements that seem to be combined to make up the phantasy of the penis baby. Like a molecule that clicks into a determinate structure on the basis of its elements, so, too, with the structure of the parthenogenic baby as its components click into place. Looked at this way, the theory gains in validity from identifying the elements in the clinical material. I think we find the following:

1 A fusional and ambivalent relationship between mother and daughter, which seems unresolved;
2 An anxiety at a loss of self, perhaps into mother, with a consequent sense of unreality in relation to herself;
3 A narcissistic pull, which can bind father and daughter together in a phallic idealization, in which the idealization of father is a wish to transcend the ambivalence in the mother/daughter relationship;

4 The father-daughter relationship can take the form of the Athene-
   Antigone complex;

I will present Miss Collins, a woman in her 20s when we began our work, with
no serious hindrances in her life. In the course of our work, she presented
vivid penis-baby dreams. They seemed to be a backdrop to her life, which did
not interfere with normality, both personally and professionally. Some way
into the work, they also shadowed her actual pregnancy with anxiety, as her
pregnancy and birth proceeded without alarm. Two nagging concerns occasioned her seeking psychotherapy following a breakdown of a relationship.
They gave a clue to the dreams that would follow. First, her ex-boyfriend said
that she was 'spiritually amputated', suggesting that a part of her had been
cut off. He was 13 years older than she and had left her after falling in love
with a woman said to be closer to his spiritual ideal. Secondly, she suffered a
persistent anxiety that, were she to become pregnant, her father would die.

These two themes uncannily match what we discussed in Chapter 5. They
bring a triangulation with it, which dealt with how a girl might come to adopt
a phallic monism. It is more robust because the clinical data from this case
long antedated my familiarity with the findings in that chapter. With respect
to the first theme, *she* did not report feeling spiritually amputated: Her
departing boyfriend said she was spiritually amputated. She, to some extent,
had either imported it or matched it to her own feeling, or some mixture of
both. With respect to the second theme, her fear that pregnancy would kill
her father sounds like a version of the same, male, anxiety, that the woman, in
procreation, takes his penis. I think we can also see Britton's Athene-
Antigone complex, with the daughter's mixture of sharing the magical phallus
to make a baby and fearing the impact of withdrawing her support for
father's security; more concretely, taking his penis. In the background, I hear
Horney's rejoinder to the female castration complex: That it is a male
invention; that it is *his* terror of castration safely pressed, into the female,
aiming to lodge it there as *her* castration complex; observed in her, not suffered by him.

I am presenting this case because it is exceptionally rich, and I have not
found anything equivalent in the literature or in clinical discussions. It does
not establish the origin of female phallic phantasies. It does, however, fit with
what I have argued in Chapter 5: That the phallic defence is an unconscious
collaboration: That male and female organize it together, with each other,
and that the organization surrounds a depressive anxiety linked to conception. The struggle to make a baby and the competition with mother, work
together with the anxiety that father, or his penis, are components to be used
in the production. The organization is isomorphic with conception, a production equivalent of conception.

To continue with Miss Collins' account. She felt unattractive as a teenager.
Her first sexual relationship was with an older man, after which she felt

attractive, at least to older men. Early in our work, she compared me with her father. Her presentation in the first session stood out: She spoke in her ex-boyfriend's words about her, a theme that returned in her feeling she was the object of my investigation, not included in it. I think we can see a clue as to the inducement into phallic idealization in her account of herself reflected through the spiritual father.

She used sex as a way to embody, stabilize and possess a moment of ecstasy, and ecstasy gave her an experience of change, of overcoming stasis. If anyone or anything got too close for too long, it would lose value for her, and a new sexual experience would restore her. I think we can see an anxiety that the 'other' (mother and father, as sites of conflict) would mingle with her, and the two, unseparated, would deteriorate as she lost herself into the other and the other remained unrenewed by her. A new, fresh, idealized other would then be needed. We remained mostly such an idealized couple, transferred from mother-daughter, to father-daughter, until late in our work. She wanted to leave with only good thoughts but also found that the emerging ambivalence towards me and our work brought a sense of reality and objectivity – I would say, a father gained substance in his own right, in the parental couple.

The question arises: What sustained the idealized father-daughter couple? I think two features of the work stood out. First, we met twice weekly, and a pattern emerged, in which she would lie on the couch for one session and sit up in the second, thereby promoting a splitting that kept the idealized apart from the denigrated. Splitting was also facilitated by the periodicity of work, with its weekly and termly rhythms; thirdly, she brought many, vivid dreams, often with sexual content, which gave us a supply of fresh work akin to the refreshment of sexual affairs. Moreover, her dreams, old and recent, often had to do with pregnancy and childbirth, and she thought of them as thresholds into adulthood.

A common thread ran through her many pregnancy and childbirth dreams. She wished for a perfect baby, but the reality of the pregnancy would dissolve, or it was distorted. She dreamt of swelling up, with geometric shapes of deformed babies inside. Sometimes there was no one around to help and she wouldn't know whether she had given birth (because there was no one to confirm it). When once she had a 'normal' pregnancy in a dream, she was overjoyed, but she deflated like a balloon and the pregnancy evaporated when some female relatives of her husband's doubted its reality (note the mingling of mother-daughter and father-daughter ambivalence).

In these dreams, she was often pregnant with angular shapes, and rarely did she give birth. When she was pregnant in reality, she had a series of dreams, as well as anxieties in waking life, suggesting biting and tearing apart: Cars scraping each other, birds tearing their prey, cats with voracious appetites. She was also confused about whose pregnancy it was: Hers or her mother's, especially when she visualized it on an ultrasound scan, where it could be seen 'objectively', but at a distance from inside her.

In one dream, she was pregnant with a child of about two, whom she could move back and forth through her vagina, removing it from and replacing it in her womb, in which the baby was a penis. The baby's age, far from conception, seemed to replace the mystery of conception with the actuality of a baby as a penis, instead of a penis associated in an unknown way with the origination of a baby. This theme was repeated in another dream, in several parts.

A woman friend is carrying a baby (ambiguous at first: pregnant? on her back?), who is closed off from the world, apart from any adult's interest. Then she is with a baby alone. The baby speaks fluently and self-assertively of his plans, as if he were 18 or 25 years old. Then her friend with a baby is with her, as vague and confused as she is brusque and organizing, like father or the baby, though she has heard her friend speak of her as without ambition.

In the session, she spoke of having no self-assurance. The unreliability – even unreality – of her pregnancies, and with them, of the self-assurance of her stable, autonomous existence, lay in her relationship to women, ultimately with mother. Mother seemed to reclaim her daughter from her wished-for motherhood. In Klein's (1928) formulation of this conflicted core of mother-daughter relationship, they struggled over everything associated with the capacity to be a mother: Father's penis, mother's internal objects, mother's reproductive organs, mother's internal babies. For Klein, father's penis, confused with father as an ego-ideal, is a guide into maturity (195–196), but we can also see a seduction into an idealization, which casts her as Athene-Antigone.

If mother and father absorb masculine and feminine capacities from each other and form a couple, and the daughter can tolerate their relationship, she can harbour the parental relationship, expressed in parental intercourse, as an internal object. In this way, she both experiences their love as a parental couple and fulfils her hope from infancy that she 'can bring them together and unite them in a happy way' (Klein 1952, 79 n. 2; Britton 1989).

The parthenogenic baby can appear in a struggle between an internal mother and father, or to find freedom from mother in a leap to an idealized father, as Athene-Antigone, or in a transition to a nurturing father in an internal parental couple. We will follow up these aspects, beginning with Miss Collins' vivid dream of a parthenogenic baby.

She found a baby in the woods. It was all wrapped up, and it looked like a little man. She felt she had a right to raise it and took it to a basin in a loo to clean it up. The loo reminded her of the one in the building where my consulting room was located. Her mother was involved; perhaps they were going to raise it together. Then a man came around. From the way he dressed, she judged that he was a circus performer. This man took back the baby, saying he knew how to take care of him, and implying a right to it. The concrete equation between the baby and a penis was vivid and unambiguous in the dream. The unconscious confusion as to the origin of a baby was registered in both mother's and father's sense of a right to it.

Note that mother and daughter acquired a baby in the woods, as if from nature, and that this natural source was the father's penis. That was what they needed from him. When he appears, he comes to claim the child as his. It seems that childbearing is the (parthenogenic) product of either mother or father, the object of struggle, not fulfilment of sexual union. Her confusion with mother is signalled in the dream by the understanding that she and mother would raise the penis baby together. Other dreams, to which I have referred, document the struggle between them, and females generally, over pregnancy. She also seemed to identify with her mother in her pelvis. Reflecting on dreams in which she puzzled over whether she actually had given birth, she wondered whether her mother had felt that giving birth to her – mother's daughter – had seemed unreal. Mother told her that labour with her had stopped and started. She – daughter – wondered whether this theme – mother's anxiety – was in her birth dreams. In addition, when she was actually pregnant and received a scan report, she felt that it was also mother's scan report, and mother raised worries about it, as if she were repeating her own difficult pregnancy rather than listening to her daughter's report on her pregnancy. She also wondered whether bearing a perfect baby would damage mother.

The unreality of her pregnancies along with the threat to them of a lapse in maternal support or from maternal opposition are consistent with the fraught mother-daughter relationship. They say nothing about her actual mother, though her mother did seem to add anxiety to the mix: They are nonetheless expressions of unconscious phantasy. She also gave voice to the paternal dimension in her first session, when she reported the – at the time – puzzling worry that, should she fall pregnant, her father would die. We can now translate that worry as the girl's phantasy that she has taken the father's penis to make her baby and has become liable to sustain it/him. So, now she has a double turmoil: She must both fight to keep the penis (baby) claimed by mother and to sustain the father who has lost this essential part of himself. Her Athene threatened father, requiring her Antigone to care for him.

I want to take up the separation of genitality from anality because it marks the transition from a fraught, retaliatory relationship with the internal mother into the aegis of a parental couple. This transition can be undermined by transporting the maternal ambivalence into the father-daughter relationship and it can be avoided by fleeing from it into an idealized father. [3] It can be mitigated, stabilized and facilitated by a masculine identification. In this case, an internal father gains substance and supports objectivity over phantasy and the transition to internalizing a fertile parental couple. Such a transitional moment found representation in Miss Collins' 'mound' dream.

> She was on a cycling journey. Father was ahead. They were in a landscape with building works, as for a road – mud and muck, signs of purposeful activity. She came to a kind of a coal bunker, like a mound with a door she could open by pushing the mound itself to either side, as if the mound itself opened. The mound was dark to either side of the entry. Inside, where she might have found coal, she found instead beautiful roses. She was not so much surprised as delighted. These events were included within another part, so much so, as for her not to be sure whether they took place separately from this other part. Here, she was with me, sitting by a fire and telling me the story of her journey. I was on a chair, she on the floor. The most important thing was to try to tell me about the flowers. I did not seem to know about them, though she was sure I did.

She connected the journey and the building works with something for the future. The landscape also reminded her of the past, of a regular path she walked with her mother. She remembered slag heaps, which had been unintelligible to her. She knew coal was dug and all the activity had meaning, but the slag heaps remained a mystery. What stood out in her telling me about the flowers was the sense of a gap between us, which she tried to fill with words. She said the dream showed her she had something good from the therapy.

The imagery suggested vividly the female genital but I did not refer to this aspect. The fireside setting, while potentially seductive, was more a father with his daughter. She seemed to be trying to work out something that involved him, possibly her feeling good and attractive to him, and needing him to help separate her from mother (walking the old paths). She wanted also to believe in the goodness of our relationship – the delightful, beautiful flowers – which was threatened by contamination from her ambivalent fusion with mother. She found an internal 'good' inside the dark mound (reminiscent of slag heaps from her childhood), surrounded by anal detritus, but safe, deep inside, not tarnished by it. Her sitting on the floor while I sat in a chair also suggested some idealization, but also a warm, protective, father-daughter relationship. Her belief (in telling the story of her journey to me), that I did know but might not know, what happened inside her (in the mound), suggested that father might be able to guide his daughter into adult motherhood, but might not. So, we have an idealized, sexualized father to take over the fraught mother-daughter relationship, with whom she identifies to sustain her idealized interior, but also the paternal father who knows she is his daughter and whom she knows is her father.

I have referred Miss Collins' unreal pregnancies in several dreams, seemingly fuelled by a confusion between her and her mother. The birth of a sibling can upset the child's assurance of her parent's love and her guaranteed place in their mind.[4] In the first session back after a break on account of illness, we got a sense of a conflicted dimension in this relationship, magnified by the birth of her brother. She reported a trip back to her childhood home city. She passed the hospital where she was born and commented that the view of the window where she waved to her mother when her brother was born wasn't as she remembered, which made her feel a bit shaky.

I connected her shakiness with her return to her sessions, with which she agreed, then she spoke at length. She said she wanted her mother to write her autobiography, then recounted a film she saw. There was a beautiful girl, treasured by her father. Mother was displaced. The daughter dressed up as a woman and danced with her father in the bedroom. Father died of a heart attack. Daughter had a sexual relationship with a friend of her parents. Mother raged with jealousy and died. She spoke again about her mother's pregnancy: How it might have been unreal for her, with labour starting and stopping, which seemed similar to her own birth dreams.

In recounting this film in connection with her wish to know more about mother and the sense of unreality around mother's pregnancy (and her own pregnancies, fancied and actual), she was connecting her impact on the parents with a consequence for her. Her oedipal enactment killed mother, by taking father's penis from her; and father, by taking it from him. The death of both parents becomes the death of the internal parental couple. Together, they threatened her pregnancies. But pregnancy is also hopeful, reparative. Phallic pregnancy is both a defence against depressive anxiety and a transitional movement into genital pregnancy.

Her actual pregnancy intensified an underlying conflict, disappointment, and resentment, which had been hidden in an idealized transference. In addition, 'three in everything', which had been an old theme, was now with us as well. In a dream, she had come to see me. I changed into a waiter in a restaurant where she ate, including recently, where she had been treated in a haughty manner and had fantasized throwing her food all over the waiter. In her dream, I was not concerned about her. She used to feel sorry for, but annoyed with, the owner's inability to make a go of the restaurant. His wife was expecting a baby. The mother-baby unit, sufficient to itself if the father is excluded, now seemed to need the father for there to enough food for the baby.

As in her dream of recounting her journey to me, father's stabilizing presence might be robust enough to counter the maternal ownership of pregnancies, but it might not. She feared her actual pregnancy would leak away, as had happened in her dream of her deflated pregnancy when her husband's female relatives doubted its existence. She decided well in advance of the birth that she would end her psychotherapy in her eighth month. She was annoyed with me for not agreeing with her wish to end our work. She feared a leaking away of her sense of self-determination as well, but it was clearly linked concretely to her pregnancy (though she had not yet told me she was pregnant). She wanted our work to end in goodness, uncontaminated by bad feelings and also to protect me from the impact of her decisiveness. She proposed reducing her sessions but increasing my fee.

She was angered at what she took to be my wish to hold onto her and at times despairing that her hopes for change had been lost. She was fearful that her pregnancy and her sense of herself could leak away if she did not stand firm in decisiveness. She felt she had to get away to have anything for herself. For several months before she did finish when she was 6 ½ months pregnant, she resented my retaining an analytical attitude towards her decision. It seemed that, in my appearing not to understand (agree with) her decision, I was threatening her conviction that she could finish the job of becoming a mother herself, as if otherwise, she would be left in a struggle for autonomy against her mother's power, girded by an unstable idealization of father.

This dilemma made it difficult to ensure she could hold onto something good. Bad thoughts could still ruin goodness. She believed she must transcend them, and she felt more impelled to do so because she also could feel cynical and distrustful. Her 'mound' dream, late in our work, brought out her wish to hold to the good. Along with her resentment that I seemed not to take seriously her concern that her capacity to assert herself, to be herself, would leak away, as did her dream pregnancies, she also sought an objectivity through me. She spoke of her capacity to excite a man, then feel contempt for him (as she did with me in an early dream).

These themes were recurrent, but in one session we returned to a dream from the previous session, in which a woman and a man appeared, both doctors (other figures entered in reviewing the dream). She associated the man with a mix of figures from George Eliot's *Middlemarch* or *Daniel Deronda*, someone authoritative, with exacting standards, though not sadistic, not seducible – a universal figure on whom Dorothea, from Middlemarch, or Gwendolyn, from Daniel Deronda (she became confused), had no impact, as she had none on me. What she could do was decide the ending of our work. But we could see her wish for an objectivity that would stabilize her sense of self.

In the language of oedipal conflict, she sought a protection from maternal retaliation for her replacing mother in the primal scene. In the language of her unstable, possibly unreal, dream pregnancies, she sought an objective, internal father's protection from her internal mother's claim on her own body, its contents and its capacities. The parthenogenic – penis – baby avoids oedipal intrusion into parental intercourse and incestuous intrusion into procreation. In its omnipotence, it aims to transcend the primal power of both an internal mother and an internal father. But it is also transitional, as father's objectivity draws her into reality.

It was likely that the underlying dilemma in my not agreeing with her wish to end or work ahead of the birth and infancy of her child undermined her confidence that she could achieve the autonomy she sought. In transference terms, she could be left with an idealized father likely to die once her pregnancy proved to be real. She could also be left in a conflict with maternal control, with the only hope of escape dependent on an unstable father. Having progressed in securing a reasonably stable, objective father, she wanted to feel the task was well enough completed. We did end our work; her pregnancy did persist, as did a second pregnancy; she did marry and consolidate a family with the father of her children.

Conclusion

I have aimed to show that the penis baby is part of phallic idealization in the girl. It need not be driven by a female castration complex nor pens envy. Instead, it can arise from a conflicted mother-daughter relationship along with a strong concern for the well-being of a fragile father, which could intensify an internal insecurity that cannot be checked against perceptual reality. This insecurity renders the girl susceptible to becoming the repository of male projective identification aimed at enhancing male internal security by forcing her to bear it. She can become confused with it, intensifying, an internal insecurity, and to wishing that she, like the boy, possessed an externally validated genital intactness. The concrete, anatomical, location of security underwrites an omnipotent, phallic phantasy of impervious security, based on phallic idealization. In any event, the temptation of omnipotence binds male and female into a collaborative defensive phallic couple.

Beneath this collaborative, phallic defence lies the dread of depressive collapse, also shared by male and female. The parthenogenic baby as a defence also, however, forms a transition to becoming a parental couple, based on a benign internal parental couple whether or not one has children). In Part IV, we move away from the phallic world to the depressive world of fertility, the threats to it and the desolation that stalks it. We also change our focus. The aim of this book is to explore the nature of masculinity, through its aggressive extreme in toxic masculinity. We move squarely to the father, and with that move, we take up the theme of masculinity based on his unique, seminal contribution to natality, but also its ambivalence, with the destruction of life. It is also a way to introduce, in Part V, the theme of masculinity based on misogyny and the annihilation of the feminine. Finally, we will generalize this ambivalence of masculinity to the depressive dread of desolation and, with Freud's use of the pathological as an extreme that highlights the normal, we come back to ordinary masculinity.

Notes

1   For Horney (1933), girls denied knowledge of the vagina because it was evidence of vulnerability to injury. Klein provides evidence that, for both boys and girls semen is an enigma. For 13-year-old Felix (Klein 1923, 72), it was not like the world of physics: It was invisible, like air. For 17-year-old Lisa (1923, 71), it was like the second unknown of a mathematical equation.

2   There is extra-clinical, empirical support for the penis baby in adult women.
     Rosalind Jones (1994) carried out an experiment with 149 women and 33 men,
     university students. She played subliminal and supraliminal messages conveying three
     distinct images: Pregnancy, penetration without sexual content and penetration with
     sexual content. The subjects then responded to ink blot images. She found
     that subliminal pregnancy messages correlated with phallic imagery – penis-like
     imagery – and not with sexual imagery. Penetration messages, whether sexual or not,
     did not correlate with phallic imagery. Moreover, supraliminal – *conscious* – preg-
     nancy or sexual-penetration messages increased sexual but *not* phallic imagery
     (correlations among men were small). In other words, women *unconsciously* associ-
     ated pregnancy with the penis (checks were made to assure the investigators that the
     messages were not infiltrated by conscious recognition of themes in the messages).
        Of course, her study reveals correlations, not mechanisms. They say nothing
     about any individual, nor about the mechanism of association. Inside the correla-
     tions, there is plenty of scope for mechanisms of defence. They could embrace, for
     example, a defence in which the penis baby is one form of anality, perhaps in the
     anal stage of ordinary, 'normal' women. Such a formulation would fit with Klein's
     thinking, discussed later in this chapter, which associates the penis baby with
     anality. Jones allows that the phallic imagery can 'indicate that women's phallic
     concerns potentially implicate both primitive anatomically based longings, as well
     as more symbolic strivings' (134). Similarly, although the anality of the penis baby
     is concrete, it can extend into a symbolic form. In Birkstead-Breen's (1996) for-
     mulation, the penis can move from phallus to a link. The importance of this study
     lies in its confirmation of what, otherwise, might seem bizarre and the product of
     male bias in psychoanalysis.
        Jones finds similar correlations among men, but they were insignificant. There is
     evidence – albeit scant – that males as well as females can hold to the phallic idea of
     forming a baby from the penis (Basch-Kåhre 1987; Boehm 1930; Van Leeuwen
     1966; Little Hans was among them; Jacobson (1950) says the wish for a child
     precedes the wish for a penis in boys and girls).
3   As we previously noted, Freud (1933, 119) detected an early, pre-oedipal, fraught
     mother-daughter relationship, which can be carried over into her relationship with
     father, in women 'who remain till a late age tenderly dependent on a paternal
     object, or indeed on their real father ... We have established some surprising facts
     about these women with an intense attachment of long duration to their father.
     We knew, of course, that there had been a preliminary stage of attachment to the
     mother, but we did not know that it could be so rich in content and so long-
     lasting, and could leave behind so many opportunities for fixations and disposi-
     tions ... Almost everything that we find later in her relation to her father was
     already present in this earlier attachment and has been transferred subsequently
     on to her father.'
4   Freud (1933, 122) lists the unassuageable reproaches of the daughter against her
     mother, one of which is the betrayal of bearing a sibling. Her 'grievance against
     the faithless mother' for her being 'dethroned, despoiled, prejudiced in [her] rights'
     can feed on mother's reserving her milk for the new baby.

References

Arendt, H. (1958) *The Human Condition*. Chicago: University of Chicago Press.
Balsam, R. (2018) 'Castration Anxiety' Revisited: Especially 'Female Castration
     Anxiety'. *Psychoanalytic Inquiry* 38(1): 11–22.

Basch-Kåhre, E. (1987) Forms of the Oedipus Complex. *Scandinavian Psychoanalytic Review* 10: 103–115.

Bion, W. R. (1992) *Cogitations*. London: Karnac.

Birksted-Breen, D. (1996) Phallus, Penis and Mental Space. *International Journal of Psychoanalysis* 77: 649–657.

Boehm, F. (1930) The Femininity-Complex in Men. *International Journal of Psychoanalysis* 11: 444–469.

Britton, R. (1989) The Missing Link: Parental Sexuality in the Oedipus Complex. In Steiner, J. (ed.) *The Oedipus Complex Today Clinical Implications*. London: Karnac, 83–101.

Chasseguet-Smirgel, J. (1986) The Archaic Matrix of the Oedipus Complex. In *Sexuality and Mind: The Role of the Father and Mother in the Psyche*. NY/London: New York University Press, pp. 74–91.

Dahl, E. (1996) The concept of penis envy revisited: a child analyst listens to an adult, *Psychoanalytic Study of the Child* 51: 303–325.

Fenichel, O. (1936) The Symbolic Equation: Girl = Phallus. In *The Collected Papers of Otto Fenichel, Second Series*. NY: W. W. Norton & Company, Inc., 1954, 3–18.

Figlio, K. (2000) *Psychoanalysis, Science and Masculinity*. London: Whurr; Philadelphia: Brunner Routledge, 2001.

Figlio, K. (2003) Getting to the Beginning: Historical Memory and Concrete Thinking. In Radstone, S. and Hodgkin, K. (eds) *Regimes of Memory (Routledge Studies in Memory and Narrative, vol. 12)*. London: Routledge, 2003, 152–66; pb *Memory Cultures: Memory, Subjectivity and Recognition*. New Brunswick/London: Transaction, 2006.

Fox, E. (1983) *The Five Books of Moses: Genesis, Exodus, Leviticus, Numbers, and Deuteronomy*. London: The Harvill Press.

Freud, S. (1908) On the SexualTtheories of Children. *The Standard Edition of the Complete Psychological Works of Sigmund Freud* 9: 205–226.

Freud, S. (1910) A Special Type of Choice of Object Made by Men (Contributions to the Psychology of Love I). *The Standard Edition of the Complete Psychological Works of Sigmund Freud* 11: 161–175.

Freud, S. (1933) New Introductory Lectures on Psycho-Analysis. *The Standard Edition of the Complete Psychological Works of Sigmund Freud* 22: 1–182

Horney, K. (1933) The Denial of the Vagina: A Contribution to the Problem of the Genital Anxieties Specific to Women. *International Journal of Psychoanalysis* 14: 57–70; reprinted in *Feminine Psychology*. NY: Norton, 1967, 147–161.

Jacobson, E. (1950) Development of the Wish for a Child in Boys. *Psychoanalytic Study of the Child* 5: 139–152.

Jones, R. J. (1994) An Empirical Study of Freud's Penis-Baby. *The Journal of Nervous and Mental Disease* 182: 127–135.

Klein, M. (1923) The Role of the School in the Libidinal Development of the Child. In *The writings of Melanie Klein*, vol. 1. London: The Hogarth Press and the Institute of Psycho-Analysis, 1975, 59–76.

Klein, M. (1928) Early stages of the Oedipus conflict. In *The Writings of Melanie Klein*, vol. 1. London: The Hogarth Press and the Institute of Psycho-Analysis, 1975, 186–198.

Klein, M. (1932) The Psychoanalysis of Children. In *The Writings of Melanie Klein*, vol. 2. London: The Hogarth Press and the Institute of Psycho-Analysis, 1975.

Klein, M. (1945) The Oedipus Complex in the Light of Early Anxieties. In *The Writings of Melanie Klein*, vol. 1. London: The Hogarth Press and the Institute of Psycho-Analysis, 1975, 370–419.

Klein, M. (1952) Some Theoretical Conclusions Regarding the Emotional Life of the Infant. In *The Writings of Melanie Klein*, vol. 3. London: The Hogarth Press and the Institute of Psycho-Analysis, 1975, 61–93.

Squitieri, L. M. (1999) Problems of Female Sexuality: The Defensive Function of Certain Phantasies About the Body. *International Journal of Psychoanalysis* 80: 645–660.

Van Leeuwen, K. (1966) Pregnancy Envy in the Male. *International Journal of Psychoanalysis* 47: 319–324.

Part IV

The Seminal World

Chapter 7

Seminal Masculinity

The Enigma of Procreation

In Part III, we concentrated on the phallic realm. We now switch our focus to the non-phallic dimension, and specifically to the masculine. We introduced this dimension in Chapter 2, with the idea of a complex, internal male genital – something equivalent to the internal female genital, which psychoanalysts had for some time described as a feminine reality quite apart from the attribution of a phallic stage. Psychoanalytic attention then laid stress on the femininity of the male, unrecognized and unacceptable to his phallically defended character. In this chapter, we look at the distinctively male, but non-phallic capacity of his internal genital: What I call seminality.[1]

It is good to remember that the phallic defence, and the phallic monism, against which there has been a robust reaction, were a feature of the part-object, part-instinct world of the phallic stage. Whole-object, composite-instinct-relating, which included loving and hating, were, for Freud, the domain of genitality. From Freud onwards, genitality has referred to a psychic accomplishment, in which the pre-genital levels of functioning are mitigated and integrated into a more stable, more consistently loving personality. But genitality also introduces something new. The main psychic achievement is to transform the belief that children are created, as parthenogenic – narcissistic extensions, or produced as a crafted product from everyday material, such as feces – into accepting the need of an other to procreate a child.

In addition, as set out by Klein, male genitality is beset by the anxiety of the deep-rooted conflict of the femininity phase, by envy-driven aggression towards the mother and by insecure masculine identification. His capacity for generosity is based on orality. It is difficult to understand how the male shifts his psychosexual character from the oral, nurturant base to a genital base, or what is specifically masculine about it. Orality supports phantasies such as milk-in-the-nipple, sucking, biting, swallowing. It bases the self-experience of the infant in mouth-toning and a mouth-orientation towards the object world, which supplies concepts from orality to describe, misleadingly, the phantasy structure and experience of genitality.

DOI: 10.4324/9781003455790-11

Phallicism, with its narcissism, is a defence against the fragility of genitality (in my view, as seminality). From Jones onwards, its defensive, as opposed to developmental, character has been emphasized. Based on oral functioning, it is built on the experience of fullness. Engorgement of any erectile organ, including the penis, is modelled on the fullness of the mouth, throat and belly, with the lips holding the nipple. The lips are the equivalent to the sphincter musculature that restricts venous outflow from an erectile organ and causes its engorgement and the associated experience of passive pleasure of fullness.[2] The feeding situation is a fundamental biological and psychological unit: Lips grasping the engorged nipple, held in a full mouth and producing fullness in the belly. It brings together aggression, in muscular discharge, with the pleasure in the release of tension. It models the fusion of aggression and love: The merger of life and death drives. But it is difficult to see how we can derive a specifically masculine or feminine character from it. The dominance of phallic thinking, perhaps in psychoanalytic theory as well as in the individual and in Western culture, has obstructed the expression not only of a feminine character, but also of a masculine character.

Recognizing seminality has profound psychical consequences. The phallic defence offers a haven from seminal anxieties deeper than castration anxiety as fear for the penis. The bedrock male castration anxiety is what we always knew to be castration: The loss of fertility. Freud points out that it is 'remarkable what a small degree of attention the other part of the male genitals, the little sac with its contents, attracts in children. From all one hears in analyses, one would not guess that the male genitals consisted of anything more than the penis' (1923, 142, n. 1). What is striking is the extent to which this 'small degree of attention' to the whole male genital has extended to the neglect of semen as the most obvious male attribute, in psychoanalysis as well as in culture more widely.

In reviewing the cultural evidence for the Oedipus complex, Boehm (1931, 449) said, 'I am almost inclined to believe that the child's jealousy of the parent of its own sex is due less to the idea of pleasurable sexual union than to envy of the capacity to beget and give birth to children.' And as we saw in Chapter 4, although the five-year-old 'Little Hans' sought the pleasure of his earlier life with mother, mainly he could not, and was not helped to find out, what his father's function in making babies was (449–50). And as Moses Laufer says of the adolescent boy, 'The actual ability to impregnate ... means normally that the defence against the incestuous wishes [would] now [be] tested within a new context ... of genitality ...' (Laufer, M. 1976, 301).

Genitality is an achievement, not just in accepting parental sexual intercourse, with the exclusion of the child, but also – perhaps fundamentally – the inexplicable nature of union and the creation from it of pregnancy. For the male, the genital father is proud both of his wife and of his daughter, for each unique pregnancy: One having brought a daughter, the other bringing a grandchild. The proud father is Meltzer's (1973, 74–80) 'testicular father', what I call the 'seminal father', to highlight the seminal function in particular. This father is not the phallic father who invites or sustains a daughter's identification through the phallus as a shared magical instrument, but the uniquely male father whose semen is generative and reparative, in a union.

The various expressions for a more rounded masculinity, such as 'feminine side', 'curative intercourse', 'parental couple' disregard this seminal function and the anxiety of losing seminal function.[3] The anxious anticipation of loss of seminal function is subsumed under (phallic) castration anxiety. In a disavowal, it narrows castration to a phallic loss housed in the lost penis. Castration proper, with the loss of seminal function, is an essential moment/ expression of loss itself – loss of being, not of an object. The phallus-as-penis is an object, while semen represents 'being', in the continuance of life; its loss signifies the failure of life to continue.[4]

Were we to dim the glare of phallic material, we might see more clearly that men dread seminal failure and seminal aggressiveness, and convert them into an anxiety over sexual performance. Anxiety over phallic potency would then refer, at the deepest level, to this dread of seminal inadequacy or destructiveness. Klein (1950, 45) speaks of castration anxiety as a phallic persecutory anxiety (paranoid-schizoid), which is distinct from the depressive anxiety, related to the loved object, and specifically in an incapacity to fertilize a woman.

> Thus, the fear of being devoured, of being poisoned, of being castrated, the fear of attacks on the "inside" of the body, come under the heading of persecutory anxiety, whereas all anxieties relating to loved objects are depressive in nature. However, persecutory and depressive anxieties, although conceptually distinct from one another, are clinically often mixed. I have defined castration fear, the leading anxiety in the male, as persecutory. This fear is mixed with *depressive anxiety in so far as it gives rise to the feeling that he cannot fertilize a woman*, at bottom that *he cannot fertilize the loved mother and is therefore unable to make reparation* for the harm done to her by his sadistic impulses. (my emphasis)[5]

Masculinity and Semen

I have argued that masculine internal, genital space, while it supports the idea of femininity in the male, such as masculine receptivity, is uniquely male, in producing semen. Semen completes the penetration of the female as an extension of phallic aggression and simultaneously brings fertility and reparation. It is 'inside' the female in a wholly different way from inside the territory occupied by the penis. The penis is expansive, takes up space and is quantitative in its narcissism. Semen effects a merger. It is absorbed and assimilated; in this non-dimensional way it represents the male – it is the male – in his distinctive, qualitative character. Following Chapter 3, we might say that semen goes into a space beyond dimension, 'O', infinity, a thing-in-itself, which leaves the man uncannily bereft of himself, unless there is a pregnancy. Pregnancy then returns himself to himself, realized as the capacity for engendering, sustaining and repairing life. But what if there is no pregnancy? In later chapters, we will explore the relationship between this incapacity and depressive desolation.

Phallic potency cannot wholly conceal this dimension, including dread of seminal inadequacy. Klein (1950, 45) said that men often suffer from severe depression if they cannot make reparation to the mother by fertilizing a woman. Keylor and Apfel (2010), referring to the research literature as well as to their clinical findings, conclude that '[w]hereas women respond [to infertility] with overt feelings loss and grief as well as anxiety and injury, the initial reaction in men is chiefly one of anxiety rather than depression or a sense of loss'(71), but 'the assault on their sense of masculine sexual potency and the anxiety that it creates is... ... not repaired as it sometimes is for women by the birth of a child'(74). In other words, phallic defence against infertility doesn't work very well. They conclude that in 'every analysis of a man, there are issues that relate to fertility, whether directly or metaphorically'(73).[6]

Ferenczi (1924) set out a theory of seminal function. In his theory, seminal function was on loan from urethral and bowel functions and its libidinal investment was the resultant of these libidinal investments. He argued that ejaculation comprised two counter-posed forces, located in two erotized organs: The urge to empty, in the bladder; and the urge to withhold, in the bowel. But the erotic satisfactions were also displaced from their erotized organs: Urethral release into the bowel, counter-posing the bowel's libidinal investment in retention; bowel retention into the bladder, endowing it with the libidinal satisfaction of retention. The penis originated in both organs, anatomically, physiologically and psychologically, and ejaculation partook of both retention and release. He called the mixing of libidinal currents, amphimixis.

Beneath the excitation of the penis as a focal and visible libidinal foundation of masculinity, lay a more fundamental but also diffuse source of sexual and existential security. Following Ferenczi, specific internal organs of seminal masculinity have been studied: Scrotum, testicles, prostate gland and connecting structures. These internal organs of seminal masculinity – the organs of the male internal genital space – do not 'fix in' the penis, as Hans explained, but produce semen and participate in procreation. Unlike phallic masculinity, which can always be recouped, seminal masculinity could be lost into a mysterious internal space. Unlike the boy's penis, which differs only in size from father's, seminal masculinity appears at a certain time, marking a qualitative acquisition. The shape and appearance of the pre-pubertal testes and scrotum, for example, differ from those of the adult (Yazmajian 1966). The appearance of semen and the seminal dimension of the Oedipus complex also marks out the adult. M. Laufer (1976) argues that, for the adolescent, the mature male genital refers to the capacity to impregnate a woman, and that the wishes and prohibitions connected with this seminal function bring internal incest conflicts to a head.

Clinical Cases of Seminality

Fenichel (1925) reported an analysis of a 28-year-old woman with hysterical symptoms, who was also plagued with insatiable hunger, sometimes for anything and sometimes for sweets, cakes, milk, eggs, chocolate and fat meat. She was told by her older brother that her sexual theory, which included cutting open the abdomen, was not true; that 'there was something about a seed' (44). She then thought that children grew in flower pots, until a rhyming association, which included the phrase that children 'come from there', brought semen to mind: *Daherkamen* rhymed with *Samen* (seed or semen). She liked eggs, especially in periods of intense hunger; and after breaking up with a potential lover, she stayed in bed and had an egg brought to her. Fenichel interpreted this episode as an introjection of the lost object (the German for egg is slang for testicle) and a regression to infancy. In her intense hunger, she was also gnawed at by an introjected object (penis eaten in penis envy).

Fenichel established an association between the lost breast and her missing penis, and between her wish to eat her mother's breasts and whole body and her wish to castrate her father and other men by biting off the penis. Her penis envy was not only envy of the breast, but principally milk envy (54, 56, 65). He and his patient could confirm 'the symbolic equation *object of hunger—proof of affection—milk—urine—sperm— child—feces—penis*'(45).

Fenichel's case clearly shows phallic and seminal aspects of her theory of sexuality. He had shown that she felt primarily deprived of milk (65, 68), that semen was equivalent to milk and that she thought that children came from semen (45), that she asked her father about the meaning of the penis (65), and that she thought the penis represented what was most essential in a man (68). Despite these connections, Fenichel did not equate castration with cutting off the supply of semen. Despite the abundance of material suggesting her wanting to internalize the penis, along with testicles and semen, he interpreted her fellatio fantasies as a cover for wanting mother's milk, and for wanting to bite off the penis (56): A phantasy of phallic castration.

What decisively divides the experience of semen from excreta (as opposed to an intimation of its procreative function) is ejaculation. Although the phallic reassurance of erection can occur from an early age, ejaculation erupts as a new experience only around puberty. Something absolutely new breaks into consciousness, as semen appears suddenly in the first experience of ejaculation. and it can be traumatic: An absolute breach of the continuity of experience; an eruption of overwhelming internal forces, boding good or ill. I reported earlier a case of Bird's (1957, 258, 265), in which a young man's first serious relationship with a woman stirred up intense feeling and also a sense of unreality. Ejaculation had made his sexual strivings and ensuing oedipal conflicts real to him, but they had been marginalized until his relationship with a woman brought them back. Initially, his anxiety had arisen from the internal male genital, focused on semen and then, later, more focally, on the penis. His relationship brought back his anxiety, transferred to phallic castration anxiety.

What we see is that ejaculation forces seminal function into the open, but phallic castration anxiety typically overshadows the discovery of healthy masculinity. Seminal clinical observations are difficult to hold in view, mixed as they are with the more sharply delineated, phallic or excremental phantasies. As Freud (1908, 222, 224) observed, even adults often don't recognize that ejaculation and urination are mutually exclusive; also, that, with 'the position of the genitals—inter urinas et faeces— ... [t]he excremental is all too intimately and inseparably bound up with the sexual' (Freud 1912, 189). Moreover, as Ferenczi argued, seminal emission can cause extreme anxiety because it can bring the male ego, identified with his semen, into an identification with the female and, therefore to the brink of extinction. In 'psychogenic aspermia', semen is defensively withheld in an orgasm. Ferenczi called it avariciousness; that is, a compelling need not give it up, because ejaculation was a self-castration (1924, 29).

In my view, the confusion of semen and excreta is evidence that a regressive, phallic world predominates against the horror of feminization, as Horney and others have implied. But it also defends against seminal aggression and the utter desolation of seminal inadequacy in the child and seminal failure in the adult, which accompany it. In his treatment of 'polymorphous tendencies in adult sexuality', Meltzer (1973, 64–73) distinguishes testicular from phallic roles, including identifications with father in his reparative, as opposed to denigrating, soiling relationship to mother. The seminal father tends to be neglected or is subservient to the phallic father. For Meltzer, father relates to mother in two ways. He services her but he possesses her; he promotes her creativity, but he tries to have it as his own. Meltzer captures these two poles of paternal function in his distinction between the testicular and the phallic father in the psyche of the child, including the adult as a child. He describes polymorphous tendencies that form the basis of sexuality through a range of identifications with feminine and masculine aspects of the internal mother and father and their sexual relationship. He distinguishes between identifications that enrich the fecundity of the internal parents and, therefore, ground and support adult sexuality, and those that perversely attack and denigrate them and, therefore, undermine adult sexuality.

Adult polymorphous identifications differentiate between the internal father's penis and his testicles, which become parts of the internal mother's body. The penis, on its own, merges with the sphincters at the entry to mother's three spaces: Mouth, anus and womb; his testicles supply the semen whose function is to repair her three spaces: To supply material for milk, to flush out the rectum and to feed her internal babies. The reparative function of semen, he argues, can be better understood as the basis of adult identifi-cations separate from those associated with the more infantile, phallic iden-tifications with the penis. Adult identifications, based on the testicular father, protect and nourish mother's fertility and nurturance; infantile identifica-tions, based on the phallic father, strive to denigrate and replace them. Father, in relation to mother, also carries the super-ego ideal, the possessor of lost narcissism; and as super-ego ideal, father's relationship to mother also includes knowledge of her, a rendering in objectifying terms of her coe-naesthetic, unconscious union with the baby, which moves between phallic and seminal poles. These maternal and paternal functions refer to the baby's emerging internal world, in which the seminal paternal function is not in his femininity but is distinctly masculine.

Meltzer (74–80) reports two dreams, separated by 12 months. In the first dream, a male patient insecurely followed another man, dressed in a sou'-wester that looked like a penis, into the sea to retrieve a milk bottle.[7] It is vividly phallic and the contents of the sought object are oral, not genital. The milk says 'not semen'. In the second dream, he did not follow, nor seek milk: He admired a 'Dr Ball', who was similar to the analyst. Together, the dreams showed a movement from phallic enthralment and deference to testicular admiration.

Extended Case Study

I will describe this unique, seminal quality of the male through key moments from an eight-year analysis of a man, beginning when he was in his 40s.[8] Mr Harris is a farmer in a long line of farmers who have farmed a historic site with ancient buildings for generations, and he feels a responsibility towards this tradition. He lives on the farm with his wife and three children, one at school, two at university; and with his father, mother, sister, brother-in-law and nephew. Following his father's dictum, he wants to leave the farm in as least as good shape as it was given to him. He went to agricultural college, and, at his father's insistence, he also trained in land surveying, but felt that he had to return to the farm to help his parents, mainly his father. Later, he came to realize that he had wanted to return home and to farming. In addition to farming the land, he also builds and converts buildings on the land for office space and for storage, to such an extent that the financial viability of the enterprise depends mainly on what he calls the 'business', as opposed to the farm.

The overall business is run by his natal family as partners, among whom he often feels junior, despite his carrying total responsibility for its daily running and for initiatives. Although they do not all live in the same house, he speaks of them as 'on top of each other'. He struggles to sort this agglomeration of three generations of kinship into a natal family and a procreational family with his sense of obligation to his natal family and his commitment to his procreational family, with his wife, who has been the object of his passionate love since his youth, figuring prominently. He seeks to bring into clear focus his need to be at home in it and his need to get away to be at home in himself. He feels beset by confusions between being a boy to his parents, a brother to his sister, a husband to his wife and a father to his children. He is clearly a responsible adult but feels like an adolescent.

His unconscious life history is more varied and much more ambivalent than this sketch portrays, but there are some organizing themes, something like a small number of 'selected facts' (Britton and Steiner 1994). The two selected facts that concern me here are the conflict between staying at home and getting away, and the presentation of oedipal conflict, with a mix of paranoid-schizoid and depressive material, in the form of seminal, rather than phallic potency. There is a unifying strand, in that he is drawn into an adolescent phantasy in which he will be free by getting away from an oppressive, dependent relationship with his parents rather than by being the husband and father that he overtly is. If he leaves the farm, his father will die; if he stays on the farm, his father oppresses him with constant criticism.

A confusion of psychosexual stages and zonal gratifications resides in conflicts on the farm. By his hard work, the riches of the farm should flow in abundance. He is frustrated and dissatisfied that they do not, and that everyone but him gets their 'draw down'. The farm has become a displaced form of being at home with the confused family, which satisfies his oral needs, in the food that it supplies; his anal needs, in the soil and fertilizing the soil; and his genital needs, in sowing and harvesting. In that sense, the farm, by blurring the focus of his ambivalences and anxieties, also acts as a psychic retreat (Steiner 1993).

Maintaining and improving the farm, and creating an organic vegetable business with his wife, seemed to express Mr Harris' wish to establish himself as husband and father (both of which he had actually achieved, with his wife and three healthy children in a loving family). He talked endlessly about the farm, encapsulating both his striving and his retreat. He was devoted to growing seeds, restoring buildings, making things better, establishing a heritage. The farm provided an explicit representation of his wish to plant seeds that grew. He had big plans to make the farm special, such as running a shop, selling organic vegetable boxes and attracting visitors.

His wife was essential to his plans, but more than that: She was 'absolutely vital to him'. He spoke of her unique contribution, adding that the way she arranged the boxes – their aesthetic – *was her*: He seemed to identify her with the organic vegetable boxes. I would say that this identification extended to identifying her with a phantasy of organic. He wanted her to be organic for him and the guarantor of his organic self, and was deeply wounded at any sign of her enjoyment of others, including their children. He was keenly sensitive to her mood. If, to him, she felt desolate, he felt desolate. He wanted her to be happy and made happy by their life together.

Their organic initiative seemed to be the fertile offspring of themselves as a parental couple. He was dedicated to maintaining organic standards and developing the prospects for organic farming. His determination to succeed with organic farming snared him in a constant struggle against the weather, crop failures, machine failures, labour and management failures, standards authorities, seed contamination, competitors, the bank. He also struggled with an underlying despair and social awkwardness, for whom life often seemed pointless and himself worthless. But he remained hard-working and optimistic, devoted to his wife and children. His good feelings sometimes would slide into feeling virtuous, then into worrying that concealed aggression and pride could spoil his good feelings. The seminal dimension was seldom the explicit object of analysis. The bond between the seminal and the farm was so tight, that they were, together, the constant object of analysis.

Despite his devoted labours, the farm in general – and the organic vegetable business in particular – fell deeper into debt, not only in not turning a profit, but also in satisfying the apparently insatiable needs of family members, who seemed to live off his labours. Despite the apparently substantial assets of the family, there was a constant insecurity in daily life. In his sessions, the farm seemed to be a collusively sustained illusion of a cornucopia breast, represented by the mystery of the large, but fragile business. He seemed alone in worrying about the actual state of depletion. The association between farm and breast was sustained partly by the overt analogy of providing food, but also in the 'female' – his wife and his mother – seeming to be well-off financially, while the male – he and his father – appearing to be poor, working as if to fill the farm-breast.

The idea of a generative, reparative lineage came vividly clear in a session following a fire on the farm, which destroyed a barn. He said that, being 100's of years old, the barn was especially valuable to father, who had lived with it all his life. On his account, however, he was in a quandary over how to think about it. Had it burned down 500 years ago they would just have rebuilt it. The barn, however, was not among the six listed buildings, so they would not have to rebuild it, but that was not the point.[9] It was special. His father wanted to hand on the farm in at least as good condition as he had inherited it from his father. The lineage was ancient. He described a site nearly sacred with ancestors. There had been archaeological finds, suggesting that people had farmed there 5000 years ago.. When he thought of similarly handing on the farm in at least as good condition as he had inherited from his father, he had in mind mainly an obligation to his father, not his children. Lineage implied an obligation of son to father.

The following session began with his feeling he could not accomplish what needed doing. Everything piled up. A policeman had come about the fire that destroyed their barn. He discovered his bean crop was mouldy and might not be salvageable. His father's words were in his mind: One job should be finished before starting another, but he felt he carried a burden that father did not. He detailed how it came about that the beans were mouldy, as if exonerating himself from a criticism he attributed to my comments, as I offered transferential interpretations. He seemed to spiral out of control, feeling unable to keep up with all that needed doing. I drew his attention to the fire and repeated his saying that father wanted to hand on the farm in at least as good condition as he had received it. I wondered whether he was taking on this onerous responsibility for what father might have felt was a failure. He agreed there was a sense of fault around, but he blamed himself. He then described getting up early this morning and going outside to find father trying to fix the gutter on a building. He said that *father* never said he'd done his utmost to hand on the farm in at least as good condition as he had received. *Rather, he thought it about his father* and about the farm in general. He's said it to himself *for* his father.

What stands out in this vignette is that, although there is an atmosphere of reproach, there is also a decidedly *internal, reparative* tone. Father is not just standing outside, criticizing his son: He is working to make things better. And this reparative father is also an internal father in his son's mind. He is a helping figure, idealized by his son, despite the competitive father-son relationship, and valuing his son. Mr Harris identified his actual father with an ideal, making father an ego-ideal; more than that: He recognized his ego-ideal as, in part, his identification. For all the paternal scrutiny that dominated his experience of father, he also embraced a generous father-ego-ideal that nourished him, his generosity and his reparative urges (I have encountered such an internal parental object in other patents as well).

In his providing for everyone, Mr Harris' construction of an ego-ideal fits Diamond's account of the son's paternal genital ego-ideal (2021, 91–99). His phantasy-world, however, was also decidedly seminal: In his wish to plant seeds that grew, rather than overflow with milk; in his anxiety that it would not succeed; and in his being a link in the paternal lineage of pro-creation and reparation. One could say that the farm also operated as a psychic enclave in which he lived his venture into adult parenthood. His endless talking about the farm encapsulated both strivings and retreat. At the same time, the farm was the object of his devotion. It was not (only) an avoidance of his internal world, but a projection of it, in which its internal existence could be experienced in doses of immediacy.

He tried continuously to make a success of one innovation after another, but in his accounts of them, each seemed to fail. A rebuke attributed to his parents rang in his ears. At first, only father seemed to rebuke him, but in one session, the criticisms of both parents, with their unique qualities, came out. Father would say that he'd always done it wrong; mother would say things never seem to work out for him. Father seemed to emphasize his getting things wrong; mother to anticipate it. Father's voice was crisp and aimed to obstruct his son's plans; mother's was sympathetic, redolent with her deep understanding of her son's nature, what he had been like from the beginning. Father's voice was clearly separate from his voice, aimed at him; mother's seemed to be more interior, more akin to his sense of himself, embedding a profound mutual identification that also found expression in his tying his moods to what he 'observed' in his wife.

His mood, which fluctuated, sometimes abruptly, from optimism to desolation, was not just tied to his wife's: He 'found' his mood in her. Returning home, he would anxiously approach her, alert to evidence that she was depressed. He would also anxiously approach his mother, expecting her to disregard his hope to be close to her. Similarly, he described a moment of startle when he turned suddenly around to discover his sister smack up behind him, as if he had run into himself. He was thrown from enthusiasm to desolation by his mood swings, both in his belief in farming and in his inner life. In his tight bond with mother and wife as an adult, he dwelt as an infant inside mother and felt mother to be inside himself, being part of himself, in what Britton (1994, (1214)) calls 'attributive projective identification'. It seemed consistent with a maternal confusion, insufficiently mitigated by paternal identification, in which his wife, mother and sister seemed to be well-off financially, while both he and his father seemed to be impoverished.

There was also a reparative dimension to his maternal identification, shrouded in mystery, I think because of an underlying oedipal conflict. The conflict involved a male relative. He often mentioned, as the cause of estrangement from this relative, a lawsuit for a substantial amount of money, which he was pursuing on behalf of his mother. The nature and size of the lawsuit only gradually came clear over a prolonged period as did his feeling that he could not fully recompense his mother (in addition, his mother held him accountable for debts to her). Similarly, an air of mystery surrounded the size of the family business. Although the farm seemed always at risk, the family seemed well-off and an esteemed part of the community. He, seemed, however, not to benefit from it. Even more, he sustained the family at his cost. He also seemed vulnerable to feeling impoverished by other, apparently minor losses.

He began a session in the second year of our work, saying he was grieving a bit, giving the impression both of an important, unguarded revelation to share with me, and of marginalizing it. He had a tooth extracted and he missed it. It was a molar. He would never see it again. It was part of him for 49 years.[10] He never said good-bye. Losing a tooth seemed to be part of a general sense of deterioration: His painful shoulder, his chest infection; five years later, he came back to the extraction as the loss of part of himself. He found his mother going through his diary. She asked about an entry: Who was Dr. C., rendering it in a critical, surprised way (his chiropractor, treating his shoulder). He told her it was none of her business; she should get out. Mother retreated after this, no doubt worrying, but he thought, also ridiculing him.

There followed a 'funny' period, with word play that, in my perplexity, I asked him to explain. He replied that it was a game he and a friend played as children. I played a hunch that it was a communication, and said that the game might have been humorous, but that he also might have been wanting to know whether I was aware of his feeling vulnerable – precarious – as he had said previously. It all goes back to being nine or ten when he went to boarding school, he said. As a ten-year-old, too much was expected of him. He was only a boy. He has always thought eight to ten were the happiest of his life. Maybe they weren't. Pause. Maybe he was eleven. He said he had an operation when he was eleven; one of his testicles had not descended, and they repaired it. They took out his appendix at the same time. *It* had been *grumbling*, so perhaps *he had not been so happy*. After the operation, he tore open all the stitches. Then he couldn't go back to the football team. He couldn't see why. He'd been first rank. He thought he was better and playing just as well, but they wouldn't let him.

'Because of the operation?' I asked. 'Yes.' He remembered lying in the bath when his parents must have chosen the moment to tell him (about his undescended testicle). His mother asked whether he'd noticed he had only one testicle. No, he hadn't. He guessed he could have felt that his scrotal sac was empty on one side, but he hadn't – for ten years. If he had said that at school, he would have been ridiculed. He said it in the present tense. I pointed out his saying it in the present, as if he could feel ridiculed now, sharing personal feelings with me. He took it up and spoke of feeling responsible for others. At 49 years old, he was seen as capable of shouldering his responsibilities, but often he did not feel capable, and that seemed ridiculous. He often did not feel manly enough or strong enough. He muddled through school with a stiff upper lip. Replying to his wife's asking whether he ever cried, he said he was sure he could, and did at school, but then stopped because he was ridiculed.

Note the flow of associations. Mr Harris spoke of his deep identification with mother, wife and sister and of a sense of impoverishment, but also of his capacity to take on a male relative on behalf of his mother. It sounds like a perfectly normal oedipal configuration. We then hear of his tooth extraction, which narrows down the loss to a part of himself, the loss of which he mourned. Even without Freud's association of tooth-castration with seminal loss, we can see the drift of his concern from the tooth-phallus to his feeling vulnerable, to his testicles and to feeling he was not capable. His feeling incapable of adequate reparation to mother, his feeling inadequate in general, had a clearly generative, not a phallic, root.

Two months after this session, he recounted delivering a box of organic vegetables to a woman, who asked for an additional box, making an unwelcome demand on him. 'I'll get my kids to do that,' he said. Afterwards, he felt self-critical. He thought that maybe she had no children and might not have been able to have children. By saying 'kids', maybe he had been taunting her, as if, with his kids and organic farm vegetables – his produce – he had taken from her what she now didn't have. He was anxious that he had been triumphal as fertile man. I think his self-criticism is complex. Perhaps he was priding himself on a phallic co-opting of female productivity (*He* had produced children). Perhaps he was also giving the fruit of his body, in a phantasy of reparative identification with her wish to be fruitful (another box). Perhaps he was defending himself against retaliation for triumph, by reassuring himself that he had plenty more (apples, children, semen).[11]

A phallic superiority now replaced the depressive feeling of adequacy, but quickly evaporated, as feeling inadequate and depleted found a place. He went on to deciding to take off the afternoon to watch his son play rugby, in which he was thwarted, caught up in lots of jobs. He had checked on his farm manager, to satisfy himself that the manager had ploughed enough field. Then his tractor ran out of petrol. Then he nearly ran out of petrol on his motorbike as he went to collect petrol for the tractor. He seemed unable just to be happy. He said he was 'short ... short tempered'. I drew attention to his preoccupation with being short when he moved from primary to secondary school (being short was a recurrent theme). He sent his boys to the same schools, and they were doing well. He was amazed at this turn in the session.

He began the following session saying how happy and good he had felt after the previous session; how surprised he was at all that had followed my taking up 'short' with him. He had told his wife about it and had gone to bed happy. But next morning he began to feel child-like and timid, and it was getting worse. I remained silent; he said he felt 'on the edge'; he puzzled over how well he felt leaving the session, now coming back with a big struggle.

Over the next few minutes, I offered an interpretation around the theme of his having taken something big from me, which I took back, leaving him small again. He replied to the effect that he was trying to understand what I was saying. I interpreted that he felt made small by me, as if I were taking back his feeling he was the big man, happy with his wife, leaving me as the child. Various clarifications followed, including my linking his being big with knowing how to plough a field; that he was knowing in sexual matters, with a big penis, but that he seemed to feel that he had taken these ideas from me. The emphasis again was phallic.

He said I had made him wonder if he had sexual hang-ups as well as [knowing how to] plough fields. He then told me (again) about the operation when he was eleven for an undescended testicle. They stitched it to his leg to keep it descended, but he had torn it loose a couple of times in careless play. They also removed his appendix at the same time, though it was unnecessary (he had complained to his mother about stomach pains, but he was just unhappy). He always thought he could not have children. Before they married, he and his future wife, living together, rarely took precautions and she did not fall pregnant until three months before they married. Notice the drift back to seminal capacity and the legitimizing of pregnancy by marriage.

I continued with the interpretative line that there seemed to be a competition between us to be big and father-like, with associations to father's continuous presence, judging his plans. His wife (as oedipal mother?) thought father was an intelligent man. I, apparently as father, left him feeling small, but he brought back 'big' problems (which would challenge my 'big' interpretations). He said he followed bits of what I said but did not understand it all together. More followed on father's intelligence and qualifications and his own. His father's school had said he – father – would not achieve a qualification, and he didn't; his – son's – school now said the same to him, but he did (oedipal triumph). He continued in this vein, as if unpersuaded by his qualifications, despite his greater school achievement (oedipal submission), and it reminded me of his doubts that he could ever have children. I pointed out his doubts, uncorrected by the evidence (provided by his three healthy children), which I connected with the presence of his father in his mind, for which I stood (I act as a reassuring father).

'Big(ger)/small(er)' was a recurrent theme for Mr Harris. Typically, one thinks of measures of size as measures of grandiosity and power; as a narcissistic feature of a borderline/schizoid personality; as phallic narcissism. Rey (1979, 8–9) sums it up concisely. Such personalities find it difficult to maintain warm relationships. They overly identify with their objects and hence lose their identity, including a 'firm sense of maleness and femaleness'. They

> accuse society and others for their ills and are easily persecuted. This may be associated with grandiose ideas about themselves. In fact, their feelings are dominated by phantasies of relative smallness and bigness [and they suffer] a sense of futility ... which is characteristic of them... reflected ... in [a] special kind of depression ... , a form of depersonalized depression, that is, boredom, uselessness, lack of interest, with a marked deadening of the pain aspect of true depression.

But Mr Harris' associations to big and small led in a different direction. These sessions show Mr Harris' organic, fertile aspiration. They show that his confidence in his fertility could easily be shaken, leaving him desolate, dashed by mother's intrusion into his interior with her 'unnecessary' operations and by father with his 'bigger' qualifications. But his mood was already depressive in a Kleinian sense – reparative – not depressed. What appears as phallic was a reconstruction of seminal potency and the uncertainty that surrounded it, despite the confirmation bestowed on it by external reality. His 'special kind of depression' was not futility and boredom, but desolation and an intense urge to make life better. Projected into the farm, it was to work hard to plant and nourish seeds, to enhance fertility and to add it to the paternal lineage. His anxiety turned on his distinctly masculine – seminal – potency, lodged in his testicles, but overlain with a phallic defence. It supports the idea that his oedipal insecurities, rivalries and anxieties were seminal and that the phallic aspects were a defence against a dread of seminal catastrophe.

In a session just after a break, he said he had had two dreams, one on the night of the final session before the break, and another recently. He said nothing about these dreams, however. The session was, instead, dominated by his shyness at feeling short, rekindled by recently meeting a short man at a party who was gregarious. He liked him but was also sceptical: Maybe the man was gregarious in order not to lapse into retreating, as he did. I should add that Mr Harris did not strike me as a short man, rather as of average hight, sturdy and fit.

At the start of the next session, I opened the door to his broad smile and friendly greeting, which seemed a bit exaggerated. He began enthusiastically, saying that his uncertainty about coming back to his sessions yesterday had vanished. He was very enthusiastic, really looking forward to them, wanting to continue with yesterday's theme, his shortness. He was bothered by it when he was younger. He was surprised he hadn't told me before how much it bothered him [he had told me a long time ago, reported in the previous vignette], to the point that he had wanted to go to the doctor to see if some kind of hormone injection might help him grow. When he was young, he worried he would be teased. He was no longer bothered by it, but now worried whether his children were worried. He referred to the man he met at a party, who put himself forward, maybe in order not to feel bothered by being short. He thought maybe he shrank away from social situations, even though he had no reason to think that anyone would tease him for being short. He acted as his mother did. He, like she, always wanted to be accepted by everyone. He fell silent and stayed silent for a long time. I thought silently that maybe he felt he was short on things to say. Eventually, I said that, while I gave no indication of being critical of him, perhaps he felt that I was critical anyway, and he was shrinking back as if I were about to criticise him.

He said he had been thinking he had said all he wanted to say about it. He then told of an incident that had just occurred with a tenant, a very aggressive woman, who was always complaining. She was now complaining about a bill. He didn't think she had a leg to stand on, but he was nonetheless mortified by her dissatisfaction. After going over what happened, he suddenly said he would like to read me the two dreams he had not been able to tell me yesterday, if that would be OK. I said nothing; he got out the dreams and began to read the first dream.

He and his wife had taken a holiday trip to X [he did take such a holiday, and the dream was about that sort of a setting]. He was lying on a sunbed. He described his exact position, though I could not follow it exactly: Something like lying partly across it. His wife was lying on a sunbed next to him. There were other sunbeds in front of them. There was a man standing there, looking smug, rubbing his private parts, but there was nothing there, just a flap of skin. Everything had been cut off and stitched over. He emphasized the man's rubbing himself in this smug way, when all he was rubbing was a flap of skin. He looked away, and when he looked back, there was at least a penis. The man was bending over, sucking, but it wasn't really sucking, it was more like licking an ice cream cone.

With his grievance in mind, I said he seemed to be saying that this man was a right prick but had no balls. I said a month had just ended, during which he had been away, and I thought he might be wondering whether I had the balls to raise with him his long-standing grievance against me for charging when he was away; that he thought I was a prick for doing it, but perhaps he also thought I should have the balls to raise it and we both needed to have the balls to bring his aggression out in the open.

He said that, yes, he did have this long-standing annoyance with me, but had come to think that it was the way I did things. He even thought that it was a good thing, because it was an effective instrument for bringing out his feelings. There followed a lengthy section on his grievance with the aggressive woman and me, including his mortification, which seemed to go beneath the aggression to his feeling intimately injured.

I pointed out that having balls means to be able to persist but also to be fertile; that the man in the dream was a prick but couldn't use it in a generative way because he had no balls. I thought he was saying we needed balls both to deal with his concern that he would wreck our doing good work.

He began the next session in an aggrieved state. Unlike yesterday, when he was beaming and full of enthusiasm, today he was subdued as he entered. He began by saying there was something from what I said yesterday that was on his mind. He was trying to recollect it – something about getting anger into the open – and pretty quickly got to saying that it was connected with my billing him for the sessions he missed. He said that he expected it and that it was my arrangement and if he wanted to continue, he had to accept it.

I sensed a discordance between his acceptance and what sounded like a rejection. I said the way he spoke reminded me of his exchange with his tenant, who maintained she was right and nothing he could do would change her view, and that he had felt mortified. Perhaps he felt that my terms humiliated him, and maybe that is how we might understand his focusing on shortness recently. It wasn't whether he was tall or short, but short meant humiliated. He agreed that it could be so.

I reminded him of how he had, yesterday, wanted me urgently to hear his dream, so perhaps we needed to look at it again. The man had no balls; a penis, but no balls, and he was using his penis like an ice cream cone. He seemed pleased with himself, but others saw him as having no balls and, licking an ice cream cone, saw him as like a child.

He seemed now to engage. He filled out the dream. He said that the man acted like Lord X, a very important person, but others looked on with disdain. Also, his penis was very large, but he had no balls. So, I said, he thinks he's big, but actually he is infantile. Big penis, but he doesn't use it like an adult, instead, like a child. You and your wife are next to each other on sun beds, sunny beds, I said, implying a parental couple.

'That's a new perspective,' he said.

I continued. 'The no balls is interesting. Having balls means ... ' He filled in for me, 'stalwart,' he said. 'Yes, stalwart,' I said, 'persisting, but there is another dimension. Balls are generative. The big penis without balls is not; there is no change, nothing new, stuck, no baby. Perhaps you are saying that you are concerned that you cannot change, that our work will not produce any change.' The session ended soon after. The dream depicts castration in the proper sense of the word – cutting off the testicles with consequent infertility, and the illusory nature of phallic castration as a defence.

Conclusion

The fact that Mr Harris was a farmer provided an opportunity for seminal anxiety to find a route into expression in his ordinary working life. His love of the soil and his lineage and his reparative drive could come together in his struggle to improve the farm and secure its organic health. For a farmer, planting seeds and nourishing growth was routine. Despite the vivid references to his physical and psychological 'organic' health, he rarely spoke directly about an anxiety that *his* fertility might be damaged, though he clearly referred to it. The obstructions to fertility and the anxieties attendant upon them were mainly lodged in the farm, but they put fertility squarely in mind. And though farming offered Mr Harris a route by which seminal anxiety could surface, I think we should in general approach our understanding of male oedipal anxiety and phallic defence as rooted in seminal anxiety and depression as a desolation that stalks the dread of infertility. I agree with Keylor and Apfel (2010, 73), who have proposed that in 'every analysis of a man, there are issues that relate to fertility, whether directly or metaphorically.'

Before leaving the clinical features of seminal anxiety and looking more broadly into the cultural dimension, I want to connect it to reparation more immediately. The penis as an object, embodying the phallus, can be stolen and repatriated. An attack on the creativity of the union of semen and ovum is different. This seminal/conceptive union is not an object and is not a possession. The violation of creativity can impel reparation but repatriation of a stolen object cannot stand in for it. For Melanie Klein, reparation is driven by guilt; guilt, in the depressive position, not persecutory anxiety and not the pathological depression that Freud called melancholia. It is driven by the recognition that one has damaged the good object. It is a psychic reality in which love and hate settle on the same object and that love itself is challenged by hate. That is ambivalence.

Psychoanalysis now embraces the idea that the phallus does not adequately account for either masculine or feminine genitality. The penis is a weapon but also a link (Birksted-Breen 1996; Blass 2010; Diamond 2021). In his genital, generative urge, a man also loves with his penis. Genitality involves assimilating the penis-weapon into using the penis in the expression of love (Diamond speaks of 'modulated phallicism', 100; Meltzer of a 'tool of procreation, 1973, 68). Genitality is ambivalent and, therefore, reparative as well as destructive. I think, however, that male linking is not an attribute of the penis alone, but of the entire male genital, and that it is ultimately rooted in his semen. The male genital is complex, internally and externally, providing an anatomical and physiological base for seminal as well as phallic masculinity. In Mr Harris' case, his family history, his medical history and his occupation as a farmer, together, presented the occasion for expressing seminal anxiety and a phallic defence against it. The farm was a psychic anatomy with oral, anal, phallic and genital zones.

The phallic defence not only repudiates the feminine and the woman as the overt bearer of the feminine: It defends against the dread of seminal incapacity. In this chapter, I have sought to bring the idea of a complex male genital into our thinking. I have aimed to support it with theoretical and clinical evidence. Psychoanalysts have argued that misogyny follows from, and reinforces, a repudiation of the feminine, and that genital masculinity needs to be more open to its feminine, receptive side. I agree but want to supplement this appeal to femininity with an appeal to being more open to its uniquely masculine, seminal dimension. Semen carries love into the woman (Diamond refers to 'seminal linking, 101), but it also carries hate. It is the substance in which ambivalence resides. That is the topic of the next chapter. Embracing genital masculinity is important in clinical theory and practice, and it is also important in mitigating the cultural – in all its dimensions – oppressiveness of phallic masculinity.

Notes

1 Seminal, seminary and seminar share the Latin root for seed, semen (*Samen* in German). Given that only males produce semen, we can speak of this quality as masculine, just as we can speak of receptive, as Steiner (2020) does, as feminine. Male anatomy and physiology ground a symbolic elaboration around the production and delivery of semen, a set of qualities of insemination, including their particular capacity of natality and of reparation, and particular vulnerabilities among men who doubt these capacities. Next to seminality, I would recast 'receptive' as 'conceptive', as a uniquely feminine capacity. In this book, I have argued that the phallic defence defends, not just against feminine vulnerability, but against seminality. I see phallicism as paranoid-schizoid, in Kleinian thinking, and seminality as depressive. Everyone, male and female, and of whatever gender identity, has a seminal capacity as a metaphor for stimulating inciting, evoking, inspiring, seeding, generative, enlivening, new ways of thinking; or of novelty itself, as in Arendt's concept of 'natality'; but only the male, in his masculinity, is seminal at the root.

2 In a personal communication, psychiatrist and analyst, Sebastian Thrul, Senior Psychiatrist and Head of the Gender Clinic at Psychiatrie Baselland, Switzerland, suggests that the

> trend in cosmetic surgery over recent years with so called fillers and lip surgery in women seem a very interesting and contemporary phenomenon to consider in connection to these observations. After the boom of constant engorgement by Viagra, it seems that women have followed the trend of having constantly engorged body parts as well.

3 I am using these concepts loosely to give a sense of the imagery of reconstructed masculinity in the literature. The 'feminine side', for example, is commonly used.

4 In a personal communication, Sebastian Thrul wonders whether

> 'the cut' of circumcision actually serves to underline this displacement. The symbolic 'castration' of cutting the foreskin would be much more threatening if it were closer to the testicles. So, I wonder if circumcision is a compromise formation between symbolizing the threat of castration, but in an area that is in a comfortable enough distance from the site where actual castration would take place.

5 Magical properties, such as we attribute to phallic omnipotence, can also be attributed to semen. Karl Abraham took up the theme of seminal omnipotence in his comparative study of myths and dreams. He sees in creation myths a 'deification of the male power of procreation', really of semen, the nectar of the gods. The intoxicating and exciting de-repressing power of alcohol is identified with semen, which is the 'divine power of creation' (1908, 85; 1909, 63–69). But unlike phallic potency, which can only support omnipotence, including parthenogenic creation of children, semen contributes the masculine part of union, procreation and reparation.

6 The concept of seminal ambivalence is relevant here. It suggests that, in addition to the dread that sperm will give out or fail in the capacity to repair the damaged mother, there is a horror that sperm is itself destructive; that the bringer of life is the bringer of death. It is a phantasy of poisoning by insemination. Phallic aggression can subdue femininity, semen poisons it. Instead of a blunt offensive instrument, semen can be a pollutant, a contaminant. Healthy semen engenders new life and repairs the female genital; distorted semen brings infertility. I focus on the ambivalence of seminality and its reparative quality in the following chapter.

7 A sou'wester looks distinctly like the glans of a penis. Freud (1900 IV, 360–362) reports a dream of a woman, in which a penis appears as a hat.

8 There was an abundance of phallic oedipal conflict in our work, including deadly knife fights, but I will concentrate exclusively on the rich seminal content of his sessions.

9 In the UK, buildings of exceptional historical or architectural significance, of national importance, can be protected as 'listed' buildings.

10 Freud (1900, IV, 387n. 1, 388, 391) thought that a tooth extraction conveyed both castration and emission. He doesn't elaborate on the coincidence, but it does suggest, with Ferenczi's thinking, that the loss of semen in ejaculation is a castration. It combines phallic and seminal castration: Phallic in the removal of an aggressive organ, seminal in the loss accompanying the (generous) emission of semen.

11 In his classic case of obsessional neurosis, Freud (1909, 295), reports the following:

> Quite unexpectedly he told me that one of his testes was undescended, though his potency is very good. In a dream he had met a captain who only had his badge of rank on the right side and one of his three stars was hanging down. He pointed out the analogy with his cousin's operation [his beloved underwent a double ovariectomy].

Potency could only refer to phallic potency with its capacity to defend – with a hint of triumph – against an anxiety of deficient fertility: In himself, in his beloved and in a paternal figure.

In the next chapter, I will argue that anxiety over seminal adequacy is not only concealed by a phallic defence, but undermined in a distinctively depressive countervailing force, a state I call "seminal ambivalence". In seminal ambivalence, good, generative semen is subverted by bad semen.

References

Abraham, K. (1908) The Psychological Relations between Sexuality and Alcoholism. In *Selected Papers on Psycho-Analysis*. London: Hogarth; reprinted London: Karnac, 1979: 80–89.

Abraham, K. (1909). Dreams and Myths: A Study in Race Psychology. NY, New York: *The Journal of Nervous and Mental Disease Publishing Company*, 1913; repr. Kessinger, n.d.

Bird, B. (1957) Feelings of Unreality. *International Journal of Psychoanalysis* 38: 256–265.

Birksted-Breen, D. (1996) Phallus, Penis and Mental Space. *International Journal of Psychoanalysis* 77: 649–657.

Blass, H. (2010) *Wann ist der Mann ein Mann? oder: Männliche Identität zwischen Narzissmus und Objektliebe* [When is the Man a Man? Or: Masculine Identity Between Narcissism and Object-Love]. *Psyche–Zeitschrift für Psychoanalyse* 64(8): 675–699.

Boehm, F. (1931) The History of the Oedipus Complex. *International Journal of Psychoanalysis* 12: 431–451.

Britton, R. (1994) Publication Anxiety: Conflict Between Communication and Affiliation. *International Journal of Psychoanalysis* 75: 1213–1224.

Britton, R. & Steiner, J. (1994) Interpretation: Selected Fact or Overvalued Idea? *International Journal of Psychoanalysis* 75:1069–1078.

Diamond, M. (2021) *Masculinity and its Discontents: The Male Psyche and the Inherent Tensions of Maturing Manhood*. London/NY: Routledge.

Fenichel, O. (1925) Introjection and the Castration Complex. In *The Collected Papers of Otto Fenichel. First Series*, 39–70. NY, New York: W. W. Norton, 1953.

Ferenczi, S. (1924) *Thallassa: A Theory of Genitality*. NY, New York: *Psychoanal. Q.*, 1938; repr. London: Karnac, 1989.

Freud, S. (1900) The Interpretation of Dreams. *The Standard Edition of the Complete Psychological Works of Sigmund Freud* 4 & 5.

Freud, S. (1908) On the Sexual Theories of Children'. *The Standard Edition of the Complete Psychological Works of Sigmund Freud* 9: 205–226.

Freud, S. (1909) Notes Upon a Case of Obsessional Neurosis. *The Standard Edition of the Complete Psychological Works of Sigmund Freud* 10: 153–318.

Freud, S. (1912). On the Universal Tendency to Debasement in the Sphere of Love (Contributions to the Psychology of Love II). *The Standard Edition of the Complete Psychological Works of Sigmund Freud* 11: 177–190.

Freud, S. (1923) The Infantile Genital Organization: An Interpolation Into the Theory of Sexuality. *The Standard Edition of the Complete Psychological Works of Sigmund Freud* 19: 139–145.

Keylor, R. and Apfel, R. (2010) Male Infertility: Integrating an Old Psychoanalytic Story with the Research Literature. *Studies in Gender and Sexuality*, 11(2): 60–77.

Klein, M. (1950). On the Criteria for the Termination of a Psycho-Analysis. In *The writings of Melanie Klein*, vol. 3. London: The Hogarth Press and the Institute of Psycho-Analysis, 1975, 43–47.

Laufer, M. (1976) The Central Masturbation Fantasy, the Final Sexual Organization and Adolescence. *Psychoanalytic Studies of the Child* 31: 297–316.

Meltzer, D. (1973) *Sexual States of Mind.* Strath Tay: Clunie Press.

Rey, H. (1979) The Schizoid Mode of Being. In LeBoit, J. and Capponi, A. (eds) *Advances in the Psychotherapy of the Borderline Patient.* NY: Jason Aronson, 449–484; In *Universals of Psychoanalysis in the Treatment of Psychotic and Borderline States.* London: Free Association Books, 1994, 8–30.

Steiner, J. (1993) *Psychic Retreats: Pathological Organisations in Psychotic, Neurotic and Borderline Patients.* London: Routledge.

Yazmajian, R. (1966) Reactions to Differences Between Prepubertal and Adult Testes and Scrotums. *Psychoanalytic Quarterly* 35: 368–376.

Chapter 8

Incapacity and Ambivalence in Seminal Masculinity

Seminal Anxiety

In the previous chapter, I built on the recognition of an internal male genital as a ground of male, seminal identity. I aimed to show that what I called seminality was tied to the continuation and sustenance of life in material reality through semen, which was also the basis of masculinity in symbolic, psychic reality. The capacity to inseminate is fundamental to masculine identity, regardless of whether an individual man wishes to father a child. In this chapter, I set out the nature and consequences of seminal incapacity for masculine identity. I add unconscious seminal ambivalence to seminal incapacity, as form of primal ambivalence in which semen, in psychic reality, provokes the depressive anxiety of harming the fertility of the mother, harming life itself. The guilt of seminal ambivalence drives either reparation or misogyny.

A leading theme of this book has been that, for all that seminality is fundamental to masculine identity, the stereotype of masculinity remains persistently dominated by an image of the phallic man. He is a big man, shamed if smaller than another man. He is, at least in phantasy, powerful in his physical, mental and economic capacities, and the object of women's thrall. This (self) image sits on top of the seminal man. The ill-repute into which masculinity has fallen is, on the surface, a reaction to phallic masculinity, a reaction to its grandiose self-regarding, narcissistic pleasure in its omnipotent phantasy of being more than big: Being wholly self-reliant, being a lure to women and a well-spring of idealization for others. The magic companion to the phallic narcissist is the penis: An anatomical structure confused with a phantasy of self-enthralment and the enthralment of others. In my view, this focus on phallic masculinity, whether by advocates or critics, is locked in place as a defence against the catastrophe of seminal failure. Phallic anxiety is paranoid-schizoid in Kleinian theory. It carries an anxiety of extinction but can magically recover. Seminal anxiety is depressive. It carries hope but also desolation. Both reach back to the existential instability of formation of the ego in its object world and, nachträglich, assimilate it into higher psychic functioning while retaining traces of existential anxiety.

DOI: 10.4324/9781003455790-12

Castration anxiety, in Freud's account of psychosexual development, is the terror of an attack on the phallic penis. As I argued earlier, castration anxiety would better be located where it always has been located outside the theory of the phallic stage: Loss of the testicles and, therefore, of fertility. Phallic castration anxiety is a terror of narcissistic depletion. It can be replenished by waiting for its regeneration or by depleting an other, in narcissistic competition. Seminal castration anxiety, by contrast, is a dread, a desolation at the loss of the capacity for engendering and sustaining life, which cannot be replenished by waiting or by competition. Seminal desolation is more fundamental than what we normally call depression.

We get a lead to this desolation in Freud's formulation of melancholia, in which the ego is totally – narcissistically – identified with the object, sinking it in a murky hopeless confusion. One of the features of melancholia is ambivalence. It is not the dilemma of loving and hating the same object, faced by a mature ego, urged towards reparation by a mature superego-conscience. It is a primal ambivalence that takes the ego back to the existential turmoil of its formation. We can get a sense of this primal ambivalence and existential turmoil from Freud's (1917) paper, Mourning and Melancholia. In melancholia, the loss of a relationship follows a peculiar route.

> [O]wing to a real slight or disappointment coming from this loved person, the object-relationship was shattered. The result was not the normal one of a withdrawal of the libido from this object and a displacement of it on to a new one, but something different … [T]he free libido was not displaced on to another object; it was withdrawn into the ego. There, however, it was not employed in any unspecified way, but served to establish an "*identification*" of the ego with the abandoned object. Thus the shadow of the object fell upon the ego, and the latter could henceforth be judged by a special agency, as though it were an object, the forsaken object. In this way an object-loss was transformed into an ego-loss and the conflict between the ego and the loved person into a cleavage between the critical agency of the ego and the ego as altered by identification. (249; Freud's emphasis)

Note that Freud refers to the *abandoned* object. Although Freud says that the melancholic directs 'plaints' against the object, then suffers low self-esteem by identification with the demeaned object, he also implies that the ego is itself grievance-ridden and pins it on the object. In addition, the identification is a total, narcissistic identification – a confusion – with the object. The ego in a melancholic state is a regressed ego: An ego thrown back to its nascent state, when it was emerging as an ego from an internal unease of the id, by differentiating and extruding 'not-ego' as the primal object.

The 'special agency' – the precursor of the ego-ideal and superego[1] – looks critically upon this confused ego-object. At the core, an ego totally absorbed into its object, and the object absorbed totally into the ego, is ambivalent: Not the ambivalence of a mature ego in loving and hating the same object, but a primal ambivalence in which existence is at stake. The loss that a mature ego could feel, and the urge for reparation that a mature superego might arouse in this ego, have regressed to an internal, narcissistic system, mired in turmoil and unanchored from reality. The unease cannot be thrown out of the ego, objectified; it is therefore without hope. It suggests an aggrieved identification with the object as a germ of projective identification, a concept not yet developed in 1917, in which the object becomes, in Klein's words, 'the bad self'. But as a total projective identification (such as described by Rosenfeld 1987, 163), the bad self is not hived off, but inside. The narcissistic identification at the root of melancholia is pre-objectal, primal, beneath projective identification.[2] The melancholic ego is a tarnished ego, in a state of primal ambivalence and unease, existentially insecure and desolate.

I connect this primal ambivalence with a specifically masculine depressive anxiety of creating, sustaining life and destroying life. It is what I call seminal ambivalence, which occurs in primal and mature forms. It is primal at the existential level just described; Later, it is conscience-driven, in its guilt and reparative urge. The first ejaculation, with its intimation of procreative capacity and the threat of psychotic terror echo the primal form; later ejaculations in intercourse can actually bring life and reparation and also contamination. Fertile/infertile form a pair. It is life-enhancing/life destroying as seminal ambivalence at a primal level and, *nachträglich*, in genital loving and hating. Keylor and Apfel's (2010) conclusion, that in 'every analysis of a man, there are issues that relate to fertility, whether directly or metaphorically' (73), implies such an elemental place in the male psyche. But we have to look for them, because primal seminal insecurity and desolation, as well as mature guilt and reparation, lie beneath the thrill of triumph and the fear of defeat of phallic narcissism.

Seminal Pollution: Clinical Studies and Popular Culture

Although seminal ambivalence is not covered in the psychoanalytic literature, there are occasional references to seminal failure and clues to ambivalence in relation to it. Perhaps Freud set the trend, not only of concentrating on phallic function, but in hinting at the seminal substratum. In analysing his 'specimen dream', he interpreted his examination of Irma, which included her mouth, in terms of competition among professional men, responsibility for Irma's not getting better and irresponsible medical behaviour in using a dirty syringe for an injection. Anzieu (1986, 140–56) carried the analysis further, interpreting the dirty syringe in seminal terms. What Freud looked into was not her mouth, but her womb and he saw semen and a pregnancy, in the composite figure that included Irma, his wife and his mother and he hinted at the ambivalence of semen = infection.

Typically, however, male sexual ambivalence has been moved away from semen and tied to excretory function. Freud referred to a common confusion, even in adults, between semen and urine (1908, 222, 224). Abraham (1917, 295–6; 1920, 351) brought it closer to semen by identifying a wish to soil the woman by ejaculation, attributing it to confusing semen with urine. Jones (1912) provided extensive evidence from folklore on the confusion of semen and urine. Ferenczi (1924, 29, 37, 64) suggested that, while a procreative component could be separated out, and semen accorded an autonomous psychic value, seminal function derived from urethral and anal roots. He attributed psychogenic aspermia, in which semen was defensively withheld in orgasm, to an avaricious need to withhold it. From its anal-erotic roots, the ejaculating penis borrowed the urge to withhold from the bowel, its ana-tomical, physiological and psychological origin. Seminal function was a mixing – what he called 'amphimixis': (Releasing) urethral- and (withholding) anal libidinal currents.

The confusion of seminal and excretory function is clear in this vignette from the analysis of a young boy, just under five years old, who

talked about chimneys, funnels, etc. which squirted smoke or fumes, sometimes said they would squirt at the therapist. He wanted to put soot from the chimney, and other dirt on [the therapist]. He wanted to put plasticene on her, and chopped lumps of it in her hand. These activities were interpreted as expressions of [his] idea that in intercourse the partners urinate and defaecate on each other. (Anna Freud Centre, Hampstead Index; a more precise citation is not possible)

Shifting attention from anal aggression and phallic masculinity to seminal masculinity brings into observation a different form of aggression: Not the attacking penis of phallic aggression, but seed withheld or seed as polluting or poisoning. Mr F, a businessman, complained of feeling uncreative and often fell into despair as he let his house fall into disrepair and untidiness. In ses-sions, he picked wax from his ears and dirt from under his fingernails, dropping them to the floor. He was fascinated by his anal smells, but also perceived such smells in women, and found them repugnant, and he mas-turbated on the loo after defecation. Although his phantasy life was domi-nated by anality, he did not anally masturbate. He seemed not to merge semen and feeces. Perhaps he confused them, in that both occurred on the toilet, but otherwise, they were separate.

There is abundant evidence associating insemination with poisoning or infection. To the backdrop of insemination by the ear (Jones 1914), we might add Freud's (1897, 273) suggesting an oedipal theme, Hamlet 'suffering the same fate as his father of being poisoned [through the ear] by the same rival'. Taylor (2016, 58; author's italics) presented a patient who had recurrent dreams of snakes, including a dream of a '*small poisonous snake on the side of his ear'*. In a 19th century erotic poem, a woman catches a fish in her net, which transforms into a snake that insinuates its way into her womb. 'I must have venom,' she cries out in ecstasy (Eisler 1914, 191). A character in *A Game at Chess*, by the 17th century playwright, Thomas Middleton, was 'poisoned ... with child' (Taylor 2000, 89). An often-cited, joint anthropological and psychoanalytic study of a semen cult in Papua New Guinea, explores the life-enhancing, masculinizing power of semen (Stoller and Herdt 1982). In a letter to Karl Abraham (7 June 1908, Freud 2002, 44–45) referred to 'the vitalizing effect of semen', but also, in his letter to Ludwig Binswanger (17 May 2009, Freud 2003, 19–22) he referred to pregnancy as a poisoning or infection. Abraham (1908; 1909, 63–9) adduces evidence that the nectar of the gods and intoxicating beverages represented semen. The excretory imagery of Freud's dirty syringe, in his 'specimen dream', suggested a seminal anxiety of both unwanted pregnancy and the equally seminal anxiety of infection (1900, 106–20; Anzieu, 140–56). Hunter (1954, 306) reported a patient saying of his semen, '"Sixteen million sperms per cubic centimetre, and every one malevolent." ... Here was the quintessence of persecution. His sperms contained his impulses. He contained them and they threatened him. As Mrs. Klein would say, his sadistic and cannibalistic desires were expressed by his parts and by his products.'

Other references cover a range of themes to do with semen as excretion, poison, pollution or, by contrast, with its idealization (Bergler 1935; Boehm 1930; Bonaparte 1952, 380; Eisler 1914; Gonzalez 1953; Grosz 1993; Hägglund and Piha 1980; Karpman, 1922; Kestenberg, 1968; Needles 1966). The prevalence of syphilis and gonorrhoea in the late 19th and early 20th centuries meant that insemination carried the threat of infection as well an unwanted pregnancy. Freud's (1909) classic *Notes Upon a Case of Obsessional Neurosis* portrays the agony of ambivalence, in which defending against the undermining of love spreads throughout one's life. He describes a young man's unconscious assaults upon his beloved, which, for me, gives also evidence of seminal ambivalence. His patient was horrified at the obsessive thought that his beloved's anus was chewed into by rats, which nucleated several strands of genital (seminal) love subverted by hateful thoughts. Anal erotism displaced his sexual object from her vagina to an anal sewer. His penis attacked it, but also poisoned it with its rat-filthiness, rendered consciously as a dread of syphilis. He hesitated pursuing marriage with her on account of her sterility, as a result of ovariectomy, but the operation was obscured in obsessional doubt, suggesting unconscious ambivalence.

Perhaps HIV and Herpes would be more recent versions.[3] Perhaps it also builds on an oral root. Freud (1933, 122) touches on frustration inciting ambivalence: 'The fear of being poisoned is also probably connected with the withdrawal of the breast. Poison is nourishment that makes one ill.'

Ambivalence carried in semen defiles the object, but also puts the subject at risk. Freud's patient, Wolf Man, classified his gonorrhoea as castration

(Freud 1918, 100; on a dream of a syringe as a penis for injecting a castrating substance, see Abraham 1920, 349). Ferenczi (1924, 29) thought that an emission could create an identification with the female through the semen, so that the ejaculation became a self-castration. Bergler (1935; 1937) hypothesized that, in intercourse, there was a seminal ambivalence between the wish to identify with, and the dread of dissolving into, the (maternal) other. A man who suffers a traumatic, intruding flow of milk as a baby can reverse, in phantasy, his infantile helpless passivity by identifying his seminal emission with mother's feeding, and inhibiting the feeding by retaining semen. In this case, semen can also be used for a sadistic attack, for dirtying the woman inside, and also for defending against castration anxiety by projecting helplessness into the woman. Kestenberg (1968, 498) described such a case, including an improvement in sperm count with analysis (also Sinha 1954).

In her concept of the archaic matrix of the Oedipus complex, Chasseguet-Smirgel (1986) speaks of the wish to eliminate the contents of the mother's body, rendering her womb smooth, devoid of any trace of father and siblings. The son can then merge into an archaic womb in a 'before' state, available just to him. She presents a dream of a male patient – one of several in support of her thesis – which shows the wish to render analyst/mother barren. It is a dream of destruction of the mother's womb by pollution. I connect the pollutant with semen because semen is the substance injected into the female reproductive system, albeit rarely spoken about explicitly. Seminal pollution is part of the ambivalence of seminality: It is fertile and life-giving *and* contaminating and life-destroying.[4] In the dream, the pollutant is grass. It is green and alive *and* it pollutes.

> I am mowing a lawn. I throw the grass into a river. This grass pollutes the waters in such a way that it destroys the fauna and the flora forever. Then I see a mass of jelly. Maybe a small calf.

Chasseguet-Smirgel follows up the dream.

> The patient's desire to make his mother sterile is then interpreted in order to show the analysand that this desire endangered the analytical process itself. The patient entirely agrees with this interpretation. He goes on about the calf as a fetus and his mother's miscarriage. Then he associates with the excitation he feels when he imagines intercourse with a woman with shaven genitals [like the genitals of little girls]. To mow the lawn means therefore to make the maternal genitals smooth and to deprive her of her secondary sexual characteristics, which are proof of her capacity to contain children and to give birth. (78)

Segal (1983, 271) presented a case in which ejaculation projected need, greed, aggression and envy, by implanting little homunculi that would torture women forever with a need of the man. Her patient seemed caught in seminal ambivalence. For him, a man '… needed to project into a woman a needy, greedy, aggressive and envious infant part of himself. He had a phantasy that in ejaculating, he was putting into women little homunculi that would possess them and he was implanting a need for [him] that would torture them forever'. The myriad little people in semen suggests an association between semen and fine particles, but Segal leaves open whether it is a seminal or an oral phantasy. 'One phantasy underlying his relationship to women is that he had removed a nipple from the breast; his penis has become the nipple; the woman's breast with the hole gets filled with his projected hunger and desires and becomes a vagina'.

Taylor (2016) reviews the concept of castration anxiety, showing its continuing importance in clinical work. He thinks of the anxiety of an attack on the genital organs as a metaphor for diminished self-esteem, in which men feel less masculine and more feminine. Their sense of masculine potency is expressed in castration anxiety, demonstrated in three vivid cases in which psychodynamic therapy led to substantial improvement. In this case and others to follow, I draw a conclusion from clinical cases that were not the authors' aims or interpretations. In my view, such unintended, contrasting versions sharpen the definition of our concepts and the robustness of evidence.

In two of the cases, a dominating, even brutal, father undermined the son's self-esteem. In the third case, the harsh critic who undermined the son's self-esteem was more linked to a high-achieving, critical mother, who also favoured his older brother, and who also suffered severe depression. Father was a gentle man who did not protect him, the younger brother, from mother. Although he shared with the other cases a (castration) anxiety of aggression and conflict with men, he also suffered a strong depressive streak. He thought circumcision would help by 'cleansing him of toxins'. He had recurrent thoughts of escaping to a peaceful, tropical island, followed by 'recurrent dreams of being at a desolate lakeside setting' (60), which Taylor connected with his depressed mother and which, he hoped, would remove this feeling. Later, the lakes in the dreams reminded him of the tiles on the hospital floor where he, at age three, visited his depressed mother, who was convalescing from surgery. He thought of his penis as a site of toxicity that could damage his mother. In my view, this case starkly stands out from the others in its depressive, seminal, as opposed to phallic, character. It makes the case by contrast with them, as if – perhaps unconsciously – the group of three cases could serve to test the hypothesis of a phallic defence against seminal anxiety.

In terms of unconscious phantasy, one might focus on the aim of controlling mother from the inside by projective identification, as well as on its stage-specifics attacks on her, and I would add the bad, poisonous quality of semen to Klein's (1946, 8) formulation of pregenital attack on the mother, in which the 'phantasied onslaughts on the mother follow two main lines: One is the predominantly oral impulse to suck dry, bite up, scoop out and rob the mother's body of its good contents ... The other line of attack derives from the anal and urethral impulses and implies expelling dangerous substances (excrements) out of the self and into the mother.'

Although – as with Chasseguet-Smirgel and Taylor – it was not his aim, Antonino Ferro (2012) has provided the most vivid evidence of seminal ambivalence. His clinical material is even more compelling because he used it to demonstrate the importance of fertility, not of semen but of the relationship between analyst and patient, in which emotional aliveness moves the analysis further, even overcoming an impasse. One of his patients was a man who inhibited his thinking to such an extent that he could 'only express positive and submissive emotions' [not, consciously, ambivalence] (261). He had been a violent man, who inhibited his thinking to restrain its violence.

As it happened, his patient also suffered diminished fertility because some of his sperm were defective – had 'monstrosities in the head' (262) – and an attempt at *in vitro* fertilization with his filtered sperm failed. Union of sperm and egg occurred, but the embryo did not survive. His worry about his monstrous sperm and the course of treatment were, for Ferro, occasions to reflect on infertility in the analytic relationship and to concentrate on moments of fertility engendered by the analyst's reverie (his conceptiveness?).

I recognize Ferro's formulation of impasse as an infertility in the analytic relationship and moving forward in moments of fertility in my clinical work, but my emphasis in this chapter is on a primary ambivalence, experienced in the uniquely male, seminal function. In particular, I am interested in the possibility that his patient might have felt his infertility as a desolation lodged deep within him, in his very capacity to engender and sustain life. He was 'terrified by what was in his head, in his interior world' (262), and in the heads of his sperm. An anxiety attending his aggression inhibited his thinking, the amelioration of which was attached to the filtering his sperm. It was an anxiety at the idea that ambivalence is a fact of life, in which monstrosity cannot be filtered out from love and eliminated.

Ferro's patient, a man in his third year of analysis, brought a 'frustrating problem of burning importance' (261), which could either erupt into a violent attack or bring him into a fertile emotional relationship. He learned that he could not have a child because his wife had '*closed tubes* ... and that he had testicular calcifications [and] that 10 percent of his spermatozoa are good and the rest have "monstrosities in the head"' (261; Ferro's emphasis). Addressing the question of what makes a session creative, Ferro draws attention to untransformed emotion, the 'beta elements [that] infiltrate and elude the process of alphabetization' (257–258), 'those quanta of never-transformed protoemotions of sensoriality' ... which – if not sufficiently transformed – give rise to more serious pathologies' (258). Ferro thinks of the sperm as 'potentialities of the self, which [his patient] fears will be dangerous if they develop and come out into the open' (261). He 'did not know whether the analysis would be fertile or whether he was, in fact, capable solely of producing monstrous emotions (or protoemotional states)' (262). Or monstrous sperm.

Violence was near the surface. The patient relates having sent a message to his father, about his brother, *Antonio* (Ferro's emphasis; his first name is Antonino), warning that, if Antonio again touches his things, he will 'smash his face against the wall and smear it with his brains'. Ferro says he hopes that 'Antonio's auditory tubes are sufficiently "open" to take in [his] intense emotions' (263), thus acknowledging the patient's fury and fear: That his wife's fallopian tubes were closed to his monstrous sperm, that they might become a couple made infertile by his aggression, and that this fear was entering the transference in a fury that Ferro's ears were closed to him.

Ferro's patient was sent into the toilet to ejaculate – a 'sordid' place – with his 'little jar', so that they could try to filter out good sperm from bad sperm. He moved on to speak of a man, called Mr Jar, who had been expelled from a community because of his violence. He reported more on this violent man and on his own wishing his father dead, as well as a dream in which doctors accused him of murder. There is, in other words, a lot of murderous aggression, needing to be filtered out. Later, after saying that he 'jumped for joy' at hearing that his sister-in-law was pregnant, he reported that, in the case of the artificial insemination of his wife with his filtered sperm, the 'spermatozoon and the egg-cell had fused, but then the embryo had not developed' (265). The analysis stood at a threshold of a successful implantation and development, in which its fertility was subject to a sterilizing, seminal attack.

While the material suggests a confusion of sperm with anal and urethral excretions, which are dangerous (note his revulsion at the implied closeness of sperm to excreta), it also signifies the destructive power of his sperm, as he and the doctors sought to separate good sperm from bad sperm with monstrous heads. The ambivalence that threatens the good object at the oral and anal levels can also endanger it at the genital level. It is conveyed *in* the semen, not only in the confusion of semen with feces, urine or milk.

The 'big' (violent) patient threatened to smash the head of the little analyst/brother, thereby destroying the monstrous heads of his bad sperm in the analyst by projective identification. His big man violence threatened against the little analyst/brother acts as a phallic defence against the desolation of infertility. It is backed up by 'Mr Jar', containing his ejaculate, whose phallic violence sits very close to his seminal capacity, able to bolster a phallic replacement of seminal desolation, should he be diagnosed as infertile. The pair, big/little, is a phallic structure that can pass back and forth between phallic competitors, as domination/submission on a quantitative scale, which conceals the qualitative difference between fertile and infertile.

What stands out for me is the expression of ambivalence, concretely, in the dual nature of sperm: Good and bad, fertilizing and anti-fertilizing, creative and monstrous, healthy and toxic. The sperm penetrates the ovum, and inside the ovum an embryo either develops or its development is destroyed. Fear of violence is also fear of poisonous sperm. One could say that sperm can symbolize a weapon. As a symbolic equation (Segal 1957), to ejaculate is literally to attack the inside of the mother. At the same time, the patient's threat to his brother/analyst is a phallic defence: He is bigger than the analyst/ brother and the aggression of his superior size defends against the depressive desolation left by sperm that undermines life.

I suggest that the phallic defence, for all its dominating intent – perhaps, in its dominating intent – also aims to create a good self by pressing the bad self into the object and annihilating it there, in a parthenogenic version of conception, which overcomes the desolation depressive of seminal ambivalence. Ferro's patient aimed to dominate people who, he thought, did not accept (fertile intercourse with) him. They included his wife, whose fallopian tubes were closed to him, and his analyst, whose ear canals were closed to him. He aimed to force them to receive him. He aimed to dominate his monstrous sperm and behaviour by their submission. He wanted to be good by a projective identification that put the bad into an object.

Oedipal triumph and injury, which we are accustomed to observing and interpreting, can, therefore, also be seen as phallic residues that carry the child's illusion of seminal capacity and incapacity. Keylor and Apfel (2010, 69-70) report on a man who came for treatment for 'irrational and groundless fears that he would be fired' and that 'his [thriving] son would be physically harmed … ' Sensitive and musical, Mr C. was unlike his working class father, and he also 'shouldered the job of keeping his mother entertained in order to rescue her from her disappointment that his father's income had not moved the family as she had hoped into a higher social class … '. Unprepared, he underwent surgery for an undescended testicle when he was six. Recovery was painful and difficult, with repeated inspection and manipulation of his genital. He also had a tonsillectomy in latency, during which the surgeon had accidentally cut his tongue. He was, again, unprepared for the operation and aftermath.

Mr C. put these traumata aside in an otherwise successful, healthy and happy life, which was punctuated by discovering, in his mid-thirties, that he and his wife could not conceive.

A recommendation was made for him to undergo repair of a varicocele[5]… He was unpleasantly surprised and quite anxious about the painfulness of the recovery period but the pregnancy that ensued once again pushed feelings about defect and damage to his body into the background. As his son grew, Mr. C.'s awareness of pride in him and love for him made Mr. C. feel increasingly vulnerable. He began to imagine that something or someone would come out of the blue and take from him the "best thing I've ever done." In addition, his wife's growing complaints that they didn't have enough income to live the way she felt they should made him feel guilty and fearful of being fired by the boss he struggled to please. Depressed and anxious, Mr. C. sought help for these bewildering fears. When an economic downturn resulted in his becoming unemployed, Mr. C. felt deeply depressed and deserving of his wife's rejection and contempt. (70)

Mr C feared he might physically harm his son, who was so precious to him. He seemed to be caught in a bind. As his mother's saviour, he would, in phantasy, replace his father in an oedipal triumph. But his wife's complaint about him was the same as his mother's complaint about his father. That would reinforce an identification with an oedipally defeated father. So he was confused: Oedipally triumphant (replacing father in mother's eyes) and oedipally defeated son (injured, lost, fired by boss); oedipally triumphant (in his unconscious wish to injure son) and oedipally defeated (as the replaced) father.

The underlying, seminal current, is clear. His wife's pregnancy temporarily reassured Mr C that his body had not been damaged. Oedipal anxieties followed as his son grew up and pushed his seminal anxieties into the background. But the medical interventions were attacks, in phantasy, on his testicles, not on his penis. What stands out, therefore, is that the wounded genital is not the phallic genital of oedipal triumph and defeat, but a seminal genital. He suffered an undescended testicle, a testicular operation, infertility and a second testicular operation. The oedipal scenario, brought to a head by losing his job, was, therefore, an instantiation, not of phallic castration anxiety, but of seminal castration anxiety. The harm that he might inflict on his son might be seen as a paternal oedipal triumph, in identification with a retaliatory father; or defeat, in his identification with the father who did not satisfy mother's wish for upward social mobility. It would not, however, be a consequence of phallic triumph – not phallic castration, which would be like, say, a broken limb, amputation or some other visible injury – but rather, it would be a mysterious, possibly internal – possibly seminal – injury, just as his own fear, as a son, was of seminal injury.[6]

Keylor and Apfel's patient suffered from a vulnerable testicle linked to oedipal anxiety; Ferro's patient suffered from anxiety connected to 'bad' sperm, which poisoned any possible conception. Their infertility and medical procedures to overcome it unmasked aggressiveness that jeopardized loving feelings and a hoped-for conception. Their conditions point to ambivalence expressed through insemination. In a case reported by Winship (2009), seminal ambivalence is managed by splitting.

Winship's patient suffered severe depression and a breakdown in his early 20s. Years later, he married and fathered a daughter, followed by a son. Shortly after his son was born, he was diagnosed with testicular cancer, which was successfully treated by removing the 'bad' testicle. 'The experience of having cancer treatment, and recovering, gave him a new lease of life. He felt inspired, believing he had received a spiritual "calling"' (31). He had suffered manic-depressive swings in his past, and they now recurred, with very intense depression. Winship ties the breakdown to an oedipal anxiety, that he had succeeded in fathering another child after the birth of a daughter, while his parents had lost a child after his birth. Dates were significant: He remembered the date of his breakdown precisely. It was the same day and month as the birth of the lost child.

Winship's interpretation is compelling, but another feature of the case stands out for me, and, once again, I take this different conclusion, drawn from the same material, to bolster belief in its robustness. I interpret the post-operative reaction to the removal of a bad testicle, leaving a good testicle intact, to be a radical splitting, in which depressive mourning was avoided to the point of manic defence. Further evidence lies in his feeling elated but tearful in reaction to a letter from his father, giving him information about his lost sister. The therapy began to uncover his unconscious belief that his fertility was both positive and negative: He had children but there was a depressive shadow cast on his procreativity. With the birth of his daughter, 'was it possible that there was some extreme anxiety that could not be managed, that death somehow became lodged in the male receptacles of his family's continuity, that then became manifest with the birth of his son (32)?'[7]

Let us return to Mr Harris, the organic farmer from the previous chapter. In that chapter, I provided extensive evidence of his seminal concerns and anxieties. Seminal concerns are also reparative. The anxiety at damage to the organs and processes of fertility – the ambivalence in seminality – stirs up guilt, and guilt drives reparative urges. The phantasy that one has damaged the good object drives the ego to make it better. Since we are talking about damage to the organs and processes of the generation and sustenance of life, and since they are seminal in the male, we can speak of seminal ambivalence as a primary ambivalence. Ambivalence-driven guilt and consequent repar-ative urges were clear in Mr C, and barely hidden by splitting in Ferro's and Winship's patents.

I will present a vignette from a two-week period in the second year of our work, which directs our attention to his conflicted seminality and its repar-ative dimension. In the background were his mood swings, which could leave him feeling desolate and also elevated to an enthusiastic high. In my view, they expressed, at root, his belief and disbelief in the capacity of his internal genital to generate and preserve life. They were connected to an ambivalence of fertility – a seminal ambivalence – in which he swung between a desolation of damaged and damaging seminality, and a manic – phallic – defence against this seminal desolation.

He began the session with an intense worry about telling me two secrets to which he had referred at the end of the previous session. He had taken drugs in college and he had contracted herpes. At first, he dwelt on the herpes. He told his parents about it but not about the drugs. How desperately anxious he was when, stammering and almost unable to speak, he told the woman, whom for years he had wanted to (and did) marry. Now she might reject him. He continued to rebuke himself as he expected rebuke from others. He seemed unrelieved by telling me his secret and by my interpretations, and he returned to his intense worrying. The herpes still recurred occasionally (as it does). Although he was reassured that it recurred only occasionally, he was not reassured by its seeming to recur more frequently when he was worried, seemingly connected with stress. Bear in mind his close scrutiny of his wife, intent on discerning her mood, in which he experienced his own mood, with which he feared he had infected her.

I commented that he hoped to be treated sympathetically, as he would treat others, but seemed to have a lingering concern that he undermined or devalued whatever or whomever he cared for, and I included his psychotherapy. He said he had a whale of a time at college, with the girls and with drugs. He spoke of specific drugs, then added 'other drugs', which he'd tried once and given up. He then seemed to absorb himself into a stream of speech about being sensible: Just a boy with drugs and a young man with girls. I referred to the 'other drugs': Perhaps he wished me to accept him without rebuke, but, apparently, I might either accept him or rebuke him utterly. I might think, 'Well, these other drugs were not just being a boy having a good time.' He said he did not understand me. I commented that I now faced being the misunderstood child whose behaviour scandalized his parents and potential wife. He said he felt guilty; that he couldn't be sure how his mother would react if she knew all about him.

I think the herpes was a symptom for him of a toxicity in his seminal genitality, not his phallic genitality, and that he could not separate his seminal genitality from his psychic state. He could not, therefore, free it from ambivalence and from the wish that ambivalence did not damage his love object. His worry about his mother's reaction to the whole of him, rather than just to what he might reveal, suggested that the whole of him included good and bad, and that mother might reject the bad, leaving it unmitigated and active. The toxic chemicals of the 'other' – the not necessarily sensible or normal – drugs, and the genital toxicity of herpes, were 'bad', while sensible drugs, boys with girls, and semen, were good, unless contaminated (with herpes or with bad drugs). The greater secrecy about the bad drugs detoxifies the confession of herpes and boys with girls.

The next session (Tuesday) began with his excitement, albeit nervousness. He had felt total wellbeing over the weekend, maybe because of his session, but he also had had a few cigarettes the night before his session.[8] His mood, however, was blunted on Monday morning. Partly, he was irritated with his farm manager, who was away. He would set him straight when he got back. He went to the gym to work it off, with some success, but, returning home, he saw his wife and felt down. He did not blame her but seeing her made him feel down. It's not her; it's him. Also, another woman in the office made him feel irritable.

I wondered whether I was to be added to people who might irritate him. I said he seemed to be trying to identify what made him feel good and what made him feel bad; he'd like to reclaim the good and get rid of the bad. He agreed and went back to his irritation with the farm manager. His criticism was directed both at himself and the farm manager, in that he wanted to tell his manager that he had not managed him very well. He returned to thinking of his wife, of how to make things better, but they didn't know what to do. I interpreted that he thought I did not realise that when he felt down, miserable, he didn't know how he would ever feel good again. He returned to the impact of his wife's mood on him; how he puts up a wall to defend himself.

The intimate tie between his mood and the mood attributed to his wife – both that he believes he infects her with his mood and that she infects him with her mood – was a recurrent theme in our work (with reparative overtones, for example, in feeling guilty at not giving her a hug when she is unhappy). His insight into the dynamics was brought out in his thinking his irritation with his farm manager stemmed, at least in part, from his treatment of his manager: That he saw an unwelcome aspect of himself in his manager. The confusions between self and object are moments of projective identification.

The object created by projective identification attacks the inside of mother's body as a bad object inside her. In Klein's formulation, it becomes the bad self, inside the mother's body. Mother is loved in introjective identification; by projective identification, she is seized, not loved. She is attacked inside by projective identification which forces the bad self into her, making her not only bad, but his bad self, inside her. Mother and baby love by an assimilation of each other, but mother is also sullied by projective identification. They are forms of infiltration, the one benign, the other malign. The sullying of the inside of mother is a contamination.

The language of toxicity conveys the idea of damage as sullying, contaminating, corrupting, infecting. The wild-fire spread of the language of toxicity, including toxic masculinity, suggests an unconscious sense of aptness, as if it has captured a significance that was swirling around in the culture, and brought a sense of coherence to what commentaries in many sectors were getting at. Toxicity, as the expression of ambivalence, occurs at several psychosexual levels. Oral love is countered by oral greed, which attacks the providing mother. Anal and urethral love is also sadistic and attacks the mother, ballistically and by poisoning. What I am adding is the idea that seminal ambivalence, in which the male procreates and sustains life, and repairs the mother's inside, also corrupts her, inside. Semen is both life-giving and life destroying, rendering fertility infertile.

Seminal ambivalence, in my view, reaches back to primal ambivalence, bringing it into the depressive position, with the desolation of a depressive catastrophe. Projective identification, carried in semen, pollutes the fertility that semen also enlivens. Freud's concept of narcissistic identification, which he proposed in 'Mourning and Melancholia', leads us to the idea of regressed, total confusion of self and other and of the primal ambivalence that goes with it.

In the next chapter, I extend the range of seminal ambivalence and the defensive cover of phallic narcissism, to the roots of misogyny. Masculinity, in its unique seminality, aims at enlivening and reparation, driven by its ambivalence. 'Normally' it is adequate. But that is a risky, open-ended route, lacking a sense of achievement through decisive action. The denigration of woman aims, not only to rid the male of his femininity with its receptivity, but also to retrieve omnipotent control of the depressive desolation to which seminal ambivalence has subjected him.

Notes

1   Freud (1914) had already introduced an observing agency, in what he called 'delusions of observation.

2   It isn't clear how projective identification and narcissistic identification sit together. I see narcissistic identification as primary and pre-objectal, on which object-relations a built and as a haven of primary narcissism to which the ego defensively seeks to return. Perhaps it is also akin to Gaddini's psycho-sensory perception, which is not object-related, but a recovery from a disturbance into primary narcissism. Perhaps it also is akin to Bion's 'O' or infinity. Projective identification may be driven by the same mechanism but is object-related and seeks to eliminate ambivalence. Narcissistic identification denotes the failure to elim- inate ambivalence, and the inner pollution that results. This failure reinforces the power of the phallic defence, with its repetition of a reparative aim as well as an omnipotent defence against depressive desolation. Ulrike May (2019) has explained the difference between Abraham, Ferenczi and Freud on the melan- cholic relationship to the object, highlighting the fundamental importance, for Freud, of narcissistic identification rather than oral incorporation.

3   Moss (2012, 82–97) examines the intensification of homophobia that accompanied the outbreak of HIV. The unconscious aim seemingly was to displace outwards a fear of infection, into homosexuals, whose expulsion from heterosexual society would isolate the threat of contamination. '[Harry Stack] Sullivan writes that vague ideas about poisoning in American culture frequently result from autistic thinking about semen. Great importance is attributed to the quality of potency in establishing the symbolic equivalence of poison and semen. Poisons unquestionably are potent agents affecting human welfare. Since semen ejaculated during sexual orgasm is necessary to the creation of human life, it, therefore, possesses the signification of an ultrapowerful substance' (Orbach 1974, 277).

4   Although this interpretation is mine, not intended by Chasseguet-Smirgel, it gains in credibility by its *not* being her intention, as long as the imagery is persuasively clear.

5   A varicocele is a lump in the testicle, formed of a network of enlarged veins around the spermatic cord. It is benign, but sometimes associated with infertility.

6   Friedman (1996) presents a substantial body of clinical evidence, showing the development of symptoms around anxieties centred on loss of the testicles, including the consequences of cryptorchidism. One conclusion he draws is that the

male body image, which has been taken to be unproblematic – based, as has been thought, on the penis – is not so secure. With Bell and Kestenberg, he argues that it is undermined by testicular anxieties, which reinforce phallic masculinity as a defence. This phallic defence leaves these inner anxieties unrecognized and, without an adequate integration of the phallic and testicular dimensions of castration anxiety, only insecurely mitigated.

7   In addition, in personal communications between Winship and me, I offered my interpretation, to which he replied that it was 'worth noting that the idea that his testicular cancer was somehow related to unresolved grief, was his assertion in the first place. Any ideas thereafter where I have referred to trauma related cancer were based on his hunch.' Winship added that, though he 'hadn't thought of it like that, ... the idea of good testicle bad testicle would be entirely consistent with a Kleinian rendering' and that I had not distorted his meaning in my rendering of his account. The psychic consequences of a difference between the two testicles deserve further study. Recall Mr C's varicocele and Mr Harris' undescended testicle, which affected just one testicle. Freud's 'Rat Man' also had an undescended testicle (testicles and their differences are discussed by Bell 1961, 1965).

8   The toxicity of cigarette smoke, and the ambivalence in his persisting to inhale it, had figured frequently in our work, but had remained unconnected with seminal ambivalence.

References

Abraham, K. (1908) The Psychological Relations between Sexuality and Alcoholism. In *Selected Papers on Psycho-Analysis*, 80–89. London: Hogarth; reprinted London: Karnac, 1979.

Abraham, K. (1909) *Dreams and Myths: A Study in Race Psychology*. NY, New York: The Journal of Nervous and Mental Disease Publishing Company, 1913; repr. Kessinger, n.d.

Abraham, K. (1917) Ejaculatio Praecox. In *Selected Papers on Psycho-Analysis.* London: Hogarth Press, 1927, 280–298.

Abraham, K. (1920) Manifestations of the Female Oedipus Complex. In *Selected Papers on Psycho-Analysis*. London: Hogarth Press, 1927, 338–369.

Anzieu, D. (1986) *Freud's Self Analysis*. London: Hogarth and the Institute of Psycho-Analysis.

Bell, A. (1961) Some Observations on the Role of the Scrotal Sac and Testicles. *Journal of the American Psychoanalytic. Association* 9: 261–286.

Bell, A. (1965) The Significance of the Scrotal Sac and Testicles for the Prepuberty Male. *Psychoanalytic. Quarterly* 34: 182–206.

Bergler, E. (1935) Some Special Varieties of Ejaculatory Disturbance Not Hitherto Described. *International Journal of Psychoanalysis* 16: 84–95.

Bergler, E. (1937) Further Observations on the Clinical Picture of 'Psychogenic Oral Aspermia'. *International Journal of Psychoanalysis* 18: 196–234.

Boehm, F. (1930) The Femininity-Complex in Men. *International Journal of Psychoanalysis* 11: 444–469.

Bonaparte, M. (1952) Some Biopsychical Aspects of Sado-Masochism. *International Journal of Psychoanalysis* 33: 373–384.

Chasseguet-Smirgel, J. (1986) The Archaic Matrix of the Oedipus Complex. In *Sexuality and Mind: The Role of the Father and Mother in the Psyche.* NY/London: New York University Press, pp. 74–91.

Eisler, R. (1914) Der Fisch als Sexualsymbol [The fish as a sexual symbol, with an appendix by Otto Rank]. *Imago* 3: 165–196; summarized by Brink, L. (1919) in *Psych. Rev.* 6: 460–64.

Ferenczi, S. (1924) *Thallassa: A Theory of Genitality.* NY, New York: *Psychoanal. Q.,* 1938; repr. London: Karnac, 1989.

Ferro, A. (2012) Creativity in the Consulting Room: Factors of Fertility and Infertility. *Psychoanalytic Inquiry* 32(3): 257–274.

Freud, S. (1897) Letter to Wilhelm Fliess, 15 October. In Masson, J. M. (translated and ed.) *The Complete Letters of Sigmund Freud to Wilhelm Fliess 1887–1904.* Cambridge, MA: Belknap Press, 270–273.

Freud, S. (1908) On the Sexual Theories of Children. *The Standard Edition of the Complete Psychological Works of Sigmund Freud* 9: 205–226.

Freud, S. (1909) Notes Upon a Case of Obsessional Neurosis. *The Standard Edition of the Complete Psychological Works of Sigmund Freud* 10: 153–318.

Freud, S. (1914) On Narcissism: An Introduction. *The Standard Edition of the Complete Psychological Works of Sigmund Freud* 14: 73–105.

Freud, S. (1917) Mourning and Melancholia. *The Standard Edition of the Complete Psychological Works of Sigmund Freud* 14: 237–258.

Freud, S. (1918) From the History of an Infantile Neurosis. *The Standard Edition of the Complete Psychological Works of Sigmund Freud* 17: 1–122.

Freud, S. (1933) New Introductory Lectures on Psycho-Analysis. *The Standard Edition of the Complete Psychological Works of Sigmund Freud* 22: 1–182

Freud, S. (2002) *The Complete Correspondence of Sigmund Freud and Karl Abraham 1907–1925,* Falzeder, E. (ed.). London: Routledge; also *PEPWEB.*

Freud, S. (2003) *The Sigmund Freud-Ludwig Binswanger Correspondence 1908–1938,* Fichtner, G. (ed.) London: Open Gate Press; also *PEPWEB.*

Friedman, R. (1996) The Role of the Testicles in Male Psychological Development. *Journal of the American Psychoanalytical Association* 44: 201–253.

Gonzalez, J. (1953) Screen Memory, Symptom, and Transference. *Revista De Psicoanálisis* 10: 277–307; extracted in *Psychoanalytic Quarterly* 24: 321–2.

Grosz, S. (1993) A Phantasy of Infection. *International Journal of Psychoanalysis* 74: 965–974.

Hägglund, T.-B. and Piha, H. (1980) The Inner Space of the Body Image. *Psychoanalytic Quarterly* 49: 256–283.

Hunter, D. (1954) Object-Relation Changes in the Analysis of a Fetishist. *International Journal of Psychoanalysis* 35: 302–312.

Jones, E. (1912) The Symbolic Significance of Salt in Folklore and Superstition. *Imago* 1: 361–454; repr. in *Psycho-Myth, Psycho-History*, vol. 2. NY: Stonehill, 1974, 22–109.

Jones, E. (1914) The Madonna's Conception Through the Ear. In *Psycho-Myth, Psycho-History: Essays in Applied Psychoanalysis*, New York: Stonehill, 1974, 266–357.

Karpman, B. (1922) On Stuper and Allied states. *Psychoanalytic Review* 9: 337–361.

Kestenberg, J. S. (1968) Outside and Inside: Male and Female. *Journal of the American. Psychoanalytic Association* 16: 457–520.

Keylor, R. and Apfel, R. (2010) Male Infertility: Integrating an Old Psychoanalytic Story with the Research Literature. *Studies in Gender and Sexuality*, 11(2): 60–77.

Klein, M. (1946) Notes on Some Schizoid Mechanisms. In *The Writings of Melanie Klein*, vol. 3. London: The Hogarth Press and the Institute of Psycho-Analysis, 1975, 1–24.

May, U. (2019) In Conversation: Freud, Abraham and Ferenczi on 'Mourning and Melancholia' (1915–1918). *International Journal of Psychoanalysis* 100: 71–98.

Moss, D. (2012) *Thirteen Ways of Looking at a Man: Psychoanalysis and Masculinity.* London/NY: Routledge.

Needles, W. (1966). The Defilement Complex–a Contribution to Psychic Consequences of the Anatomical Distinction Between the Sexes. *Journal of the American Psychoanalytic Association* 14: 700–710.

Orbach, C. E. (1974). Ideas of Contamination in Postoperative Colostomy Patients. *Psychoanalytic Review* 61: 269–282.

Rosenfeld, H. (1987) Projective Identification in Clinical Practice. In *Impasse and Interpretation: Therapeutic and Anti-Therapeutic Factors in the Psychoanalytic Treatment of Psychotic, Borderline and Neurotic Patients.* London: Tavistock, 157–190.

Segal, H. (1957) Notes on Symbol Formation. *International Journal of Psychoanalysis* 38: 391–397.

Segal, H. (1983) Some Clinical Implications of Melanie Klein's Work—Emergence from Narcissism. *International Journal of Psychoanalysis* 64: 269–276.

Sinha, T. (1954) 'A Case of Aspermia'. *Samiksa*, 8 (1); summarized, *International Journal of Psychoanalysis* 36: 434.

Stoller, R. and Herdt, G. (1982) The Development of Masculinity: A Cross-Cultural Contribution. *Journal of the American Psychoanalytic Association* 30: 29–59.

Taylor, Gary (2000) *Castration: An Abbreviated History of Western Manhood.* NY/London: Routledge.

Taylor, Graeme (2016) Varieties of Castration Experience: Relevance to Contemporary Psychoanalysis and Psychodynamic Psychotherapy. *Psychodynamic Psychiatry* 44(1): 39–68.

Winship, G. (2009) The Testes: Theoretical Lacunae and Clinical Imperatives. *British Journal of Psychotherapy* 25: 24–38.

Part V

Masculinity as Repudiation of Femininity

Chapter 9

Misogyny in the Production of Masculinity

Introduction

The work of Melanie Klein has redirected our understanding of masculine ego development from dis-identification from the mother through identification with the father, to a never wholly resolved struggle with the complexity of the femininity complex. Secure masculine development depends heavily on whether a generous relationship between mother and son can mitigate the aggressiveness of this struggle, a generosity transferable to other women in adult relationships. In my view, misogyny is related to an insecure resolution of the femininity phase. The 'production of masculinity' is a response.

Father has a crucial place in the boy's development, as the complement to mother in the parental relationship and as the father in mother's mind. Together, they form a template of generous or withholding, competitive, relationships. But since father also struggled with the femininity complex, he bears the residue of his own immersion in it, as he becomes the source of masculine identification for his son. Overall, masculinity as a lineage perpetuates a core instability, and, as a result, is inclined to react assertively, as if to establish its own identity. At the beginning of the beginning, as a mainly male phantasy, one is present at one's origination; not only present but the fabricator of oneself. In this formulation, I extend Freud's oedipal theory, in which the boy phantasies that he has fathered himself with mother, into saying that he replaces fertile union with production (I think this phantasy also goes a step further than the parthenogenic phantasy of fashioning a child from a body part, such as feces or the penis, and becomes fabrication as activity). One consequence of this active production is competitiveness with women and an imperative to outdo them.

Unequal treatment of women compared to men is so much in the news that it needs no documentation to support the importance of investigating it. 'Unequal' is, however, often more sinister, more hate-driven, for which misogyny is the better descriptor. Misogyny is the active demeaning of women by men, including violence. Misogyny is also found along with other forms of hate. For example, a recent report on corruption the British

DOI: 10.4324/9781003455790-14

Metropolitan Police, by Louise Casey, found, 'Sadly [more than] 20 years after Macpherson[1], there remains a clear racial disparity and systemic bias throughout the system, and within that, there is clear evidence of misogyny' (Dodd 2022, 2). I suggest, in Chapter 10, that misogyny, not only accompanies other forms of hate-driven denigration but could be the template for them.

Each case of male violence towards women can seem especially shocking because women are also the constant objects of love. But if we bear in mind ambivalence, which is central to psychoanalytic thinking, observation and theory, it should be no surprise to find that the most loved can also be the most hated. And as I have developed in previous chapters, there is a primal ambivalence, in which love and hate are not yet relevant. The nascent ego does not love or hate, but urgently holds to the primal object, to the point of being the primal object, opposed by an equal urgency not to be the primal object. The ego exists in the tension between having/being the good object/self and expelling the not good/self. The pairing is an existential necessity and the germ of a later crisis.

In this formulation, the template of love is making the ego good by introjective identification, and the template of hate is extruding the not-good – the bad – by projective identification. From this angle, loving and hating women builds on loving and hating mother, which builds on assimilating good to the ego as the good-mother-self and extruding the bad from the ego as the bad-mother-self. So, the woman-mother is both the source of the good self and the repository for the bad self, in whom not-self is eliminated. For the male, the good self is also identified with masculine, and the bad self is identified with feminine, in a paradox of taking everything from mother and depositing everything that undermines the masculine self in the same mother object. As I argued in Chapter 8, primal ambivalence is not wholly resolved. A kernel of confusion of ego and object leave the ego blemished by the 'bad' self it seeks to expel. Toxic masculinity, as seminal masculinity, reaches back to this primal ambivalence. It identifies the primal object with the feminine. Life-giving- and sustaining semen also poisons the feminine from within.

We will take up misogyny in three steps: First, in the current chapter, we aim to understand misogyny in the dynamics of male development; secondly, in chapter 10, we will extend misogyny into social movements in which (principally white) men dominate in a way that seems intrinsic to masculine identity. Finally, in chapter 11, we will turn to a case study of an incident – the financial crisis of 2008 – in which the masculine nature and vulnerability of a sector of society was unmasked. We will also follow up the hypothesis that misogyny is the template for other hate-relationships.

I speak, not just of misogyny, but of 'the production of masculinity', to highlight a core of identity formation shared by male and female alike, but more unstable for the male. The production of masculinity offers an imagery for the idea of creation as production. Men make themselves, as in the self-made man, with an emphasis on self = making. Misogyny intensifies this meaning, by projective identification, into masculine self-making, often connected with abolishing the feminine.

A Masculine Imperative: Bringing the Feminine into Sight and Under Control

In my view, misogyny is characterized by an imperative to pin down the feminine; that is, to *have* the feminine to the extent of *assimilating* it – to *be* it – while asserting *autonomy* from it. It is an expression of primal ambivalence towards the mother.[2] In misogyny, tolerating both the need for the feminine and the dread of losing the masculine self into the feminine has been compromised. The resolution is to attack the feminine, to have the feminine by possession, and to assert autonomy from it by annihilating it, symbolically or concretely.

Misogyny, in this formulation, is a deviation from normal development in managing the complex consolidation of masculine identity from its origins in the mother (we will examine 'normality in' chapter 12). The masculine ego 'normally' grows in union with the feminine, as a complement to it, based on introjective identification. The misogynistic ego grows by the imperative, continually to negate the feminine, based on narcissistic and projective identification. I have associated 'normal' masculine development with the positive side of seminal masculinity and misogyny with the negative side: Together, as in chapter 8, they constitute a seminal ambivalence. A phallic defence sits on top of ambivalent, seminal masculinity.

Misogyny demeans women, whether emotionally, intellectually or physically. At root, the masculine – an attribute more prominent in men – aims, in misogyny, to eliminate the feminine, an attribute more prominent in women, while stealing its core identity. The aim is extinction, whether or not it ends in murder. It is akin to hatred, rather than to aggression more generally, as a reaction to primal ambivalence. This definition shifts the problem from male and female to what we mean by masculine and feminine, whether in a man or a woman.[3] Although masculinity is a vague concept, and no doubt one could include many attributes associated with maleness within it, it gains in clarity by a particular feature that has a clear tie to misogyny.

I locate misogyny in an extreme projective identification into the feminine. By projective identification, I refer to an imposition upon the interior of the feminine, predominantly as Britton's (1994) attributive projective identification of a particularly virulent sort or Meltzer's (Meltzer et al. 1982) 'intrusive identification'. By the feminine, I refer to receptivity and vulnerability to being a repository for this projective identification. I say that the masculine is more prominent in the male and the feminine in the female because of an alignment between the anatomical distinction between the sexes and these processes. The penis functions by incursion into the female interior, both phallically and seminally, and the latter is uniquely male. While vulnerability to incursion is not uniquely female, receptivity to insemination is uniquely female.

There is, in addition, a deeper layer to the relationship between the masculine projective identification and the feminine repository for projective identification. As I argued in Chapter 3, in primal ambivalence, the yearning to get back inside mother becomes thinkable as it becomes dimensional. It can take the form of claustrophobic terror at being cramped; that, too is dimensional: Inside a box-like space; uncomfortable, even terrifying, but visualizable. Inside and outside contain the very idea of a somewhere. But such an idea of a somewhere in space must be grounded as an extraction from not anywhere. 'Inside', 'outside', 'before' and 'after': They give an external – in the sense of objectified – dimensional reality to what can only be an intimation of shapelessness and timelessness.

In my analysis, the masculinity of projective identification lies in the dissolving into the 'inside' of the uniquely feminine, conceptive inside, to seize and control it. Toxic masculinity goes beyond phallic incursion into a dimensional interior, which is genderless. It is not just a phallic encroachment but the corruption of conceptive union, and misogyny is a waystation. One could say that they are forms of experience, transforming the 'beyond' into the thinkable, but based on degradation.

This view of misogyny takes us back to Chapter 3, where we addressed the idea of a topography of the interior. We will now look at this topography again, with an eye to a suspicion that stalks the craving for representation: That the satisfaction of this craving, and therefore the 'beyond' that it captures for thinking, are being cruelly withheld by the feminine.

Bion (1970, 10) speaks of experience as a realm reduced from infinity or 'O'. It points to an intimation of a realm beyond what language can specify, sometimes in the form of emotion, which is not anywhere. I think he was getting at this idea of a somewhere with his geometry of emotion:

> [I]f the geometer's concept of space derives from an experience of "the place where something was" it is to be returned to illuminate the domain where it is in my experience meaningful to say that "a feeling of depression" is "the place where a breast or other lost object was" and that "space" is "where depression, or some other emotion, used to be".

Internal objects are the places where emotions are, and sensing them might be thought of as recognizing an emotion, [4] for example, anxiety as a sensation in the heart, shame in the face, greed in the mouth, excitement in the bladder, defiance in the bowel. Bion suggests that such cravings for representation drive even abstract intellectual work. The formulations that result transform the infinite beyond into the thinkable. What about union, as in the parental couple, as the core of the ego? The resolution of the Oedipus complex instals – or tolerates – the parental couple, as the oedipal child accepts his parentage in the couple and his dwelling outside it. For Britton (1995), the parental couple is located in a place, in 'the other room'. But it also remains beyond the expressible. Bion (1992, 372–373; Bion's emphasis) says,

> This crisis of "I and You", or "We and They", can indeed be one of very great proportions, partly because there is no language with which it can be expressed. I could try to put it this way: the fundamental reality is "infinity", the unknown, the situation for which there is no language – not even borrowed from the artist or the religious – which gets anywhere near to describing it. Nor can it be assumed that there is a relationship between Smith and Jones, because "Smith and Jones" is a language that is used to describe a physical reality in which there are *physical* boundaries, but not a *mental* reality; we do not know where the mental boundaries are, nor do we know where the impulses commence.

This pre-dimensional world is the world that we posit when trying to grasp the idea of a beginning, of primary narcissism, of 'before'. The intimation of a pre-dimensional world seeks representation and evokes a craving to get to a creative source that is 'before' union. The omnipotent phantasy of self-creation, which Freud (1910, 173) recognized as one form of an oedipal phantasy, is such an attempt, *nachträglich*, to imagine one's origin as an omnipotent act of self-creation. It happens 'inside' the mother, not as a location – that would be a form of bringing it under control in dimensional reality – but by replacing her conceiving and nurturing as the subject's self-creation.

Conception as a sexual union is beyond the power of language to express. Oedipal jealousy captures a part of it, in the emotion-infused idea of putting oneself 'inside' a scene in which only superficial behaviour can be observed. Being inside the scene can then capture a dim feeling memory of infantile fulfilment and perhaps actual memories of a pregnant mother. They are at the edge of expressible meaning, hinting at the inexpressible idea of a beginning (of life). Masculinity aims to resolve the paradox of being at the beginning by transforming it in several stages. Life begins with the feminine, or with union, as the source of it; then woman as the bearer of the feminine; then the location of it in space and time, perhaps inside mother as inside the next room. In this sense, we are speaking of thinking itself, perhaps a masculine dimension of thinking, not of misogyny.

The drive to represent may have a masculine inclination to it, but that is not necessarily misogynist. The idea of beginning in the inside of the mother, in which mother is a space – mother's womb is the place where we begin – supports the phantasy, not only of being there at one's beginning, but of producing oneself there. One can imagine such a space and what might be done there, rendering the mysterious process of conception and embryological development thinkable.

There is a recognizable theme, in which the male's activity in intercourse contributes to, but does not engender, the foetus. Although there may be a residue of the enigma of conception, it is beyond the activity of intercourse. It is kept alive in various ways. Among the Trobiands, for example, child-growing begins in the undifferentiated androgyny of a brother-sister union. The sister's brother calls upon her husband to activate, by intercourse, a separation inside his incestuous relationship to his sister (Malinowski 1916). Often the womb is the just place in which children are put or grow, in a repudiation of femininity. In a clear repudiation of feminine reproductive creativity, the Gimi people of Papua New Guinea, believe that women are pregnant with the penis of their fathers; the husband, in intercourse, cooperates with the father to create the child (I have surveyed these themes in Figlio 2000). Sexual union is allocated its place but remains outside procreation (akin to preformationism in early modern Western culture), which suggests that oedipal anxiety is not centred on the sexual act, but on the hubris of an omnipotent urge to believe in one's power to create life.

One could argue that these myths are the product of an imagination embedded in cultures uninformed by the naturalistic thinking of science. But maybe Western naturalism feeds a delusion of masculine production of children, cloaked in its naturalism, which these cultures have circumscribed and limited. Perhaps masculine aversion to feminine creativity in contemporary society buttresses a masculine identity that otherwise might dissolve into the feminine. Sivi Hustvedt (2019) draws attention to a masculine blindness to a complex, unfolding, internal relationship. Masculine phantasy, which also pervades scientific naturalism, unthinkingly presupposes a primordial child – perhaps a DNA child, implanted in the womb by the combined activity of male and female, where it is sheltered and nourished until it can be placed – potted up, so to speak – in the external world. But that is not the case. Life begins as a blastocyst: A ball of cells from which a foetus comes into being in an intimate, dynamic relationship with mother's womb.

> Pregnancy is not equivalent to a uterus. It is not a uterus that hosts a predestined DNA soul. It is an active process of ongoing metamorphosis in the mature maternal body, which initially accommodates a travelling cell ball and the "cross talk" between it and her cells that may result in implantation in the uterine lining, after which those cells may develop into a fetus and placenta and grow to term. And the myriad changes are sustained by the woman's overall homeostatic reality, her whole being, during which the placenta serves a crucial negotiator. Homeostasis is the continually shifting adjustments an organism makes to stimuli inside and outside of itself. (238)

In misogyny, there is a masculine way of entering the scene of union in the feminine. Instead of tolerating an exclusion from it or of unending imagination about it, the masculine appropriates the essential moment of coming to life from the feminine. It recasts union as a place in which the male is active to avoid passivity. And since we can think of a defence as a reaction to a wish, we can see an urgency to retain his identity in the face of the wish to merge with her. The wish and the dread of feminization is, therefore, much deeper than contiguity with the feminine. Like a symptom, misogyny, in its exhibition of male autonomy, enacts a dread of dissolving into the feminine – not the female as an embodied being in time and space, but the mysterious 'and', which Hustvedt describes so evocatively. It is a dread of replacement, not just by women in social status, but by the feminine as an erosion of identity. At the level of social movements, it is a replacement ideology, but at the level of primal ambivalence, it is an existential crisis.

In the sexual entitlement of misogyny, phallic penetration seizes the female from the inside, transformed into a dimensional world. That sets the stage, recasting 'and' as a place in which the self pulls itself into existence by its activity, and is probably universal, shared by male and female alike as the root of parthenogenic phantasies. These phantasies are phallic, and the penis can dominate because it is an instrument that can be used as a weapon. But it doesn't succeed in seizing what she has inside, in the world beyond language, where her fertility lies. Misogyny takes the next step, in which intensive projective identification consolidates this interior dimension, turning the feminine into the repository of a bad, anti-masculine self, against which masculine identity mints itself.[5] This level of projective identification is both fertile and toxic – in fertile and toxic semen – as we explored in Chapter 8. Let us now look more deeply into the toxic base of misogyny. Klein (1946, 8) gives us a lead.

> [S]plit-off parts of the ego are … projected on to the mother [the good object] or, as I would rather call it, *into* the mother. These excrements and bad parts of the self are meant not only to injure but also to control and to take possession of the object. In so far as the mother comes to contain the bad parts of the self, she is not felt to be a separate individual but is felt to be *the* bad self. (Klein's emphasis)

The mother, so essential as the bedrock of identity, is simultaneously the repository for what must be expelled from the ego for the ego to consolidate its identity. Unlike the introjection of union, projective identification is not a loving embrace and a mingling, but it is a hate-driven incursion, aiming to possess the inside of the mother while simultaneously asserting independence from her.[6] And because, along with narcissistic identification, it also creates a confusion between subject and object, it turns the object into an internal threat. Even 'threat' is too object-related, too dimensional. I would say the object turns ominous. Just as Bion points out that 'and' cannot be captured in our dimensional language of physical objects, so too the displacement by, or the extinction of, the 'and' of the parental couple, cannot be captured in dimensional language. The same incapacity applies to the separation from the mother and the yearning to be 'inside' her.

I think that this inexpressible level – shall we call it 'region', despite its geographical resonance? – ties together instances of misogyny, not only between male and female, but also in historical and contemporary social movements. Dimensional language gives a veneer of intelligibility to a primal level that is a reaction to a narcissistic wound of a particular quality for the male. As the source of an internal drive to possess woman, it merges with misogynist, largely White supremacist movements, driven by a 'replacement ideology'. Racism, anti-feminism, misogyny, antisemitism, white supremacy, the 'manosphere' form overlapping groups (see Johanssen 2022 for extensive documentation).

The Anxiety of Depletion: Misogyny as the Narcissism of Small Differences

Let's turn to clinical evidence of a distinctively male aggression towards females, through which misogynist identity is formed. Klein noted a kind of aggression of boys towards girls, which called for a specific explanation.

> A tendency in boys to express excessive aggression… has its source in the femininity complex. It goes with an attitude of contempt and "knowing better", and is highly asocial and sadistic; it is partly determined by an attempt to mask the anxiety and ignorance which lie behind it. In part it coincides with the boy's protest (originating in his fear of castration) against the feminine role, but it is rooted also in his dread of his mother, whom he intended to rob of the father's penis, her children and her female sexual organs. This excessive aggression unites with the pleasure in attack which proceeds from the direct, genital Oedipus complex, but it represents that part of the situation which is by far the more asocial factor in character-formation. (Klein 1928, 191)

It is the working-through of this early ambivalence towards the mother, which, in Klein's view, is the source of the male's later capacity for generosity in his genital relationship with a woman. Thus, although she says that aggression towards the female, based on the anxieties of the femininity phase, are extreme, she also suggests that their mitigation provides the foundation for mature love. His sexual relationship with a *'woman capable of reassuring him of the reparative power of his penis seems to be more important than his identification with his father, in bringing him into adulthood'* (Klein, 1937, 313–316; my emphasis).

She speaks of the male's capacity to play the part of the 'bountiful mother' towards a woman, thereby satisfying 'his partner's love-wishes arising from her strong attachment to her mother', then says (1932, 251):

Thus, and only thus, by sublimating his feminine components and overcoming his feelings of envy, hatred and anxiety towards his mother, which originated in his feminine phase, will the boy be able to consolidate his heterosexual position in the stage of genital dominance.

But the roots of the castration complex and of a tyrannical superego also lie in this phase, in which he envied and hated his mother's reproductive organs and capacities – precisely what he could never have – and also protested against his feminization. The 'femininity phase' 'is characterized by anxiety relating to the womb and the father's penis, and this anxiety subjects the boy to the tyranny of a super-ego which devours, dismembers and castrates, and is formed from the image of mother and father alike' (Klein 1928, 190). It brings with it rivalry with women, which can be sadistic and superior in attitude, displaced onto the penis and intellectuality – the two classical tropes of masculinity. It expresses his need to free himself from femininity and his dread of it, as a state and in terms of mother's (and father's) retaliation for his aggression. Because it is driven by primitive, pre-oedipal phantasies, his rivalry with women is far more sadistic and a-social than that with other men, which will be more on a genital, oedipal level.

Whatever progress the boy makes in growing beyond the sadism of this phase owes to his engagement with his mother and the mother in his female partners. Identification with the father, and the development of his superego, do not seem to be adequate for this maturation. Instead, the boy must become himself while carrying her (femininity) at his core. Father – and the father-in-the-mother's-mind – contributes to his maturation, but father is, himself, in the lineage of masculinity.

This deep entanglement of son with mother provides a template for struggles against identification with mother: More generally, a struggle against sameness, along with the need to have mother by being mother. Perhaps the best example of the phantasy of sameness that provokes hatred, is the elemental dread of the female that Freud identified in 'The Taboo of Virginity' (1918 [1917]). There, Freud investigated the dread in the male of deflowering a virgin – a dread that seemed universal despite the apparent pleasure in being the first to possess her, and which surfaced in the form of various taboos. In some societies, the taboo is explicit, in giving over the deflowering to someone other than the future mate, sometimes by intercourse and sometimes by hand or by an instrument. In early modern Western culture, there are references to this practice in 'seigneurial rights' (spoofed in, for example, Mozart's *Marriage of Figaro*).

The castration complex and penis envy are central to Freud's phallic theory of female sexuality and identity. The deflowering penis robs the female of her grip on narcissistic intactness, a violation that provokes her castration complex into a hostility that can be unassuageable, ruining marriages and crippling sexual potency in the male and the female. But in this paper, he also introduces the 'narcissism of small differences', according to which aggression builds up to violence as differences decrease to near sameness. In my view, we are invited to conclude that the differences between male and female are actually minor distractions from a fundamental, vanishingly small, fragile differentiation, in which male identity remains insecure and aggression against the female is maximal.

I am strengthened in this view of Freud, by his referring to the work of the anthropologist, Ernest Crawley, on sexual taboos. Freud says

> Crawley, in language which differs only slightly from the current terminology of psycho-analysis, declares that each individual is separated from the others by a "taboo of personal isolation", and that it is precisely the minor differences in people who are otherwise alike that form the basis of feelings of strangeness and hostility between them. It would be tempting to pursue this idea and to *derive from this "narcissism of minor differences" the hostility which in every human relation* we see fighting successfully against feelings of fellowship and overpowering the commandment that all men should love one another. *Psychoanalysis believes that it has discovered a large part of what underlies the narcissistic rejection of women by men, which is so much mixed up with despising them, in drawing attention to the castration complex* and its influence on the opinion in which women are held. (199; my emphasis)

Freud invites us to range the castration complex of phallic monism, the bedrock horror that turns man away from woman and incites penis envy in the woman, within the narcissism of small differences. He seems to say that, in this phallic world, the penis is the only marker of difference between male and female, and it is very significant because it is so minor.

I don't think it extrapolates Freud's meaning unduly to suggest that the antipathy of the narcissism of small differences does not arise as a consequence of difference, but in the creation of difference (Figlio 2018). Hatred drives the projection of these delusional differences into the other that it creates, there to be abolished. Overt differences, to which the delusional differences can be attached, are distractions that appeal to consciousness but mask the delusional projection and the source of hatred in sameness. Narcissism intensifies as the overt differences between people decrease. At the heart of it lies an unease that must be projected. Objects of hatred are created in the process of projection. To *create* such an other most effectively eliminates inner hatred, because it can be done anytime, anywhere, as an omnipotent phantasy.

In my extension of Freud's account, male and female differ in many aspects, but the phallic aspect has stood out because it tranches upon the narcissistic core of identity. The penis has attracted impassioned attention because it is a visible male possession. It is easy to attach both idealization and denigration to it, but it is just the signifier of the invisible, illusory phallus, as the omnipotent core phantasy; and that illusion also serves as the bastion that holds the narcissism of small differences in place. The perceived difference between male and female creates the female as a delusion enemy, based on the idealization of self (male) and the denigration of the other (female) as the repository of projection. But beneath omnipotent phantasy of absolute difference is the realty of difference-in-sameness.

The reality of sameness springs from deeper roots. On the surface, the taboo of virginity seems to enact a hatred between the sexes as an avoidance of two, paired, anxieties: That of the female's phallic deficiency and that of the male's phallic insecurity, exacerbated by fear of her castrating retaliation. But, for Freud, a taboo is a defence against a wish (Freud 1913 [1912–1913], 69–70). So, the horror of the castrated and castrating woman is, as Ferenczi (1924, 29) argued, actually a horror of wishing to be castrated in order to merge with the mother. I think there is, behind this wish, which can be articulated as the wish to return to the womb, the unrepresentable disappearance into pre-objectal primary narcissism, which I connect to the mystery of 'and' in the primal process of creation 'inside' the dimensionless womb.

The fundamental conflict is not between male and female, masculine and feminine, but between the wish to merge into the (mother) object and the dread of loss of self. The narcissism of small differences is also between the wish for sameness, as the merger and the dread of loss of self, displayed in the larger, typically social arena. Rosenfeld (1987, 161–169) describes a defensive mental realm of 'narcissistic omnipotent object relations', in which unbearable, envied separateness is avoided by a phantasy of total immersion in, with total control of, the object. Such patients 'feel they live inside the analyst's mind and body and possess his help and understanding as part of themselves' (162). They project their envy of the object into the object, thereby feeling they, not the object, is envied. He speaks of an 'almost total projective identification' (163; also Joseph 1988, 67). He also distinguishes this extreme projective identification from 'primordial forms of projective identification [that] might then be considered a forerunner of the more usual type relating to the very earliest primary states of fusion between mother and baby' (158) and of normal 'symbiotic processes [that] are similar to, but not identical with, projective identification' (167). They include an ensnaring 'symbiotic entanglement' (168), in which one can feel at the mercy of the symbiotic object, and 'overpowered by ... internal attacks against [oneself] and [the] capacity to think' (1987a, 92).

The primordial merger phantasies are essential to emerging selfhood and are seen in everyday mother-infant relating. Projective identification is also, as a communication, part of this process. But it is also, especially in extreme forms, a fraught defence, in that it deposits hated aspects of the self in the object, from which they retaliate and persecute the self. In my view, Rosenfeld's contributions to primitive mental functioning are also elaborations of Freud's narcissism of small differences. Freud speaks of the virulent hatred that erupts from vanishing difference between self and object. But the threat of blending into identicality is not just a fact to which the ego reacts: It is produced by extreme projective identification. Rosenfeld's symbiotic entanglement speaks of an extreme an inherent conflict between the urgent need – demand – for sameness, to the point of requiring the object to be identical to the self, and a violent reaction to the threatened loss of self.

The primitive process described in detail by Rosenfeld is naturally constitutive of both male and female psychic reality. But the male-female relationship seems to offer the male a specific structure in which they occur. In misogyny, the male/masculine self makes use of being essentially the same as the female/feminine, yet is open to being recreated as essentially different. Her receptiveness can be recast as not-masculine, driven by a phantasied envy of masculinity. They fit her as a repository of projective identification, which sits on top of primal merger/symbiotic wishes and the dread of loss of self. Projective identification forcefully distances the female as the repository of his yearning and his dread, locking them into her by denigration. Phallic narcissism aims to seal them off inside her, with its dramatic display of male superiority and female deficiency.

This dilemma underlies the oedipal wish to replace father's union with mother, countered by the castration threat. It is the wish, not just to enter mother, not just to possess her, but the unrepresentable wish to be at the origination of oneself: To be the mother in whom one emerged. Castration horror at the sight of the female acts as a defence, aiming to maintain the security of a visible difference between male and female, adult and foetus, against the wish to undo their difference (cf. Gabbard 1993). Difference reassures the male, because the threat now appears to emanate from the woman as an external object, not as a wish from inside. It can then be met by the overt or covert denigration of the female for her overt differences. Difference undergirds existence itself. The shock of the female-as-castrated-male is a repudiation of the drive to move right through the female to the grandiose, omnipotent phantasy of self-creation,[7] bringing with it the dread of dissolution.

The narcissistic dilemma of the imperative to be the same and the dread of dissolving into it forces its way into all human relationships. It is there from the outset of psychic life and also remains as a pole of psychic life opposite and opposed to external reality (Britton 2017). For Freud, the first object for the ego is itself, and from this standpoint, narcissism is an achievement in which the ego comes into being for itself and in itself (Freud 1914). But it comes into being in a tension between being an object for itself and being replaced by an external object. There is, therefore, a rift in the psyche from the moment one can speak of there being a psyche. In relating to an object, the ego suffers the violation of its narcissism by the external world. It must either accommodate the object or eliminate it along with the inner tension projected into it. In other words, narcissism lives in a world of phantasy, which contact with reality contaminates, but which remains necessary.[8]

In a case reported by Rhode (1994, 42), a patient spoke about

> someone he knows who is in prison—and who suffers from an unusual bone disease. The man ... appears to have two skeletons—or, rather, one full skeleton and another adjacent one that seems to shadow the first skeleton and to exist only in bits. The fragments of the second incomplete skeleton keep growing ... He believes that ... at the time he was conceived ... [a]n inseminated ovum in part began to split; a pair of twins should have been formed; but the process was somehow arrested. The other twin never reached life, but its residue, the growing bits of bone, continue to exist as a disabling physical reproach within the twin who lives – or partially lives ... He now finds himself in a prison, both actual and symbolic.

This image captures well his patient's view of himself. For Rhode, there is a 'foetal consciousness that is vulnerable to binary division' (37) at birth, in the separation of the baby from a mother who, even in the separated infant's imagination, will replace it with another. But the binary division is more powerful at the threshold between Klein's paranoid-schizoid position and depressive position. Here, the ego in relation to an object sets off a cata-strophic change. In the primitive paranoid-schizoid world, the psyche lives in an omnipotent illusion of fantastic good and bad 'part objects', split from each other and projected into the object world, which then becomes idealized or retaliatory and threatening (Rhode 1994, 37). The advent of the depressive position destabilizes this defensive splitting.

But notice that Rhode's patient suffers from the belief that he has van-quished a competitor in the womb, as if it were a battlefield. The male, in his masculinity, is vulnerable to narcissistic collapse, because of the insecurity of his identity apart from the mother. He counters this phantasy by one in which he produces himself by his own activity. He simultaneously repudiates his internal genital as a site of identification with the internal world of the mother, repudiates it along with the feminine. The male, *in his masculinity*, tends towards a phallic posture, which avoids an awareness of an internal genital world. The female, in her femininity, embraces an internal genital world, but her receptivity, characteristic of femininity, does not move so easily into a phallic posture. The masculine attitude is implemented through projective identification, a receptive 'lack' of defence opens the feminine to projective identification. She then contains the masculine, denigrated internal world, as her denigrated internal world. (Kestenberg 1977). This mechanism operates along with envious attacks upon the feminine (see also examples in Chapter 4; Steiner 2020).

At the same time as the male displaces his internal genital space by pro-jective identification, he senses his exclusion from it, an exclusion borne partly by recognizing that the female internal space is pre-occupied and mysterious in its fertility. Their turmoil is exacerbated by an unconscious incitement to return to the origin of themselves. Another dose of projective identification with the female aims to destroy the internal world that draws the male into it. In toxic masculinity, it takes the form of poisoning, carried in toxic semen as the deadly side of fertility.

On top of these anxieties, providing cover against recognizing them, lies a belief that woman drives the feminization of man. Replacement ideology – the belief that identity is being stolen by an anti-male feminist movement – runs as a thread throughout mostly male and mostly white male, right-wing conservative movements. We will look at them in the next chapter. First, let us focus on envy as an experience of not having what an other has, and of feeling deprived of it. We will bear in mind the belief that the envied female has stolen a piece of oneself.

Consolidating Misogyny: The Certainty of 'Not'

I have argued that misogyny has a primary place among the knee-jerk hatreds. Reviling the feminine, whether in women or men seems to be the template for other forms of revulsion, through which we cast outside an internal discontent and aim to extinguish it there. Since women most fully and obviously display femininity, they take the brunt of an assault by masculinity, most fully and evidently displayed by men. At the core of this hatred, driving its intensity, is the turmoil stirred up in the male psyche by the femininity phase and it points to a contradiction between repudiating and envying the feminine, as an infectious spread of masculinity as 'not feminine'.

For Britton (2008), envy is composite – a molecule, not an atom – and a reaction to entering into the depressive position (which I associate with seminal masculinity). This depressive moment stirs envy at the recognition of the separateness of subject and object, including the object's turning to a third figure. It is, therefore, triadic, in the child's exclusion from the parental relationship, though it does comprise the dyadic, paranoid-schizoid, destructive element, which commonly typifies envy. The exclusion that draws envy is of a particular, deeply internal sort, which challenges the core of the narcissistic tone of identity.

> It is the revelation that the source of life is outside, pre-exists the existence of the self, is not of the same substance, and is the essential part of an asymmetric relationship: the parental ideal figure can be worshipped but does not worship in return. It is the discovery that the parent's projected ideal child was not born out of experience of the idealized self but on an internal, pre-existing pre-concept in the parental mind. (134)

Envy includes a benign 'twinge of pain in the midst of a surge of admiration' at the 'recognition of another's qualities or abilities that we do not possess but to which we aspire' (126). But the 'disappointed wish to have the same nature as the love object' can be joined by the more primitive, destructive components. The wish for worship and 'for worship to be reciprocal', to be idealized as is the ego ideal, brings disillusionment, which arises 'where there is a persistence of the belief that *someone* possesses this ideal identity' (134; Britton's emphasis). The disillusioned reaction, in my view, can include a toxic, seminal urge to seize the inside of the feminine.

Such an internal, delusional world can be stabilized by retreating into a group as an enclave, within which, externally, one appears to act rationally. It chimes with Moss' (2001) idea, that virulent hatred crystallizes in the formation of a group, which hates 'in the first person plural'.[9] That is what misogyny does. It is not that 'Jack' hates 'Jill', but 'man' hates 'woman', or 'masculine' hates 'feminine'. An essence of the individual is distilled – or fabricated – which is the same in both masculine and feminine embodiments. Misogyny reacts to that moment of dread (misogyny as a social organization is the topic of Chapters 10 and 11).

Moss (2001, 1315) sees a particular transformation of a private longing into a public, group hatred.

On the basis of personal, cultural, and clinical references, misogyny, homophobia, and racism are conceptualized as structured forms of hatred grounded in a defensive use of the first person plural voice. This use of hatred defends against dangers associated with desires linked to the first person singular. In these hatreds, "I want" is defensively transformed into "we hate."

In this transformation, we move from wanting to the point of identifying with an object into an abrupt disidentification when it is consolidated and reinforced by an experience of sharing it with others who are identical in their absolute difference from the now-hated object. Now, a homogenized 'we' are certain in 'our' stance, clear about the nature of the hated, now, in phantasy, homogenized, abstract object, known as if immediately, rather by the uncertain and lengthy process of discovery. Moss describes the group character of a primal hatred as a form of disgust. The forms of collective revulsion – racism, homophobia, misogyny – fit this model. I think we could add replacement ideology, White supremacy and religious fundamentalisms. In all these cases, each of us, as an individual, is lured into group reaction that *is*: Is, in the absolute comfort of identity with the group; knows the object instantly, by revelation; knows one is not the object: One *is*, *because* one is *not* the object.

Moss points to the interior quality of this apprehension of the object. Referring to a 1997 documentary based on interviews of men imprisoned for murdering gays (*Licensed to Kill*):

One man ... tells of his long hatred of "whatever is inside me" that drives him to seek out homosexual contact ... No matter how painful the effects of this "whatever" that drives him, the man has been able to endure, for a long period, his own sense of its opacity. In addition to this source of pain, he spoke of the egregious insult associated with often being rejected in these encounters. He found it especially terrible to be rejected at what he "hated having to do in the first place." His solution was that the problem would vanish only if he could "rid the world of homosexual men." (1329)

I think we might align this homophobic drive with misogyny. He reviles his homosexual urges and is humiliated by rejection, but what strikes me is Moss's drawing attention to 'whatever is inside me'. The feminine is inside-ness, interiority, the inside-mother at the root of yearning, even at the breast, where her inside satisfies the inside of the baby. Moss extracts from his clinical work the case of a woman who, along with her husband and, we can imagine, with masculine society, identifies with a – masculine – revulsion towards her body. Who could stand alone, for a moment, against such a revulsion, as a fact of masculine society?

Patient: I told John [her husband] I was going to shave my bikini spot. He said he was glad. Something disgusting about all that hair. He's right, I know. He's so squeamish about women. So am I. Disgusting, that hair, covering something over. Like something icky is about to pop out. And my Dad referring to a world filled with women squirting out babies. It's so hard to take my own side against all of that ...

Physically, I'm measurably good enough. Here, though, with you just staring *inside* of me, I can't say I'm basically okay ... I did wax drips on my legs after remembering what my father said about babies squirting out. Clean myself, somehow. I didn't want to.

Analyst: You imagined the waxing would join you to me in hating you for being a woman.

Patient: That is where the safety lay. You once said if kids aren't loved, they're just repellent creatures. Love is the only thing that makes another person not ugly. I don't want to have to dye my hair, have facelifts and all that. There are always things to find fault with.

Analyst: The more fault you find in yourself, the stronger you feel.

Patient: That's the reality of it. I'm not trying to hide my feelings. I can bear what's true. It's stronger to simply accept the indictment. More dignified. Beat them to the punch. It's better than trying to defend something on faith. If you're a woman, they can always list things to hold against you. There's nothing concrete to fight back with. But last night, for just a few minutes, I had a sneaky feeling of okayness. Like I have something, something to offer. *I was alone with it. No one but me could really know.* (1331–1332; my emphasis)

Misogyny in this case, with its 'hermeneutics of transparency' (1333), provides the patient with an unassailable sense of connection: 'That's the reality of it.' That sense of connection is not at all disturbed by her awareness that she is the explicit target of the 'reality' she is affirming. 'That's the reality of it' actively transforms the private and fluid dynamics of thought, fantasy, and history into the static, and public, dynamics of straightforward perceptual certainty. By way of this sense of certainty, the singular voice fades out ('I was alone with it'), replaced by the plural. She is then united with a powerful cluster of objects, from which she derives what she feels is her only secure source of vitality.

With the feminine in the woman as the original interior, the masculine in men can band together in misogyny to deal with the revulsion of inside, whether in man or woman. But why is 'inside' revolting? Because it is envied, as in Britton's construal, but with this emphasis: The evoked hatred pollutes the good object, turning it menacing; hatred transforms 'inside', as the ultimate place of yearning, into an object, the destruction of which protects the ego from assimilation to it. It is not just that the feminine is hated because the masculine lacks it: It is hated as a defence against becoming it.

Misogyny as a Template

Misogyny offers a working model of a foundational prejudice, a template of prejudices, characterized by domination, hate and repudiation. Let's take an example: Misogyny as a template for an authoritarian character of an analysis that we will extend in chapter 10. Just after World War II, in the wake of the Holocaust, *The Authoritarian Personality*, a psychoanalytically-informed social study of antisemitism, was published in the United States (Adorno et al. 1950).[10] The investigators devised a scale of indictors of prejudice, with one of the scales (F) devoted to discerning a 'pre-fascist personality'. Moss (2012) draws attention to an interesting correlation between two apparently unrelated items on this 'F' scale:

Nowadays with so many different kinds of people moving around so much and mixing together so freely, one has to be especially careful to protect himself against infection and disease.

and

Homosexuality is an especially rotten form of delinquency and ought to be severely punished.

The two items, contagion from mixing and homosexuality, were shown to be tied together in the popular imagination. Bear in mind, that the *Authoritarian Personality* antedates by decades the outbreak of HIV AIDS, seen as a disease of homosexual sex. Moss, writing originally in 1997, revised in 2012, aimed to show that the HIV virus offered a nucleus around which pre-existing, embedded prejudice, retrospectively clustered. 'Homosexuality, rotten, disease, punish, careful' now clustered together as if by nature. It supported a legitimating narrative of nature's reaction to homosexuality. In Freudian terms, it was a day residue, a conscious narrative that concealed an unconscious, repressed, prejudice. The 'Jew's nose, "Negroe's" hair, the female genital, the HIV virus' were pointers towards this nature... ...*For psychoanalysis, the paradigm of this narrative category is the female genital'* (85; my emphasis).

Moss builds on a model of anti-Black racism proposed by Brian Bird (1957). Bird coined the term, 'incorprojection', to name a process of identifying with an envied object (by incorporation) and dispensing with the envy by repudiating an undesired identification (by projection). An anti-Black racist identifies with an envied White, and passes the envy on to a Black, now seen to envy whiteness. Similarly, in *The Authoritarian Personality*, Adorno had argued that all race hatred was based on envy. Bird's model focused on the subject – the 'I' who could sustain a self-idealization by projecting envy onto the object of racism (what Moss 2021 calls 'vertical splitting'; also Steiner on the gap between the ideal and the real 2020, 15–52).

Moss extends Adorno's and Bird's thinking to sexuality: To homophobia and femininity. 'A single object toward which one simultaneously has passive yearnings and envious destructive ones – this is the unstable conundrum from which homophobia and other structured prejudices offer an exit.' The repository of contradictory wishes, 'whether woman, homosexual, or person of color, is then hated for the insatiety of his/her appetites ... [Here is] the core character of the homophobe's homosexual, the misogynist's woman, the anti-Semite's Jew. Their passivities mark them as sly and insidious, their envy as insatiable' (96, 97)

I agree with Bird's and Moss's model, but I think it is not yet elemental. For Moss, incorprojection resolves the conundrum of ambivalence by driving envious hatred into the object of desire. I have argued that there is a primal ambivalence at the nascent core of the ego. The ego comes into existence in the creation of an object, against which it manages the turbulence of becoming a subject. It must forego its primal omnipotence as it becomes aware of the object as not-self, experienced as a truncated self. Or it can carry forward this primary ambivalence by continually attacking the object as the bearer of its not-self: A not-self that it wants for itself and simultaneously dreads and hates becoming that not-self. In my view, misogyny repeats this primary Ambivalence in the male's repudiation of the female genital as an existential threat, but *nachträglich*, at a more advanced psychosexual level.

I think the elemental level can be discerned in the several aspects of narcissistic dilemma that we discussed earlier in the chapter, with Freud's narcissism of small differences at the core. The more difference diminishes, the more primitive states of mind erupt, including the twinned illusion of omnipotence and helplessness. The immediate expression of narcissistic eruption is violence. In a moment of omnipotence, it projects an illusion of difference and helplessness, consolidates them in the targeted enemy and eliminates them, thereby achieving a stabilization, albeit transiently. I suggest that the best example of the disjunction between a conscious perception of difference and an unconscious phantasy of sameness, which provokes the narcissistic dilemma, is that between male and female. Masculinity tends towards misogyny as a simplified route to identity: Taking it from the mother while repudiating the very identification on which his identity is built.

The conscious perception of difference, the apparent cause of misogyny, is actually a reassuring patch over the narcissistic dilemma, in which difference, in the limit, vanishes, thereby satisfying a primal urge that is also dreaded. Castration horror at the sight of the female acts as a defence against the wish to undo difference (cf. Gabbard 1993). It aims to maintain the conscious difference between male and female, adult and foetus, and to assume control of this difference by phallic supremacy. Castration anxiety, in this sense, is a signal anxiety, through which the supremacy of the penis supports an action to maintain difference. In this way, difference reassures the male. The threat now appears to emanate from external object, not as a wish from inside, and can be met by phallic performance, by the enacted taboo of virginity or by the overt or covert denigration of the female.

From this angle, observed difference undergirds an omnipotent illusion of existence itself. The shock of the female-as-castrated-male can then function as a repudiation of the drive to move right through the female to the grandiose, omnipotent phantasy of undifferentiated self-creation. It specifies Freud's (1914) theory, that in relating to an object, the ego suffers the violation of its narcissism by the external world, as an unconscious phantasy. Similarly, for Britton (2017, 35), the body, existing in time and space is too much reality. A mind-self sees the body only as *its* – the mind self's – idea. Narcissism, 'in the sense of the abolition of object relations ... , is a psychic immune response to the ingestion (introjection) of objects that are not identical with the self.'

Craving identicality brings dread of dissolving into the not-quite-me-other. Observed difference, paradoxically, reassures because it fixes what would be a deeper foreboding of depletion even to extinction. In the world of narcissism, objects are replicas that steal the essence of the self. To the narcissistic ego, the object is a replica of itself, and, to the extent that the object also continues to exist in its own right, it can only signify extinction of the ego. Freud says that the phallic woman reassures the male that there is no castration, because she is the same as he; but as a woman, she also represents an unstable delusion of difference along with the wish to be the same. At a primitive level, it refers to the anxiety of extinction in assimilating to, and differentiating from, an object (Figlio 2000, pp. 61–72, 78–82; Figlio 2010; Freud 1915).

The female is a delusional enemy; the perceived difference between male and female is a creation of a difference between the idealization of self (male, nation, white) and the denigration of the other (female) as the repository of projection identification. I think it is reasonable to find in Freud's theory of phallic monism the germ of the idea that what can be seen – what is consciously perceived – can function as the surface narrative for a comforting denial of sameness: 'I (male) am *not* same as you (female).' There is the denial. 'I am reassured that you wish to be the same as me. I am at one with myself; you are unstable, disoriented, at odds with yourself.' It hides the dread of instability at wondering, 'If I am the same as she, then who am I?' – a dread brought to a head by a male's reaction to a female because he is, at his origin, her.

In the next chapter, I want to extend the treatment of misogyny as a social consolidation of masculine identity. I have suggested that misogyny is the fundamental hate-driven prejudice, acting as a hate-driven, group repudiation in society. As Moss (2012, 85) said, 'the paradigm of this narrative category is the female genital'. We will go on to argue that they are replacement ideologies, rooted in misogyny as a primal replacement anxiety. They share a feature associated with the narcissism of small differences: The difference that draws denigration and repudiation – skin colour, Semitic features, sexual orientation or identity – conceals the root of denigration in narcissism of small differences.

I have claimed that surface differences are actually reassuring guarantors for perpetrators, underwriting the belief in their solid reality. We will now aim to show how whiteness becomes the prime signifier of superiority across the board, on the basis of male supremacy, based on misogyny. Within this reality, women (Blacks, Jews, gays) cannot/should not be considered the equal of White (men), because they are patently not equal (in ability, in ancestry, in national purity). But these defensive assurances, as patches over psychotic anxiety, aim to consolidate a psyche in relation to into solid, external, perceptual reality.

Notes

1 A report, published in 1999, of an enquiry into racism in the Met, following the murder of the Black teenager, Stephen Lawrence, which accused the Met of 'institutional racism'.
2 Freud seems to have been pre-occupied with the dilemma of the ego retaining itself while wanting to have the primal object, to the point of being it. I have referred to a 'primal ambivalence' several times, and connected it to Freud's ideas on the development of the ego (Freud 1915; 1917b). In his late notes on various themes (1938, 299), he comes back to this vexed relationship to the desired object.

July 12

"Having" and "being" in children. Children like expressing an object-relation by an identification: "I am the object." "Having" is the later of the two; after loss of the object it relapses into "being". Example: The breast. "The breast is a part of me, I am the breast." Only later: "I have it"—that is, "I am not it" …

3 We cannot ignore the anatomical, genital distinctions between the sexes. The penis is an instrument that can also be a weapon of incursion; the vagina is a particular receptive, conceptive organ. One version of the controversy on this point came alive in recent UK law. A bill on gender self-identification was approved by the Scottish Parliament, only to be blocked by the UK government. Shortly after, the Scottish government transferred a transgender female, previously convicted as a rapist, from a women's to a men's prison, following protest (see 'UK Blocks Scottish Law: Gender Recognition Bill', at https://www.gov.scot/news/gender-recognition-reform-bill-passed/, Accessed 1 February 2023; 'Trans Double Rapist Isla Bryson Transferred Out of Women's Prison After Row Over Safety of Female Inmates', at https://www.lbc.co.uk/news/isla-bryson-female-prison-scotland/ (by Kieran Kelly), Accessed 1 February 2023.

4 One occasionally glimpses the organization of the ego through spatial differentiation in the consulting room, as patients attribute different qualities – perhaps comforting on one side and frightening on the opposite side, or investing objects in the room with desirable or undesirable qualities, partly on the basis of where they are. Parts of the body, as internal objects, can suddenly harbour an emotion, for example, as a mutilation in place of feeling attacked. Such a phenomenon corresponds, in Kleinian thinking, to the evolution of internal objects from localized organ sensations, and of the skin holding the self together, inside. Their defensive eruption in analysis girds up a vulnerable psyche, and points to dimensional structuring in the development of the psyche (see Hinshelwood 1997a, 1997b). Deborah Wright (2022) has explored these structuring, spatial attributes in detail.

5 I use the metaphor of minting, as in minting a coin, because the figures are produced by striking an unformed disc, pressing the non-figure down, thereby elevating the figure into existence.

6 Hate is the appropriate word for the full-blown misogyny of, say, replacement ideology, but not for the existential root. Freud (1915) makes clear that we need a language appropriate to the stage of development. Hate, like love, is genital stage, whole-object relating, and is not the negation of love. I am suggesting that we embed misogyny in its existential roots, albeit revised *nachträgich*. Hate might best express the force of the expulsion, if not the emotion. Freud adds to the confusion, however, by also using hate to describe the first expulsion of 'not me', in the formation of the ego.

7 This interpretation is consistent with Freud's (1915) account of the mechanism of projection. Projection transforms the unrepresentable, relentless pressure of the drives into an external, representable form. The non-objectal world of the former is transformed into a representable, object-relating form.

8 Freud (1915) embraces the initial paradoxical need of, and yet a depletion by, the object, with the *Aufheben* – the suspension – of the object: To hold it in being while annulling its presence. Anality brings a later, decisive attack on, and control of, the object. Winnicott brings out the paradoxical nature of the earliest, formative relationship of the emergent ego with its emergent object in several of his writings (eg, 1949). Indeed, it becomes a kind of axiom in his theory of psychic development. The sense of self emerges as a reaction to impingement, which is a breach in continuity of the ego. The object, as for Freud, appears as an obstacle, and, as for

Freud, the ego normally manages the paradox of needing (to remove) the object, which is inherent in its very existence. For Freud, however, this originary *Aufhebung* is the kernel of ambivalence, which remains at the core of the psyche; for Winnicott, it is the kernel of paradox, as of transitional objects and phenomena, which remains at the core of the psyche.

9 Moss' (2001; 2021) concept of 'hating the first person plural' focuses on the solidaristic uniformity among individuals who coalesce in hating and ostracizing others, coalesced, in their view, into an equally homogenized group. Such a process of group formation follows from Freud's (1921) concept of group formation based on individuals identifying with each other in their egos, when they invest their individual ego-ideals in the same object, forming a collective ego-ideal. Moss adds, as an impetus for group formation, the creation of an external group as a repository for projection of the non-ideal. This projection reinforces, by denigration of its opponent group, its own collective ego-ideal. There can be only one ego-ideal within a single psycho-social universe; a competing ego-ideal must be debased to support this idealization. Hating in the first person plural can be put with Moss's concept of 'vertical splitting', in which an individual or group idealizes itself by splitting its object, and the ego, into ideal and debased. This splitting follows from Klein's (1946) concept of splitting the object into a good and a bad object, keeping them separate to avoid the ambivalent contamination of the good object. Moss emphasizes the self-idealization that accompanies it, in the way Freud (1914) speaks of the ideal-ego in identification with the ego-ideal. He contrasts this splitting from 'horizontal splitting', which maintains a separation without the pairing them as idealized and debased (see also Steiner 2020, 15–52).

10 Funded by the American Jewish Committee.

References

Adorno, T. W. et al. (1950). *The Authoritarian Personality*. New York: Harper & Row; London/New York: Verso, 2019.

Bion, W. R. (1970) *Attention and Interpretation*. London: Tavistock; Karnac, 1984.

Bion, W. R. (1992) *Cogitations*. London: Karnac.

Bird, B. (1957) A Consideration of the Etiology of Prejudice. *Journal of the American Psychoanalytical Association* 5: 490–513.

Britton, R. (1994) Publication Anxiety: Conflict Between Communication and Affiliation. *International Journal of Psychoanalysis* 75: 1213–1224.

Britton, R. (1995). Psychic Reality and Unconscious Belief. *International Journal of Psychoanalysis* 76: 19–23; revised version in *Belief and Imagination: Explorations in Psychoanalysis*. London: Routledge.

Britton, R. (2008) He Thinks Himself Impaired: The Pathologically Envious Personality. In Roth, P. and Lemma, A. (eds) *Envy and Gratitude Revisited*. London: Karnac, 124–136.

Britton, R. (2017) Disconnection: A New Look at Narcissism. In Bronstein, C. and O'Shaughnessy, E. (eds) *'Attacks on Linking' Revisited: A New Look at Bion's Classic Work*. London: Karnac, 25–37.

Dodd, V. (2022) Met Failings Let Corrupt Police Officers Stay on Force. *The Guardian*, 17 October, 1–2.

Figlio, K. (2000) *Psychoanalysis, Science and Masculinity*. London: Whurr; Philadelphia: Brunner Routledge, 2001.

Figlio, K. (2010) Phallic and Seminal Masculinity: a Theoretical and Clinical Confusion. *International Journal of Psychoanalysis* 91(1): 119–139.

Figlio, K. (2018) Fundamentalism and the Delusional Creation of an Enemy. In Krüger, S., Figlio, K. and Richards, B.(eds) *Fomenting Political Violence: Fantasy, Language, Media, Action*. London: Palgrave, 2018, 149–166.

Ferenczi, S. (1924) *Thallassa: A Theory of Genitality*. NY, New York: *Psychoanal. Q.*, 1938; repr. London: Karnac, 1989.

Freud, S. (1910) A Special Type of Choice of Object Made by Men (Contributions to the Psychology of Love I). *The Standard Edition of the Complete Psychological Works of Sigmund Freud* 11: 161–175.

Freud, S. (1913[1912–13]) Totem and Taboo. *The Standard Edition of the Complete Psychological Works of Sigmund Freud* 13: 1–165.

Freud, S. (1914) On Narcissism: An Introduction. *The Standard Edition of the Complete Psychological Works of Sigmund Freud* 14: 73–105.

Freud, S. (1915) Instincts and their Vicissitudes. *The Standard Edition of the Complete Psychological Works of Sigmund Freud* 14: 109–140.

Freud, S. (1918 [1917]) The Taboo of Virginity (Contributions to the Psychology of Love II). *The Standard Edition of the Complete Psychological Works of Sigmund Freud* 11: 191–208.

Freud, S. (1921) Group Psychology and the Analysis of the Ego. *The Standard Edition of the Complete Psychological Works of Sigmund Freud* 18: 65–144.

Freud, S. (1938) Findings, Ideas, Problems. *The Standard Edition of the Complete Psychological Works of Sigmund Freud* 23: 299–300.

Gabbard, G. (1993) On Hate in Love Relationships: The Narcissism of Minor Differences Revisited. *Psychoanalytic Quarterly* 62: 229–238.

Hinshelwood, R. (1997a) The Elusive Concept of 'Internal Objects' (1934–1943): Its Role in the Formation of the Klein Group. *International Journal of Psychoanalysis* 78: 877–897.

Hinshelwood, R. (1997b) Catastrophe, Objects and Reparation: Three Levels of Interpretation. *British Journal of Psychotherapy* 13(3): 307–317.

Hustvedt, S. (2019) What Does a Man Want. In *Mothers, Fathers, and Others*. London: Sceptre, 2021, 225–253.

Johanssen, J. (2022) *Fantasy, Online Misogyny and the Manosphere: Male Bodies of Dis/Inhibition*. London/NY: Routledge.

Joseph, B. (1988) Projective Identification: Clinical Aspects. In Sandler, J. (ed.) *Projection, Identification, Projective Identification*. Madison, Ct: International Universities Press, 65–76.

Kestenberg, J. S. (1977) Psychoanalytic Observation of Children. *International Review of Psychoanalysis* 4: 393–407.

Klein, M. (1928) Early Stages of the Oedipus Conflict. In *The Writings of Melanie Klein*, vol. 1. London: The Hogarth Press and the Institute of Psycho-Analysis, 1975, 186–198.

Klein, M. (1932) The Psychoanalysis of Children. In *The Writings of Melanie Klein*, vol. 2. London: The Hogarth Press and the Institute of Psycho-Analysis, 1975.

Klein, M. (1937) Love, Guilt and Reparation. In *The Writings of Melanie Klein*, vol. 1. London: The Hogarth Press and the Institute of Psycho-Analysis, 1975, 306–343.

Klein, M. (1946) Notes on Some Schizoid Mechanisms. In *The Writings of Melanie Klein*, vol. 3. London: The Hogarth Press and the Institute of Psycho-Analysis, 1975, 1–24.

Malinowski, B. (1916) Baloma: The Spirits of the Dead in the Trobriand Islands. In *Magic, Science and Religion and Other Essays*. Glencoe, IL: The Free Press, 1948; Garden City, NY: Doubleday Anchor, nd.

Meltzer, D. et al. (1982) The Conceptual Distinction Between Projective Identification (Klein) and Container-Contained (Bion). *Journal of Child Psychotherapy* 8: 185 –202. In *Studies in Extended Metapsychology: Clinical Applications of Bion's Ideas*. Strath Tay: Clunie, 1986, 50–69.

Moss, D. (2001) On Hating in the First Person Plural. *Journal of the American Psychoanalytic Association* 49:1315–1334.

Moss, D. (2012) *Thirteen Ways of Looking at a Man: Psychoanalysis and Masculinity*. London/NY: Routledge.

Moss, D. (2021) On Having Whiteness. *Journal of the American Psychoanalytic Association* 69: 355–372.

Rhode, E. (1994) *Psychotic Metaphysics*. London: Karnac.

Rosenfeld, H. (1987). Projective Identification in Clinical Practice. In *Impasse and Interpretation: Therapeutic and Anti-Therapeutic Factors in the Psychoanalytic Treatment of Psychotic, Borderline and Neurotic Patients*. London: Tavistock, 157–190.

Steiner, J. (2020) *Illusion, Delusion, and Irony in Psychoanalysis*. Abington, Oxon/NY: Routledge.

Winnicott, D. W. (1949) Birth Memories, Birth Trauma, and Anxiety. In *Through Paediatrics to Psycho-Analysis*. London: Hogarth and the Institute of Psycho-Analysis, 1975, 174–193.

Wright, D. L. S. (2022) *The Physical and Virtual Space of the Consulting Room: Room-Object Spaces*. London: Routledge.

Chapter 10

Social Misogyny

Toxic Misogyny in Society

I have argued that misogyny[1] is rooted in a primal hatred of, and yearning for sameness. It is a version of the narcissistic dilemma, with the narcissism of small differences at the core, most acutely instantiated in the relationship between masculine and feminine. The female, as the other half of humanity, and the first object, is the elemental repudiated object. The narcissism of small differences evokes the denigration of the feminine as a homogenized group, in the way Moss characterized hating in the first person plural, with vertical splitting: The (male) masculine, as an abstract group, denigrates the (female) feminine, as an abstract group. Misogyny is perpetuated by an apparent paradox: The difference that draws hatred – penis/no penis; penis/vagina breast/no breast – is actually a reassuring, defensive cover, and a distraction from the underlying sameness. They stand for solid, external reality, in the face of psychotic unreality. It is the lack of difference at an elemental level brings dread: Dread of dilution of masculine into feminine.

In this chapter, I want to extend the treatment of misogyny. As I suggested in the previous chapter, I see it as the template for hate-driven, group repudiations in society; they are replacement ideologies, rooted in misogyny as a primal replacement anxiety. At this level, it is, at root, racism as well.[2] They share a feature associated with narcissism of small differences: The difference that draws denigration and repudiation – skin colour, Semitic features, sexual orientation or identity – conceals the root of denigration in narcissism of small differences. The surface differences are actually reassuring guarantors for perpetrators, that their beliefs are anchored in solid reality. They make hating this assured reality seem rational, in line with solid, external, perceptual reality.

A blatant eruption of violence in support of such a 'solid' reality occurred in an incident that was widely reported in the British press. Vigilantes attacked the home of a local female paediatrician in 2000. The word 'paedo' was daubed on the windows of her cottage. Their ire was kindled, apparently, by their belief that they were punishing, not a paediatrician, but a paedophile,

DOI: 10.4324/9781003455790-15

in an eruption of righteous fury against her sinful behaviour. In my view, she was neither a paediatrician nor a paedophile in their minds: Even 'paedophile' would have suggested an individual with a personality, albeit one whose behaviour crossed a moral threshold and drew their censure. Instead, there was an eruption of violence based on a piece of a word. An intolerance of meaning stripped 'paediatrician' (or paedophile) of its coherent reference to reality in an explosion that left meaningless pieces that could only be evacuated; could only be an action. It broke the linking – of thoughts into thinking, of parts of speech into grammatical constructions and of perceptions into connections with reality – to unburden the mind (Bion 1962). Thinking and belief were reduced to a vanishing point, homogenizing subjects (individual actors) into an abstract group that hated a paedo in the first person plural, as an equally abstract group (see Figlio 2018, where this case was reported along with an elaboration of the idea of creating delusional enemies).

Later, the BBC reporter of the incident wrote that it was 'time we put the paedo-paediatrician morality tale to bed' (*Press Gazette* 2012). I think that this appeal to reasonable, common sense reproduces the defensive appeal to reality. The vigilantes *may* have *mistaken* this woman for a paedophile, so let's move on from self-righteous exaggeration of their offence. But what they *did* was scrawl 'paedo' on the paediatrician's windows. 'Paedo' was a meaningless utterance, not even a word. It was a violent attack. The paediatrician was, in that violent act, neither a paedophile nor a paediatrician, but the meaningless particle, 'paedo', having no symbolic nor representational meaning. Their moral outrage was then locked in place by the moral outrage of the counter-vigilantes who denounced them. The whole incident coalesced a psychotic eruption against a delusionally created object, hiding securely inside an apparently reasonable language. The aim was to deposit, by projective identification, this delusionally created object inside a perceived object – a house with its occupant – and to explode it.

At the psychotic level of functioning, the meaningless and shrill 'paedo' has kin, treated equally or even more savagely. It includes 'Jew', 'Homo', 'Black', 'Muslim', 'Heretic', 'Infidel'. It also includes, I think at the core, 'female', 'feminine', 'feminist'. The coherence of thinking and reference to reality are exploded, revealing a catastrophe. The catastrophe, with its scattered fragments of what was coherent psychic and social life, is agglomerated into a facsimile of coherence by rationalized justifications. Groups that hate in the first person plural are mainly populated by men – white men, in particular – but their main feature is that they are masculine, to which the labels, 'hegemonic masculinity' and 'toxic masculinity' also apply. On-line sources have facilitated their gathering into networks that are continuously reinforced by the immediacy of on-line communication. Johanssen (2022) labels such an overarching movement with a White supremacist, misogynist character, a manosphere (57–64, 98–103). The instantaneous amassing into a group creates and is facilitated an omnipotence of hating in the first person plural.

Not only are the misogynist agents of this cluster of virulent – often violent – oppressions and denigrations typically male: They are characterized by phallic narcissism. Misogyny is the core replacement ideology because the female, in her femininity, is the immediate target of denigration. Not only is half the population of the world female, but everyone is born of a female. The male works through – or does not work through – the tortuous route into male identity, with its dominant masculine character and defensive organization, rooted in the femininity phase. One way or another, every male has to relate to a female, even if it is to renounce such a relationship, as in the MGTOW (Men Going Their Own Way) movement (Johanssen, 122–143).

Let us briefly work back from extreme, white, masculine social movements, characterized by hate-driven denunciation. I see a thread running through them. They are tied together by a conviction of a shared reality behind their attack on an object, but which is a defence against a psychotic core that is dreaded. The fundamental instance of this dread is the loss of masculine into feminine. The psychological process of this loss, which kindles the explosive reaction against it, is the narcissistic dilemma, with the narcissism of small differences at the core. Misogyny works as a defence because the female is nearly the same as the male, but with a visible marker of difference. I think it is significant that Freud introduced the narcissism of small differences in his essay on the dread surrounding the first entry by a male into the female (in 'The Taboo of Virginity'). Phallic masculinity dramatically proclaims its immunity to this danger, only revealing its vulnerability and also its underlying dread.

Let us now draw this cluster together, and bring it into the extreme, interior dimension, inherent in seminal and toxic masculinity. Not only is the feminine a danger by retaliation, in the way many psychoanalytic theorists have argued: It is the scene of a depressive catastrophe – a failure of the capacity of depressive masculinity to sustain life. In this world, semen is a toxic as well as a healthy seed. The ubiquity of the epithet, toxic masculinity, for every sort of aggressive male attitude and behaviour, is also a repression. The ubiquity of 'toxic' for everything egregious, with 'masculinity' tacked on, explicitly or implicitly, is a phallic performance, a glare that hides its fundamental fragility in blindingly bright view. This seminal ambivalence, hidden inside the phallic proclamation of toxic masculinity, brings a dread of depressive collapse. I characterize misogyny as this interior, toxic expression of ambivalence in the relationship of masculine to feminine.

We begin with the wound to the boy's self-regard, which his mother can inflict on him by rejecting his libidinal impulses (Horney 1932). His fury at rejection can combine with pre-genital impulses, adding up to a destructiveness with a phallic character. In that case, the vagina, as the retaliating object of phallic attack, becomes the agent of his castration anxiety, a source of dread to the point of denying the existence of the vagina, and a buttress to his phallic narcissism, with its dominating, possessive attitude towards women. In Horney's account, wounded narcissism, not male phallic superiority, grounds a superior attitude towards women, based on dread, which women, in turn, do not feel towards them.

Felix Boehm (1930, 469) draws out this difference between an overt male contentment at his superiority and a concealed the inner fragility of a wounded narcissism. He turns on its head the idea that a woman takes on herself the 'contempt felt by men for a sex which is the lesser in so important a respect [, and by so doing] she clings obstinately to being like a man.'

> But men, who do not bear the mark of this wound to their narcissism, ought, one would think, to have no difficulty in admitting that the vagina represents to them an organ productive of pleasure and therefore worth coveting, even though the fact that they themselves lack this organ is something of a blow to their narcissism. (p. 469)

His wry comment hits home. The male, if so confident in his superiority, should find it easy – even enjoyable – to acknowledge the female attributes that he absolutely and irretrievably lacks. But not only does the phallic narcissist not acknowledge her unique attributes: He denigrates her and, as Horney pointed out, forces her to denigrate herself. It suggests a defensive posture that needs constant reinforcement. His unique attributes are not hers. He has to tolerate a union with her without appropriation of her. At root, his intolerance degrades her from within, in a toxic incursion.

Triangulating the Theme: A Philosopher's View

We can add a confirming example from well outside psychoanalysis. Martha Nussbaum (2018), a philosopher with a special interest in ethics, the law and politics, groups sexism and misogyny together as a 'toxic brew' of male self-interest, fear, denigration and disgust, pressed into women. The brew, now woman herself, is excluded from male-dominated society. At root, men fear the mortality, so manifest in bodies, in the loss of acquisitions, such as income, and in the loss of privileged status. Mix them together, find them in women, and they become the toxic brew in their bodies, especially the fluids that leak from them, as well as in their aspiration to have what belongs to men.

Nussbaum distinguishes misogyny from sexism. Sexism is the attribution of qualities to women by nature, a claim she easily dismisses. By nature, so the claim goes, women are not fitted to public or intellectual endeavour. She dismisses this claim easily. Borrowing from J. S. Mill on the subjection of women, she points out how nature seems spectacularly unable to keep women in their place. It seems to need all the help men can provide – legislation, exclusion from education and occupations, moral pressure – to supplement its ineffectual power. Misogyny helps out, immediately and directly. It simply puts reasons aside, and depreciates women, in an exclusionary attitude towards them. Misogyny is a

> determined enforcement of gender privilege, which can sometimes be motivated by hatred but is more often combined with benign paternalistic sentiments. Its primary root is self-interest, combined with anxiety about potential loss. (177)

Her definition is gentler than her analysis of misogyny. She builds her account on three stories, having fear in common: Fear-blame, fear-envy, fear-disgust. In fear-blame, the woman should serve the man, from boyhood on, and the expectation is laced with a 'deep anxiety [that] gets blended with rage' (185). In fear-envy, women have what men should have, both the privilege that women might competitively take from them, but also inalienable capacities such as a womb and fertility (171, 190). In fear-disgust, women embody corruption, decay, stench, mortality, pollution (193).

For Nussbaum, these abhorrent traits of woman are embodiments of male anxiety and fear. Misogynist disgust at women's bodily fluids are not only wrongly attributed to women, to distance them from man: They are attributes of man, objects of disgust in himself, pressed into woman. She draws on a legal theorist, William Ian Miller, to raise the question, 'is it the fact that men leave their own fluids behind in the woman and therefore think of her as a receptacle of the sticky stuff they discharge' (193)? Of disgust misogyny, Nussbaum adds, that it is 'clearly fear-driven, like all projective disgust' (194).

To my mind, Nussbaum comes close to describing what I have called toxic masculinity. That sticky discharge into women can only be semen – toxic semen. Our coming at it from two, quite different angles and knowledge-bases adds to the confidence with which we can embrace such an idea. We need, however, to attend to some nuances around which we might differ, to bring out the key themes more clearly. Nussbaum, for example, explains the inspiration for her book. It was a night of 'political anxiety', on the eve of Trump's election, which led her to an awareness that 'fear was the issue, a nebulous and multiform fear suffusing US society ... [which led to ideas] about how fear is connected to, and renders toxic, other problematic emotions such as anger, disgust and envy' (xii).

The spine of her thinking, however, seemed to be her realization that her father loved and supported her in all her aspirations but would cut her off if she transgressed boundaries of prejudice she could only see as racist. Father was an admirable man but harboured prejudice against minorities, including Blacks and Jews. She, as woman, was loved but she had also to stay in place, and her father contradicted himself on what that meant. For example, he encouraged her to follow aspirations that he would not tolerate in a woman he married. Father's love and the self-esteem that goes with it was, for Nussbaum, uncannily compromised.

Three currents of her thinking stand out to me: First, that fear drives people into extreme, divisive positions; secondly, that men press their fear, often inchoate and self-contradictory, into women, and seek to hold onto self-confidence through distancing themselves from women, the repositories of their fear; thirdly, that misogyny is racism, or *vice versa*.

I think her reflections and analysis call out for psychoanalytic partnering. First, I don't think fear is primal. Fear has an object. In that sense, it is already an organized defence: One can act against a feared object, albeit sometimes mistaken about the actual object (as in phobias). I think she is closer to the primal when she speaks of rage and of anxiety: Gut reactions that have no object, that are dreaded rather than feared. This was also the area that Freud was approaching with his *Unbehagen in der Kutur* (1930; translated misleadingly as *Civilization and its Discontents*). *Unbehagen* refers to a dissatisfaction, but it has a more interior sense of an uneasiness or malaise, while the 'and' in the translation puts the dissatisfaction in conjunction with civilization. It marginalizes its inherence *in* civilization, while drawing attention to the enigma of 'and'; like 'toxic', it is a form of repression.

Unbehagen presses for external representation, objectifying its internal, inchoate, inarticulable quality. For Freud, the instincts differed from external sources of excitation, in that they did not arise from identifiable objects but from diffuse organic sources. There was, therefore, no object to which the ego could turn to quell its demand or from which it could turn to avoid its demand. The ego resolves this dilemma by recasting the internal world as if it were external. It casts it onto an object – *projects* it – then relates to that object (Freud 1915).

Secondly, Nussbaum says that men press their fear into woman in their 'projective disgust' (194). The projection that she and Miller allude to is, in my view, 'projective identification'. In projective identification, the object as repository not only is corrupted by what is put into it: It *becomes* the bad, corrupted self. And, as Klein said, it is a projection *into*, not onto. It is an interior incursion, not an external assault. Nussbaum's use of the expression, 'toxic', articulates the peculiarly incursive pressure of misogyny, and invites the concept of projective identification to bring out this interior quality. Men feel – or behave in a way that expresses a feeling of which they are unaware – that they lack the feminine capacity of fertility, of countering death, of caring in a reparative way. They lack the capacity to mitigate their own, internal, pollution. They can – in the midst of their own appreciation of femininity – feel displaced. They react with hyper-masculinity (toxic and phallic-narcissistic masculinity), in which they secure themselves by denigrating woman as the repository of their *Unbehagen*. And at the root of the *Unbehagen* is the narcissistic dilemma.

On the third point – misogyny as racism – I argued in Chapter 9 that misogyny might be thought of as the template of replacement ideologies, including racism. Nussbaum does not make this additional claim, but she does speak of feeling on the edge of transgressing father's gender boundaries as racist moments.

Racism as Replacement Ideology: Replacement Ideology as Misogyny

White supremacism is based on the belief that the homogenized group of whites – the white 'race' of racist ideology – is being replaced by others, themselves homogenized into races. It was firmly held in Nazi anti-miscegenation sentiment and legislation. But even today, the Hungarian prime minister, Victor Orbán, for example, nods to replacement ideology and says, 'We [Hungarians] are not a mixed race ... and we do not want to become a mixed race ... [With mixing, countries are] no longer nations' (Walker and Garamvolgyi 2022). But the manosphere movement makes the same claim against a feminist ascendancy in culture.

The absolute demand to reclaim a lost primacy must have primitive roots, in which an object comes into being as a threat to the ego. There is an absolute core to this belief, in which the ego experiences, not just depletion, but extinction, by the very presence of an object. There are three steps. First, the individual subject feels his personhood is secured and augmented by his abstract-group-identity. Secondly, the racial other is an abstraction, into which individual personhood disappears, as a person becomes an object along with the race with which he/she is identified. Thirdly, the elimination of the object, also an abstraction, secures the identity of the racializing abstract group subject.

Replacement ideology is a common thread throughout many extremist groups. They form a phalanx of rage in their conviction that they are under threat of extinction by replacement. The other common thread is misogyny. (Belew 2018; Johanssen 2022). In their hate-driven character, extremist groups react to a belief that they, in their various social locations, are threatened with extinction. Together, in the manosphere, they unofficially agree that women threaten them all. Consciously, in replacement ideology, they feel empowered by right to dominate the object, and fear being out-numbered by minority populations, or swamped by feminism. In the Unconscious, it is an equation: Self = – racialized object (see Figlio 2017, 73–100, esp. 94).

This way of thinking converges on definition of race as a homogeneous group, characterized by a 'racial object' (Davids 2011), a single, or minimal, signifier. A racial object is an internal object that represents the homogenized ideal, existing by right and with certainty. It manifests in the internal world whenever ambiguity or tension destabilizes the ego, as an agent of certainty with which the ego can identify or call upon as an ego-ideal. I have postulated that it has its origin at the origin of the ego. I draw on Freud's (1914, 94) concept of ego-ideal as a reserve of primary narcissism, retained as the ego engages with realty and enters into object relations; and as a critical agency next to the narcissistic identification of ego and object, in melancholia (1917). In both cases, the nascent ego-ideal stands for an entrenchment of a feeling of self in the presence of an incursion of and into the other. The mature ego can release into its imperilled, originating state.

This line of thinking is also consistent with Freud's concept of the narcissism of small differences, in which hatred grows in proportion to perceived likeness between groups. Here we see another version of defence that replays, in reverse, the nascence of the ego. At the birth of the ego in the emergence of an object world, the first object is 'suspended', then hated, as the repository of everything not-ego, and therefore, bad by definition (Freud 1915). Later, the more two groups are like each other, the more virulent the antagonism between them, as they approach the natal condition in which the ego emerges along with the object that it repudiates in hatred. I take it a step further: Race is not an object that is eliminated to secure the self from replacement: Race is *created* as an abolished object at the primitive core of becoming a self.

A stable difference would not arouse the hatred of the narcissism of small differences. It might provoke a stable – mature – ego's anger at unwanted (unbearable) aspects of an other, but not arouse hatred of the other, dressed up as reality. An unstable ego, by contrast, needs a repository for the inner discord of primal ambivalence. Typically, an unstable ego seeks relief by pairing the disposal of its inner tension with an identification with a desired quality – Moss's (2021) 'vertical splitting' (see also, Figlio 2006; Steiner 2020, 15–52). Patrick Wolfe (82), for example, shows that, in post-Reconstruction United States, anti-Black racism reinforced White solidarity: Through its 'shared obsession with excluding Black people [, it] was part of the consolidation of a White proletariat out of the fractious human mix engendered by the convergence of old and new migrations. Racial overlordship compensated for common deprivations.'

Wolfe shows that Blacks became an easy target for denigration because they resolved an inner discord in the racial overlords from the influx and amalgamation of immigrants. Skin colour marked them out as not white, but the delusional aspect was clear, for example, in identifying Black as the 'blood quantum': One drop of Black blood. Not only was it invisible: It was an imaginary creation that seemed to confer the reality of an essential difference on which domination could be based. The perceptual reality, that Blacks are darker than Whites, was a cover for the delusion, anchoring it to what one could see. The evident difference, as the marker of an apparent, essential difference, diffused the internal discord within the white population by *creating* harmony in suppressing the Black population, now equally *created* as *Black* more than seen to be black.[3] The projective core of delusion is clear. If only one drop of blackness could undermine the dominating majority race, how powerful must it be, and how much has it taken over the secure, self-affirmation of the dominating race.

Wolfe traces racism as a thread through disparate historical situations, different from Black slavery in the USA. Studies, such as Wolfe's, aim to distil the common features of different historically specific forms of colonial domination; that is, situations in which one group encroaches upon another. Economic and territorial domination pushes indigenous people into the margin, taking their land, its wealth and their wealth as producers, whether labourers or slaves. But these factors are not enough to create racism.

> Race ... is a trace of history: Colonised populations continue to be racialised in specific ways (2)... Whether presented juridically or geographically ... the threat to social space is no mere metaphor. Rather, in the most concrete of both practical and geographical senses, and often simultaneously, race and place are inextricable. (16) ... [Extending Mary Douglas' idea that dirt is matter out of place], race denotes certain peoples as being out of place, rendering the subordinate populations concerned inherently dirty ... The *primal threat* posed by *contamination* sheds some light on the barbarity characterising colonisers' treatment of subject populations. *To contaminate is to invade.* Race's deep anatomical moorings bring together geographical and physiological mappings so *that a people in the wrong place*[4] *is experienced as an assault on the body*, summoning a reflex response, which though collectively enacted, is *personally experienced at a powerfully intimate level.* (17; my emphasis)

The common thread in the colonialisms that Wolfe studies is that the coloniser wants the territory and everything thing that it yields, but more than that: The native population is not to exist. Except that it does, and its alterity is to be eliminated, sometimes by dilution into the settler population (as with indigenous populations in Australia and the US), sometimes by segregation as a distinct and totally dominated 'race' (as with Backs after the abolition of slavery in the US), sometimes by eliminating it physically (as in the Holocaust). Racism is the category that ties together the different historical situations of domination. One way or the other, the self is equated with the extinction of the other. Consciously, it might be seen only as domination. In the Unconscious, it is an equation: Self = – other.

The most egregious example of this equation, in which a delusionally created object condenses an array of relationships into one, hated, form, is the Holocaust. Wolfe asks how the age-old Judaeophobia became modern antisemitism in the 19th and 20th centuries. Jewish emancipation gave rise to a rival workforce, as did the emancipation of the slaves in the United States. Eastern and Western European Jews, so different in appearance and in assimilation into gentile society, coalesced as 'Jew'. Projective identification based on delusion is clear here, as it was in the case of anti-Black racism. The character of the Jew became the negative equivalent of the capitalist. 'When applied to capital, the negative qualities of the Jews acquired positive complements: Cunning, cupidity, parvenuism, pushiness and related vices figured as the market virtues of shrewdness, enterprise, innovation and drive. So long as it was not Jewish, greed was good'. The unbounded, universal circulation of capital was the virtuous side of the bad cosmopolitan Jew with no allegiance (the bad self, in Klein's theory of projective identification). The national state could create a boundary in which the Jew was an outsider, to maintain the good inside by extruding the bad, in a version of a colonial mentality and repressive apparatus.

In the sense of externalization, colonialism created race (101). Wolfe uses Freud's concept of condensation and of paranoid delusion as an attempt to reconstruct a bond with reality, along with Arendt's insistence that anti-semitism was not about the Jews. He concludes that this new, racial Judaeophobia, involved

> an ideological condensation, the channelling of a confused welter of latent resentments onto a single, clearly defined and locally available hate-object. Refracted through the embodied, intensely cathected prism of race, antisemitism mobilized an emotional language intense enough to give vent to the diffuse discontents of a deeply disturbed class. Each and every Jew gathered all this unto him- or herself. It is in this concentratedness, I wish to suggest, that antisemitism partook of its mystic potency, inscribing its mark of Cain upon and within every Jew. (105)

The Jew is, in Wolfe's formulation, a paranoid reconstruction of reality, not the reality of anyone or any perceived piece of reality. The Jew, as opposed to Jews, organizes perplexities, confusions, discontents, internal dissonance, into a unity as a hate-object. A hate-object is a homogenized condensation of individuals, as in Moss's hating in the first person plural, an object of action, not of thinking – like a paedo, or the feminine. Just as Wolfe traces racism through diverse historical situations, and finds a colonial mentality and practice behind it, through which property – land, labour, products, identity – can be estranged and taken, so to with the Jew who lives among the colonizers. So, too, I propose, with the feminine, which lives intimately with white, male, misogynist toxic masculinity. The feminine – not females, not this female, not this woman – is the hate-object; not of males, this male, this man, but of toxic masculinity.

Toxicity in the Depressive World

Bear in mind the association between racism, anti-feminism and primal threat of contamination. It is more than matter out of place or in the wrong place. It bespeaks a deeply internal invasion, 'experienced at a powerfully intimate level'. It transforms Wolfe's idea (17) that race is 'an assault *on* the body' into an incursion *into* the body. That is the world of toxicity, which, in my view, is what tags the unconscious dread of depressive catastrophe. The phallic world is a world of omnipotence, in which what is lost can be magically regained, and it parades itself openly and proudly; the depressive world is hidden, both humble in its concern for the object and on the edge of lonely despair at the depletion of life by a toxic attack that contaminates it.

The world of toxicity, with the dread of contamination inherent in it, is repressed in the logic of domination as the exercise of power, whether imposed physically or by 'law', as in economic relations. Domination creates a belief in superiority and inferiority. It seems rational, in the sense of easily understood and legitimized. The epithet, 'toxic', obscures the very meaning to which it gives voice. As a repression, it brings the unconscious into consciousness, but distorted. The dread of contamination by toxic attack is expressed, barely masked. The power to impose laws or control minority groups hides the internal, toxic incursion and the dread of contamination that follows upon it, but it shows through. The 'blood quantum' is a glaring example of toxicity that shows through the suppression of power. In the case of anti-Black racism in post-Reconstruction United States, the one-drop rule was codified in legislation, defining 'Black' as one-drop: No matter how diluted with settler blood, Black blood could contaminate bloodlines and spread throughout the bloodstock. The paranoid structure and defence is clear. Hatred seizes the interior of the Black person, homogenized into the Black race, and creates the contaminated – now feared as contaminating – object. It is projective identification that creates the Black racial object, implemented by Davids' internal racial object as the ideal who represents the right and the certain.

That interior dimension of projective identification was brought out in Klein's definition, in which she spoke of projecting *into* and of the object *as* the bad self. This account of projective identification, along with that of envy and narcissism, takes us squarely to the internal dimension, which is carried inside the economic and territorial drivers of racism. It gives us a handle on the barbarity, the dehumanization, the infliction of inferiority. It is the territory of replacement ideology. The rage of replacement ideology, as a White supremacist movement, betrays the unconscious existential threat of depleted whiteness as depleted identity. The ego is existentially threatened by the object – contaminated by it, at the level of narcissism and envy. The indigenous population – even the slave – possesses, not only the land or the productive power that can be usurped as geographical or physiological territory. It has something more, something interior, in its very substance, which the colonizer is driven to acquire. The display of domination and the privileges that attend it are implemented with the gloss of superiority, but the intense denigration and suppression bespeak, not the confidence of secure power, but a forever looming existential crisis.

White supremacist group are protective of their own women but an overly zealous protectiveness suggests an idealization and idealization conceals contempt. The trace of denigration – perhaps unconscious – of women, really woman – is easily found. The overtly racist Ku Klux Klan, for example, has persistently alluded to the threat of rape of white women by non-white men, which suggests a projective element. In one murder trial of Klansmen and neo-Nazis in Greensboro, North Carolina, in 1979, the 'non-white' threat came from the Communist Workers Party, several members of which were killed. The defendants were freed in two trials and the shooting unified the white power movement (Belew, 55–76). The projection was complete.

The Pollution of (Mother) Nature

Up to now, I have argued throughout that the primal threat to male (White supremacist, misogynist, replacement ideologue, toxic masculine) identity is the feminine of the female, not as a stable difference, but in the dilution of masculine identity in the narcissism of small differences. They are all forms of replacement ideology, which gain emotional intensity by reaching back to the primal ambivalence at their root. The toxic incursion into the feminine by primal (seminal) ambivalence evokes a dread of a contaminated object, which then appears everywhere, in the way Rosenfeld (1987, 167) describes the persecutory object of projective identification.

It might seem strange to range the pollution nature with replacement ideologies, and to ground it, as well, in misogyny. There is a history of the human relationship with nature as both bounteous and enervating, draining every drop of energy and deadly at any moment when one's guard is relaxed. I will just point out this tense, endangered relationship to nature untamed, and turn to what I previously (Figlio 1996) called 'the ominous in nature'. With this expression, I mean to capture the uncanny sense of something dreaded in nature, whose capacity to absorb and neutralize the assaults upon her had been compromised; she no longer recovered her nurturing provision, but turned nasty. Nature is typically treated as feminine – mother – writ large, perhaps the final, crucial repository of ambivalence, ample enough to manage it, until ... (see also Searles 1972). I now put the ominous in nature squarely with seminal ambivalence: The pollution of the feminine internal world, including nature, creates a feminine that threatens to absorb the masculine who yearns to blend into her and reacts with narcissistic rage against her.

As in my earlier use of a philosopher's analysis to triangulate my psychoanalytic thesis, I draw now on the large-scale empirical work of McCright and Dunlap (2011). They review a large literature on climate change denial, which concludes consistently that it is predominantly espoused by conservative white males. From this research, they adopt the unemotional, cognitive terms, 'risk perception', 'identity-protective cognition' and 'system-justifying tendencies' for the attitudes of these men. They are men who tolerate risk, root their views on climate change in a group identity and stick to it. This earlier research also identified an affinity with hierarchy and trust in authorities to manage risk (also characteristic of *The Authoritarian Personality*; Adorno et al. 1950).

McCright and Dunlap accept these findings and set out their research goal on the basis of it.

> The parallel dynamics of identity-protective cognition and system-justifying attitudes also suggest that heightened emotional and psychic investment in defending in-group claims may translate into misperceived understanding about problems like climate change that threaten the continued order of the system. [W]e thus expect a positive association between conservative white males' self-reported understanding of global warming and their climate change denial. (1165)

Their expectation was confirmed by yearly data, covering 2001–2010, collected by The Gallup Poll on climate change denial in the United States. Climate change deniers were overwhelmingly conservative white males. Even more striking, a subgroup of about 30% of these men, who were confident in their knowledge of climate change, raised the correlation between conservative male and climate change denial substantially. These men held a variety of views: Global warming would not occur, recent temperature rises were not the effect of human activities, the media exaggerated it, they were not worried about it, there was no scientific consensus on climate change.

The last two views stand out: These men seemed unconcerned about risk, and they were clear that there was no scientific basis for the worry that others felt. The authors draw attention to the tolerance of risk of these white men risk but also to the power of entrenched belief and resistance to change. This final point was reinforced by a later study (McCright, A. et al. 2015), which examined the effect of climate change denial messages on belief in the reality of climate change and positive outcomes that could flow from acting on the basis of it. Females believed in the reality of climate change more than males and supported more strongly policies to reduce greenhouse gas emissions. Climate denial messages significantly reduced belief in the reality of climate change and reactions to that belief among extreme conservatives, an effect that diminished in proportion to liberal beliefs, to the point of no effect among extreme liberals. The conservative group were also more anti-reflexive; that is, less given to critical self-evaluation of their adherence to the presumed tenets of modern western capitalism.

Thus, climate change denial messages attract conservatively inclined people – typically men – away from believing in a demonstrated reality and its harmful impact. It suggests a triumph over realty by misinformation, turning away from evidence and entrenching oneself in group ideology. It suggests the power of illusion, even delusion, and the cohesive strength of bonding through shared emotion. Lying, as distinct from distortion, endows it with exceptional power (Figlio 2021).

McCright and Dunlap's quantitative research work is supplemented by Veldman's (2019) qualitative study of climate scepticism among traditionalist evangelicals in southern USA, based on interviews and focus groups. She found, to her surprise, that they created an 'embattled mentality', in which they fought what they construed as anti-Christian thinking and action by believers in climate change: In government, in schools, among scientists, among liberals, in secular society at large. The embattled position of traditionalist evangelicals in defence of Christianity encouraged and justified a sometimes virulent denunciation of secular culture. Moreover, their embattled position was self-justifying. They were driven, not just by attitudes towards the natural world, but by embattlement itself: By their attitude towards environmentalists, against whom they could maintain a favourable identity. Environmentalists were 'radicals', 'crazy people', concerned with matters not of ultimate concern, secular, spiritually suspect. It was not just a matter of embracing different ideas, but of continuing social 'identity work' (115–122).

Veldman did not focus on gender and cannot speak to the connection between misogyny and anti-environmentalism shown by McCright and Dunlap. Other studies confirm the relationship between masculinity and a reactive conservative force in US society (Belew 2018; Du Mez 2021), without dealing with anti-environmentalism. Du Mez, for example, complements Veldman. She does not deal with climate change but shows the religious and political influence of conservative evangelicals, reacting to feminism and to a sense of weakness of American society, by consolidating an image of patriarchal, patriotic, militaristic masculinity, especially in post-World War II. I think, however, we can begin to put together a picture of a thread of misogyny running through the extreme conservatism of various groups, strongly influenced by white males.

Let's look more closely at the belief that human activity contributes to climate change. McCright and Dunlap (2011) based the assessment of attitudes towards the human contribution to climate change on the Gallop Poll question, 'And from what you have heard or read, do you believe increases in the Earth's temperature over the last century are due more to—the effects of pollution from human activities OR natural changes in the environment that are not due to human activities?' Note that the keyword is 'pollution'. The authors don't make anything of the penumbra of ideas evoked by the word, pollution, but Anne Pesek (2021) identifies a network of climate change denying organizations that aim to create a powerful image of carbon dioxide – one of the main greenhouse gasses – not only as *not* a pollutant, but a necessary, healthy component of the ecosystem. The concentration of CO_2 should, if anything, be increased. She names this movement, 'carbon vitalism', which 'has been institutionalized within a network of conservative policy, science, and communications groups, composed almost entirely of white men' (5).

Carbon vitalist climate denial began in 2006, with the airing of a short climate denialist commercial, entitled *Energy*, produced in 14 US cities by the conservative think tank, Competitive Enterprise Institute. It was screened contemporaneously with Al Gore's film, *An Inconvenient Truth*, which dramatically portrayed the impact of global warming from human CO_2 production, and a US Supreme Court ruling in Massachusetts vs EPA (Environmental Protection Agency), which required the EPA to act to restrict CO_2 production. Previously, the EPA did not include CO_2 within its jurisdiction within the Clean Air Act because Congress had not included it as a pollutant.

As Pesek (2021, 2) reports, *Energy* invites viewers to think differently of CO_2, with these two advocates of reducing CO_2 in mind.

At first, this molecule is presented as a mysterious link between seemingly unrelated images: sunbathers, a jogger, antelope, forests, and a young white girl blowing on dandelion seeds. The narrator explains, "There's something in these pictures you can't see. It's essential to life. We breath it out. Plants breath it in. It comes from animal life, the oceans, the earth, and the fuels we find in it." The music transitions to long pastoral chords as the invisible connection is named:

"It's called carbon dioxide—CO2 …Now some politicians want to label carbon dioxide a pollutant."

[Returning to the girl with the dandelion], "We … call it life."

Carbon vitalists drive their argument home, not by engaging with climate science, but by appealing to a vital contribution that carbon dioxide makes to modern life. More fundamentally, carbon dioxide is 'the stuff of life itself' (5). They claim that 'the global combustion of fossil fuels will produce a net benefit for all people and organisms, given the resulting increases in food productivity and the modest (>1°C) expected global rise in temperatures associated with this CO_2 "enrichment"' (6). They appeal beyond this claim to the vital contribution that human activity makes, even the contribution that you and I make by exhaling carbon dioxide.

These empirical studies complement the psychoanalytic view that I am putting forward: The widespread currency of toxic masculinity represses the dread of seminal failure and pollution. In doing so, it also provides a conduit for its expression in a distorted, unrecognized form. Extreme conservative – mostly white male – belief consolidates as a group identity around this repression. It is a masculine identity, reinforced by asserting a misogynist anti-feminine posture, vividly captured in a recent email from Andrew Tate, prominent in social media for his masculine, anti-feminine stance, to the environmental activist, Greta Thunberg. He provocatively asked for her email address, so he could send a list of his cars with their 'their respective enormous emissions'. Her curt reply suggested that she was well aware of his exhibitionist masculine posture. (reported by Solnit 2022). Experimental work also brings out the association between a masculine sensitivity to a gender challenge and behaving in less eco-friendly ways than women (Brough and Wilkie 2017).

This confrontational masculine identity is also impervious to evidence, and reinforced by the need continuously to resist evidence. Pollution must not enter the belief system, nor must evidence that could incriminate conservative identity be recognized. The desideratum to repress any such implication is more determined because it stirs up unconscious ambivalence of contaminated thoughts. They are projected into people who, so to speak, admit to having contaminated thoughts, clearly revealed in the pollution with which they are preoccupied. Environmentalists, in Veldman's research, were 'causing moral decay by promoting secular values' (123). In psychoanalytic terms, they were guilty of debasing the good object, located in God, by attending too much to the earth itself. They could then serve as the repository for the projected guilt that would, unprojected, motivate reparation (Klein 1937).

Climate scepticism is, in my view, a particular target of dispute with environmentalism because greenhouse gases are invisible. What we see are the reactions of nature: Nature contaminated, injured on the inside by bad seed, perhaps beyond recovery in herself or by reparation; the good object undermined by an ego not good enough to make her better nor able to feel restored by her recovery. It is a depressive catastrophe.

Conclusion: Misogyny as the Foundation of Replacement Ideologies

I have proposed that toxic masculinity lies at the core of a cluster of replacement catastrophes. Based in primal ambivalence, it is the site where misogyny erupts; misogyny becomes the template the broader social forms of replacement ideology. I have located them in a narcissistic dilemma, with the narcissism of small differences at the core, which re-runs the primal process of emerging from primary narcissism in reverse. Some similarity between the two groups, of no significance in itself, re-kindles an existential dread. As the ego approaches its double, it begins to lose its identity into it. As in the nascent ego's emergence from narcissism, it calls up the imperative to abolish the object. More typically, as in racism, some marker of difference, also insignificant in itself, justifies a virulent reaction. For the male ego, the narcissism of small differences struggles against an entangled relationship with object, threatening the resolution for which it strives as it matures in the more complex stages of psychosexual maturation. Every male must come into some sort of relationship with the female: The masculine with the feminine.

Masculine advocacy has various tags: The manosphere, toxic masculinity, White supremacy, (some) climate change denial, Incel grievance, misogyny, racism and many others. I see them as varieties of replacement ideology. I mean by this, that they give voice and action to an underlying anxiety, not only of diminished status and weakened identity in society, against which they reassert their identity – that is conscious – but to an anxiety of elimination, in the Unconscious. Their denigration of liberalism, effeminacy, women, femininity, science and democracy is a conduit from a primal, narcissistic vulnerability in the earliest stages of ego formation and object relations, into compelling political, ideological or religious stances.

My point is not that misogyny is more serious, more violent, more hating than other racisms; rather, that it is a template. At the extreme, *phallic* masculinity has become the performative, dramatic expression of its opposite, *toxic* masculinity: Brandished as the near-universal epithet for a phallic maleness, idealized in particular male circles, and denounced elsewhere for its demeaning, often violent assault on the feminine. Toxic masculinity has also crystallized a widespread anxiety over toxicity in every corner of everyday life. This anxiety, gathered into toxic masculinity, gives a masculine quality to degradation by poisoning: Of culture and nature, and of personal, social and economic relations. The toxic is insidious: Not an assault from the outside, not an impact *on*, but an erosion *inside*. Toxic corrodes life. It suggests an effluent of waste that must be separated from the processes of the healthy organism, of which it was once part. Toxic reminds us that the bad is mixed with the good. It suggests dangerous feelings and behaviour that ride inside good feelings and behaviour, akin to the poison that medicines become if we overdose. Male fertility and reproductive organs and processes produce semen, which is life-giving and poisonous.

In the next chapter, we will look into a specific case study: The financial crash of 2008. Popular opinion saw it as a crash of the masculinity of the banking system. I will argue that it was a crash of phallic masculinity, in which toxic masculinity became visible, revealing a dread of a depressive crisis from seminal failure.

Notes

1   I am using misogyny to cover all forms of masculine predominance. That might seem too narrow and extreme. Men do not necessarily hate women when they press a view that dominates women's views. I need a single concept to express the superiority and the denigration, whether mild or aggressive, that it implies. Misogyny does that.

2   Hustvedt (2019, 226) quotes from a Twitter experience reported to Amnesty International by the British writer and producer, Danielle Dash.

> "The Violence," she said, "is at the intersection of everything that I am – for example – 'I am going to rape you, you black bitch. You have the misogyny, and you have the racism and you have the sexual violence all mixed up into one delicious stew of cesspool shit.'"

In his monumental, classic study of racism in the United States, *An American Dilemma*, Gunnar Myrdal (1944, 1073) made an immediate connection between race and sex:

> In every society there are at least two groups of people, besides the Negroes, who are characterized by high social visibility expressed in physical appearance, dress, and patterns of behavior, and who have been "supressed." We refer to

women and children. Their present status, as well as their history and their problems in society, reveal striking similarities to those of the Negroes.

Both blacks and women, as a category, were to be held in an inferior position by the paternalism of whites as a group. Myrdal's analysis is partly economic, but also in terms of status, in particular the status of one group next to another, not one individual next to another. In the case of white racism, he shows that, where two groups are more immediately in competition and insecure in status, aggression is intensified. Lower-class whites vent on blacks the frustration that finds no outlet among whites (597). They nonetheless identify with higher status whites, and the 'two white groups agree upon the Negroes as a scapegoat and the proper object for exploitation and hatred' (598). The driver of suppression, denigration and exclusion was a dread of dilution of racial purity, with miscegenation at the root. Miscegenation took on the 'popular magical concept of blood', hedged by taboo, and was severely suppressed and punished as the insidious source of dilution. 'Sex becomes in this popular theory the principle around which the whole structure of segregation ... is organized' (587).

If miscegenation, as the source of the dread of dilution, fuels racist hatred, might we postulate that it fuels misogynist hatred as well? Myrdal (1078; my emphasis) says that paternalism subjected women and blacks to a parallel position, woman hindered in competition by the 'function of procreation', black people by the 'doctrine of unassimilability. *But note*: 'The second barrier is actually much stronger ... But the first *is more eternally inexorable.*'

Sex with 'woman' (an abstract group, not any individual female) – that intimate moment of being 'inside', with semen absorbed into it – is ominously dangerous, unless buttressed by the superiority of race or misogyny. Myrdal's research is into the situation in America but is likely to find more general application (see, for example, Wolfe 2016). In an equally monumental and classic study of women, *The Second Sex*, Simone de Beauvoir (1949) said of *An American Dilemma* and discussions with the black writer, Richard Wright, that (as Kirkpatrick 2019, 237–238, reports) they

> had inspired her book on women. This book ... made her "begin to think again about the book I began about women's situation. I should like to write a book as important as his big one about Negroes." She wanted to do for women what Myrdal had done for African Americans, showing the way racism and sexism were rooted in the contingencies of culture – that with women, too, people were hiding behind alibis.

With hints of Ferenczi's claim that men identify with their semen, de Beauvoir (1949, 21) begins her study in vivid terms.

> Woman? Very simple, say those who like simple answers: she is a womb, an ovary; she is a female: this word is enough to define her ... The word "female" evokes a saraband of images: an enormous round egg snatching and castrating the agile sperm ...

I am grateful to E. S. Lyon for directing me to Myrdal and Beauvoir and these connections in their thinking (also see Lyon 2004 for an analysis of Myrdal's classic study of racism in America).

3   This mechanism of racism is vividly portrayed and cogently explained in psychoanalytic terms. The classic, extensive, empirical study of oppressive ideology, the multi-authored, *The Authoritarian Personality*, sponsored by the American Jewish Committee (Adorno et al. 1950), converges on a psychoanalytic understanding (not a total surprise, because it also draws on psychoanalysis). In it,

Adorno (613) speaks of the Jew of antisemitism as an 'imaginary foe', the target of 'omnipotence fantasies projected upon a whole outgroup', upon whom the application of 'such ideas to factual experience comes close to paranoid delusion'
4   Freud (1908, 172) said, 'Dirt is matter in the wrong place.'

References

Adorno, T. W., et al. (1950) *The Authoritarian Personality*. NY: Harper & Row; London/NY: Verso, 2019.

Belew, K. (2018) *Bring the War Home: The White Power Movement and Paramilitary America*. Cambridge, Mass./London: Harvard University Press.

Bion, W. R. (1962) A theory of Thinking. In *Second Thoughts: Selected Papers of Psycho-Analysis*. London: Heinemann, 1967; Karnac, 1984, 110–119.

Boehm, F. (1930) The Femininity-Complex in Men. *International Journal of Psychoanalysis*, 11: 444–469.

Brough, A. R. and Wilkie, J. E. B. (2017) Men Resist Green Behavior as Unmanly: A Surprising Reason for Resistance to Environmental Goods and Habits. *Scientific American* 26 December. https://www.scientificamerican.com/article/men-resist-green-behavior-as-unmanly/, Accessed 2 January 2023.

Davids, M. Fakhry (2011) *Internal Racism: A Psychoanalytic Approach to Race and Difference*. London: Karnac.

de Beauvoir, S. (1949) *le deuxième sexe* [*The Second Sex*], translated by C. Borde and S. Malovany-Chevallier. London: Random House, 2009.

Du Mez, K. (2021) *Jesus and John Wayne: How White Evangelicals Corrupted a Faith and Fractured a Nation*. NY: Liveright Publishing Corp.

Figlio, K. (1996) The Ominous in Nature. *Free Associations* 6(2): 276–296.

Figlio, K. (2006) The Absolute State of Mind in Society and the Individual. *Psychoanalysis, Culture and Society* 11(2): 119–143.

Figlio, K. (2017) *Remembering as Reparation: Psychoanalysis and Historical Memory*. London: Palgrave Macmillan, 2017.

Figlio, K. (2018) Fundamentalism and the Delusional Creation of an Enemy. In Krüger, S., Figlio, K. and Richards, B. (eds) *Fomenting Political Violence: Fantasy, Language, Media, Action*. London: Palgrave, 2018, 149–166.

Figlio, K. (2021) Lying in Autocratic Society. *Free Associations: Psychoanalysis and Culture, Media, Groups, Politics* 83: 15–28.

Freud, S. (1908) Character and Anal Erotism. *The Standard Edition of the Complete Psychological Works of Sigmund Freud* 9: 167–176.

Freud, S. (1914) On Narcissism: An Introduction. *The Standard Edition of the Complete Psychological Works of Sigmund Freud* 14: 73–105.

Freud, S. (1915) Instincts and their Vicissitudes. *The Standard Edition of the Complete Psychological Works of Sigmund Freud* 14: 109–140.

Freud, S. (1917) Mourning and Melancholia. *The Standard Edition of the Complete Psychological Works of Sigmund Freud* 14: 237–258.

Freud, S. (1930) Civilization and its Discontents. *The Standard Edition of the Complete Psychological Works of Sigmund Freud* 21: 57–146.

Horney, K. (1932) The Dread of Women: Observations on a Specific Difference in the Dread Felt by Men and Women Respectively for the Opposite Sex. *International*

Journal of Psychoanalysis 13: 348–360; reprinted in *Feminine Psychology*. NY: Norton, 1967, 133–146.

Hustvedt, S. (2019) What Does a Man Want. In *Mothers, Fathers, and Others*. London: Sceptre, 2021, 225–253.

Johanssen, J. (2022) *Fantasy, Online Misogyny and the Manosphere: Male Bodies of Dis/Inhibition*. London/NY: Routledge.

Kirkpatrick, K. (2019) *Becoming Beauvoir: A Life*. London: Bloomsbury Academic.

Klein, M. (1937) Love, Guilt and Reparation. In *The Writings of Melanie Klein*, vol. 1. London: The Hogarth Press and the Institute of Psycho-Analysis, 1975, 306–343.

Lyon, E. S. (2004) Researching Race Relations: Myrdal's American Dilemma from a Methodological Perspective. *Acta Sociologica* 47: 203–217.

McCright, A. and Dunlap, R. (2011) Cool Dudes: The Denial of Climate Change Among Conservative White Males in the United States. *Global Climate Change* 21: 1163–1172.

McCright, A., et al. (2015) Examining the Effectiveness of Climate Change Frames in the Face of a Climate Change Denial Counter-Frame. *Topics in Cognitive Science* 8: 76–97.

Moss, D. (2021) On Having Whiteness. *Journal of the American Psychoanalytic Association* 69: 355–372.

Myrdal, G. (1944) *An American Dilemma, Volume II: The Negro Problem and Modern Democracy*. NY: Harper and Row/New Brunswick NJ: Transaction, 1996.

Nussbaum, M. (2018) *The Monarchy of Fear: A Philosopher Looks at Our Political Crisis*. Oxford: Oxford University Press.

Pesek, A. (2021) Carbon Vitalism: Life and the Body in Climate Denial. *Environmental Humanities* 13: 1–20.

Press Gazette. (2012, May 11). A Tale Told Too Much: The Paediatrician Vigilantes. Retrieved from http://www.pressgazette.co.uk/a-tale-told-too-much-the-paediatrician-vigilantes/

Rosenfeld, H. (1987) Projective Identification in Clinical Practice. In *Impasse and Interpretation: Therapeutic and Anti-Therapeutic Factors in the Psychoanalytic Treatment of Psychotic, Borderline and Neurotic Patients*. London: Tavistock, 157–190.

Searles, H. F. (1972) Unconscious Processes in Relation to the Environmental Crisis. *Psychoanalytic Review* 59: 361–374. In *Countertransference and Related Subjects: Selected Papers*. NY: International Universities Press, 1979, 228–242.

Solnit, R. (2022) Greta Thunberg Ends Year with One of the Greatest Tweets in History. *Guardian* 31 December. https://www.theguardian.com/commentisfree/2022/dec/31/greta-thunberg-andrew-tate-tweet, Accessed 2 January 2022.

Steiner, J. (2020) *Illusion, Delusion, and Irony in Psychoanalysis*. Abington, Oxon/NY: Routledge.

Veldman, R. (2019) *The Gospel of Climate Skepticism: Why Evangelical Christians Oppose Action on Climate Change*. Oakland: University of California Press.

Walker, S. and Garamvolgyi, F. (2022) Viktor Orbán Sparks Outrage with Attack on 'Race Mixing' in Europe. *The Guardian* 24 July. Available at https://www.theguardian.com/world/2022/jul/24/viktor-orban-against-race-mixing-europe-hungary

Wolfe, P. (2016) *Traces of History: Elementary Structures of Race*. London/NY: Verso.

Chapter 11

Toxic Masculinity in the Financial Crisis

A Case Study

Financial Toxicity

I turn now to a case study of toxic masculinity in a specific social situation: The financial crisis of 2008. It was a moment at which, suddenly, the value of financial assets vanished. One minute, these assets had value and were the source of confidence in the clever strategies of the market men, the investment bankers; the next minute, they were worthless, without an assignable value. Not only were they worthless: They poisoned the entire financial system. Trust between financial institutions collapsed and they suddenly refused to lend to each other. The extent of 'leverage' was laid bare and support for this over-extended, unsecured lending vanished. With their assets valueless, so – at least briefly – confidence in their possessors and manipulators collapsed. These assets, which poisoned the financial system, were called toxic assets.

But market instability was also well-known, and the looming crisis was both no surprise, and an unforeseen catastrophe. Some actors no doubt both knew it and continued in practices that would provoke it, hoping to get out before it hit them. Others managed not to know what they knew: The defence of disavowal, in psychoanalytic terms. Still others rejected what they knew: The defence of denial, in psychoanalytic terms. Yet others created a magical belief in the power of the financial system that was about to crash: An omnipotent, manic defence. In a knowing ignorance, however, they might all have been astounded at the crash that nearly wrecked economies across the world. They were nearly all men, behaving masculine.[1]

The crisis was a specific incident in which toxic masculinity, joined to phallic narcissism, irrupted into popular consciousness. The investors in toxic assets were mainly men. At the time, the connection was often made between the toxic assets and the toxic masculinity that poisoned them. Confidence had included the assured status of men next to women, whose status was to be based on their servicing men, practically and in deference and admiration. The masculine character of the financial markets and the reaction among some men to the collapse added strength and virulence to an already rising

DOI: 10.4324/9781003455790-16

tide of anti-feminist, anti-woman aggression and hatred. The financial crisis was, therefore, also a chapter in the history of misogyny.

According to Lord Turner (2009), author of the Financial Services Authority report on the 2008 global financial crisis, the makers and traders of financial products precipitated the crisis by disregarding economic models that demonstrated an intrinsic instability in markets, especially markets for financial products. Instead, they had concocted forms of risk management that reinforced their belief in innovation, but which concealed fundamental flaws, buried in inconceivable complexity. They constructed abstract models of risk, in which risk could not be calculated. Far from expertly anticipating the movements of a robust, rational market, they were creating a world of illusion, buttressed by an accumulation of wealth that seemed to confer material reality upon illusion, but in fact merely compounded it.

Douglas Kirsner (1990) had already drawn attention to the related omnipotent belief in a sound economy following the 1987 stock-market crash. He argued that this belief was an illusion – a wish-fulfilling conviction, in Freud's definition of the term – that ignored the reality of economic cycles and the unpredictability of the market. People lived in a phantasy in which an intrinsically 'good' sound market was split from the 'bad' extrinsic factors that caused the crash. The crash was a blow to the market's narcissism, which produced denial rather than a recognition of reality accompanied by a sense of responsibility for repair. The 2008 financial crisis moved this sort of illusion to a new level, in that the products traded in the market were not goods but financial products, which generated powerful illusions themselves. These illusions were toxic in themselves, but also in the belief that 'bad' extrinsic factors caused the crash, while they were in fact inside the market, corrupting it.

A key component of this illusory world is what Mark Stein (2003) has called 'organizational narcissism'. It involves a self-inflation that rests on demeaning an 'other', but that demeaned other is a projection, also an illusion. This self-inflation expands without limit, because the projected other grows monstrous by the projection, and must continuously be overcome by greater self-inflation, greater wealth, to confirm its superiority. This organizational narcissism is characteristically masculine.

Commentaries on the crisis provide considerable evidence that it was produced by men. Of the 159 'characters' in the cast of Sorkin's (2009) commentary on the financial crisis, for example, just eleven are women. Similarly, there are only two women in Paulson's (2010, vii–xii) cast of 55 characters (excluding politicians and non-economic advisers). Many commentators have remarked on the dominating masculinity of the crisis and the greater vulnerability of women to its effects: Not only was it produced by men, but men would be relatively protected from the consequences of their mismanagement. Some women have claimed that they would not have created such a mess, and that the stability of the financial system depends on employing more women. The news media, professional as well as popular, have tagged the crisis a masculine catastrophe.[2]

Both popular and professional writers saw a market personality that was masculine, not only in the gender bias of its management but also in the sense that it was characterized by certainty and risk-taking, without regard for reality or for the damage that might have resulted. Claims of superiority are actually claims to omnipotence. In an identification of the ego with the ego-ideal as an idealized object, the ego becomes, in Freud's terminology, an ideal-ego. From the status of the ideal-ego or a group of ideal-egos in identification with each other, ordinary, non-ideal figures – and more specifically, women – are denigrated by vertical splitting. Accounts of the events of the crisis read like thrillers – a form of fiction that is crisis-ridden and whose protagonists are typically male.

The financial crisis was a dual crisis: A crisis of masculinity as well as a crisis of the capitalist economy. The crisis magnified and opened for study the illusory dimension of both the financial market and of masculine phantasy.[3] In line with psychoanalytic convention, 'phantasy' here signifies an unconscious creation, as opposed to conscious fantasy. The masculine stereotypes attributed to the actors in the drama of the crisis were conscious, but I am referring to the unconscious dimension. In this unconscious realm, inflation and deflation of the economy reinforced a stereotype of masculinity as the inflation and deflation of phallic narcissism. In turn, this stereotype, already pervasive in the culture, normalized the behaviour of market innovators and traders of financial products. The stereotype is of a confident, single-minded, self-aggrandizing, fierce competitiveness, unconcerned about consequences beyond demonstrating superiority in achieving market advantage through the phantasy of creating wealth as if from nothing. [4] Business cycles are no more debilitating than cycles of phallic potency. The magic in the reciprocal reinforcement between markets and masculinity is phallic.

As I have argued throughout this book, phallic masculinity defends against a procreative – seminal – masculinity. The disregard that follows is total; it is a not-seeing, what psychoanalysis calls a scotomization, a defence mechanism by which the subject utterly fails to see something about itself or its situation. The scotomization of seminal masculinity occurs in the literature and practice of psychoanalysis as well as in the culture at large. We can therefore observe this process in the detail of clinical work and use that insight to understand it in a wider context. The internal dynamics of psychoanalysis offer a reflection point for culture; and their accessibility to detailed psychoanalytic observation offers a model for cultural analysis (Figlio 2004; 2017, 45–72). In this case, because the clinical and cultural spheres share a phallic scotomization or occlusion of seminal masculinity, observing the eruption of seminal phantasies in the clinical situation helps us to characterize a parallel eruption in culture. The financial crisis was a particular expression of this scotomization and eruption of seminal phantasy. By investigating this clinical/cultural congruency, we can contribute to a reappraisal of both markets and masculinity, giving more prominence to their seminal aspect.

The congruency on which I will focus is captured during the global financial crisis in the sudden spread of references to 'toxic assets'. Toxic assets destabilized economies throughout the world and intruded into everyday life. They had become part of culture, even in the language of bankers, before the crisis, as a way of thinking, a source of dread of an invisible agent, like a pathogen, which contaminated the healthy life of societies.[5] 'Toxic thoughts' appeared in our vocabulary even earlier than toxic assets, further suggesting the contamination of the inside of society as we became aware of these new ideas. Shortly after the financial crisis, in the middle of anxiety about recovery, 'toxic' erupted into banking language. Reporting for *Market Business News*, Tom Petruno (2009) remarked:

> The use of "toxic" to describe high-risk mortgages has been *de rigueur* for the last two years. Now it looks like **Countrywide Financial** Corp. founder **Angelo R. Mozilo** might have coined the term. In the Securities and Exchange Commission's civil fraud case filed today against Mozilo, the agency includes excerpts from e-mails Mozilo wrote in spring 2006 to other Countrywide executives, describing his concerns about some of the lender's unconventional mortgages ... He wrote that the lender's program of granting subprime loans for 100% of the value of a borrower's home was "the most dangerous product in existence and there can be nothing more toxic and therefore requires that no deviation from [underwriting] guide-lines be permitted irrespective of the circumstances [and] [i]n all my years in the business I have never seen a more toxic product [sic]." ... But when Countrywide's risk-management department in April 2006 recommended increasing minimum credit scores for the loans ... the idea allegedly was opposed by **David Sambol**, who then headed the lender's production units (and who also is a defendant in the SEC's case). Sambol ... "noted that such an increase would make Countrywide uncompetitive with subprime lenders such as **New Century**, **Option One**, and **Argent**," the SEC says. (Petruno's emphasis)

'Toxic masculinity' had already been coined in the 1980s by Shepherd Bliss, a writer on masculinity, but only later, after the financial crisis, did it spread into culture, and then it spread quickly. Harrington (2021) has linked the currency of toxic masculinity to the feminist search for what goes wrong in masculinity – in my thinking, what poisons the relationships between men and women. I would add that women quickly seized on the financial crisis as a crisis in masculinity. In this feminist critique, aggressive masculinity had already infected culture, then it infected the very material foundation of society as well: The two crises were one crisis, a crisis borne of toxic masculinity. In my view, the financial crisis was a moment in which an ominous sense of there being something wrong – something toxic – in masculinity exploded into consciousness. It fractured the material base of society and in this devastation and the insecurity that spread from it, it also destabilized the culture and psychic realities of everyday life. The way it crept into the material and non-material worlds, then erupted, was akin to a toxic degradation.

I am treating the financial crisis as an event, a sudden, unrecognized, toxic incursion, against the background of a gradual toxic encroachment. In chapter 8, I located the toxicity of toxic masculinity in 'seminal ambivalence'. I aimed to show that this life-giving fluid also carried, in phantasy, a destructive force that could contaminate life from the inside – inside the female in the generation of new life. Semen enhances life; toxic semen destroys life. Semen is fertile; toxic semen is infertile. The toxic masculinity that has spread through our language is, for me, the material and psychic reality of toxic semen. The material and psychic infertility of toxic seminality lies beneath – defended by – the bluster of phallic masculinity. It is a deep dread of desolation, covered over by the fear of losing phallic masculine credibility.

We have noted that some analysts quicky rejected a phallic stage in girls in technical detail (Horney 1926; see also Abraham 1920).[6] With respect to phallic thinking in culture more broadly, it is noteworthy that Karen Horney also drew on the work of the sociologist, Georg Simmel, to point out that the theory was a product of, and represented, the masculinity of culture. It did not portray the experience of femininity but the male's horrified belief about what it was like to be a female. In 1946, Viola Klein, a sociologist and student of Karl Mannheim's, took up Horney's idea and inaugurated the cultural and technical critique of an implicit phallic masculinity in psychoanalytic theory. What stands out from this debate for me, however, is that both phallic monism and its repudiation scotomize seminal masculinity. The uniquely male contribution to procreation and the psychic reality of a generous masculinity also go unnoticed, including a concern for growth as a form of flowering or maturation, as opposed to an increase in size.

Theoretical Review

Just quickly to review the theoretical base of my argument, I associate phallic monism with Melanie Klein's concept of the paranoid-schizoid position. I see it as a defence against seminal masculinity, which I associate with her concept of the depressive position. Briefly, the paranoid-schizoid position entails a splitting of the ego and its objects into two forms, 'good' and 'bad', or, we might say, nurturant and destructive. This phantasy reinforces a defensive sense of superiority through the splitting of the ego, with idealisation of the self-sustained by projection of 'bad' objects and ego fragments, so that the repository-object becomes the bad self. The phallus represents such a superior positioning. It is an illusory, idealized object with which the ego identifies, threatened by the equally illusory, 'bad' paternal phallus with which it competes, and over which it assumes superiority by vertical splitting.

By contrast, 'seminal' masculinity, associated with Klein's concept of depressive anxiety, refers to a more integrated ego that perceives the object-world as damaged. The object is not split but both loved and hated, as the object of guilt and concern for damage. The procreation and sustenance of new life recreate concern for the state of the good internal object and for making it better, as in Klein's (1935) reparative impulse. I have also argued, however, that the tension in the depressive character of seminality carries forward, *nachträglich*, a primal, existential ambivalence that is worked through, with greater or lesser success, in the femininity phase. As a result, the insecurity of masculinity in its seminality is challenged at two levels.

Clinical findings support the division of masculinity into phallic and seminal. Phallic masculinity is supported by the phantasy of a single penis, simultaneously possessed by father and son. In the narcissistic world of phallic masculinity, there is only bigger and littler, only more or less, only accretion or depletion. Each male is threatened by the other with theft of his emblem of narcissistic intactness. Seminal masculinity, by contrast, is accompanied by phantasies of a qualitative capacity or incapacity. The normally fertile and reparative ego can be thrust into anxieties associated with seminal injury or destructiveness, such as experiencing the first ejaculation as a terrifying injury or insemination as poisoning, signalling an inability to sustain life or an unconscious wish to destroy it.

I have drawn attention to the comparative rarity of seminal phantasies in the psychoanalytic literature. I attribute this paucity to the power of the phallic stereotype inside as well as outside the consulting room. Briefly put, phallic phantasy is an illusion of unlimited expansion or collapse. Seminal phantasy, by contrast, engages with making good the depredations of the fertile soil and the feared destructiveness of bad semen. Phallic illusions are paranoid-schizoid, in that either the ego or the object is at risk of annihilation. Seminal phantasies are deeply ambivalent but include reparative urges to restore the good object.[7] The market crisis stripped its phallic narcissism of the thrall of its magic – only for a moment – followed by its recovery. The drama of a global economic collapse as a failure of phallic narcissism, however, also exposed the lack of seminal masculinity in enhancing and protecting life. It also brought a reactive surge of misogyny in the manosphere.

Market Magic: The Thrall of Illusion

Let us return to the financial crisis. For Flavia Morante (2010), the financial crisis was spurred on by 'the collective need to escape the reality of an increasingly complex and vulnerable global world and find an illusory refuge in the ownership of money and property' (18). It was – and is – a world that fosters a 'psychic retreat', in which 'reality is neither fully accepted nor completely disavowed' (Steiner 1993, 88). Morante argues that this illusory condition was sustained by the absence of the father, which encouraged a quick, magical replacement of the father in the financial hierarchy, rather than a gradual, maturational assuming of authority. A similar process was charted by Stein (2002) in his detailed analysis of the 1995 collapse at Barings Bank brought about by the rogue trading of Nick Leeson. Stein argues that the bank compensated for its conservatism – a conservatism that threatened its existence – by hiring a 'shadow' whose extreme risk-taking would save it. The bank, consciously, remained the same, but, unconsciously, acted wildly and irrationally, with its illusory omnipotence lodged in Leeson as its saviour (also, see Bootle 2009; Sorkin 2009; Tett 2009).

I see the instability of the financial market, not as the absence of the father *per se*, but a phallic organization, steeped in arrogance and illusion, with a belief in magical recovery. In its paranoid-schizoid superstructure, the principal anxiety is of annihilation, and the principal defences are splitting and projection. Market men create and attack bad projected objects that threaten an idealized ego, which is identified with an idealized object. The sense of an external threat to be counter-attacked was apparent shortly before the crash. In February 2007, Lehman's 'top distressed-debt trader', Larry McCarthy, said: 'The current risks in the Lehman balance sheet put us in a dangerous situation. Because they're too high, and we're too vulnerable. We don't have the firepower to withstand a serious turnaround' (Sorkin, 123). Equally, the president of Lehman Brothers employed splitting and projection as defences in August 2008, when he drew up 'possible scenarios, most of which included some variation on dividing Lehman in two: A "good bank" that they'd keep and a "bad bank" that they'd spin off, thereby ridding themselves, at least on paper, of their worst real estate assets' (Sorkin, 213). In economic terms, this is creative accounting. At the same time, it separates good from bad absolutely – not in the real world, but in omnipotent phantasy. The phantasy of splitting reinforces the belief that creative accounting can save the bank from bad objects, and bad objects can be annihilated by the ballistic firepower of projective identification.

The paranoid-schizoid phantasy is that growth is without limit; that threats are eliminated by relentless competition, girded by superior predictions; and that loss can always be recouped. The market expands or contracts according to an autonomous reality, unconnected – at least for the financial sector – with the material reality of the production of goods in a creative, seminal system.[8] Market men produce virtual financial products, and the growth of these products is realized in deals between financial institutions, which lock them into complex systems of illusion. That is why collapse is so unforeseen, so quick, so total (Turner, 42–43; on Lehman's sudden and unforeseen loss of major trading partners, and the urgent attempts to forge new deals, see Sorkin, 185–187). It is also why the collapse seems so easily overcome, at least in the actors' minds (though the defence was ultimately unsuccessful in Lehman's case). Financial markets recover, even while credit to business is strangulated (BBC News 2009; Wilkie 2010). Market men feed off their objects, whether or not they destroy them in the process. Market trading gratifies the wish for expansion; retraction humiliates the wish for expansion, but only temporarily. In the end, neither retraction nor expansion seems connected to solid events. Banks did fail, but the market men could scarcely believe it when it happened.

In a project on the future of capitalism, David Tuckett (2008, 2009) interviewed financial managers who were caught up in the financial crisis. He found two characteristic psychological traits: They were in search of, and believed they could acquire, a 'fantastic' object; and they 'split' their ego- and object-worlds in such a way that feelings were kept separate from risk. The fantastic object was their superior financial product, and they claimed it without any sense of precariousness or of guilt or concern for the damage that their risk-taking might produce. In their own conviction and in the conviction they inspired in their clients, they could consistently achieve fantastically higher returns on investment than others, because they were exceptions from the market.

In my view, the fantastic object Tuckett describes is phallic, as is the magical replacement for father described by Morante. The grandiosity of the trader's ego lies in identifying with the magical expansive power of the fantastic object, the market's magical expansive power. It is an illusion in which expansion and contraction does not represent any intrinsic value beyond financial gain and loss, and in which loss is insubstantial and transient. Market deflation as a form of phallic castration is recouped in the phallic competition of the market. As Green (1990) and Laplanche (1980, 61–65, 133–134, based on Rank 1924, 20–22) have argued, there is no castration in the world of the phallus: It too is an illusion. Financial institutions take risks in a phallic competition akin to the single-penis phantasy. They live in the illusion of recovering from loss by passing debt from one to the other until it seems to vanish.[9]

The world of finance that produced the crisis is confident, self-aggrandizing, domineering, aggressive, usurping. The Royal Bank of Scotland, for example, largely publicly owned and with reported losses of £5 billion, was planning to pay bonuses of £1.3 billion in 2010 (Treanor 2010, 25). Major Wall Street banks also planned large bonuses, with a bonus pool at Goldman Sachs, JP Morgan and Morgan Stanley up by 31 per cent for 2009 (Clark 2010, 23). According to the *Financial Times*, banks shifted from capital investment towards the currency exchange market, receiving commissions through supporting speculation by financial institutions such as hedge funds and pension funds. In addition, this currency trading is highly leveraged; a currency trader might be trading with a hundred times the funds actually held. The shift in banking policy has helped to push daily forex (currency) trading to about $US 4000 billion (Garnham and Hughes 2010, 15; Meyer 2010). The illusion of expanding financial wealth is phallic, and like phallic thinking, it transiently substitutes the excitement of phallic robbery and an illusion of wealth creation for the fertility it does not have.

But surely, one might argue, the financial crisis was not caused by a masculine state of mind: The market men were striving for success in a system with a rational structure. Indeed, their strength was in grasping its rationality faster than anyone else, and competition tuned the rationality of the system. Not only would their competition create more wealth: It would also protect the market from collapse. The market was, after all, an inherently stable, self-correcting, lawful system. The mixing of tranches of debts and assets into novel financial products added to the belief in stability and rational control. Indeed, in April 2006, the IMF's Global Stability Report claimed that 'the dispersion of credit risk by banks...has helped make the banking and overall financial system more resilient' (Turner, 42). At a conference in 2005, 'One brave attendee, Raghuram Rajan (of the University of Chicago, surprisingly [because of its free-market monetarism]) presented a paper ['Has Financial Development Made the World Riskier?'], warning that the financial system was taking on potentially dangerous levels of risk. He was mocked by almost all present' (Krugman 2009, 136; Tooze 2018, 69). At its meeting on 21 July 2007, the board of the huge Merrill Lynch organization felt quite secure.

But two weeks later, when Gregory Fleming, president and chief operating officer, and Ahmass Fakahany, chief administrative officer wrote to them about the deteriorating position, the reality disappeared (Sorkin 2009, 146). In August 2007, the availability of credit evaporated after France's largest bank, BNP Paribas, suddenly halted withdrawals from money market funds worth $2 billion because the assets were largely backed by US mortgage loans (88). But even long before the financial crisis, the traders' phantasy of continuous market expansion was known to be illusory in economic circles, and nonetheless, apparently, not known. From the 1950s on, Hyman Minsky (2008)[10] had shown that markets were inherently unstable (see also Papadimitriou and Randall Wray 2008). The financial world 'knew' that deflation was inevitable. There was particular concern for so-called 'collateralised debt obligations' (CDOs) and financial 'derivatives', which were forms of selling packages of debt on to other banks or insuring them. As the packaging of debt moved further away from the original institution and client, it became more difficult to assess the assets from which the debt could be repaid. *The Banker* had raised an alarm in 2004. It drew attention to reports from rating agencies, 'one from Fitch claiming that credit derivatives are too volatile to be useful as risk measures and one from Standard & Poor's suggesting that they had done little to effect the transfer of risk away from the banking system' (De Teram 2010).

The chair of the US Federal Reserve, Alan Greenspan, described himself as being bewildered by 'the complexity of the instruments that were going into the CDOs... ... And I figured that if I didn't understand it and I had access to a couple hundred PhDs, how the rest of the world is going to understand it sort of bewildered me' (Sorkin, p. 90). There was no empirical basis for pricing such instruments, but the 'market men' nonetheless generated 'rational' models to set prices, and assess and insure against risks. The models bore little relation to real economic conditions. Psychoanalytically speaking, they were illusions; that is, they were driven by omnipotent phantasy. The risk calculations were fantastic; they reinforced the financial market man's confidence in his quest for the fantastic object in an illusory world. In reality, no price could be put on the debts that brought down the banks and insurance companies, and no valuation could be made of the assets that would need to be realized if the institutions were to pay them off.[11]

Toxicity, Masculinity and Depressive Anxiety

This phallic illusion obscures the depressive seminal phantasy in which market expansion signifies material production that is generative, fertile. Recession in the market does not just signify deflation in financial value, but damage to the process of creating growth, damage to lives: Damage that causes guilt and awakens reparative impulses. The frenetic activity of the market reveals, like a geological outcropping, a depressive layer that now lies exposed. Exposed with it is a phantasy of desolation with attendant depressive anxiety. The curious expression, 'toxic assets', crept into the vocabulary of both the professional and the popular media during the crisis. These burdensome assets were a contaminated, poisonous version of normally healthy assets. Interestingly, the term 'toxic asset' seems to have been borrowed from assets that actually were toxic, in the form of land that had lost value because it was polluted with toxic waste. Banks that lent money for the purchase or development of such land were left with an asset whose value had plummeted, so that they could no longer underwrite the debt they had incurred in buying it. It became a toxic asset in their portfolios.

In May 1990, the *United States Banker* headlined an article 'Toxic Waste Is Banks' Latest Hazard: Banks are mobilizing their political strength to fight open-ended liability for environmental problems'. The report began by likening the risks 'seeping up' for bankers as a result of legislation that extended liability for contaminated land to 'toxic waste that suddenly oozes up from long-forgotten underground tanks' (58). In the references to toxic bonds, toxic debts and toxic assets that appeared with increasing frequency, especially from 2007, the use of the term 'toxic' to refer to debt accrued from financial trading maintained the link with contamination, pollution, poisoning.

Unproductive commercial property, partly derelict, still cripples the banks' capacity to invest in productive ventures in the USA, Britain and many parts of Europe. In Britain, the commercial property market collapsed, leaving banks facing serious 'negative equity'. Banks not only lent developers up to 90 per cent of the value of their properties but also added loans for 'equity capital', which would appear as the developer's equity. The banks' partnerships with these property developers bypassed the empirical testing that a loan application would usually undergo. The banks then repackaged the debts into small bundles and sold them on. The value of the investment on which the banks expected a return moved beyond any empirical assessment into phantasy. The banks' financial position was also phantasy, because the debts did not show up in their books but were distributed as equity owned by their developer partners and as debts carried by the purchasers of their repackaged debt bundles. The banks could not foreclose on property developers without exposing the extent of the debts they carried. These debts still limited the banks' capacity to lend for other purposes, starving the economy of investment (Robinson 2010).

For years, the thrall of expansion overrode the toxicity of the assets, along with the associated depressive concern and anxiety. Traders continued to produce financial products far removed from a sustainable economic base, as if they were themselves the creators of wealth and not dependent on the economic work of producers, including 'primary' producers of food who are dependent on the soil. The traders behaved as if the chain of dependency hung from the opposite end, from them as creators of wealth.

The complexity and obscurity of 'creative' packages of debt, laden with unassessable risks, corrupted the assets and began to poison the economy. Hence my emphasizing that, early on, 'toxic assets' were poisoned land – land that could have been fertile and could have sustained generative activity. This pollution of a good object, which I associate with depressive anxiety and with seminal masculinity, carries a fear of toxic, polluted semen that destroys fertility. The notions of 'toxic asset' and 'toxic debt' are eruptions from the unconscious of depressive anxiety, to use Klein's term. They suggest the contamination of the land as the source of life and portend the intrusion of depressive anxiety into the phallic illusion of expansion, deflation and recovery. They shift the imagery from inflation and deflation to poisoning.

Phallic narcissism seeks independence from the sources of life, and the accompanying dread of contaminating them. Even more: The magical capacity to recover, which the hallmark phallic narcissism, claims to reverse the dependency on them. Carbon vitalism, which I discussed in chapter 10, is a good example of this thinking. For carbon vitalists, CO_2 is not a pollutant (whoever said it was?), but a necessary and good component of the life cycle (as if that had ever been denied). Moreover, here is the reversal: Human CO_2 production is good for life. Reduced to the skeleton of the argument, carbon vitalists seem to say that humans are not dependent on nature and need not limit their contamination of nature, which climate change advocates exhort us to do: Nature depends on us, on our producing healthy CO_2.

In my view, it is appropriate to call the phallic reversal of a form of destructive narcissism, in the post-Kleinian usage of that term by Herbert Rosenfeld (1987, 105–132). Destructive narcissism aims to sustain the illusion of self-creation and to undermine the libidinal ties that hold ordinary relationships together. It creates an illusory enclave inside which anything is possible; external objects are obstructions to this illusion, to be destroyed. In phantasy, it reverses dependency. Moreover, it takes pleasure in its supremacy.

This inversion of reality attacks the fertility of the parental couple. Manic excitement defends against the depressive anxiety that accompanies the vulnerable seminal phantasy. The intensity of the repudiation – scotomization – of seminal masculinity indicates the extent of the damage done to it, but the unconscious preoccupation with this damage nonetheless pushes itself into expression. Toxic assets, toxic waste and toxic debt have spread throughout popular and business commentary. As I pointed out in chapters 1 and 8, there is toxicity everywhere. They signify a poisoning of seminal function, which is breaking though a phallic cover. The excitement of operating in a super-charged atmosphere, trading assets of unknown value, supported by risk assessments of great obscurity and complexity, also suggests that phallic masculinity has a perverse aspect, which links it to negative narcissism.

The phallic is empty of content. It is inflation or deflation, in which nothing substantive is lost or gained. In the paranoid-schizoid world, any disruption of the illusion is immediately projected outside the ego. In the world of financial market trading, this projection is enacted in asserting competitive advantage over others who are not as clever, but who would, given half a chance, usurp one's cleverness and destroy one's illusory assets. There is no collaboration, only a jostling for advantageous buy-outs or mergers, with the aim of eliminating the other or appropriating whatever the other has that is valued. It is consistent with Morante's (2010, 13–14) pointing out that investment banks, rather than building reliable and long term client relationships by assisting and consulting with corporations and government, moved to risking capital and non-existent capital for the sake of making money quickly. It is also consistent with Stein's (2002) account of the way Barings Bank transcended its vulnerability (ultimately unsuccessfully) by depending on a world of illusion, created by a wildly expansive trader.

Seminal masculinity, by contrast, hovers between procreating and sustaining life on the one hand, and either failing, or when corrupted, destroying it from within on the other. It is deeply ambivalent and therefore troubled by guilt, which sustains the impulse to repair the object and contribute to its fertility. Clinical findings support the idea that seminal phantasies are pro-creative and reparative, but also poisoning and polluting. Seminal masculinity is not omnipotent. It does not create or usurp anything: It only procreates or pollutes. In its depressive character, it is concerned about the state of its object world. It is infused with desolation and anxious for the maintenance, repair and reproduction of life. Although it suffers guilt, it has no control over the outcome of its own or others' actions. It cannot take over the object, whether by dominating it or merging with it; it can only collaborate.

Illusion, Greed and Reparation

I have emphasized the illusory nature of the phallic phantasy and its equally illusory defence against seminal despair. The bankers worked the capitalist system, priding themselves on greater intelligence and on the use of complex, rational models in which, at the conscious level, debt was dispersed. Unconsciously, the claim to be more intelligent and more rational was a primitive phantasy in which debt- indebtedness - vanished. It was a phantasy of possessing the sources of wealth, based on possessing and replacing the primal source of wealth in new life.

One might call this phantasy of possession greed. For Roger Bootle (2009), a prominent financial commentator and former group chief economist at HSBC, the crisis was a 'tale of greed, illusion, and self-delusion on a massive scale' (4). 'Although some individuals were culpable for both their greed and their incompetence', he suggested, 'all bankers were operating in a culture of poisoned values' (121). He believed that this culture surfaced in the 1980s, with 'the combination of deregulation and the doctrine of "greed is good"' (246). Bootle's reference to 'poisoned values' recalls the toxicity of the financial products that contaminated the financial system. I link the theme of toxicity in this period with the greed to which Bootle attributes so much of the crisis.

Psychoanalytically, greed does not just refer to compulsive hoarding, disregarding the needs of others. In Kleinian thinking, it is an oral defence against depletion. 'The violence of the oral incorporation ... leads in phantasy to the destruction of the object'. Greed therefore fails to achieve oral satisfaction, because it renders the incorporated object 'worthless, [which] gives rise to a greater and greater hunger for "good" objects to alleviate the internal state of dominance by "bad" objects and by hated and destructive impulses' (Hinshelwood 1991, 313). Greed provokes more greed, because the very attempt to acquire and retain good objects undermines their goodness (Klein 1952, 62). The good objects that might form the basis of a stable relationship to a good world, a world of concern, have been savaged and turned persecutory. In Kleinian terms, depressive responsibility for restoring good objects has been traduced into a frenzy in which massive incorporation aims to quell the revenge of the objects that have been incorporated.

The failure to satisfy the need to internalize good objects is greater if the object is idealized; that is, if it is felt to be good because it has been created by the ego's own goodness. In such cases, Klein says, the hunger for objects is more indiscriminate and driven to get the best from anywhere; but such idealized objects exist only in illusion and turn persecutory (Klein 1957, 193).

The trade in financial products is similarly a trade in idealized illusory goods that turn on the traders. Bootle (2009) captures this situation, quoting the economist Paul Samuelson. Samuelson, referring to Greenspan when he was head of the US Federal Reserve Bank, said, 'He actually had an instruction, probably pinned on the wall: "Nothing from this office should go forth which discredits the capitalist system. Greed is good"' (22).

Following a devastating economic collapse that ruined so many lives, it is appropriate to think, from a psychoanalytic angle, of making things better. One would in this case speak of the psychoanalytic concept of reparation. To make my argument clearer, I will use the paired Kleinian concepts of reparation and manic reparation (Klein 1937; Segal 1981). Reparation is an aspect of the depressive position, an internal psychic moment in which an internal object is experienced as damaged by the ego and in which depressive anxiety at the state of the object arouses a wish to repair it (Klein 1935). Guilt is intrinsic to the depressive position. Manic reparation seems to be the same as reparation, but it differs internally. In the paranoid-schizoid world, the urge to make better – the reparative impulse, in Kleinian thinking – becomes a manic reparation. Manic reparation is narcissistic and riven with ambivalence. Making the object better becomes an omnipotent act, to be accomplished instantly and perfectly, in order to reinstate the illusory perfection of the original object and its reflection of the narcissistic perfection of the ego. In that sense, greed is also a form of manic reparation. The depressive motivation to repair good objects is replaced by the attempt to overwhelm persecutory objects with good objects, which instantly turn persecutory through the violence of their incorporation. But the object is also hated, since, to the narcissistic ego, the restored object obtains its perfection by depleting the ego. The object must be magically restored to confirm the ego's omnipotence, but then denigrated, so that the omnipotent ego is not depleted by it (Ahumada 1982, 65–82).

From a psychoanalytic angle, the 'poisoned' social values to which Bootle refers are the bad objects produced by greedy incorporation itself, as it aims, not just to acquire and sustain the good object, but also to create an idealized object. The bad objects are not separate and pre-existing but produced by the violence of the greedy attempt to incorporate good objects. Because the good object is assailed by bad objects in the moment its incorporation, the greed must continue in a hapless striving to defend the narcissistic ego against them by filling it with a goodness that is immediately corrupted. But this system aims also to keep depressive anxiety at bay. We need to study the financial crisis, therefore, not just to learn lessons about financial regulation. We need, primarily, to analyse it as a social instance of a phallic defence against depressive catastrophe, to speak of the depressive underbelly of culture. The 'greed is good' of financial market arrogance is a defiant and illusory assertion that the next piece of incorporated wealth will dispel both depressive anxiety about deterioration and paranoid-schizoid anxiety that the process of incorporation itself has created more monsters. More than that: It is to parade greed as the creation of an idealized object, acquisition of which garners our devotion.[12]

It seems likely that there are moments or situations in which a state of mind can be carried and reflected in a social system, and in which it even structures the social system. Stein (2002) demonstrated such an occasion in the case of Nick Leeson, who carried, for the whole organization, a risk-taking, even profligate, side of a conservative banking institution. Market men and analysts attribute a mind to the market all the time, and pride themselves on their interpretative skill in knowing what the market thinks. We have reason to think that they have idealized themselves, their rationality, their own organizations (or parts of them) and the market itself, and that they have projected their uncertainty, doubted competence and irrationality onto others, as denigrated, 'bad' objects, in order to maintain their conviction of their own rationality, superior intelligence and skill. The market becomes the phallus – their phallus – that they have possessed by taking it from the losers in the unconscious competition that goes on beneath the conscious strategies of financial trading.

Structure releases the individual from tension, or, psychoanalytically, from anxiety. This protective cover of normalisation reinforces the individual's sense of the rationality of his work, including the rationality of trading in financial products. The fact that this defensive – phallic – masculinity fits a cultural stereotype of masculinity buttresses the belief in the 'normality' of the defensive structure and absorbs any tension between the phallic and the seminal that the individual man might feel.

The Financial Crash and Misogyny

In chapter 10, I explored ways in which misogyny infiltrates social organization and proposed the hypothesis that it was the root prejudice, a kind of ur-racism. I referred to digital networks of men who felt marginalized and aggrieved by feminism and by women in general. The digital networking expanded and reinforced men's sense of masculine identity through mass identification as men in a sustained, lived present. Individual men could instantly coalesce into groups to support each other, to react to slights to masculinity and buttress the solidity of masculine identity. In their various formations, such as PUA (Pick-Up Artists), MGOW (Men Going Their Own Way) and Incel (Involuntary Celibate), a coalition of men in the mass set themselves against an insecurity of masculine identity by aiming to dominate or to demean women. Johanssen and Krüger (2022, 145–154) also connect the extensive digital networking of the manosphere with negative narcissism.

The 2008 financial supports the belief in a link between phallic masculinity, social organization and misogyny. A crisis in a dominant social institution was followed quickly by a distinct shift in sectors of the manosphere – an immediacy that supports a belief a link between them. The crisis was a discrete event, an irruption in the financial world, as was the shift in the manosphere. So, we have two distinct events, the one following the other in rapid succession. I suggest we see this occurrence as a natural experiment, in that historical forces have contrived a bounded phenomenon that can be observed, as if under controlled conditions, akin to a scientist's experimental design. In this natural experiment, the independent variable was the 2008 financial crisis, a sudden collapse in investment banking. The dependent variable – the event that followed upon the crisis – was a shift in the manosphere, as the PUA movement collapsed, and the Incel movement grew and turned violent towards women.

The 'PUA industry' (Bratich and Banet-Weiser 2019, 5003) began in 2007 with a reality television programme, VH1, for men with difficulties establishing sexual relationships with women. The men were mentored in techniques of seduction by the host, Mystery. Their sexual success was monitored and the failures eliminated from the programme. Becoming a PUA burgeoned on-line and with global mentor training. 'The Pickup Artist debuted during neoliberalism's peak, and the series ended with the season 2 finale in November 2008, in the immediate wake of the global economic crashes and anxieties' (5013). The whole PUA idea crashed, provoking an anti-PUA site, PUAHate. Its misogyny erupted with the closure of the PUAHate site and its reappearance as sluthate (5014). Incels began as a men's support group around 2009. They increasingly shared the cultural space of the PUA. But Incels were very different from PUA, who aimed to attract women. Incels carried a grudge at their perceived deprivation, then turned hating and violent towards woman, who, in their view, deprived them of their right to women's bodies. Bratich and Banat-Weiser document Incel-driven mass shootings in which women were the principal targets (5015–5016). De Cook and Kelly (2022) review the vast literature on Incels and argue against seeing it as a homogeneous group. The organizing intent is misogyny.

The growth and violent turn in the Incel movement followed from the failure of the PUA movement, as a misogynistic shift in the manosphere. For Bratich and Banat-Weiser, it was a reaction to the failed promise of neo-liberalism. Masculinity was confident. Neo-liberalism made men subjects, confident agents of their lives and of the social order, aware of themselves as effective performers within their inherent, superior status. Performance in the globalized world instantiated their confident subjectivity. Women served their confidence, and sexual availability confirmed their inherent right to their status. The collapse of this world order betrayed their confidence and gutted them of their masculine ascendency. Incels saw the cause of the betrayal of their masculinity, not just as a betrayal by neo-liberalism, but by women in their feminism, and specifically, in their withholding their bodies from men.

On the surface, there is a logical flaw in this account. The financial world was a world of men. The collapse of trust was between men. If there was a betrayal, it was between men, as when banks suddenly refused to lend to each other. But treachery was re-assigned to women. Picking up the theme of chapter 10, I would say that the grievance was not deflected only from the market failure to women but found its way back to the mother as the original object of grievance. Freud and Klein rooted the drive to explore in a knowledge drive – an epistemophilic drive – that aims, at root, to explore the mother's body, and is diverted ever outwards from the mother's body by the prohibition of incest. The collapse of masculine confidence was a second betrayal of narcissistic intactness. It tapped the primal ambivalence of the nascent male psyche, now in an adult body and mind, intensifying grievance into destroying the betraying object in an unconscious primal replacement ideology: Self (masculine) = – object (feminine).

Notes

1 Adam Tooze (2018) has written an extensive, detailed history of the crash, in its national and international contexts, including the various levels of awareness of instability. It becomes clear that the economic base of the unstable financial system was mortgaged property, that it comprised a large proportion of national economies and that a crash threated to spread quickly. Tooze's history is sufficiently fine-grained to pair with a psychoanalytic analysis of defences that allowed the instability to proliferate. He doesn't impute a masculine character to economics, but others, to whom I will refer, do.

2 References to the view that men or machismo contributed in a major way to the collapse include Ruth Sunderland, 'Focus: Women and Recession', *Observer*, 15 February 2009, 24; Mathew Syed, 'What Caused the Crunch? The Sex of the City', *The Times*, 30 September 2008, 2; Avivah Wittenberg-Cox, 'Banks Must Make Gender Balance a Priority to Avoid Another Fall', http://www.20-first.com/940-0, n.d., Accessed 30 October 2010; this article was taken up by many journalists in 2009.

3 I am allowing a certain confusion between the market itself and the market traders, because the market is their illusion and it has no autonomous existence wholly apart from the people who trade through it. Graeber (2011) has made this case.

4 Connell (2012) has drawn attention to the 'abstract organization', which concentrates on turning a profit to the exclusion of all other considerations. It is 'fractal', in that this abstract profit-seeking is repeated at every level in the organization. It is masculine, not only in the gender-profile of the staff, but also in relying on female service both in the organization (e.g., personnel) and in the home, relieving men of any responsibility outside the closed system of the abstract organization.

5 In psychoanalytic terms, they were simultaneously known and not known, disregarded until the crisis hit. In psychoanalytic thinking, they were 'disavowed'. One might say that they infiltrated thinking, undermining it from the inside well before symptoms of the illness erupted.

6 In a way, she also rejected phallic stage in the boy. The putative female phallic stage was, in her view, a projection of the boy's fear of castration: To be a girl was the boy's nightmare. The penis would, therefore, serve as a defence against the nightmare for both sexes.

7 Klein (1963, 281) draws an interesting comparison on this score between Freud and herself.

Freud (1916) has described a type of individual who cannot bear success because it arouses guilt, and he connects this guilt in particular with the Oedipus complex. In my view, such people originally meant to outshine and destroy the mother's fertility.

8 I have not attempted an analysis of production itself. I will simply distinguish between fabrication, as an assembly of items into a product, from production, more as Marx conceived of it, as an investment of the self into a process as living labour. The fabricating workman is under no illusion of his/her alienation in the productive process: Reduced to abstract labour power, no more than a machine-like realization of a designer's plan with elements not of his/her own making or understanding. At the opposite pole is the illusion of the financial market, in which the market men stand above fabricating workers, or even the designers of the labour process, as if the creators and owners of the mystery of production. It is from nothing to nothing, not an investment of living labour in a labour process that fashions a material reality within the laws of material reality. Creative labour, seminal labour, is humble, in organizing natural elements into new products in a spirit of wonderment at nature. A craftsman, a scientist and an artist all take part in such processes. They are accompanied by the phantasy of making better; that is, they are urged on by a reparative drive. On the idea that money displaces quality as an inherent value, with a narcissistic sense of more or less as an insatiable need for more, see Figlio 2023.

9 There is clinical evidence that men with an insecure relationship to their fathers find it difficult to persist in ordinary work. Ordinary work, along with marriage and family, is for them a field of masculine achievement that they replace with grand fantasy projects (Axelrod 1994).

10 Minsky (2008, 11)

The major flaw of our type of economy is that it is unstable ... not due to external shocks or to the incompetence or ignorance of policy makers [but] due to the internal pressures of out type of economy.

11 We have nonetheless to be cautious in attributing the financial crisis to narcissism, omnipotence and illusion. MacKenzie and Spears (2014) extensively analysed the mathematics of the modelling of financial product trading and interviewed the modellers, the so-called 'quants'. They found that there was an allure of the magnificent abstract models but also a hard-nosed, hard-working commitment to making it work – and it did work, at least in bank profitability, for some time. Despite the image of recklessness, banks strived to achieve economic stability through hedging adjusted to what they could predict of the economy and through hours of computational time preparing for each day's trading. Despite the allure, the bankers were focused on practical ways to remain profitable in an extra-ordinarily complex market with risky fluctuations of asset prices. Yet, modelling also sought simplification. The models could be more easily used but at the cost of departing farther from empirical reality, where there was already a strain. The system also depended on a common understanding and participation by a large number of institutions, among which risk cold be spread. Quants contributed to common culture by moving among the institutions.

The whole assembly was, however, a 'bricolage', a composite of many, diverse interests, including career interests. These factors added up to an unstable system, kept going until a spanner fell into the works. That spanner was the sub-prime mortgage market. Gillian Tett (2018), an anthropologist who studied financial institutions and also became US Editor-at-Large of the Financial Times, said that when the extent of credit, hanging in mid-air, caught the attention of BNP Paribus and IKP bank, trust among institutions collapsed and the system with it. She remarked on the 'sudden loss of trust', which was 'akin to a food-poisoning scare'. Mortgage defaults erupted, but 'because debt had been ... diced into new products, nobody knew where the poisonous risks sat in the financial food chain.'

Here is where we need to look for narcissism, omnipotence and illusion. The bankers were not dreamers, but they were enmeshed in the apparent fruitfulness of a human production – the modelling of financial markets. They did not notice that stability depended on a more sure-footed anchoring in empirical reality and on the human need of trust. Neither empirical reality nor trust could be interpolated into their equations, to become outcomes of their solution. Illusion infused reality and gave it its most powerful property: To seem to be reality. That is also a phallic illusion. It covered a 'poisonous' – in my view, ambivalently seminal – infiltration of the economy.

12 I see the root of this analysis in Freud's (1930) *Civilization and its Discontents*, better translated as *The Unease in culture*. Guilt plagues human society in Freud's analysis and mine, and the avoidance of guilt becomes a force of social organization, partly in driving reparation. The Paranoid-schizoid defence against depressive anxiety externalizes this internal process, replacing guilt with aggression towards the other groups that now embody bad objects, and reparation with manic reparation.

References

Abraham, K. (1920) Manifestations of the Female Oedipus Complex. In *Selected Papers on Psycho-Analysis*. London: Hogarth Press, 1927, 338–369.

Ahumada, J. (1982) The Unconscious Delusion of 'Goodness' (1982). In *The Logics of the Mind: a Clinical View*. London/New York: Karnac, 2001, 65–82.

BBC News (2009) 'More Credit' For Homes and Firms, http://news.bbc.co.uk/1/hi/business/7978434.stm, Accessed 3 September 2009.

Bootle, R. (2009) *The Trouble with Markets: Saving Capitalism From Itself*. London/Boston: Nicholas Brealey.

Bratich, J. and Banet-Weiser, S. (2019) From Pick-Up Artist to Incels: Con(fidence) Games, Networked Misogyny, and the Failure of Neoliberalism. *International Journal of Communication* 13: 5003–5027.

Clark, A. (2010) Wall Street Bonuses Top $20bn. *Guardian*, 24 February, 23.

Connell, R. (2012) Inside the Glass Tower: The Construction of Masculinities in Finance Capital. In McDonald, P. and Jeanes, E. (eds) *Men, Wage Work and Family*. NY/London: Routledge, pp. 65–79.

De Cook, J. R. and Kelly, M. (2022) Interrogating the 'Incel Menace': Assessing the Threat of Male Supremacy in Terrorism Studies. *Critical Studies in Terrorism*: 15: 706-726.

De Teram, D. (2010) Fools' Gold. *The Banker*, 5 April 2004, https://www.thebanker.com/Archive/Fools-gold/(language)/eng-GB

Figlio, K. (2004) Psychoanalysis, Politics and the Self-Awareness of Society. *Psychoanalysis, Culture and Society* 9(1): 87–104.

Figlio, K. (2017) *Remembering as Reparation: Psychoanalysis and Historical Memory*. London: Palgrave Macmillan.

Figlio, K. (2023) Money as the Currency of Value. In Jacobsen, K. and Hinshelwood, R. D. (2023) (eds) *Psychoanalysis, Science and Power: Essays in Honour of Robert Maxwell Young*. Abingdon Oxon/NY Routledge, 164–183.

Freud, S. (1916) Some Character-Types Met in Psycho-Analytic Work. *The Standard Edition of the Complete Psychological Works of Sigmund Freud* 14: 309–333.

Freud, S. (1930) Civilization and its Discontents. *The Standard Edition of the Complete Psychological Works of Sigmund Freud* 21: 57–146.

Garnham, P. and Hughes, J. (2010) Banks Shift from Risk Helps Push FX Trading to $4,000bn a Day. *Financial Times*, 1 September, 15.

Graeber, D. (2011) *Debit, the First 5,000 Years: Towards an Anthropology of Value.* Brooklyn/London: Melville House Publishing. 3rd edn, 2014 and Kindle edition.

Green, A. (1990) *Le complexe de castration* [The Castration Complex]. Paris: PUF.

Harrington, C. (2021) What is "Toxic Masculinity" and Why Does it Matter? *Men and Masculinities* 24(2): 345–352.

Hinshelwood, R. D. (1991) *A Dictionary of Kleinian Thought* 2ndedn London: Free Association Books.

Horney, K. (1926) The Flight from Womanhood: The Masculinity-Complex in Women, as Viewed by Men and by Women. *International Journal of Psychoanalysis* 7:324–339; reprinted in *Feminine Psychology*. NY: Norton, 1967, 54–70.

Johanssen, J. and Krüger, S. (2022) *Media and Psychoanalysis: A Critical Introduction.* London: Karnac.

Kirsner, D. (1990) Illusion and the Stock Market Crash: Some Psychoanalytic Concepts. *Free Associations: Psychoanalysis, Politics, Culture, Society* No. 1, 31–59.

Klein, M. (1935) A Contribution to the Psychogenesis of Manic-Depressive States. In *The writings of Melanie Klein*, vol. 1. London: The Hogarth Press and the Institute of Psycho-Analysis, 1975, 262–289.

Klein, M. (1937) Love, Guilt and Reparation. In *The Writings of Melanie Klein*, vol. 1. London: The Hogarth Press and the Institute of Psycho-Analysis, 1975, 306–343.

Klein, M. (1952) Some Theoretical Conclusions Regarding the Emotional Life of the Infant. In *The Writings of Melanie Klein*, vol. 3. London: The Hogarth Press and the Institute of Psycho-Analysis, 1975, 61–93.

Klein, M. (1957) Envy and Gratitude. *The Writings of Melanie Klein*, vol. 3. London: The Hogarth Press and the Institute of Psycho-Analysis, 1975, 176–235.

Klein, M. (1963) Some Reflections on The Oresteia. In *The Writings of Melanie Klein*, vol. 3. London: The Hogarth Press and the Institute of Psycho-Analysis, 1975, 275–299.

Krugman, P. (2009) How Did Economists Get it So Wrong. In *Arguing with Zombies: Economics, Politics, and the Fight for a Better Future*. NY: Norton, 2020, 130–148 Originally in the New York Times *Magazine*, 2 September 2009.

Laplanche, J. (1980) *Problématiques II: castration–symbolisations* [Problematics II: castration–symbolizations]. Paris: PUF.

MacKenzie, D. and Spears, T. (2014) 'The Formula That Killed Wall Street': The Gaussian Copula and Modelling Practices in Investment Banking. *Social Studies of Science* 44(3): 393–417.

Meyer, G. (2010) Backlash Prompts Rethink on Forex Rules'. *Financial Times*, 1 September, 33.

Minsky, H. (2008) *Stabilizing an Unstable Economy*. New Haven, Ct: Yale University Press/NY: McGraw Hill (first edn 1986).

Morante, F. (2010) Omnipotence, Retreat from Reality and Finance: Psychoanalytic Reflections on the 2008 Financial Crisis. *International Journal of Applied Psychoanalytic Studies* 7: 4–21.

Papadimitriou, D. and Randall Wray, L. (2008) Minsky's Stabilizing an Unstable Economy: Two Decades Later. In Minsky, H.(2008) (ed.) *Stabilizing an Unstable Economy*. New York, McGraw Hill, xi–xxxv.

Paulson, H. (2010) *On the Brink: Inside the Race to Stop the Collapse of the Global Financial System*, New York/London: Hachette.

Petruno, T. (2009) *Market Business News*, 4 June. https://marketbusinessnews.com/financial-glossary/toxic-assets/, Accessed 13 September 2021.

Rank, O. (1924) *The Trauma of Birth*. NY: Harper & Row, 1929.

Robinson, M. (2010) The Next Banking Nightmare?, File on Four, BBC Radio 4, 9 February 2010.

Rosenfeld, H. (1987) Destructive Narcissism and the Death Instinct. In *Impasse and Interpretation: Therapeutic and Anti-Therapeutic Factors in the Psychoanalytic Treatment of Psychotic, Borderline and Neurotic Patients*. London: Tavistock, 105–132.

Segal, H. (1981) Manic Reparation. In *The Works of Hanna Segal: A Kleinian Approach to Clinical Practice*, NewYork: Jason Aronson; London: Free Association Books, 1986, 147–158.

Sorkin, A. (2009) *Too Big to Fail: Inside the Battle to Save Wall Street*. London: Penguin.

Stein, M. (2002) The Risk Taker as Shadow: a Psychoanalytic View of the Collapse of Barings Bank. *Journal of Management Studies* 37: 1215–1229.

Stein, M. (2003) Unbounded Irrationality: Risk and Organizational Narcissism at Long Term Capital Management. *Human Relations* 56(5): 523–540.

Steiner, J. (1993) *Psychic Retreats: Pathological Organisations in Psychotic, Neurotic and Borderline Patients*. London: Routledge.

Tett, G. (2009) *Fool's Gold: How Unrestrained Greed Corrupted a Dream, Shattered Global Markets and Unleashed a Catastrophe*. London: Little Brown.

Tett, G. (2018) Have We Learnt the Lessons of the Financial Crisis? *Financial Times*, August 31, 2018. https://www.ft.com/content/a9b25e40-ac37-11e8–89a1-e5de165fa619, Accessed 30 April 2023.

Tooze, A. (2018) *Crashed: How a Decade of Financial Crisis Changed the World*. London: Allen Lane.

Treanor, J. (2010) Anger Escalates Over Royal Bank of Scotland Plan to Pay £1,3bn Bonuses. *Guardian*, 25 February, p. 25.

Tuckett, D. (2008) Phantastic Objects and the Financial Market's Sense of Reality: a Psychoanalytic Contribution to the Understanding of Stock Market Instability'. *International Journal of Psychoanalysis* 89: 389–412.

Tuckett, (2009) *Addressing the Psychology of Financial Markets*. London: Institute for Public Policy Research and the Friends Provident Society.

Turner, A. (2009) *The Turner Review: A Regulatory Response to the Global Banking Crisis*. London: Financial Services Authority.

United States Banker (1990) *National Edition*, May.

Wilkie, B. (2010) Bank Loan Complaints More than Double. *British SME*, 16 August 2010.

Conclusion

Chapter 12

The Unease in Normal Masculinity

Between Desolation and Hope

By way of conclusion, I want to pick up some themes from the book, to further illustrate them and add a dimension to them. In particular, I want to place misogyny in a spectrum of masculinity, which includes its normality. Nina Power (2022, 4) is a philosopher who writes of masculinity:

> There are, of course, a *small number* of men who behave as if the world, and the women in it, owe them something. Some men are extremely violent. Some men are in power. *These men, however, are not most men …* Bashing men is also *easy*. It is much more difficult, but ultimately much more worthwhile and, I would suggest, necessary, to wonder how we might live together better, about how men and women might be reconciled to one another's existence. (Power's emphasis)

I agree with the gist of Power's project of reconciliation, but I do not accept the alternatives of wondering how to live together or man-bashing. There is another option: to build the essential groundwork of reconciliation by bringing into consciousness the destructive forces that seem to inhere in masculinity. That is a difficult job.

I am not concerned with the statistics of good and bad men, but with a tension within masculinity. A 'normal' man emerges from an adequate resolution of the tension documented and interpreted in Melanie Klein's definition and account of the femininity phase. But even normal masculinity is complex and vulnerable to enticement into a reactive posture with respect to femininity, a reactivity that shade into misogyny and, in the extreme, into aggressive repudiation, denigration and violence against women. This misogynist current in masculinity is consolidated in groups that cohere through emotion-driven – often hate-driven – prejudice. In earlier chapters, I have sought to show links of this sort between various forms of misogyny, environment crisis denial and racism.

At the same time, with Freud, I see the extreme, or pathological, as a magnification, which throws the normal into relief, revealing its contours more clearly and opening it to closer scrutiny. Later, we will also see that

DOI: 10.4324/9781003455790-18

Freud struggled with the feminine, with misogynistic overtones, and therefore, embedded a struggle with the feminine in the origin of psychoanalysis.

Let us first further develop the idea of the toxicity of toxic masculinity, in order to move to the normal. Toxic suggests poison, pollution, contamination. It seems at odds with the superior, dominating, condescending phallicism of masculinity. It suggests degradation by an erosion of the health of the cultural body as well as the female body; that is, from the inside, rather than by attack from the outside. The seemingly ubiquitous use of toxic and of toxic masculinity suggests that a toxic substance poisons the female, or, more abstractly and generally, the feminine. And what could a toxic, masculine substance be, other than semen? In the unconscious, the fertilizing, life enhancing fluid is also poisonous.

As I have argued throughout this book, I see in toxic masculinity a deep and shocking dread that is cloaked by a stereotype of aggressive masculinity – real in its own right, but also a defence against depressive desolation, to which Klein has drawn our attention. It points to an 'intimate' misogyny, effected inside the woman, which verges on the unrepresentable.

Intimate Misogyny

Referring to the philosopher, Martha Nussbaum and the anthropologist, Mary Douglas, Siri Hustvedt (2019, 243, 244) speaks of disgusting fluids, male and female, which hint at mortality and waste products. She points out that 'Many contemporary popular treatments of misogyny do not discuss human reproduction. They emphasize power structures that reproduce themselves and keep women in their place.' She directs us to an avoidance of the deeply interior, intimate relationship between mother and foetus, mediated by the placenta, which derives from and belongs to both (She also associates the placenta with Winnicott's potential space; Hustvedt 2022).

Hustvedt uncovers a misogyny in the abstract, a cleansing of disgusting intimacy by age-old western myth, in which man implants himself in the womb as in a vessel. For Aristotle, man implanted the immaterial form of the child in the material supplied by the female. In a modern, scientific, genetic version, the genetic implant, albeit composed of male and female genes, also uses the womb as a vessel, as surely as, in myth, man implants himself in the womb. In both versions, the woman is reduced to her womb and her womb is reduced to a vessel. Both versions ignore the intimate mother-baby relationship, embedded in their separate and shared substance.

For Hustvedt, both versions are misogynistic, and she puts this misogyny down to the conviction that women – and their insides, their wombs – must be available to men. Women were in fact made for men:

> the absurd demand that I, the woman, exist only *for* you, the eternal man-child … And if I do not perform this part to your full satisfaction, I am a

spoiled, wicked, heartless bitch – a witch ... The idea that they were once inside a woman, and that a woman's body was instrumental in *making* them, has to be suppressed in mythical cultural ideas, which bleed into what is supposed to be stripped of all myth – parts of science. And if male heterosexual desire for women enters the picture, the need to embrace the mixed angel-demon creates a poisonous stew. (249–250; Hustvedt's emphasis)

In this reduction of mother to a womb, the womb becomes a kind of room inside the mother. As a room, a space in three dimensions, the inconceivable union that creates becomes conceivable, albeit with lost dimensions. Those lost dimensions are what Hustvedt tries to recreate with an imaginative language that evokes a sense of intimacy in an anatomical and physiological location. The kind of exclusive, male occupation of the womb, to which Hustvedt refers, points to an omnipotent state of mind, one that not only suppresses the mother's fertility, but also reverses it and reduces it to a form of intrauterine activity. That way, the male re-inserts himself into the intimate mother-placenta-foetus relationship from which he has been excluded.[1]

The mechanics of intercourse are observable. One can easily form an idea of what is going on, and whether it is tender, passionate, or violent. It is an activity that fits with the idea of a phallic father. Hustvedt puts her finger on a grandiose male phantasy, in which mother is reduced to a womb, the place into which the male inserts himself, both to control her and to plant himself as pre-existing the intimate relationship in which he was brought to life, nurtured and matured.

But note her language. Whether intended or not, her reference to a 'poisonous stew' evokes the idea of toxicity. She implies that the aggressiveness of the masculine demand for the woman's absolute availability is poisonous; that it is toxic; that, in psychoanalytic terms, it turns her into a feared witch by projective identification. In my view, she has recovered the phantasy of toxic poisoning of that deeply interior process and the deeply interior relationship between mother and foetus, which has been concealed by the abstract womb as a place.

I have argued that the deeply interior process and relationship of child-creation can turn toxic in a phantasy of omnipotent semen turned poisonous, and I have called the combination of creative and toxic semen, seminal ambivalence. It is ambivalence at a primal, existential level, and it is normal. It is normal, that is, if it is assimilated to a conceiving relationship between a conceptive mother and a testicular father. Seminality gets us to the interior processes of natality, sustenance, and reparation.

Such a 'poisonous stew' can breed an intimate misogyny, which girds up a masculine identity in the face of an overwhelming maternal intimacy. For Klein, the stage is set for her son in his femininity phase, which, she says, is more important to the boy's psychosexual development than the father. I would add that it also includes mother's and son's attitude towards semen. Klein speaks of the reparative function of semen, but not of the mother's receptivity to it, in its conceptive, reparative and destructive potentials. I stress this point, because psychoanalysis has emphasized the resistance of men to femininity, particularly to its receptivity, but not the recognition, by male and female, mother and father, of the uniquely masculine, seminal function.

So, we have to step back a generation or two, to include the lineage of ambivalence towards masculinity, and with it, ambivalence towards seminal function. Recall from Chapter 4, that Freud described a fraught relationship of woman to man. She might transfer her ambivalent relationship with her mother over to her father. She might attach herself undyingly to him, idealizing him. But she might also identify with her mother's ambivalence towards her father; that is, her mother's husband. Bound to her father in an idealized union, she might then, by identification with her mother, transfer this ambivalently-held father, over to her own husband. In that way, in her relationship to her own husband/partner she becomes mother to a son captured by an overwhelming feminine.

If that woman, whose husband has become a dominated son, now has a son, his masculine identity would be compromised by the overwhelming and ambivalent feminine. Suppose such a son – now a man – marries a woman who, as above, already carries an ambivalence towards masculinity, inherited from her mother and with whom she identifies. The marriage becomes an inter-generational moment in which both the woman and man of this third generation are submitted to an overwhelming feminine power. As parents, the maternal and the paternal lineages, leave masculine identity of the fourth generation insecure, in an overwhelming feminine environment. And so on.

With respect to seminal masculinity, does the son of such a lineage welcome his semen when he first unexpectedly expels it from somewhere inside his body; does it horrify him; does it just puzzle him? Do his internal parents, as a couple or separately, welcome it, or does it horrify them.

Normal and Pathological Masculine Identity

Although toxic masculinity has become the epithet called upon for all sorts of masculine aggression, that does not make masculinity a pathology. Let's take two extreme reactions to this struggle for masculine identity. Let us look first at ordinary, 'normal' boyhood with ordinary, 'normal', loving mothering. Perhaps the seeds that will ripen into compassionate or toxic masculinity have already been sown at this early time. Max is a healthy boy, three-years-nine-months-old at the time of his sister's birth, with loving parents, available to their son's mixed feelings as he ponders what is going on. Max can work with his feelings, because his mother is sensitively aware of his wavering moments, when his internal and his external worlds wobble, and he recovers his stability with her help. She may be bringing the challenge of a little sibling into his world, but she remains a good object.

Although we don't have similar vignettes with his father, what information we have suggests that he is an able partner to his wife, helping to consolidate Max's identity as a boy in his mother's presence, secure in his 'place' within her (mind). The vignettes are snippets from everyday life, reported by his mother, not part of an analysis, but they allow one to imagine an early, secure relational environment – the kind that can mitigate misogyny in culture. I ask the reader to allow an imaginative entry into a little boy's managing a radical restructuring of the future he expected.

During his mother's pregnancy with their second child, they often discussed the baby's development and how it would come into the world. Upon first hearing that a surprise was on the way, when his mother was 13 weeks pregnant; we hear

Mom: Max, we have a surprise!
Son: (very excited) Is it a fire truck?!
Mom: No, we are having a baby...
Son: (utterly disappointed) I don't want a baby, I want a toy!
Mom: (comforting) But Max, can you imagine, you are going to be a big brother!
Son: (grumpy) But I want to be an ordinary boy!

His disgruntlement at an expected displacement is clear. In a later interaction, his annoyance at anticipating the baby's intrusion triggered a hint of guilt, from which he quickly recovered. It was a moment in a normal depressive position with its toleration of ambivalence and recognition of reality. He accepted, annoyed but also woefully, the actuality of his little sister's presence in his restructured future. Playing at home, during an ordinary afternoon, he raised an anxiety with his mother, which must have unsettled him for some time.

Son: (a bit worried) Mom, the baby is going to step on my train track!
Mom: No, don't worry, the baby can't even walk.
Son: (shocked) doesn't it have any legs?!
Mom: (laughing) yes it does, but at first it mostly lies, and then crawls before it can walk.
Son: (woeful) well, then the baby will crawl on my train track!!

We see Max confronting reality, which meant bearing the complex feelings it evoked. His appraisal of what the future would bring could become more of a realistic prediction. We can hear him oscillate between the intrusion of reality, the annoyance it evoked, the guilt at his angry thoughts, the sadness brought by his anticipation of the reality of his lost, ideal world, and his grievance against his not-yet sister (sure enough, his nightmare was realised; as soon as his little sister was able to crawl, she went straight for his train track).

He wanted to see inside his mother, presumably out of curiosity, but also to check to see that she was alright and would be alright in the process of producing a sister who might break through her belly or otherwise cause her harm. But at least such an eruption from a place inside mother to a place outside mother is conceivable, akin to passing from any inside space to an outside space. Passing between spaces is much the same as his train moving along a track – also to be damaged by the new arrival. The damage caused mother and, reciprocally, his train track, would follow from his phantasied attack on his 'treacherous' mother for bringing this intrusion into their lives. We can hypothesize that such an attack was embodied in a projective identification into his sister, as an internal object also in mother. His sister, inside mother, would then be his 'bad self' inside mother. But his love of his mother and his guilt at his angry thoughts towards his sister – towards his projective identification – meant that both she and his mother would be reparable. Still, he wanted to have a look inside, to check it out.

Mom and son taking a bath:

Son: how will the baby come out? Will the belly burst or what?!
Mom: no, it will come out through the vagina.
Son: can we take a look at the baby?
Mom: um, no that's not how it works... but you can touch the belly if you want?
Son: (a bit disappointed) Alright...

With a secure idea of dimension, of inside mother as a space like a room, explanations of the inconceivable were readily to hand, albeit as imaginative constructs, not as empirical reality. A baby develops inside mother, just as food is taken inside and things – perhaps babies – are made from it. The idea of space can transform these great mysteries into a visualizable form. It is also consistent with clinically discernible, parthenogenic theories, which remain in the Unconscious of the adult, which also dispel the mythic mystery of natality.

Mother had many times referred to 'when the baby is here'. At one of the hundred times Mom referred to 'when the baby is here':

Son: But mom, the baby is already here.
Mom: (surprised) Oh really?!
Son: yes, it is in the attic.
Mom: then what is this? (pointing at belly)
Son: you have just been eating too much, mom (laughing)

His reasoning is perfectly sound. It brings together eating, making feces, making babies – all mysterious, yet transformed into three-dimensional space.

These interpretations are mine. Readers will make their own judgments. Here is a little boy, reacting to the news that he will share his mother with a little sister, and to the ambivalent feelings that this news evokes in him. Both are unsettling: The news disturbs his security in the external world; his ambivalence unsettles the security of his internal world. We hear his endearing inquisitiveness; his jealousy at anticipated replacement in parental affection; his anxiety about the inside of the mother, confused with depressive anxiety at harmful thoughts; and his reparative inclination. They all pivot around the boy's preoccupation with what is going on inside mother, which he suspects is linked to the special feature of mother: A process in the interior of the feminine. He is, after all, a boy, unlike his mother and his new sibling.

We also see the capacity to face a tough reality, nourished by an intimate relationship, in a vivid observation of a little boy by Henri Rey (1994, 221). He was not only one of several siblings: He was fundamentally different from them; he was adopted. Yet he preserved a reparative process of love and concern.

> A female patient had the following experience. After the birth of a Down's syndrome child, she had adopted a little Chinese boy. She also had other children. The little Chinese boy adored his adoptive mother, who well returned this love. When still very young, he said to his mother, "I wish I could go into you and come out like the other children, then I will really be your little boy." That story is disturbingly touching. The fact that objects and situations are projected into mother for transformations that the infant or child cannot achieve by themselves is a well-known process, but it must be linked with reparation … (Rey 1994, 221)

What a beautiful example of a boy's wish to make his damaged mother (evident in her Down's syndrome child) better, while she, in getting better, makes him better in his rebirth. They share a mutual loving, introjective, reparative relationship. He is aggrieved at his perceived, deficient status, but his reparative towards his mother's damaged state is clear. In his reparative urge and his reliance on his good mother, he relinquishes his grievance against her while sticking to the actuality that he is not her child in the way her other children are her children.

Perhaps boyhood gives rise to additional anxiety about one's place in a new order of things. Boys explore feeling of self, of masculinity, under the watchful eyes of females, with anxiety charged with uncertainty about their attitude towards them. To me, it is a revised rerun of the primal state of the boy in his mother's embrace, *nachträglich* in Freud's thinking. Extending this interpretive line, we can postulate that the boy is identifying with his father, situating himself in a lineage of masculinity.

The lineage of the boy on the way to manhood raises another issue. His father is in the same lineage, presumably also seeking to identify with a father in that lineage. Does this lineage ever achieve the solidity of the lineage of female identification? Earlier, I put forward the view that it does not, and I suggested that one source of misogyny lies in its shakiness. Men form networks in the hunt for a stable masculine identification. Social media have made easy the coalescence of shallow masculine identifications organized around misogynistic themes. In the manosphere, white men magnify these identifications with racist themes.

Let us turn to the unfortunate case, in which the environment exacerbates the aggression between mother and son. I will draw upon a thought-provoking short story by Freud's literary double, Arthur Schnitzler, called *The Son* (1892; Figlio 2007). A man has attacked – ultimately killing – his mother. Her doctor is called. Before she dies, she explains what has happened. She begs him to plead in court for her son's innocence. She confesses that she had tried, unsuccessfully, to suffocate him at birth, but with the next morning came her life-long devotion and love. So also began his defiance.

Her account is compelling. It is more than a description of her state: Schnitzler induces the reader to think as she does, as she captures the doctor, inducing him to take up her cause. In a live encounter, it would be projective identification. The doctor does come to think that there can be a foundational, internal assault, which embeds a murderous mother inside an infant's mind. The mother, then, is not a clear perception of separate person for him, but a swirling, overwhelming internal, threatening confusion. The existential threat, now an ominous unease in the infant, calls out his defiance as a desperate grip on survival and identity.

Reflecting on how he might act in court, the doctor muses,

> Do we retain confused memories from the first hours of our existence, which we can no longer make clear and yet which do not vanish without trace? ... Is perhaps a ray of sun that falls through the window the earliest source of a peaceful disposition? – and if a mother's first glance embraces us with infinite love, does it not gleam unforgettably back in the sweet blue eyes of the child? – If, however, this first glance is a glance of ambivalence and hatred, does it not burn with destructive force into the soul of that child, which absorbs thousands of impressions long before they can be deciphered? ... [N]one of you ... can know what of the good and the bad that he bears he owes to the first breath of air, the first ray of sun, the first glance of the mother ... (Schnitzler 1892, 2039; my translation)

Schnitzler also tells the tragic story of a woman's plight: On her own, shamed by an unexpected pregnancy. She is guilty in the eyes of a moralistic, harshly judgmental culture, and she reacts to it by trying to erase the shaming of its condemnation. Her story elicits sympathy. Surely she is guilty of no more than a moment's passion in the past and, at her son's birth, a moment of deranged frenzy: The attempted murder is actually blood on the hands of a misogynistic culture, which singles her out, condemns her and takes no notice of the father. But for the child, she is the very origination of himself and she tries to extinguish him, to erase his existence.

The child's defiance becomes his identity. His defiance replaces the mother as the origin and guarantor of his existence, including his masculine identity. It feeds on extracting his every wish from her, which peaks at the moment of yet another demand, which this time she cannot meet and which seals her fate. His demands, justified in his defiance, also feed on extracting her life, just as, in his unconscious phantasy, she tried to reclaim her virtue by extracting his life. Schnitzler casts the story around events: She did fall pregnant; she did react with shame; she did try to kill her child; he did absorb her murderousness; her love was not, for him, reparative. But what Schnitzler adds, with deep insight, is the possibility of an unconscious introjection of a bad object – a topic that has only recently been explored in detail by psychoanalysts.

Critics of psychoanalysis have argued for years that Freud was responsible for the neglect of actual abuse, usually by men, when he seemed to replace his seduction theory with one based on phantasy. The history of this limited appraisal is not relevant to my analysis (see Whitebook 2017, 220–21). Schnitzler's insightful, psychoanalytically-near account, allows us to attend to a moment before external reality has been secured by perception, when phantasy is mixed in with sensation, when sensation itself has no clear location from which it originates. The infant is simply besieged. He invites us to translate behaviour, which is in the realm of conscious experience, into an unconscious realm of a psychic dread of a murderous internal object. In the world of phantasy, such an internal object might have been intruded by an external object or might have been a phantasy of retaliation by the object for murderous impulses, which Klein described with her concept of projective identification. Or maybe it is just dread, to be mastered by a phantasy of putting it outside and attacking it in the repository – the first object. One way or another, it is embedded in the psyche, (re)projected into an external object and attacked in that object. The first internalized object and repository of projective identification is, by definition, mother.

The (Masculine) Crisis of 'And': Individual and Social Misogyny

Schnitzler's harrowing story recreates such a moment. But as I have argued, everyone – every male – begins life 'inside' mother, with mother also inside the child at the beginning. The intimacy of which Hustvedt speaks can nurture or subvert his identity; in any event, the intimacy is uneasy, the bedrock of love and dread. The contexts and forces of history, important as they are – so compellingly demonstrated in Wolfe's comparative historical analysis – do not operate apart from the crucible in which misogyny is brewed.

In her analysis of the Nazi mind, extreme in its brutality beyond imagination, Wieland (2015) connects these two levels. She scales up the primal
threat at the core of idea male identity. A defensive male group identification
spread through German society, based on an unconscious phantasy of the
nation as a *male* womb. She sees the racist extremity of Nazism as a monstrous expansion of a male drive to save and amplify itself by replacing the
female from the very beginning.

> The fascist group acts both as a *womb and as its denial* portrayed as a war
> machine – both as a big mother and as a huge machine for manufacturing
> new men – the men of steel. It both affirms and denies the wish to be one
> with mother ... The homogenised group has the advantage of being a
> concrete symbol (a "symbolic equation") of the womb in which the
> members can immerse themselves and lose their identity *but at the same
> time* retain their sense of being masculine, or perhaps more than that,
> enhance their masculinity ... a masculinity bigger than life and truly
> omnipotent. (42; Wieland's emphasis)

At a primal level, misogyny is the source of replacement ideology, both in
the individual and in society. I have argued in this book that men – principally white men in western culture – begin the route to dominating society by
dominating women, and they enter onto that route in reaction to being inside
a woman. All men begin that way. A primal, existential ambivalence is carried in the phantasy that the male inside the female holds a contradiction
between engendering new life with her and sustaining her as a good object, on
the one hand, and destroying her, on the other: A phantasy linked to the
devouring feminine that can absorb him.

The phantasy of this existential ambivalence is carried by the semen, with
its procreative, sustaining, reparative capacity, on the one hand, and its
toxicity, on the other. This primal ambivalence, in which the male colonizes
the inside of the mother in reaction to his absorption into her, is the source of
an existential anxiety. In that sense, it is an unthought, proto-replacement
theory. Replacement ideology conveys, in an adult language, a deep anxiety
that its language cannot comprehend. The 'replacement' in this language does
not speak to competition with women for jobs. Such a sense of disadvantage
is within consciousness. It does not, on its own, cause dread: Not the dread of
being replaced. Replacement language points to an existential crisis that it
cannot name or represent: The dread of no longer existing because one's
identity has been stolen – literally stolen – and that is inconceivable.
Conscious replacement language cannot encompass dread: It can only
exacerbate it by continually intimating, and thereby evoking, what it cannot
comprehend.

I have approached this primal beyond representation in a variety of ways.
I have seen it as primary narcissism, as union, as fertility, as conception in

procreation, as 'inside' without dimensions to be inside of; as an intimation of a primal yearning to return or to retrieve a primal state of 'before' coming into being; as getting to the beginning of the beginning, at the origin of natality; as a quest for natality as an activity, a production – a self-production. These ideas are all attempts to represent what lies beyond representation. They are intimations of such a place, which is beyond the dimensions by which we designate place. The losses of which we can speak, such as losing the breast, exclusion from oedipal triumph, loss of body parts, all give voice to such a primal displacement from existential security.

This line of thinking is consistent with the interest in Bion's (1957) work on the psychotic aspect of the psyche – an aspect of every psyche – adjacent to the 'normal' neurotic side of the psyche (see, for example, Bergstein 2019; Mawson 2011; Meltzer 1988). The reality-hating, psychotic side reacts to reality by exploding in fragments that invade reality and the ego attached to it, distorting perception by the intrusion of these 'bizarre objects'. Reality itself then portends an infinity that breaches the capacity to integrate it into the ego, encompassing it in ordinary perception.

What I have called the 'reduction in dimensionality' is to one side of a duality of reality (explored in Chapter 3). It aims to bring a 'beyond' into perceptual reality, to comprehend it. I associate this beyond with Bion's 'O' or infinity, Kant's thing-in-itself and the 'and' of union, represented by the parental couple. They become, as the beyond, the eternal object of curiosity and unfulfillable longing, incarnated in the intimate involvement with natality. Natality, with all its elaborations – social and internal – brings concern and guilt with it. Phallic narcissism aims to subsume the helpless submission to these realities under omnipotent mastery.

Masculinity confronts this duality of reality in its own way, in a struggle to mitigate the unease of masculine identity in the femininity phase, embodied in the feminine. The backbone is the lineage of masculinity: The father, the father's father, the father in the mother, the father in the father's mother. It is a lineage never fully firmed up as its own structure outside the femininity phase in which the fathers grew up. Misogyny is one stance, a somewhat manufactured masculine identity, standing against mother in woman and consolidated in networks of masculine identification in groups. It can find the feminine everywhere and in the extreme it becomes toxic masculinity. One place where the feminine is found, and against which toxic masculinity takes a stand, is nature, to which we turn in the next section.

Masculinity in the Desolation of Mother Nature

Let us move from mother as the primal object to mother nature. There are anti-nature-activists with a misogyinistic leaning, who participate in the wanton destruction of nature, or deny its precarious state, or seem unmoved by the evidence of it, or say that nature is in God's hands. They stand above the fortunes and misfortunes of a sustained relationship with nature, of its realities, of their responsibility for her. They also attribute to nature a maternal capacity to survive their ruthlessness, and in that way, continue to live in an infantile phantasy of maternal robustness, reinforced by an absolute repudiation of the fragility of nature in the face of their destructive incursions.

Nature is robust in surviving, but only within the eyeshot of blinkered vision. Their repudiation can be so complete – as we saw in Chapter 10, in discussing the pollution of nature and 'carbon vitalists' – and their vision can be so blinkered, as to equate her survival with their creative efforts. They thereby apear to reverse their dependence on nature into nature's dependence on them. Also, creativity realized in destruction implies an unconscious equation of annihilation with creation. Together they feed an omnipotent phantasy of triumph over mourning the desolation of nature.

The idea of toxicity and toxic masculinity as a poisoning incursion into the interior of the feminine makes sense of an aspect of the wanton destruction of nature, beyond the self-interest of economic exploitation. The pathway to consciousness of the toxic follows a typical route of defence, in that it allows representation of the unconscious content while shielding consciousness from view. Repression accomplishes this double-act by displacing the content from the emotional charge. Disavowal achieves it by splitting the ego. Negation does it by attaching a repudiating particle, such as 'not' to the unconscious content. 'Toxic' manages all three deceptions. The aggression of toxic masculinity is internal, based on what I called seminal ambivalence. It is depressive, urging engagement, guilt, concern and mourning. The more toxic masculinity is shielded by phallic masculinity, the more an ominous sense of depressive collapse remains hidden and evaded. The more phallic masculinity satisfies this defensive function, the wider the scope of depressive anxiety it gathers into it.

Psychoanalytic thinking suggests that defences are also unconscious communications in search of a listener who can receive, understand and translate them, and mitigate their impact: That is, contain it. 'Toxic' as the name of an aggressive masculinity, is, I suggest, such an unconscious communication. Toxic is just that – poison – but packaged as phallic, with all its dramatic, omnipotent, exhibitionistic overtones, which create a climate of magical recovery from the depressive desolation of a poisoned world and the mourning of a world lost to the point of desolation.

Harold Searles (1972, 242) captures the omnipotent phantasy of triumph over mourning by a predilection for a final, apocalyptic annihilation of the world.

The greatest danger lies in the fact that the world is in such a state as to evoke our very earliest anxieties and at the same time to offer the delusional "promise", the actually dangerous promise, of assuaging these anxieties by effacing them, by fully externalizing and reifying our most primitive conflicts that produce those anxieties. In the pull upon us to become omnipotently free of human conflict, we are in danger of bringing about our extinction.

I want to tie in two aspects of his analysis with the thesis of this book. First, he refers to the resurgence of the very earliest anxieties. Secondly, he speaks of getting free of human conflict. The link, in my view, is that the very earliest anxieties are the existential anxieties at the emergence of the ego and of its managing the femininity phase, and that the original conflict is ambivalence, in particular, a primal, existential ambivalence. Bear in mind that these anxieties and these omnipotent defence mechanisms, in their dangerous realizations, are typically masculine and misogynistic.

Searles is bringing to our attention an ultimate catastrophe of extinction produced by omnipotent defences against recognizing the reality of our embeddedness in nature, the responsibility for nature and the consequences of repudiating this responsibility. But that connectedness, and the repudiation of it, is rooted in a repudiated engagement with each other: More particularly, with misogyny in mind, of the masculine with the feminine or, in its indescribable reality, in Goethe's words, of the masculine with the eternal feminine. The internal catastrophe is depressive desolation, the incapacity for, or the rejection of, depressive, reparative concern for the good object.

Masculinity and the Desolation of Social Nature

While the environment can be recast as external – out there – the episodic terror of both overpopulation and depopulation, which ripples through society, recreates a link to an internal catastrophe. There seem always to be too many of us or too few of us. When our fertility is too great, it threatens the external environment; when it is too low, it reveals a threat at work deep inside our internal environment. The mother's body is the first natural body and the first natural environment for the foetus. It is either enriched into over-production or inadequately enriched, or even poisoned, just as surely as the external environment can be enriched or poisoned by man-made chemicals. And, at root, it is never wholly external.

The Google ngram viewer documents words and phrases over time, in writings of all sorts, contained in the vast repository of the Google search engine (English language in my queries). By selecting key words and phrases, and comparing when they dramatically come into use, one can get a sense of correlated, if not causal, topics. We can, for example, see that 'population decline', 'sperm count', 'sperm motility' and 'feminization' move almost in synch (accessed 18 December 2022). 'Population decline', 'sperm count', 'sperm motility' level off around 1980, while 'feminization' continues to rise until the early 1990s, then falls. 'Toxic masculinity' came to prominence in the 1980s, rising starkly in 2012. In 2019, the latest year for which figures are available, it is still rising sharply, while 'population decline' has levelled off and 'feminization' is declining. It then stands at 11% of 'feminization', but if the heavily US spelling is replaced by the British, 'feminisation', then feminisation falls into the same range as the others, and they all cluster together in the extent of their usage.

'Misogyny' rises along with the registering of 'feminisation', 'population decline', diminished 'sperm count' and diminished 'sperm motility'. It then continues to rise as the others level off, overtaking them dramatically. Meanwhile, toxic masculinity was brewing in the background for some time, registering along with feminization. So, misogyny and toxic masculinity seem to register, and react to, an anxiety around feminization and declining seminal capacity across English-speaking cultures A repository search can only establish correlations, and also lacks context and the intentions of authors. It nonetheless indicates a level of aggregated preoccupation.

Even a cursory look at the popular press shows anxiety at both an impending, unsustainable over-population and an impending unsustainable under-population. Anxiety at overpopulation, and the disaster that it would bring through the depletion of nature, is matched by the anxiety that population is declining and will continue to decline, weakening a nation and leading ultimately to extinction. Coleman and Rowthorn (2011) provide a comprehensive overview of population changes across the world, and the projected consequences of population decline. They begin by noting that

> Fear of population decline, censuses to warn of it, and pronatalist and other policies to avert it are almost as old as states themselves. Rulers and states ... and stateless tribal societies, found affirmation, strength, and protection in population growth and cause for alarm in decline as symptom and cause of failure and weakness. (217)

Population declined in Western Europe and the United States between World War I and World War II, jumped with the baby boomers, then declined again and still declines. Decline is widespread across the world, and even where population is now increasing, it is likely to decrease in the future. It also stands out that the modern decline is down to decreased fertility, not to an ageing population. There are too many factors to allow firm conclusions of advantage or disadvantage. As might be expected, however, over-population does deplete the health of the environment, and in any event, 'population' acts as an abstract trigger of anxiety of both over- and under-population.

But, as Coleman and Rowthorn point out, a reasoned overview of population dynamics and their impact on the economy does not necessarily correspond to popular perception and to anxieties connected to population increase or decrease. Some factors lie near the surface, such as imagined military strength (consider the decline of population under Russian control since the break-up of the Soviet Union) and impact in international fora, such as the EU. In fact, these considerations seem to command more urgent attention than the catastrophic degradation of the environment.

A review article in *Science Daily* (24 August 2021) reported a population peaking in 2064, with a 50% drop in this century. Levine et al. (2017) carried out a large-scale analysis of sperm count between 1973 and 2011, showing a 50% - 60% reduction in North America, Europe, Australia and New Zealand (no consistent results for South America, Asia and Africa). Picking up and expanding on this work, Niciola Davis (2022), writing in the *Guardian*, headed her article: 'Humans Could face Reproductive Crisis as Sperm Count Declines'. Natalie Huet (2022), writing in *Euronews Next*, reported on the same study. She reported the decline as world-wide and included extracts from an interview with some of the authors. They were astounded by what seemed like a pandemic, a population collapse predicted at the very moment that global population passed eight billion.

The decline in population has been noted in many countries, sparking a concern at the ultimate outcome and policies to reverse the trend, despite the ever-increasing population (most recently in China, the most populous country; Zhang and Master 2023). In a study by van Dalen and Henkins (2011), as the world population hit seven billion, the wish for a decline in population, even in the densely populated Netherlands, was in the minority. Although there was majority support for a decline in the world population, only 31% supported a national decline, a figure that dropped to 16% among local populations. The data suggest that 'we' – my group – want to remain strong – populous – against 'them'; that is, all others. It was supported by two, opposing, extreme groupings: Right wingers who opposed immigration, and left wingers who feared for the environment.

Regardless of attempts at causal explanations, such as the destructive influence of human overpopulation, perhaps through chemicals discharged into the environment, or even stress, there seems to be an unstable oscillation between a dread that overpopulation will lead to the extinction of human life on earth and a dread that population decline will also lead to extinction. Overall, human life is eroding its own foundation. I link it – though not exclusively – with dread of a depressive – seminal – catastrophe. It is covered by the stereotype of masculine activity, superiority and bravado. The masculine lineage, in its dread of dissolution, reacts with phallic assertiveness based on an omnipotent phantasy of total control and magical recovery, a phantasy secured by diminishing the feminine, sometimes intending violently to annihilate it. 'Our' men should dominate; 'their' men should weaken.

A vivid fictional portrayal of the depressive collapse of seminality – P. D. James' novel, *The Children of Men*, published in 1992 and set in 2021 – makes the case compellingly. I contrast it with two overtly phallic films in the *Terminator* series. In *The Children of Men*, male fertility has given out and no children have been born for years. The possibility of a future depends on a fertile couple, for which viable sperm are needed. In the *Terminator* series, the future is in the hands of super-masculine cyborgs. I will sketch the films first, because we can then see the depressive desolation revealed beneath phallic masculinity.

In the second *Terminator* story, advanced microchip technology has produced an intelligent system that gains control of US defences, including all decision-making. The system is challenged by humans, and, in retaliation, it provokes a nuclear war with Russia, which destroys humanity. But time is not absolute: None of this has happened – yet – but will (could) take place in a future, from which two intelligent humanoid machines – cyborgs – have come back to the 1990s, the present-as-past. One, based on more advanced microchip technology that is just about to be invented in the 1990s, aims to make sure the future does take this course, by killing any human opposition. The other cyborg is less advanced but able to absorb human experience to the point of having human feelings and tries to prevent the 'future' human catastrophe. At some point, he begins to act from feelings as well as in accordance with his programme, while the advanced technology both increases cyborg capacity to imitate human beings and distances it from its human core. A struggle ensues between the two cyborgs.

The hope of averting this future lies with a boy who will grow up to lead a revolutionary group of human beings. He was conceived in the first film, by a couple who straddled time: The mother living in the 1980s, the father coming back from the future to try to change the as-yet unforeseen but disastrous course of history. In the second film, the mother sees this future in visions, after her lover has been killed, and she prepares to defend her son, who will carry out his father's mission. She is incarcerated in a mental hospital because of her visions, but escapes with the help of her son and the cyborg ally, and plans to kill the inventor of the microchip technology before he invents the advanced cyborg technology. In the end, as a human being with feelings, she cannot kill him, but does enlist his help in destroying all the research. The second film also accomplishes the destruction of both cyborgs, who contain potentially dangerous, advanced microchips, and all the microchip technology, so that the future cataclysm is averted. The child of human love survives, as the fruit of the human connection between present and future. Historical time is realized in a human lineage.

The films portray the usual version of male destructiveness in the masculinity of science and technology. The opposition of rational male and feeling female is clear: The boy's mother shouts at the scientist that *his* science is an empty and futile version of the simplicity of pregnancy. *She*, as a woman, cannot kill him. The revolutionary *action* was to be carried forward by a *male*, despite the fact that she had become an accomplished fighter. The problem lay in the technological mind, mainly reified into the objects – the microchips. We could see the films as the prophetic visions of a woman about the fate of masculinity. She has a vision: The cyborgs, which are the material product of masculine science and technology, actually intervene in the material world.

The Children of Men begins with a diary of an Oxford don, who gathers his life into daily accounts for no particular reason that he can discern, because all human life will soon have disappeared – not through annihilation, as in *Terminator II*, but through a total cessation of male fertility. The human species is simply winding up its existence. Living becomes meaningless – even sexual intercourse loses its interest – as the future simply falls away. The novel is also dramatic, permeated with anxiety, as violent gangs roam the countryside, but the overriding mood is desolation.

The late 20th century, when male fertility gave out, retained its science and technology. Nothing was destroyed, but semen simply gave out. That was where the real horror lay, and its demise unmasked the hollowness of phallic masculinity. The union of the parental couple was violently attacked. Anyone who might have laid claim to the fertility that would give birth to the future, died (the biological father, though a priest who did not lay claim, and the Warden of Britain, who did, were both killed). A pregnancy finally occurs, a loving couple becomes the basis of hope through their love, not through their (phallic, magical) capacity to change the future (as the penis recovers its potency after detumescence). Fittingly, the novel ends there. Unlike the films, the ultimate failure of masculinity was not phallic: It was a failure of seminality. Human love, however, has a chance to work towards the renewal of life.

The difference between the terminator films and the novel is striking: The fatalism of the films, which is produced by the fact that humankind is threatened with annihilation, as opposed to the aching depression of the novel, in which humanity is simply helpless. The former, I would say, is triumphal, even though the love child survives; the latter is depressive in the Kleinian sense. The films combat destructiveness with its own weapons: technology attacks technology; the aim is 'good', but the means are shared with evil. This kind of defence is akin to Klein's (1933, 250) account of the death instinct that cannot be disposed of by projection: 'parallel with this deflection ... outward against objects, an intra-psychic reaction of defence goes on against that part of the instinct which could not be this externalized ... A division takes place ... whereby one part of the instinctual impulse is directed against the other.' The novel, by contrast, aches with the realization of human incapacity and destructiveness.

The films embody hope through destroying destructiveness; the novel carries a seed of regeneration, nurtured by the hope for a conception that can be protected from (envious) attack. The former is omnipotent; the latter reality-orientated and object-related, in its waiting for love to renew human life. In the films, there was a loving relationship and a pregnancy, which the future as an IT system sought to destroy; in the novel, there is a loving relationship and a pregnancy. It is also attacked, but by other humans, and also protected. A child is to be born, who could overcome the desolation of non-life.

We come back to the thesis of this book. The ultimate dread, which seems to perfuse culture – at least Western culture – is depressive desolation: Life will give out; specifically, the masculine capacity to enliven, sustain and repair life through his seminal relationship to the feminine, is giving out. It is not just a matter of failing seminal capacity, but of seminal ambivalence, a failing of love, procreation and reparation to mitigate seminal destructiveness. It is more a matter of dread than of anxiety, and it is concealed beneath active, omnipotent, magically restorative phallic masculinity. The very expression, 'toxicity', is a disavowal and a denial. It registers consciously as phallic and unconsciously as an insidious, internal degradation of nature and of enlivening natality. It reduces the testicular father to the phallic father, while recognizing his seminal function and the desolation wrought by his ambivalence towards it. It reduces the 'and' of union and procreation to masculine activity inside a place.

The sharp light directed on masculinity by the phallic defence thrown up around its toxicity brings out the contours of its normal, seminal, capacity. The glare of it can also deflect our attention from ordinary masculinity. A misogynist streak pervades our culture, and Freud has been called to account for embedding it in the origin of psychoanalysis. But he struggled with it, and rightly appealed to having established a science that is sensitive to its errors and distortions. Indeed, it is a science built on the idea and the practice of correcting itself, and bearing repeated humbling moments that they bring. It is a tough job. It involves embracing the guilt of depressive concern, which can be an exemplar for society.

Struggling with the Feminine at the Root of Psychoanalysis

To conclude our study, we will turn to the struggle of psychoanalysis with the feminine, at the root, in Freud's struggle with the feminine. Joel Whitebook (2017), a psychoanalyst and philosopher, has written a fascinating intellectual biography of Freud, in which he sees the father of psychoanalysis wresting with this vulnerability. Whitebook (236) argues that Freud was undoubtedly a man of the Enlightenment, but of a late Enlightenment that did not gird itself with arid rationalism. He was alert to the irrationality of a counter-enlightenment, but in the mood of what

Yovel [1992] calls "the dark enlightenment", which was a deeper, conflicted, disconsolate, and even tragic yet still emancipatory tradition within the broader movement of the Enlightenment ... Freud, as a "dark" enlightener, sought to take the claims of the *Gegenaufklärung* [counter-Enlightenment] seriously. And this meant doing justice to the truth content of the irrational. (11, 236)

On the one hand, he took telepathy seriously, which bothered the more conventional Jones; on the other hand, he stuck to his project of disillusionment and rebutting omnipotence and magical thinking, often with Jung in mind. In his late, monumental study of Jewish monotheism, *Moses and Monotheism* (1939), Freud includes a major section, *Der Fortschritt in der Geistigkeit*, translated in the *Standard Edition* as The Progress of Intellectuality. Whitebook draws attention to the limitation of this rendering – but really, of any rendering in English – in its restriction of the scope of *Geistigkeit*: Intellectuality, yes, but also of the *Geist*, of the spirit,

> the extra-cognitive and emotional reverberations contained in the German ... Because of its polysemic nature, *Geistigkeit* can be interpreted as a "tertiary" concept, and, at its best, it prescribes us the ask of sublating or sublimating the binomial opposition between intellectuality and spirituality at a higher level of integration. (440)

Moses for Freud, and Freud in his identification with Moses, aimed to encompass the maternal, with its emotionality, drives and bodily intimacy, within the abstract, non-sensual world of the paternal. To do so, Freud had to ignore evidence that his model for Moses, the Egyptian pharaoh, Akhenaten, was displayed in sensuous, naturalistic forms with his queen, Nefertiti. He had also to ignore the paper of his close colleague, Karl Abraham (1912), which speaks of Akhenaten's androgynous character (450–451).

But Whitebook also sees a Freud in a struggle between two versions of himself. There is an 'official' Freud, in his view of himself and in its lineage through acolytes and critics, and there is an 'unofficial' version. In the official version, we see Freud as we have been trained to know him: The scientist; the *man* of reason, suspicious of the irrational, suspicious of the feminine; the creator of a science in which reason and consciousness were built on repression. In the unofficial version, we see the lover – of women and men – passionate to the point of madness. Among the women, were his young mother; his nanny; his teenage infatuation with Gisela Fluss, the sister of his close friend, Emil; Martha. Among the men were Fliess, Breuer, Jung.

For Freud, the eternal feminine is our origin and our end, a theme that he elaborated in his paper, 'The Theme of the Three Caskets' (1913; Whitebook, 333 – 342). The struggle with the eternal feminine appears in his beautiful essay, 'On Transience' (1916b), which he wrote for a commemoration of his idolized poet, Goethe, comprising 247 distinguished figures of his time, including Einstein, Hugo von Hofmannsthal and Arthur Schnitzler (Der Berliner Goethebund 2016, 37 – 38). Freud closes with the final stanzas from Goethe's *Faust* PtII (1832):

Everything transient
Is only a likeness
The unattainable
Here is achieved
The indescribable
Here is realized
The eternal-feminine
Draws us beyond
(my translation)[2]

Freud's use of the closing passage from Goethe's epic ties his thinking to the idea that our earthly life is a finite version of the eternal feminine. It adds to Freud's optimism and belief in the beauty of the transient world. Whitebook is sceptical, but we nevertheless glimpse an encompassing majesty of the feminine. In Freud's (1913) 'The Theme of the Three Caskets', it takes the form of three incarnations: The womb mother from whom we emerge, the woman of our beloved choice, and the tomb mother to whom we return. In Freud's borrowing Faust's salvation, we see the masculine, in his finiteness, embraced in the eternal feminine.

For Freud (1913, 292), however, the mythic is not a separate domain of a reality of its own, but a dimension of finite human reality.

[W]e do not share the belief of some investigators that myths were read in the heavens and brought down to earth; we are more inclined to judge with Otto Rank that they were projected onto the heavens after having arisen elsewhere under purely human conditions.

Faust's compulsion to transcend his finiteness is masculine. Mephistopheles undermines his every wish in seeming to satisfy it, and crashes his compulsive aspirations. But one can also read him as an extreme magnification of Faust's masculine striving and the emptiness of masculine omnipotence. In fact, Mephistopheles warns Faust of the illusion of his quest. In effect, he demonstrates its futility (lines 1803 – 1815) while becoming Faust's servant, working for his doom and declaring his preference for the 'Eternal-Empty' (line 11603). Faust is redeemed. His redemption lies in a fulness that renders emptiness a futile gesture against the embrace of the feminine.

One might say that Freud saw beauty and hope in the transient life of 'man', embodied in fertile relationships, but was also unable fully and squarely to address what happened in that transience between 'his' beginning and 'his' end. Reading between the lines, with Whitebook in mind, one can discern Freud's struggle with the feminine in the struggle between his official and unofficial versions. We do get an insight into the hopeless striving of masculinity on its own, the power of the feminine and the recognition that human love alone can transcend this contradiction. That is what Melanie Klein filled in with her theory of the femininity phase.

Lotto (2001), for example, argues that Freud formulated the groundwork of psychoanalysis along with consolidating his relationship to the ear, nose and throat specialist, Wilhelm Fliess, as his confidant. Freud referred a patient of his, Emma Eckstein, to Fliess for an operation on her nose, a procedure in line with Fleiss' theory of a nose-genital axis. Fliess botched the operation, leading to life-threatening bleeding and infection, but Freud supported him, offering interpretations of Eckstein's condition. Whitebook discerns a misogynistic streak as Freud struggles with this turmoil and they see a recurring triangle, 'in which he forged a homosexual bond with a male companion by jointly treating a female victim in a misogynistic and sadistic fashion' (Whitebook 2017, 211).

The struggle of reason with passion is exacerbated by the importance of the father in a man's life – in Freud's life. Whitebook also shows Freud's ambivalence towards his father – a man whom he idealized: The father, the loss of whom is the greatest loss in a man's life; and the father who did not fulfil the son's need to believe in this ideal. Freud, the son – and we may infer, all men – cover their passion for their beautiful mother, and her lineage, with their needed and imperfect, idealized fathers. Such a wrestling of paternal reason with maternal emotion drives Freud's psychoanalytic preoccupations, such as his 'Moses of Michelangelo' (1914), a Moses – his idealized father of mythic proportions – who struggles with, and masters, his fury at his wayward people.

Freud's 'On Transience', presaged the theoretically tight 'Mourning and Melancholia'. In both, he speaks of loss and mourning as realities that enliven and buttress our belief in love and the renewal of life. They are not reasons for despair, but for hope. Melancholia fights against these realities: Denying them becomes a source of rage against them and, beneath it, of despair. I think there is another dimension to this resistance, which we can also tie in with the eternal feminine: That she is a source of hope and renewal or an object of rage and, beneath it, despair. The misogyny, which I have traced in this book, including its extreme, brutal, enactments, are rebellions against her. As I have tried to show, they lead, not only to attacks upon her, as she appears in the individual women in a man's life, but also in her abstract embodiments: In nature, in the social nature of population and in human productions, such as the economy. To remain with her, in a sustained relationship, with its happiness and sadness, fortunes and misfortunes, is much harder than to destroy her, as the object in which they are placed.

The extreme of masculine repudiation of the feminine, often aggressive and even violent, is associated with the display of masculine activity, muscularity, rationality: They are all overt displays of a vigour that does not submit to the entangling emotionality of femininity. But that is also why toxic masculinity has come to represent the masculine defence. The secret is lying in plain sight: That is its concealment, as in a gripping crime novel. 'Toxic' so evidently points to pollution. Only semen, not the penis, can poison the female as the source of his life; only semen, not the penis, attacks intimately inside, not in a room inside. The penis can assault ballistically, penetrating like a bullet or an arrow: Semen mixes with the interior of the female, to share in procreation, to sustain it, to repair it – or to contaminate it.

Notes

1   Hagit Aharoni (2010, 39) offers a psychoanalytic account of the living, intimate relationship between mother and foetus, mediated by the placenta.

> I propose the term placental economy to represent both the primal intrauterine state as well as its expressions after biological and psychological birth. This economy is characterized by a paradoxical form of linkage/separateness that is defined by a combined, indivisible element between the two that is at the same time different and differentiated … . The placenta, which has its own mode of existence, may even serve as a proto-representation of what the mind will eventually conceive of as a third, already at this primal, uterine phase. The placental link, then, is always one of linkage/separateness never one or the other alone and is not static.

2   Alles Vergängliche
    Is nur ein Gleichnis;
    Das Unzulängliche,
    Hier wird's Ereignis;
    Das Unbeschreibliche,
    Hier ist's getan;
    Das Ewig-Weibliche
    Zieht uns hinan

I have used the Norton Critical Edition as a reference. The translator, Walter Arndt, renders 'Das Unbeschreibliche, Hier ist getan', in terms of 'discernment' that is 'passed by'. With my focus on Freud on transience and on his Faust, I have decided on an 'indescribable' that is 'realized'. I want to stress an inconceivability that becomes conceivable, though mysterious: Real as experience, in an essentially transient moment of union with the feminine. The feminine remains beyond complete fulfilment, and yearning holds it in being. Renewal as redemption returns; hope comes with the anticipation of the seasons.

References

Abraham, K. (1912) Amenhotep IV: A Psycho-Analytical Contribution towards the Understanding of his Personality and of the Monotheistic Cult of Aton. In Abraham, H. C. (ed.) *Clinical Papers and Essays on Psycho-Analysis*. NY: Brunner Mazel, 262–290.

Aharoni, H. (2010) Placental Economy: Thoughts on the Movement Between Linkage and Separateness and Their Paradoxical Coexistence. *Ma'arag: The Israel Annual of Psychoanalysis* 1: 39–64.

Bergstein, A. (2019) *Bion and Meltzer's Expeditions into Unmapped Mental Life: Beyond the Spectrum in Psychoanalysis*. London/NY: Routledge.

Bion, W. R. (1957) Differentiation of the Psychotic from the Non-Psychotic Personalities. In *Second Thoughts: Selected Papers of Psycho-Analysis*. London: Heinemann, 1967; Karnac, 1984, 43–64.

Coleman, D. and Rowthorn, R. (2011) Who's Afraid of Population Decline? A Critical Examination of Its Consequences. *Population and Development Review* (Population Council) 37: 217–248.

Davis, N. (15 Nov 2022) 'Humans Could Face Reproductive Crisis a Sperm Count Declines'. Guardian. https://www.theguardian.com/society/2022/nov/15/humans-could-face-reproductive-crisis-as-sperm-count-declines-study-finds, Accessed 5 December 2022.

Der Berliner Goethebund (eds) (2016) *Das Land Goethes 1914–1916: Ein vaterländisches Gedenkbuch* [*The Land of Goethe 1914–1916: A Book of Commemoration of the Fatherland*]. Stuttgart/Berlin: Deutsche Verlags Anstalt.

Figlio, K. (2007). A New Naturalism: On the Origins of Psychoanalysis as a Social Theory of Subjectivity. In Bainbridge, C. et al. (eds) *Culture and the Unconscious*. London: Palgrave Macmillan, 24–40.

Freud, S. (1913) The Theme of the Three Caskets. *The Standard Edition of the Complete Psychological Works of Sigmund Freud*. 12: 289–302.

Freud, S. (1914) The Moses of Michelangelo. *The Standard Edition of the Complete Psychological Works of Sigmund Freud* 13: 209–238.

Freud, S. (1939) Moses and Monotheism: Three Essays. *The Standard Edition of the Complete Psychological Works of Sigmund Freud* 23: 1–138.

Huet, N. (2022) Sperm Count Drop is Accelerating Worldwide and Threatens the Future of Mankind, Study Warns. *Euronews Next* 17 November. https://www.euronews.com/next/2022/11/15/sperm-count-drop-is-accelerating-worldwide-and-threatens-the-future-of-mankind-study-warns#:~:text=Sperm%20counts%20worldwide%20have%20halved,threatening%20the%20survival%20of%20humanity, Accessed 18 December 2022.

Hustvedt, S. (2019) What Does a Man Want. In *Mothers, Fathers, and Others*. London: Sceptre, 2021, 225–253.

Klein, M. (1933) The Early Development of Conscience in the Child. In *The writings of Melanie Klein*, vol. 1. London: The Hogarth Press and the Institute of Psycho-Analysis, 1975, 248–257.

Levine, H., et al. (2017) Temporal Trends in Sperm Count: A Systematic Review and Meta-Regression Analysis. *Human Reproduction Update* 23(6): 646–659. https://academic.oup.com/humupd/article/23/6/646/4035689, Accessed 5 December 2022.

Lotto, D. (2001) Freud's Struggle with Misogyny: Homosexuality and Guilt in the Dream of Irma's Injection. *Journal of the American Psychoanalytic Association* 49: 1289–1313.

Power, N. (2022) *What Do Men Want: Masculinity and its Discontents*. London: Penguin Books.

Mawson, C. (ed.) (2011) *Bion Today*. London/NY: Routledge.

Meltzer, D. (1988) *The Apprehension of Beauty: The Role of Aesthetic Conflict in Development and Violence*. Strath Tay: The Clunie Press.

Rey, H. (1994) *Universals of Psychoanalysis in the Treatment of Psychotic and Borderline States: Factors of Space, Time and Language*, edited by Magagna, J. London: Free Association Books.

Schnitzler, A. (1892). *Der Sohn. Aus den Papieren eines Arztes*. In Ausgewählte Werke (2017). Chicago: OK Publishing, 2032–2039 (English translation by I. Bamforth, British Journal of General Practice 57: 1007–1009).

Science Daily (24 August 2021) Stress from Rising Population Numbers May Cause a Decline in Human Fertility. https://www.sciencedaily.com/releases/2021/08/210824104102.htm, Accessed 5 June 2022.

Searles, H. F. (1972) Unconscious Processes in Relation to the Environmental Crisis. *Psychoanalytic Review* 59: 361–374. In *Countertransference and Related Subjects: Selected Papers*. NY: International Universities Press, 1979, 228–242.

van Dalen, H. and Henkens, K. (2011) Do People Fear Population Decline. https://voxeu.org/article/seven-billion-people-so-why-do-some-fear-population-decline.

Whitebook, J. (2017) *Freud: An Intellectual Biography*. Cambridge/NY: Cambridge University Press.

Wieland, C. (2015) *The Fascist State of Mind and the Manufacturing of Masculinity: A Psychoanalytic Approach*. London/NY: Routledge.

Yovel, Y. (1992) *Spinoza and Other Heretics*, vol. II: *Adventures in Immanence*. Princeton: Princeton University Press.

Zhang, A. and Master, F. (2023) China's First Population Drop in Six Decades Sounds Alarm on Demographic Crisis. Reuters 17 January 2023. https://www.reuters.com/world/china/chinas-population-shrinks-first-time-since-1961-2023-01-17/, Accessed 11 February 2023.

References

Abraham, K. (1908) The Psychological Relations between Sexuality and Alcoholism. In *Selected Papers on Psycho-Analysis*. London: Hogarth; reprinted London: Karnac, 1979, 80–89.

Abraham, K. (1909) *Dreams and Myths: A Study in Race Psychology*. New York: The Journal of Nervous and Mental Disease Publishing Company, 1913; repr. Kessinger, n.d.

Abraham, K. (1912) Amenhotep IV: A Psycho-Analytical Contribution towards the Understanding of His Personality and of the Monotheistic Cult of Aton. In Abraham, H. C. (ed.) *Clinical Papers and Essays on Psycho-Analysis*. New York: Brunner Mazel, 262–290.

Abraham, K. (1917) Ejaculatio Praecox. In *Selected Papers on Psycho-Analysis*. London: Hogarth Press, 1927, 280–298.

Abraham, K. (1920) Manifestations of the Female Oedipus Complex. In *Selected Papers on Psycho-Analysis*. London: Hogarth Press, 1927, 338–369.

Abraham, K. (1922) An Infantile Theory of the Origin of the Female Sex. In *Selected Papers on Psycho-Analysis*. London: Hogarth Press, 1927, 333.

Adorno, T. W., et al. (1950) *The Authoritarian Personality*. New York: Harper & Row; London/New York: Verso, 2019.

Aharoni, H. (2010) Placental Economy: Thoughts on the Movement between Linkage and Separateness and Their Paradoxical Coexistence. *Ma'arag: The Israel Annual of Psychoanalysis* 1: 39–64.

Ahumada, J. (1982) The Unconscious Delusion of 'Goodness' (1982). In *The Logics of the Mind: A Clinical View*. London/New York: Karnac, 2001, 65–82.

Anna Freud Centre (1981) Scientific Forum on the Superego: Its Early Roots and the Road from Outer to Inner Conflict as Seen in Psychoanalysis. *Bulletin of the Anna Freud Centre* 4: 77–117.

Anon. (Ferenczi)(1933) Ontogenesis. *Psychanalytic Quarterly* 2: 365–403.

Anzieu, D. (1986) *Freud's self Analysis*. London: Hogarth and the Institute of Psycho-Analysis.

Arendt, H. (1958) *The Human Condition*. Chicago: University of Chicago Press.

Axelrod, S. (1994) 'Impossible Projects': Men's Illusory Solutions to the Problem of Work. *Psychoanalytic Psychology* 11: 21–32.

Balsam, R. (2018) 'Castration Anxiety' Revisited: Especially 'Female Castration Anxiety'. *Psychoanalytic Inquiry* 38(1): 11–22.

Basch-Kåhre, E. (1987) Forms of the Oedipus Complex. *Scandinavian Psychoanalytic Review* 10: 103–115.

BBC News (2009) 'More Credit' For Homes and Firms, http://news.bbc.co.uk/1/hi/business/7978434.stm, Accessed 3 September 2009.

Belew, K. (2018) *Bring the War Home: The White Power Movement and Paramilitary America*. Cambridge, MA/London: Harvard University Press.

Bell, A. (1961) Some Observations on the Role of the Scrotal Sac and Testicles'. *Journal of the American Psychoanalytic. Association* 9: 261–286.

Bell, A. (1965) The Significance of the Scrotal Sac and Testicles for the Prepuberty Male. *Psychoanalytic. Quarterly* 34: 182–206.

Bergler, E. (1935) Some Special Varieties of Ejaculatory Disturbance Not Hitherto Described. *International Journal of Psychoanalysis* 16: 84–95.

Bergler, E. (1937) Further Observations on the Clinical Picture of 'Psychogenic Oral Aspermia'. *International Journal of Psychoanalysis* 18: 196–234.

Bergstein, A. (2019) *Bion and Meltzer's Expeditions into Unmapped Mental Life: Beyond the Spectrum in Psychoanalysis*. London/New York: Routledge.

Bion, W. R. (1957) Differentiation of the Psychotic from the Non-Psychotic Personalities. In *Second Thoughts: Selected Papers of Psycho-Analysis*. London: Heinemann, 1967; Karnac, 1984, 43–64.

Bion, W. R. (1962) A theory of Thinking. In *Second Thoughts: Selected Papers of Psycho-Analysis*. London: Heinemann, 1967; Karnac, 1984, 110–119.

Bion, W. R. (1965) *Transformations*. London: Heinemann; Karnac, 1984.

Bion, W. R. (1967) On Arrogance. In *Second Thoughts: Selected Papers on Psycho-Analysis*. London: Heinemann, 86–92.

Bion, W. R. (1970) *Attention and Interpretation*. London: Tavistock; Karnac, 1984.

Bion, W. R. (1992) *Cogitations*. London: Karnac.

Bird, B. (1957a) Feelings of unreality. *International Journal of Psychoanalysis* 38: 256–265.

Bird, B. (1957b) A Consideration of the Etiology of Prejudice. *Journal of the American Psychoanalytical Association* 5: 490–513.

Birksted-Breen, D. (1996) Phallus, Penis and Mental Space. *International Journal of Psychoanalysis* 77: 649–657.

Blass, H. (2010) Wann ist der Mann ein Mann? oder: Männliche Identität zwischen Narzissmus und Objektliebe. *Psyche – Zeitschrift für Psychoanalyse* 64(8): 675–699.

Boehm, F. (1930) The Femininity-Complex in Men. *International Journal of Psychoanalysis* 11: 444–469.

Boehm, F. (1931) The History of the Oedipus Complex. *International Journal of Psychoanalysis* 12: 431–451.

Bonaparte, M. (1952) Some Biopsychical Aspects of Sado-Masochism. *International Journal of Psychoanalysis* 33: 373–384.

Bonomi, C. (1998) Freud and Castration: A New Look into the Origins of Psychoanalysis. *Journal of the American Academy of Psychoanalysis* 26: 29–49.

Bootle, R. (2009) *The Trouble with Markets: Saving Capitalism From Itself*. London/Boston: Nicholas Brealey.

Bratich, J. and Banet-Weiser, S. (2019) From Pick-Up Artist to Incels: Con(fidence) Games, Networked Misogyny, and the Failure of Neoliberalism. *International Journal of Communication* 13: 5003–5027.

Breen, D. (ed.) (1993) *The Gender Conundrum: Contemporary Perspectives on Femininity and Masculinity.* London/New York: Routledge.

Britton, R. (1989) The Missing Link: Parental Sexuality in the Oedipus Complex. In Steiner, J. (ed.) *The Oedipus Complex Today Clinical Implications.* London: Karnac, 83–101.

Britton, R. (1994) Publication Anxiety: Conflict between Communication and Affiliation. *International Journal of Psychoanalysis* 75: 1213–1224.

Britton, R. (1995) Psychic Reality and Unconscious Belief. *International Journal of Psychoanalysis* 76: 19–23; revised version in *Belief and Imagination: Explorations in Psychoanalysis.* London: Routledge, 1998, 8–18.

Britton, R. (1999) Getting In on the Act: The Hysterical Solution. *International Journal of Psychoanalysis* 80: 1–14.

Britton, R. (2001) Forever Father's Daughter: The Athene-Antigone Complex. In Trowell, J. and Etchegoyen, A. (eds) *The Importance of Fathers.* London/New York: Routledge; revised, as Phallic Idealisation in Women. *In Sex, Death and the Superego: Updating Psychoanalytic Experience and Developments in Neuroscience,* 2nd edn. London/New York: Routledge, 2021, 50–61.

Britton, R. (2008) He Thinks Himself Impaired: The Pathologically Envious Personality. In Roth, P. and Lemma, A. (eds) *Envy and Gratitude Revisited.* London: Karnac, 124–136.

Britton, R. (2017) Disconnection: A New Look at Narcissism. In Bronstein, C. and O'Shaughnessy, E. (eds) *'Attacks on Linking' Revisited: A New Look at Bion's Classic Work.* London: Karnac, 25–37.

Britton, R. (2021) Narcissistic Problems of Sharing Space. In *Sex, Death and the Superego: Updating Psychoanalytic Experience and Developments in Neuroscience,* Second Edition. London/New York: Routledge, 121–133 (originally published in 1990, not in English, in the Brazilian Psychoanalytic Journal).

Britton, R. and Steiner, J. (1994) Interpretation: Selected Fact or Overvalued Idea? *International Journal of Psychoanalysis* 75: 1069–1078.

Brough, A. R. and Wilkie, J. E. B. (2017) Men Resist Green Behavior as Unmanly: A Surprising Reason for Resistance to Environmental Goods and Habits. *Scientific American* 26 December. https://www.scientificamerican.com/article/men-resist-green-behavior-as-unmanly/, Accessed 2 January 2023.

Burnham, L. (1971) Freud and Female Sexuality: A Previously Unpublished Letter. *Psychiatry* 34: 328–329.

Carson, R. (1962) *Silent Spring.* Boston: Houghton Mifflin.

Chasseguet-Smirgel, J. (1986) The Archaic Matrix of the Oedipus Complex. In *Sexuality and Mind: The Role of the Father and Mother in the Psyche.* New York/London: New York University Press, 74–91.

Chodorow, N. (1994) *Femininities, Masculinities, Sexualities: Freud and Beyond (Blazer Lectures).* Lexington, KY: University Press of Kentucky.

Clark, A. (2010) Wall Street Bonuses Top $20bn. *Guardian* 24 February: 23.

Coleman, D. and Rowthorn, R. (2011) Who's Afraid of Population Decline? A Critical Examination of Its Consequences. *Population and Development Review (Population Council)* 37: 217–248.

Connell, R. (2012) Inside the Glass Tower: The Construction of Masculinities in Finance Capital. In McDonald, P. and Jeanes, E. (eds) *Men, Wage Work and Family*. New York/London: Routledge, 65–79.

Crawley, E. (1902) *The Mystic Rose*. London: Macmillan.

Dahl, E. (1996) The Concept of Penis Envy Revisited: A Child Analyst Listens to an Adult. *Psychoanalytic Study of the Child* 51: 303–325.

Davids, M. F. (2011) *Internal Racism: A Psychoanalytic Approach to Race and Difference*. London: Karnac.

Davis, N. (15 November 2022) 'Humans Could face Reproductive Crisis a Sperm Count Declines'. Guardian. https://www.theguardian.com/society/2022/nov/15/humans-could-face-reproductive-crisis-as-sperm-count-declines-study-finds, Accessed 5 December 2022.

de Beauvoir, S. (1949) *le deuxième sexe* [*The Second Sex*], Borde, C. and Malovany-Chevallier, S. (translated by). London: Random House, 2009.

de Cook, J. R. and Kelly, M. (2022) Interrogating the 'Incel Menace': Assessing the Threat of Male Supremacy in Terrorism Studies. *Critical Studies in Terrorism* 15: 706–726.

de Teram, D. (2010) Fools' Gold. *The Banker*, 5 April 2004. https://www.thebanker.com/Archive/Fools-gold/(language)/eng-GB, Accessed 31 October 2010.

Der Berliner Goethebund (eds) (2016) *Das Land Goethes 1914–1916: Ein vaterländisches Gedenkbuch* [*The Land of Goethe 1914–1916: A Book of Commemoration of the Fatherland*]. Stuttgart/Berlin: Deutsche Verlags Anstalt.

Diamond, M. (2006) Masculinity Unravelled: The Roots of Male Gender Identity and Shifting Oof Male Ego Ideals throughout Life. *Journal of the American. Psychoanalytic. Association* 54:1099–1130.

Diamond, M. J. (2013) Evolving Perspectives on Masculinity and Its Discontents: Reworking the Internal Phallic and Genital Positions. In Mari, E. P. and Thomson-Salo, F. (eds) *Masculine and Feminine Today*. London: Karnac, 1–24.

Diamond, M. J. (2015) The Elusiveness of Masculinity: Primordial Vulnerability, Lack, and the Challenges of Male Development. *Psychoanalytic Quarterly* 84: 47–102.

Diamond, M. (2021) *Masculinity and Its Discontents: The Male Psyche and the Inherent Tensions of Maturing Manhood*. London/New York: Routledge.

Dimen, M. and Goldner, V. (2006) Gender and Sexuality. In Person, E., Cooper, A. and Gabbard, G. (eds) *The American Psychiatric Publishing Textbook of Psychoanalysis*. Washington, DC/London: American Psychiatric Publishing, 93–114.

Dodd, V. (2022) Met Failings Let Corrupt Police Officers Stay on Force. *The Guardian* 17 October: 1–2.

Douglas, M. (1966) *Purity and Danger: An Analysis of the Concepts of Pollution and Taboo*. New York: Praeger.

Dreher, A. U. (2000) *Foundations for Conceptual Research in Psychoanalysis*. London: Karnac.

Du Mez, K. (2021) *Jesus and John Wayne: How White Evangelicals Corrupted a Faith and Fractured a Nation*. New York: Liveright Publishing Corp.

Edgcumbe, R. and Burgner, B. (1975) The Phallic Phase – A Differentiation between Preoedipal and Oedipal Aspects of Phallic Development. *Psychoanalytic Studies of the Child* 30: 161–180.

Eisler, R. (1914) Der Fisch als Sexualsymbol [The fish as a sexual symbol, with an appendix by Otto Rank]. *Imago* 3: 165–196; summarized by Brink, L. (1919) in *Psychoanalytic Review* 6: 460–64.

Elise, D. (2001) Unlawful Entry: Male Fears of Psychic Penetration. *Psychoanalytic Dialogues* 11: 499–531.

Etchegoyen, R. (1988) The Analysis of Little Hans and the theory of sexuality. *International Review of Psycho-Analysis* 15: 37–43.

Federn, P. (1929) On the Distinction between Healthy and Pathological Narcissism. In Weiss, E. (ed.) *Ego Psychology and the Psychoses*. London: Imago, 1953; Karnac, 1977, 323–364.

Fenichel, O. (1925) Introjection and the Castration Complex. In *The Collected Papers of Otto Fenichel. First Series*. New York: W. W. Norton, 1953, 39–70.

Fenichel, O. (1936) The Symbolic Equation: Girl = Phallus. In *The Collected Papers of Otto Fenichel*, Second Series. New York: W. W. Norton, 1954, 3–18.

Ferenczi, S. (1924) *Thallassa: A Theory of Genitality*. New York: Psychoanal. Q., 1938; repr. London: Karnac, 1989.

Ferro, A. (2012) Creativity in the Consulting Room: Factors of Fertility and Infertility. *Psychoanalytic Inquiry* 32(3): 257–274.

Figlio, K. (1996) The Ominous in Nature. *Free Associations* 6(2): 276–296.

Figlio, K. (2000) *Psychoanalysis, Science and Masculinity*. London: Whurr; Philadelphia: Brunner Routledge, 2001.

Figlio, K. (2003) Getting to the Beginning: Historical Memory and Concrete Thinking. In Radstone, S. and Hodgkin, K. (eds) *Regimes of Memory (Routledge Studies in Memory and Narrative*, vol. 12. London: Routledge, 2003, 152–166; pb *Memory Cultures: Memory, Subjectivity and Recognition*. New Brunswick/London: Transaction, 2006.

Figlio, K. (2004) Psychoanalysis, Politics and the Self-Awareness of Society. *Psychoanalysis, Culture and Society* 9(1): 87–104.

Figlio, K. (2006) The Absolute State of Mind in Society and the Individual". *Psychoanalysis, Culture and Society* 11(2): 119–143.

Figlio, K. (2007) A New Naturalism: On the Origins of Psychoanalysis as a Social Theory of Subjectivity. In Bainbridge, C. et al. (eds) *Culture and the Unconscious*. London: Palgrave Macmillan, 24–40.

Figlio, K. (2010a) Phallic and Seminal Masculinity: A Theoretical and Clinical Confusion. *International Journal of Psychoanalysis* 91(1): 119–139.

Figlio, K. (2010b) The Financial Crisis: A Psychoanalytic View of Illusion, Greed and Reparation in Masculine Phantasy. *New Formations* 72: 33–46; also in Bennet, D. (ed.) *Loaded Subjects: Psychoanalysis, Money and the Global Financial Crisis*. London: Lawrence and Wishart, 2012, 34–51.

Figlio, K. (2017a) The Mentality of Conviction: Feeling Certain and the Search for Truth. In Mintchev, N. and Hinshelwood, R. (eds) *The Feeling of Certainty: Psychosocial Perspectives on Identity and Difference*. Cham, Switzerland: Palgrave Macmillan, 11–30.

Figlio, K. (2017b) *Remembering as Reparation: Psychoanalysis and Historical Memory*. London: Palgrave Macmillan, 2017.

Figlio, K. (2018) Fundamentalism and the Delusional Creation of an Enemy. In Krüger, S., Figlio, K. and Richards, B. (eds) *Fomenting Political Violence: Fantasy, Language, Media, Action*. London: Palgrave, 2018, 149–166.

Figlio, K. (2021) Lying in Autocratic Society. *Free Associations: Psychoanalysis and Culture, Media, Groups, Politics* 83: 15–28.

Figlio, K. (2023) Money as the Currency of Value. In Jacobsen, K. and Hinshelwood, R. D. (eds) *Psychoanalysis, Science and Power: Essays in Honour of Robert Maxwell Young*. Abingdon Oxon/New York: Routledge, 2023, 164–183.

Flouri, E. (2005) *Fathering & Child Outcomes*. Chichester: John Wiley & Sons.

Fogel, G. (1998) Interiority and Inner Genital Space in Men: What Else Can Be Lost in Castration. *Psychoanalytic Quarterly* 67: 662–697.

Fogel, G. (2006) Riddles of Masculinity: Gender, Bisexuality, and Thirdness. *Journal of the American Psychoanalytic Association* 54: 1139–1163.

Fox, E. (1983) *The Five Books of Moses: Genesis, Exodus, Leviticus, Numbers, and Deuteronomy*. London: The Harvill Press.

Freud, S. (1895) Draft K. The Neuroses of Defense (A Christmas Fairy Tale), January 1, 1896: [enclosed with letter]. In Masson, J. M. (translated and ed.) *The Complete Letters of Sigmund Freud to Wilelm Fliess, 1887–1904*. Cambridge, MA: Belknap Press, 1986, 162–169.

Freud, S. (1897) Letter to Wilhelm Fliess, 15 October. In Masson, J. M. (translated and ed.) *The Complete Letters of Sigmund Freud to Wilhelm Fliess 1887–1904*. Cambridge, MA: Belknap Press, 1986. 270–273.

Freud, S. (1900) The Interpretation of Dreams. *The Standard Edition of the Complete Psychological Works of Sigmund Freud* 4: 5.

Freud, S. (1905) Three Essays on the Theory of Sexuality. *The Standard Edition of the Complete Psychological Works of Sigmund Freud* 7: 123–245.

Freud, S. (1908a) On the Sexual Theories of Children'. *The Standard Edition of the Complete Psychological Works of Sigmund Freud* 9: 205–226.

Freud, S. (1908b) Character and Anal Erotism. *The Standard Edition of the Complete Psychological Works of Sigmund Freud* 9: 167–176.

Freud, S. (1909a) Analysis of a Phobia in a Five-Year-Old Boy. *The Standard Edition of the Complete Psychological Works of Sigmund Freud* 10: 1–149.

Freud, S. (1909b) Notes Upon a Case of Obsessional Neurosis. *The Standard Edition of the Complete Psychological Works of Sigmund Freud* 10: 153–318.

Freud, S. (1910a) A Special Type of Choice of Object Made by Men (Contributions to the Psychology of Love I). *The Standard Edition of the Complete Psychological Works of Sigmund Freud* 11: 161–175.

Freud, S. (1910b) Leonardo Da Vinci and a Memory of His Childhood. *The Standard Edition of the Complete Psychological Works of Sigmund Freud* 11: 57–138.

Freud, S. (1911a) Psycho-Analytic Notes on an Autobiographical Account of a Case of Paranoia (Dementia Paranoides). *The Standard Edition of the Complete Psychological Works of Sigmund Freud* 12: 1–82.

Freud, S. (1911b) Formulations on the Two Principles of Mental Functioning. *The Standard Edition of the Complete Psychological Works of Sigmund Freud* 12: 213–226.

Freud, S. (1912) On the Universal Tendency to Debasement in the Sphere of Love (Contributions to the Psychology of Love II). *The Standard Edition of the Complete Psychological Works of Sigmund Freud* 11: 177–190.

Freud, S. (1913[1912–1913]) Totem and Taboo. *The Standard Edition of the Complete Psychological Works of Sigmund Freud* 13: 1–165.

Freud, S. (1913) The Theme of the Three Caskets. *The Standard Edition of the Complete Psychological Works of Sigmund Freud* 12: 289–302.

Freud, S. (1914a) On Narcissism: An Introduction. *The Standard Edition of the Complete Psychological Works of Sigmund Freud* 14: 73–105.

Freud, S. (1914b) The Moses of Michelangelo. *The Standard Edition of the Complete Psychological Works of Sigmund Freud* 13: 209–238.

Freud, S. (1915) Instincts and their Vicissitudes. *The Standard Edition of the Complete Psychological Works of Sigmund Freud* 14: 109–140.

Freud, S. (1916a) Some Character-Types Met in Psycho-Analytic Work. *The Standard Edition of the Complete Psychological Works of Sigmund Freud* 14: 309–333.

Freud, S. (1916b) On Transience. *The Standard Edition of the Complete Psychological Works of Sigmund Freud* 14: 303–307.

Freud, S. (1917a) On Transformations of Instinct as Exemplified in Anal Erotism. *The Standard Edition of the Complete Psychological Works of Sigmund Freud* 17: 125–133.

Freud, S. (1917b) Mourning and Melancholia. *The Standard Edition of the Complete Psychological Works of Sigmund Freud* 14: 237–258.

Freud, S. (1918 [1917]) The Taboo of Virginity (Contributions to the Psychology of Love II). *The Standard Edition of the Complete Psychological Works of Sigmund Freud* 11: 191–208.

Freud, S. (1918) From the History of an Infantile Neurosis. *The Standard Edition of the Complete Psychological Works of Sigmund Freud* 17: 1–122.

Freud, S. (1919) The 'Uncanny'. *The Standard Edition of the Complete Psychological Works of Sigmund Freud* 17: 217–256.

Freud, S. (1920) Beyond the Pleasure Principle. *The Standard Edition of the Complete Psychological Works of Sigmund Freud* 18: 1–64.

Freud, S. (1921) Group Psychology and the Analysis of the Ego. *The Standard Edition of the Complete Psychological Works of Sigmund Freud* 18: 65–144.

Freud, S. (1923a) The Ego and the Id. *The Standard Edition of the Complete Psychological Works of Sigmund Freud* 19: 1–66.

Freud, S. (1923b) The Infantile Genital Organization: An Interpolation into the Theory of Sexuality. *The Standard Edition of the Complete Psychological Works of Sigmund Freud* 19: 139–145.

Freud, S. (1924) The Dissolution of the Oedipus Complex. *The Standard Edition of the Complete Psychological Works of Sigmund Freud* 19: 171–180.

Freud, S. (1925a) Some Psychical Consequences of the Anatomical Distinction between the Sexes. *The Standard Edition of the Complete Psychological Works of Sigmund Freud* 19: 241–258

Freud, S. (1925b) Negation. *The Standard Edition of the Complete Psychological Works of Sigmund Freud* 19: 233–240

Freud, S. (1926) Inhibition, Symptoms and Anxiety. *The Standard Edition of the Complete Psychological Works of Sigmund Freud* 20: 77–175.

Freud, S. (1930) Civilization and Its Discontents. *The Standard Edition of the Complete Psychological Works of Sigmund Freud* 21: 57–146.

Freud, S. (1931) Female Sexuality. *The Standard Edition of the Complete Psychological Works of Sigmund Freud* 21: 221–243.

Freud, S. (1933) New Introductory Lectures on Psycho-Analysis. *The Standard Edition of the Complete Psychological Works of Sigmund Freud* 22: 1–182.

Freud, S. (1937) Analysis Terminable and Interminable. *The Standard Edition of the Complete Psychological Works of Sigmund Freud* 23: 209–254.

Freud, S. (1938) Findings, Ideas, Problems. *The Standard Edition of the Complete Psychological Works of Sigmund Freud* 23: 299–300.

Freud, S. (1939) Moses and Monotheism: Three Essays. *The Standard Edition of the Complete Psychological Works of Sigmund Freud* 23: 1–138.

Freud, S. (2002) *The Complete Correspondence of Sigmund Freud and Karl Abraham 1907–1925*, Falzeder, E. (ed.) London: Routledge; also *PEPWEB*.

Freud, S. (2003) *The Sigmund Freud-Ludwig Binswanger Correspondence 1908–1938*, Fichtner, G. (ed.) London: Open Gate Press; also *PEPWEB*.

Friedman, R. (1996) The Role of the Testicles in Male Psychological Development. *Journal of the American Psychoanalytical Association* 44: 201–253.

Gabbard, G. (1993) On Hate in Love Relationships: The Narcissism of Minor Differences Revisited. *Psychoanalytic Quarterly* 62: 229–238.

Gaddini, E. (1969) On Imitation. In *A Psychoanalytic Theory of Infantile Experience: Conceptual and Clinical Reflections*. London: Tavistock/Routledge, 1992, 18–34.

Gaddini, E. (1972) Aggression and the Pleasure Principle: Towards a Psychoanalytic Theory of Aggression. In *A Psychoanalytic Theory of Infantile Experience: Conceptual and Clinical Reflections*. London: Tavistock/Routledge, 1992, 35–45.

Gaddini, E. (1974) Formation of the Father and the Primal Scene. In *A Psychoanalytic Theory of Infantile Experience: Conceptual and Clinical Reflections*. London: Tavistock/Routledge, 1992, 61–82.

Gaddini, E. (1976) On Father Formation in Early Child Development. In *A Psychoanalytic Theory of Infantile Experience: Conceptual and Clinical Reflections*. London: Tavistock/Routledge, 1992, 83–89.

Garnham, P. and Hughes, J. (2010) Banks Shift from Risk Helps Push FX Trading to $4,000bn a Day. *Financial Times* September: 15.

Glenn, J. (1969) Testicular and Scrotal Masturbation. *International Journal of Psychoanalysis* 50: 353–362.

Goethe, J. W. von (1832) *Faust: A Tragedy, an Authoritative Translation, Interpretive Notes, Contexts, Modern Criticism*, Second Norton Critical Edition, Arndt, W. (Translated by), Hamlin, C. (ed.), 2nd edition. New York/London: W. W. Norton.

Gonzalez, J. (1953) Screen Memory, Symptom, and Transference. *Revista De Psicoanálisis* 10: 277–307; extracted in *Psychoanalytic Quarterly* 24: 321–2.

Graeber, D. (2011) *Debit, the First 5,000 Years: Towards an Anthropology of Value*, 3rd edn. Brooklyn/London: Melville House Publishing, 2014 and Kindle edition.

Green, A. (1990) *Le complexe de castration [The Castration Complex]*. Paris: PUF.

Green, A. (1995) Has Sexuality Anything to Do with Psychoanalysis? *International Journal of Psychoanalysis* 76: 871–883.

Grosz, S. (1993) A Phantasy of Infection. *International Journal of Psychoanalysis* 74: 965–974.

Grunberger, B. (1979) *Narcissism: Psychoanalytic Essays*. Madison, CT: International Universities Press.

Grunberger, B. (1989) *New Essays on Narcissism*. London: Free Association Books.

Hägglund, T.-B. and Piha, H. (1980) The Inner Space of the Body Image. *Psychoanalytic Quarterly* 49: 256–283.

Harrington, C. (2021) What Is 'Toxic Masculinity' and Why Does It Matter? *Men and Masculinities* 24(2): 345–352.

Hess, E. (1975) *The Tell-Tale Eye: How Your Eyes Reveal Hidden Thoughts and Emotion*. New York: Van Nostrand Reinhold.

Hinshelwood, R. D. (1989) Little Hans's Transference. *Journal of Child Psychotherapy* 15: 63–78.

Hinshelwood, R. D. (1991) *A Dictionary of Kleinian Thought*, 2nd edn. London: Free Association Books.

Hinshelwood, R. (1997a) The Elusive Concept of 'Internal Objects' (1934–1943): Its Role in the Formation of the Klein Group. *International Journal of Psychoanalysis* 78: 877–897.

Hinshelwood, R. (1997b) Catastrophe, Objects and Reparation: Three Levels of Interpretation. *British Journal of Psychotherapy* 13(3): 307–317.

Horney, K. (1926) The Flight from Womanhood: The Masculinity-Complex in Women, as Viewed by Men and by Women. *International Journal of Psychoanalysis* 7: 324–339; reprinted in *Feminine Psychology*. New York: Norton, 1967, 54–70.

Horney, K. (1932) The Dread of Women: Observations on a Specific Difference in the Dread Felt by Men and Women Respectively for the Opposite Sex. *International Journal of Psychoanalysis* 13: 348–360; reprinted in *Feminine Psychology*. New York: Norton, 1967, 133–146.

Horney, K. (1933) The Denial of the Vagina: A Contribution to the Problem of the Genital Anxieties Specific to Women. *International Journal of Psychoanalysis* 14: 57–70; reprinted in *Feminine Psychology*. New York: Norton, 1967, 147–161.

Huet, N. (2022) Sperm Count Drop Is Accelerating Worldwide and Threatens the Future of Mankind, Study Warns. *Euronews Next* 17 November. https://www.euronews.com/next/2022/11/15/sperm-count-drop-is-accelerating-worldwide-and-threatens-the-future-of-mankind-study-warns#:~:text=Sperm%20counts%20worldwide%20have%20halved,threatening%20the%20survival%20of%20humanity, Accessed 18 December 2022.

Hunter, D. (1954) Object-Relation Changes in the Analysis of a Fetishist. *International Journal of Psychoanalysis* 35: 302–312.

Hustvedt, S. (2019) What Does a Man Want. In *Mothers, Fathers, and Others*. London: Sceptre, 2021, 225–253.

Hustvedt, S. (2022) Umbilical Phantoms. *International Journal of Psychoanalysis* 103: 368–380.

Isaacs, S. (1940) Temper Tantrums in Early Childhood in Their Relation to Internal Objects. *International Journal of Psychoanalysis* 21: 280–293.

Jacobson, E. (1950) Development of the Wish for a Child in Boys. *Psychoanalytic Study of the Child* 5: 139–152.

Johanssen, J. (2022) *Fantasy, Online Misogyny and the Manosphere: Male Bodies of Dis/Inhibition*. London/New York: Routledge.

Johanssen, J. and Krüger, S. (2022) *Media and Psychoanalysis: A Critical Introduction*. London: Karnac.

Johns, M. (2002) Identification and Dis-identification in the Development of Sexual Identity. In Trowel, J. and Etchegoyen, A. (eds) *The Importance of Fathers: a Psychoanalytic Re-evaluation*. Hove: Brunner-Routledge/New York: Taylor and Francis, 2003.

Jonas, H. (1966) *The Phenomenon of Life: Toward a Philosophical Biology*. New York: Harper & Row.

Jones, E. (1912) The Symbolic Significance of Salt in Folklore and Superstition. *Imago* 1: 361–454; repr. in *Psycho-Myth, Psycho-History*, vol. 2. New York: Stonehill, 1974, 22–109.

Jones, E. (1914) The Madonna's Conception through the Ear. In *Psycho-myth, Psycho-History: Essays in Applied Psychoanalysis*, vol. 2. New York: Stonehill, 1974, 266–357.

Jones, E. (1927) The Early Development of Female Sexuality. *International Journal of Psychoanalysis* 8: 459–472. In *Papers on Psychoanalysis*, 5th edn. London: Baillière, Tindall and Cox, 1948; London: Karnac, 1977, 438–51.

Jones, R. J. (1994) An Empirical Study of Freud's Penis-Baby. *The Journal of Nervous and Mental Disease* 182: 127–135.

Joseph, B. (1988) Projective Identification: Clinical Aspects. In Sandler, J. (ed.) *Projection, Identification, Projective Identification*. Madison, CT: International Universities Press, 65–76.

Kant, I. (1781/1787) *Critique of Pure Reason: Unified Edition* (translated by Pluhar, W.). Indianapolis/Cambridge: Hackett.

Karpman, B. (1922) On Stuper and Allied states. *Psychoanalytic Review* 9: 337–361.

Kestenberg, J. S. (1968) Outside and Inside: Male and Female. *Journal of the American. Psychoanalytic Association* 16: 457–520.

Kestenberg, J. S. (1977) Psychoanalytic Observation of Children. *International Review of Psychoanalysis* 4: 393–407.

Keylor, R. and Apfel, R. (2010) Male Infertility: Integrating an Old Psychoanalytic Story with the Research Literature. *Studies in Gender and Sexuality* 11(2): 60–77.

Kirkpatrick, K. (2019) *Becoming Beauvoir: A Life*. London: Bloomsbury Academic.

Kirsner, D. (1990) Illusion and the Stock Market Crash: Some Psychoanalytic Concepts. *Free Associations: Psychoanalysis, Politics, Culture, Society* 1: 31–59.

Klein, M. (1923) The Role of the School in the Libidinal Development of the Child. In *The Writings of Melanie Klein*, vol. 1. London: The Hogarth Press and the Institute of Psycho-Analysis, 1975, 59–76.

Klein, M. (1928) Early stages of the Oedipus conflict. In *The Writings of Melanie Klein*, vol. 1. London: The Hogarth Press and the Institute of Psycho-Analysis, 1975, 186–198.

Klein, M. (1932) The Psychoanalysis of Children. In *The Writings of Melanie Klein*, vol. 2. London: The Hogarth Press and the Institute of Psycho-Analysis, 1975.

Klein, M. (1933) The Early Development of Conscience in the Child. In *The Writings of Melanie Klein*, vol. 1. London: The Hogarth Press and the Institute of Psycho-Analysis, 1975, 248–257.

Klein, M. (1935) A Contribution to the Psychogenesis of Manic-Depressive States. In *The Writings of Melanie Klein*, vol. 1. London: The Hogarth Press and the Institute of Psycho-Analysis, 1975, 262–289.

Klein, M. (1937) Love, Guilt and Reparation. In *The Writings of Melanie Klein*, vol. 1. London: The Hogarth Press and the Institute of Psycho-Analysis, 1975, 306–343.

Klein, M. (1945) The Oedipus Complex in the Light of Early Anxieties. In *The Writings of Melanie Klein*, vol. 1. London: The Hogarth Press and the Institute of Psycho-Analysis, 1975, 370–419.

Klein, M. (1946) Notes on Some Schizoid Mechanisms. In *The Writings of Melanie Klein*, vol. 3. London: The Hogarth Press and the Institute of Psycho-Analysis, 1975, 1–24.

Klein, M. (1948) On the Theory of Anxiety and Guilt. In *The Writings of Melanie Klein*, vol. 3. London: The Hogarth Press and the Institute of Psycho-Analysis, 1975, 25–42.

Klein, M. (1950) On the Criteria for the Termination of a Psycho-Analysis. In *The Writings of Melanie Klein*, vol. 3. London: The Hogarth Press and the Institute of Psycho-Analysis, 1975, 43–47.

Klein, M. (1952) Some Theoretical Conclusions Regarding the Emotional Life of the Infant. In *The Writings of Melanie Klein*, vol. 3. London: The Hogarth Press and the Institute of Psycho-Analysis, 1975, 61–93.

Klein, M. (1957) Envy and Gratitude. In *The Writings of Melanie Klein*, vol. 3. London: The Hogarth Press and the Institute of Psycho-Analysis, 1975, 176–235.

Klein, M. (1961) Narrative of a Child Analysis: The Conduct of the Psycho-Analysis of Children as Seen in the Treatment of a Ten Year Old Boy. In *The Writings of Melanie Klein*, vol. 4. London: The Hogarth Press and the Institute of Psycho-Analysis, 1975.

Klein, M. (1963) Some Reflections on the Oresteia. In *The Writings of Melanie Klein*, vol. 3. London: The Hogarth Press and the Institute of Psycho-Analysis, 1975, 275–299.

Klein, V. (1946) *The Feminine Character: History of an Ideology*. London: Routledge and Kegan Paul.

Ladame, F. (1995) The Importance of Dreams and Action in the Adolescent Process. *International Journal of Psychoanalysis* 76: 1143–1153.

Laplanche, J. (1980) *Problématiques II: castration – symbolisations [Problematics II: castration – symbolizations]*. Paris: PUF.

Laplanche, J. (2007) Gender, Sex, and the Sexual. *Studies in Gender and Sexuality* 8: 209–219.

Laplanche, J. and Pontalis, J.-B. (1980) *The Language of Psycho-Analysis*. London: Hogarth and the Institute of Psycho-Analysis.

Laufer, E. (1986) The Female Oedipus Complex and the Relationship to the Body. *Psychoanalytic Studies of the Child* 41: 259–276; In Birksted Breen, D. (ed.) *The Gender Conundrum: Contemporary Psychoanalytic Perspectives on Femininity and Masculinity (New Library of Psychoanalysis)*. London: Routledge, 1993, 67–81.

Laufer, M. (1976) The Central Masturbation Fantasy, the Final Sexual Organization and Adolescence. *Psychoanalytic Studies of the Child* 31: 297–316.

Lax, R. (1997) Boys' Envy of Mother and the Consequences of This Narcissistic Mortification. *Psychoanalytic Studies of the Child* 52: 118–139.

Levine, H., et al. (2017) Temporal Trends in Sperm Count: A Systematic Review and Meta-Regression Analysis. *Human Reproduction Update* 23(6): 646–659. https://academic.oup.com/humupd/article/23/6/646/4035689, Accessed 5 December 2022.

Lotto, D. (2001) Freud's Struggle with Misogyny: Homosexuality and Guilt in the Dream of Irma's Injection. *Journal of the American Psychoanalytic Association* 49: 1289–1313.

Lyon, E. S. (2004) Researching Race Relations: Myrdal's American Dilemma from a Methodological Perspective. *Acta Sociologica* 47: 203–217.

MacKenzie, D. and Spears, T. (2014) 'The Formula That Killed Wall Street': The Gaussian Copula and Modelling Practices in Investment Banking. *Social Studies of Science* 44(3): 393–417.

Malinowski, B. (1916) Baloma; The Spirits of the Dead in the Trobriand Islands. In *Magic, Science and Religion and Other Essays*. Glencoe, IL: The Free Press, 1948; Garden City, NY: Doubleday Anchor, nd.

Marí, E. P. and Thomson-Salo, F. (eds) (2013) *Masculinity and Femininity Today*. London: Karnac.

Mawson, C. (ed.) (2011) *Bion Today*. London/New York: Routledge.

Mawson, C. (2019) *Psychoanalysis and Anxiety: From Knowing to Being*. London/New York: Routledge.

May, U. (2019) In Conversation: Freud, Abraham and Ferenczi on 'Mourning and Melancholia' (1915–1918). *International Journal of Psychoanalysis* 100: 71–98.

Mayer, E. (1995) The Phallic Castration Complex and Primary Femininity: Paired Developmental Lines Towards Female Gender Identity. *Journal of the American Psychoanalytic Association* 43: 17–38.

McCright, A. and Dunlap, R. (2011) Cool Dudes: The Denial of Climate Change Among Conservative White Males in the United States. *Global Climate Change* 21: 1163–1172.

McCright, A., et al. (2015) Examining the Effectiveness of Climate Change Frames in the Face of a Climate Change Denial Counter-Frame. *Topics in Cognitive Science* 8: 76–97.

Meltzer, D. (1973) *Sexual States of Mind*. Strath Tay: Clunie Press.

Meltzer, D. (1988) *The Apprehension of Beauty: The Role of Aesthetic Conflict in Development and Violence*. Strath Tay: The Clunie Press.

Meltzer, D., et al. (1982) The Conceptual Distinction between Projective Identification (Klein) and Container-Contained (Bion). *Journal of Child Psychotherapy* 8: 185–202. In *Studies in Extended Metapsychology: Clinical Applications of Bion's Ideas*. Strath Tay: Clunie, 1986, 50–69.

Meyer, G. (2010) Backlash Prompts Rethink on Forex Rules'. *Financial Times* 1 September: 33.

Midgley, N. (2006) Re-reading 'Little Hans': Freud's Case Study and the Problem of Competing Paradigms in Psychoanalysis. *Journal of the American Psychoanalytic Association* 54(2): 537–559.

Minsky, H. (2008) *Stabilizing an Unstable Economy*. New Haven, CT: Yale University Press/New York: McGraw Hill, first edn, 1986.

Morante, F. (2010) Omnipotence, Retreat from Reality and Finance: Psychoanalytic Reflections on the 2008 Financial Crisis. *International Journal of Applied Psychoanalytic Studies* 7: 4–21.

Moss, D. (2001) On Hating in the First Person Plural. *Journal of the American Psychoanalytic Association* 49: 1315–1334.

Moss, D. (2012) *Thirteen Ways of Looking at a Man: Psychoanalysis and Masculinity*. London/New York: Routledge.

Moss, D. (2021) On Having Whiteness. *Journal of the American Psychoanalytic Association* 69: 355–372.

Myers, W. (1976) The Psychological Significance of Testicular Problems. *Journal of the American Psychoanalytic Association* 24: 609–629.

Myrdal, G. (1944) *An American Dilemma, Volume II: The Negro Problem and Modern Democracy*. New York: Harper and Row/New Brunswick, NJ: Transaction, 1996.

Needles, W. (1966) The Defilement Complex – A Contribution to Psychic Consequences of the Anatomical Distinction between the Sexes. *Journal of the American Psychoanalytic Association* 14: 700–710.

Nussbaum, M. (2018) *The Monarchy of Fear: A Philosopher Looks at Our Political Crisis*. Oxford: Oxford University Press.

Orbach, C. E. (1974) Ideas of Contamination in Postoperative Colostomy Patients. *Psychoanalytic Review* 61: 269–282.

Papadimitriou, D. and Randall Wray, L. (2008) Minsky's Stabilizing an Unstable Economy: Two Decades Later. In Minsky, H. *Stabilizing an Unstable Economy*. New York: McGraw Hill, 2008, xi–xxxv.

Paulson, H. (2010) *On the Brink: Inside the Race to Stop the Collapse of the Global Financial System*. New York/London: Hachette.

Pesek, A. (2021) Carbon Vitalism: Life and the Body in Climate Denial. *Environmental Humanities* 13: 1–20.

Petruno, T. (2009) *Market Business News*, 4 June. https://marketbusinessnews.com/financial-glossary/toxic-assets/, Accessed 13 September 2021 (The entry has changed into a pared down definition of toxic assets, since I accessed it).

Power, N. (2022) *What do Men Want: Masculinity and Its Discontents*. London: Penguin Books.

Press Gazette (11 May 2012) A Tale Told Too Much: The Paediatrician Vigilantes. http://www.pressgazette.co.uk/a-tale-told-too-much-the-paediatrician-vigilantes/, Accessed 11 September 2023.

Rank, O. (1924) *The Trauma of Birth*. New York: Harper & Row, 1929.

Rey, H. (1979) The Schizoid Mode of Being. In LeBoit, J. and Capponi, A. (eds) *Advances in the Psychotherapy of the Borderline Patient*. New York: Jason Aronson, 449–484; In *Universals of Psychoanalysis in the Treatment of Psychotic and Borderline States*. London: Free Association Books, 1994, 8–30.

Rey, H. (1994) *Universals of Psychoanalysis in the Treatment of Psychotic and Borderline States: Factorss of Space, Time and Language*, Magagna, J. (ed.) London: Free Association Books.

Rhode, E. (1994) *Psychotic Metaphysics*. London: Karnac.

Robinson, M. (2010) The Next Banking Nightmare?, File on Four, BBC Radio 4, 9 February 2010.

Rosenfeld, H. (1971) A Clinical Approach to the Psychoanalytic Theory of the Life and Death Instincts: An Investigation into the Aggressive Aspects of Narcissism. *International Journal of Psychoanalysis* 52: 169–178.

Rosenfeld, H. (1987a) Narcissistic Patients with Negative Therapeutic Reactions. In *Impasse and Interpretation: Therapeutic and Anti-Therapeutic Factors in the*

Psychoanalytic Treatment of Psychotic, Borderline and Neurotic Patients. London: Tavistock, 85–104.

Rosenfeld, H. (1987b) Destructive Narcissism and the Death Instinct. In *Impasse and Interpretation: Therapeutic and Anti-Therapeutic Factors in the Psychoanalytic Treatment of Psychotic, Borderline and Neurotic Patients.* London: Tavistock, 105–132.

Rosenfeld, H. (1987c) Projective Identification in Clinical Practice. In *Impasse and Interpretation: Therapeutic and Anti-Therapeutic Factors in the Psychoanalytic Treatment of Psychotic, Borderline and Neurotic Patients.* London: Tavistock, 157–190.

Ross, J. M. (1992) *The Male Paradox.* New York: Simon & Schuster.

Rustin, M. (2000) Psychoanalysis, Racism and Anti-Racism. In Du Gay, P., Evans, J. and Redman, P. (eds) *Identity: A Reader.* London: Sage, 183–201.

Sayers, J. (1991) *Mothering Psychoanalysis: Helene Deutsch, Karen Horney, Anna Freud And Melanie Klein.* London: Hamish Hamilton.

Science Daily (24 August 2021) Stress from Rising Population Numbers May Cause a Decline in Human Fertility. https://www.sciencedaily.com/releases/2021/08/210824104102.htm, Accessed 5 June 2022.

Schnitzler, A. (1892) 'Der Sohn. Aus den Papieren eines Arztes'. In *Ausgewählte Werke.* Chicago: OK Publishing, 2017, 2032–2039; Bamforth, I. (English translation by). *British Journal of General Practice* 57: 1007–1009.

Searles, H. F. (1972) Unconscious Processes in Relation to the Environmental Crisis. *Psychoanalytic Review* 59: 361–374. In *Countertransference and Related Subjects: Selected Papers.* New York: International Universities Press, 1979, 228–242.

Segal, H. (1957) Notes on Symbol Formation. *International Journal of Psychoanalysis* 38: 391–397.

Segal, H. (1981) Manic Reparation. In *The Works of Hanna Segal: a Kleinian Approach to Clinical Practice.* NewYork: Jason Aronson; London: Free Association Books, 1986, 147–158.

Segal, H. (1983) Some Clinical Implications of Melanie Klein's Work—Emergence from Narcissism. *International Journal of Psychoanalysis* 64: 269–276.

Sinha, T. (1954) 'A Case of Aspermia'. *Samiksa*, 8 (1); summarized. *International Journal of Psychoanalysis* 36: 434.

Smith, J. (2019) *Home Grown: How Domestic Violence Turns Men into Terrorists.* London: Riverrun.

Solnit, R. (2022) Greta Thunberg Ends Year with One of the Greatest Tweets in History. *Guardian* 31 December. https://www.theguardian.com/commentisfree/2022/dec/31/greta-thunberg-andrew-tate-tweet, Accessed 2 January 2022.

Sorkin, A. (2009) *Too Big to Fail: Inside the Battle to Save Wall Street.* London: Penguin.

Spillius, E., et al. (2011) *The New Dictionary of Kleinian Thought.* London/New York: Routledge.

Squitieri, L. M. (1999) Problems of Female Sexuality: The Defensive Function of Certain Phantasies About the Body. *International Journal of Psychoanalysis* 80: 645–660.

Stärcke, A. (1921) The Castration Complex. *International Journal of Psychoanalysis* 2: 179–201.

Stein, M. (2002) The Risk Taker as Shadow: A Psychoanalytic View of the Collapse of Barings Bank. *Journal of Management Studies* 37: 1215–1229.

Stein, M. (2003) Unbounded Irrationality: Risk and Organizational Narcissism at Long Term Capital Management. *Human Relations* 56(5): 523–540.

Stein, R. (2002) Evil as Love and as Liberation. *Psychoanalytic Dialogues* 12: 393–420.

Steiner, J. (1993) *Psychic Retreats: Pathological Organisations in Psychotic, Neurotic and Borderline Patients.* London: Routledge.

Steiner, J. (2020) *Illusion, Delusion, and Irony in Psychoanalysis.* Abington, Oxon/New York: Routledge.

Stoller, R. and Herdt, G. (1982) The Development of Masculinity: A Cross-Cultural Contribution. *Journal of the American Psychoanalytic Association* 30: 29–59.

Taylor, G. (2000) *Castration: An Abbreviated History of Western Manhood.* New York/London: Routledge.

Taylor, G. (2016) Varieties of Castration Experience: Relevance to Contemporary Psychoanalysis and Psychodynamic Psychotherapy. *Psychodynamic Psychiatry* 44(1): 39–68.

Tett, G. (2009) *Fool's Gold: How Unrestrained Greed Corrupted a Dream, Shattered Global Markets and Unleashed a Catastrophe.* London: Little Brown.

Tett, G. (2018) Have We Learnt the Lessons of the Financial Crisis? *Financial Times* August 31, 2018. https://www.ft.com/content/a9b25e40-ac37-11e8-89a1-e5de165fa619, Accessed 30 April 2023.

Thrul, S. (2023) The Young Man and the Sea: Reflections on Male Infantile Development, Fatherhood and Psychoanalytic Training. *British Journal of Psychotherapy* 39(2): 380–392.

Tooze, A. (2018) *Crashed: How a Decade of Financial Crisis Changed the World.* London: Allen Lane.

Treanor, J. (2010) Anger Escalates Over Royal Bank of Scotland Plan to Pay £1,3bn Bonuses. *Guardian* 25 February: 25.

Tuckett, D. (2008) Phantastic Objects and the Financial Market's Sense of Reality: a Psychoanalytic Contribution to the Understanding of Stock Market Instability. *International Journal of Psychoanalysis* 89: 389–412.

Tuckett, D. (2009) *Addressing the Psychology of Financial Markets.* London: Institute for Public Policy Research and the Friends Provident Society.

Turner, A. (2009) *The Turner Review: A Regulatory Response to the Global Banking Crisis.* London: Financial Services Authority.

Tyson, P. (1986) Male Gender Identity: Early Developmental Roots. *Psychanalytic Review* 73(4): 1–21.

United States Banker (1990) *National Edition*, May.

van Dalen, H. and Henkens, K. (2011) Do People Fear Population Decline. https://cepr.org/voxeu/columns/do-people-fear-population-decline, Accessed 11 September 2023.

Van Leeuwen, K. (1966) Pregnancy Envy in the Male. *International Journal of Psychoanalysis* 47: 319–324.

Veldman, R. (2019) *The Gospel of Climate Skepticism: Why Evangelical Christians Oppose Action on Climate Change.* Oakland: University of California Press.

Vermote, R. (2019) *Reading Bion.* Abingdon, Oxon/New York: Routledge.

Walker, S. and Garamvolgyi, F. (2022) Viktor Orbán Sparks Outrage with Attack on 'Race Mixing' in Europe. *The Guardian* 24 July. Available at https://www.theguardian.com/world/2022/jul/24/viktor-orban-against-race-mixing-europe-hungary#:~:text=%E2%80%9CWe%20%5BHungarians%5D%20are%20not,in%20stark%20far%2Dright%20terms, Accessed 11 September 2023.

Weintrobe, S. (2021) *Psychological Roots of the Climate Crisis: Neo-Liberal Exceptionalism and the Culture of Uncare*. London/New York: Bloomsbury.

Whitebook, J. (2017) *Freud: An Intellectual Biography*. Cambridge/New York: Cambridge University Press.

Wieland, C. (2000) *The Undead Mother: Psychoanalytic Explorations of Masculinity, Femininity and Matricide*. London: Rebus; Routledge, 2002.

Wieland, C. (2015) *The Fascist State of Mind and the Manufacturing of Masculinity: A Psychoanalytic Approach*. London/New York: Routledge.

Wilkie, B. (2010) Bank Loan Complaints More than Double. *British SME*, 16 August 2010.

Winnicott, D. W. (1935) The Manic Defence. In *Through Paediatrics to Psycho-Analysis*. London: Hogarth and the Institute of Psycho-Analysis, 1975, 129–144.

Winnicott, D. W. (1949) Birth Memories, Birth Trauma, and Anxiety. In *Through Paediatrics to Psycho-Analysis*. London: Hogarth and the Institute of Psycho-Analysis, 1975, 174–193.

Winnicott, D. W. (1963) Communicating and Not Communicating Leading to a Study of Certain Opposites. Reprinted In *The Maturational Process and the Facilitating Environment*. London: Hogarth/Institute of Psycho-Analysis, 1965, 179–192.

Winnicott, D. W. (1966) On the Split-Off Male and Female Elements. In Winnicott, C., Shepherd, R. and Davis, M. (eds) *Psycho-Analytic Explorations*. London: Karnac, 1989, 168–192.

Winnicott, D. W. (1971) *Playing and Reality*. Harmondsworth: Penguin.

Winship, G. (2009) The Testes: Theoretical Lacunae and Clinical Imperatives. *British Journal of Psychotherapy* 25: 24–38.

Wisdom, J. O. (1983) Male and Female. *International Journal of Psychoanalysis* 64: 159–168.

Wisdom, J. O. (1992) *Feud, Women, and Society*. New Brunswick/London: Transaction Publishers.

Wolfe, P. (2016) *Traces of History: Elementary Structures of Race*. London/New York: Verso.

Wollheim, R. (1969) The Mind and the Mind's Image of Itself. *International Journal of Psychoanalysis* 50: 209–220.

Wollheim, R. (1987) *Painting as an Art*. London: Thames & Hudson.

Wright, D. L. S. (2022) *The Physical and Virtual Space of the Consulting Room: Room-Object Spaces*. London: Routledge.

Yazmajian, R. (1966a) The Testes and Body-Image Formation in Transvestitism. *International Journal of Psychoanalysis* 14: 304–312.

Yazmajian, R. (1966b) Reactions to Differences between Prepubertal and Adult Testes and Scrotums. *Psychoanalytic Quarterly* 35: 368–376.

Yazmajian, R. (1967) The Influence of Testicular Sensory Stimuli on the Dream. *International Journal of Psychoanalysis* 15: 83–98.

Yazmajian, R. (1983) On a Retractile Testis and an Infantile Umbilicus Phobia. *Psychoanalytic Quarterly* 52: 584–589.

Yovel, Y. (1992) *Spinoza and Other Heretics: Adventures in Immanence*, vol. II. Princeton: Princeton University Press.

Zachary, A. (2018) *The Anatomy of the Clitoris: Reflections on the Theory of Female Sexuality*. London: Routledge.

Zepf, S. and Steel, D. (2016) Penis Envy and the Female Oedipus Complex: A Plea to Reawaken an Ineffectual Debate. *Psychoanalytic Review* 103: 397–420.

Zhang, A. and Master, F. (2023) China's First Population Drop in Six Decades Sounds Alarm on Demographic Crisis. *Reuters* 17 January 2023. https://www.reuters.com/world/china/chinas-population-shrinks-first-time-since-1961-2023-01-17/, Accessed 11 February 2023.

Index